D0221681

Explorations in Global Ethics

Explorations in Global Ethics

Comparative Religious Ethics and Interreligious Dialogue

edited by

*Sumner B. Twiss
and Bruce Grelle*

Property of
Graduate Theological Union
Please return to
San Francisco Theological
Seminary

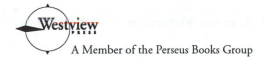

A Member of the Perseus Books Group

BJ
1188
E96
1998

S

All rights reserved. Printed in the United States of America. No part of this publication may be reproduced or transmitted in any form or by any means, electronic or mechanical, including photocopy, recording, or any information storage and retrieval system, without permission in writing from the publisher.

Copyright © 2000 by Westview Press, A Member of the Perseus Books Group

Published in 2000 in the United States of America by Westview Press, 5500 Central Avenue, Boulder, Colorado 80301-2877, and in the United Kingdom by Westview Press, 12 Hid's Copse Road, Cumnor Hill, Oxford OX2 9JJ

Visit us on the World Wide Web at www.westviewpress.com

Library of Congress Cataloging-in-Publication Data
Explorations in global ethics : comparative religious ethics and
  interreligious dialogue / edited by Sumner B. Twiss and Bruce
  Grelle.
    p. cm.
  Includes bibliographical references and index.
  ISBN 0-8133-2881-0 (hc)—ISBN 0-8133-6623-2 (pbk)
    1. Religious ethics—Comparative studies.   2. Religions—
Relations.   I. Twiss, Sumner B.   II. Grelle, Bruce.
BJ1188.E96   1998
291.5—dc21   98-9706
                                                                              CIP

The paper used in this publication meets the requirements of the American National Standard for Permanence of Paper for Printed Library Materials Z39.48-1984.

10   9   8   7   6   5   4   3   2   1

b 12596516

To
Patricia R. Twiss
and
Deborah S. Grelle

Contents

Acknowledgments   ix

Introduction: A New Venue for Comparative Religious Ethics   1

PART 1
COMPARATIVE RELIGIOUS ETHICS AND
INTERRELIGIOUS DIALOGUE

1   Four Paradigms in Teaching
    Comparative Religious Ethics, *Sumner B. Twiss*   11

2   Scholarship and Citizenship: Comparative Religious
    Ethicists as Public Intellectuals, *Bruce Grelle*   34

3   Reckoning with Religious Difference: Models of
    Interreligious Moral Dialogue, *Kate McCarthy*   73

4   A Global Ethic in the Light of Comparative
    Religious Ethics, *Sallie King*   118

5   Commentary on Part One, *Marcus Braybrooke*   141

PART 2
RELIGIOUS PERSPECTIVES IN DIALOGUE
ON GLOBAL MORAL ISSUES

6   Religion and Human Rights: A Comparative Perspective,
    Sumner B. Twiss   155

7   The Problem of Distributive Justice in World Religions,
    James F. Smurl   176

8   "Teachers of Reality": Voices of Resistance and
    Reconstruction, *June O'Connor*   197

9   Piety, Politics, and the Limits Set by God: Implications of
    Islamic Political Thought for Christian Theology, *John Kelsay*   217

10 Religions and the Ethics of International Business,
    Ronald M. Green   237

11 Environmental Ethics in Interreligious Perspective,
    Kusumita P. Pedersen   253

12 From Genocide to Global Ethics by Way of Storytelling,
    Darrell J. Fasching   291

13 Commentary on Part Two, *Dennis P. McCann*   322

About the Editors and Contributors   335
Index   337

Acknowledgments

Our gratitude to the editors of *The Annual of the Society of Christian Ethics* for their permission to reprint Chapter 1, originally published as "Curricular Perspectives in Comparative Religious Ethics: A Critical Examination of Four Paradigms" in the 1993 *Annual,* pp. 249–269.

Our thanks also to the Faculty Development Fund, Brown University, for a grant to help prepare this volume and to the California State University, Chico, for a research grant and sabbatical leave to Bruce Grelle for work on the volume.

We have benefited considerably from discussions among the members of the Comparative Religious Ethics Interest Group of the Society of Christian Ethics. Finally, we wish to thank Kathleen Pappas, academic secretary, Department of Religious Studies, Brown University, for her excellent labors in helping to pull this volume together through its various stages of production.

Sumner B. Twiss
Bruce Grelle

Introduction:
A New Venue
for Comparative
Religious Ethics

For nearly two decades, comparative religious ethics, as a nascent discipline in the field of religious studies, has been struggling for a distinctive method and identity.[1] Various approaches have been proposed, developed, criticized, and refined, but no single one has carried the day in providing a fully convincing rationale and research program. Prominent among these approaches have been: (1) the formalist-conceptual approach (using Western moral theory to analyze the moral positions and reasoning of diverse religious traditions); (2) the historical approach (using history-of-religions methods to comprehend the holistic webs of belief and practice in rich historical and cultural context); (3) the methodological-theoretical approach (involving metaethical inquiry into theories of ethics and religion with a particular concern for the problem of moral relativism versus universalism); and (4) the hermeneutical-dialogical approach (using intercultural moral theorizing and praxis involving the quest for cross-cultural understanding and the fusion of diverse moral and religious horizons). In one way or another, all of these approaches are concerned with issues of theory and interpretation in comparative moral inquiry, and all attempt to provide the discipline with a dominant rationale and method aimed at convincing insiders and outsiders of its integrity and worth. Thus far, however, for reasons of theoretical contestability and uncertainty about aims and goals, no one of these has entirely succeeded.

During the same period, but with a much longer history extending back to the late nineteenth century (e.g., to the 1893 World's Parliament of Religions), representatives of the world's major religious traditions have pursued interfaith or interreligious dialogues about substantive moral issues of general concern to the peoples of the world. Such issues have included, for example, intolerance and discrimination, war and peace, abuse of vulnerable populations, freedom of conscience and religious practice, human rights, and environmental responsibility (see, e.g., Braybrooke 1992a and

1992b). Interreligious dialogue about such issues has resulted in numerous declarations and agenda attempting to secure practical accords that, if pursued and implemented, might help alleviate human suffering and otherwise advance human well-being. Unlike the scholarly inquiries of comparative religious ethics, interreligious moral dialogues have a reasonably perspicuous and persuasive rationale—to call the world to shared responsibility for the alleviation of suffering and oppression, and are based on a practical method—dialogue about intercultural moral understandings and agreements on practical moral issues.

Most recently, for example, at the 1993 Parliament of the World's Religions, these dialogues have taken a somewhat new turn involving explicit efforts to frame and promulgate a "global ethic," which, it is hoped, can serve as a stable though somewhat minimal moral consensus among the world's religious and cultural traditions. These recent efforts have, however, exposed certain weaknesses in interreligious moral dialogue—for example, difficulty in mounting positions and arguments fully appreciative of the diversity of premises among the various traditions; some naïveté in accepting at face value the dominant voices of religious traditions while overlooking the more muted voices of oppressed minorities; and a seeming inability to move much beyond what many would regard as moral platitudes.

So we are confronted with a problematic and provocative situation. On the one hand, we have an area of scholarly inquiry—comparative religious ethics—which, despite its sophisticated tools and methods, appears to lack a unifying rationale and purpose convincing to those within and outside the field. On the other hand, we have a community of interreligious dialogue with an enormously persuasive rationale and mission that nonetheless tends to founder in its ability to mount convincing and nonparochial positions and arguments. This situation is aptly illustrated by both enterprises' recent discussion of prospects for, respectively, a common morality (a subject of scholarly interest) and a global ethic (a subject of interreligious dialogue) (see, e.g., Outka and Reeder 1993; Küng and Kuschel 1993; O'Connor 1994; and George 1994). In the first instance, scholarly discussion bogs down in technical arguments about alternative moral epistemologies, failing to address many substantive issues of practical moral concern and ultimately leading to some skepticism about the practical worth of the inquiry. In the second instance, interreligious dialogue has tended to bog down in difficulties about how meaningful moral agreements are to be secured when the parties seem unable to appreciate and work through the depth and complexity of their differences, ultimately leading to questions about the naïveté of the dialogue despite its good intentions.

What is especially provocative and stimulating about this situation is the possibility that the discipline of comparative religious ethics and the community of interreligious dialogue each has something to offer the other, if both could see their way clear to join hands in a mutually beneficial collaboration. Interreligious dialogue offers to comparative religious ethics a more persuasive rationale, agenda of issues, and practical orientation than hitherto has been the case. By the same token, comparative religious ethics offers to interreligious dialogue a number of critical tools and methods that could enhance the sophistication and effectiveness of its practical work. In this way, both theory (a dominant concern and strength of comparative religious ethics) and praxis (a dominant concern and strength of interreligious moral dialogue) could be joined together in a mutual effort, each contributing to the work of the other.

The overriding purpose of this volume, then, is to attempt to bring the discipline of comparative religious ethics into constructive collaboration with the community of interreligious dialogue. This collaboration yields a new and distinctive vision for conducting ethical inquiry in our pluralistic world, one that is simultaneously *hermeneutical, critical,* and *practical* in its dimensions. The *hermeneutical* dimension involves interpreting moral-religious cultural systems and patterns of reasoning in social and historical context, with the latter including both intracultural and cross-cultural diversity. The *critical* dimension involves analyzing the social, political, economic, and institutional influences within and on these systems and patterns. And the *practical* dimension involves identifying and developing intra- and intercultural moral procedures and resources for proposing practical strategies for advancing human well-being.

This vision combines the methods and theory of comparative ethical inquiry with a practical moral rationale and project. It is self-consciously open to methodological diversity, while at the same time introducing a constructive moral purpose and sustaining motivation for its practitioners. These practitioners, in turn, take on the role of "transformative intellectuals" who self-consciously and critically relate their inquiries to the important tasks of constructive moral practice, making common cause with the aims and tasks of interreligious moral dialogue (see Giroux 1988).

The contributors to the book include both scholars of comparative religious ethics and professionals in interreligious moral dialogue. Despite their specific locations—whether in the university or in the religious community— all share the vision of collaboration between the two fields, and all explicitly draw from both communities of discourse in a manner that crosses disciplinary and professional boundaries in order to deal with important methodological and global moral issues creatively and constructively.

Although theory and practice cannot be easily separated in the collaboration—as is evidenced by the fact that all the contributors explicitly address both sorts of issues—for purposes of clarity, the volume is divided into two main parts. One is principally concerned with methods, models, roles, and teaching in comparative religious ethics and interreligious dialogue, and the other is focused on substantive moral themes and issues, many of which were raised at the 1993 Parliament of the World's Religions by both religious representatives and scholarly participants. Taken together, the chapters in these two parts articulate and illustrate new ways of approaching contemporary moral concerns cross-culturally and yet with a rigor that is appropriate to our complex and pluralistic world.

This volume is designed to be of use to a broad and variegated readership, including scholars, teachers, and university students; participants in interreligious moral dialogues at both the international and local levels; and members of the general public concerned about contemporary moral issues in a pluralistic and global context. The editors have also attempted to be open to diverse methodologies and religious traditions so as to demonstrate and test the strengths and weaknesses of the volume's vision of collaboration between comparative religious ethics and interreligious dialogue. Thus, readers can expect to encounter pluralism at two levels: (1) in the ways that issues are approached (e.g., using different interpretive methods, social theories, genres of texts); and (2) in the diverse traditions discussed (e.g., Christian, Buddhist, Islamic, Hindu, Jewish, Confucian, Native American and other indigenous traditions). In addition, readers can expect to be challenged to reflect upon what seem to be familiar issues (e.g., justice, human rights, poverty, oppression, politics, business, environment, genocide) in unfamiliar ways that expose new angles of vision, different modes of reasoning, and diverse worldviews that may lead to an altered and more sophisticated understanding and appreciation of moral thought and behavior across the world. In this way, all of us may perhaps gain a greater appreciation of the need for a vision of collaboration in dealing with enormously important global moral issues.

The essays in Part 1 are concerned largely with methodological and educational issues. The essays in Part 2 explore significant moral issues in our contemporary world as these issues are addressed by various religious traditions. Although much would be lost by doing so, each chapter in these sections, with two exceptions, could be read as a self-contained essay, independently of the others. The two exceptions are the specially commissioned commentaries on the chapters of Part 1 and Part 2 by Marcus Braybrooke and Dennis P. McCann, respectively. These two commentators are strongly identified with the community of interreligious dialogue and are therefore well-positioned to reflect on whether and how comparative religious ethics could contribute to its work. Their commentaries refer specifically to the chapters within each part of the volume, and should be read in that context.

A few words of characterization about the essays themselves are now in order. As indicated above, the essays of Part 1 are concerned with issues of method and education. Sumner B. Twiss (Chapter 1) provides an analytical overview of different approaches to teaching comparative religious ethics, proposing that one in particular, the hermeneutical-dialogical approach, is more adequate and persuasive than the others. In distinguishing these approaches, he also introduces the diverse scholarly programs in the field. In arguing for the relative superiority of the hermeneutical-dialogical approach, he thereby links an educational (and research) paradigm with the collaborative vision of the volume as a whole. Bruce Grelle (Chapter 2) continues and deepens this educational and collaborative vision by first diagnosing some obstacles to its emergence and then proposing a transformative social role for comparative ethicists as public intellectuals. In the latter regard he analyzes and explores various institutional contexts and practical strategies for effecting collaboration between comparative religious ethics and interreligious dialogue.

Kate McCarthy (Chapter 3) provides a typology for construing different modes of interreligious relationship and thus for understanding the diversity of types of interreligious moral dialogue. She identifies certain conditions and virtues necessary for viable interreligious dialogue and concludes by underscoring the special importance of dialogue within traditions. Sallie King (Chapter 4) takes up one of the prominent subjects of interreligious moral dialogue—namely, the development of a global ethic—and critically examines its content and production in the light of moral-theoretical problems explored in comparative religious ethics and from the perspective of the politics of process. She concludes by identifying and assessing the potential usefulness of such an ethic in a variety of institutional and social contexts. Concluding this series of essays is an assessment by Marcus Braybrooke (Chapter 5) of their strengths, weaknesses, and insights. His commentary is a practical one deeply informed by the history of interfaith movements as well as by ongoing experience with their trials and prospects. His contribution is intended to provoke critical reflection on the issues and positions articulated in the foregoing essays.

The essays in Part 2 explore significant moral issues in our contemporary world, particularly as they are seen and handled by various religious traditions. In addition to pursuing substantive inquiry into global moral problems, these essays also present and probe the types of methods that can contribute to the collaborative vision of the volume as a whole. Sumner B. Twiss (Chapter 6) examines the connections between human rights and religious traditions by first forging a historicist and pragmatic re-visioning of human rights in the international context and then demonstrating how even apparently resistant and unpromising traditions (Confucianism and indigenous religions) can affirm these rights. James F. Smurl (Chapter 7), after identifying ethnocentric problems in usual discussions of distributive justice, explores how three traditions (Theravada Buddhism, Christianity, and Islam) deal with distributive justice on their own terms in three religiously informed social movements. Continuing with the themes of human rights and justice, June O'Connor (Chapter 8) explores problems of poverty and oppression by carefully considering the testimonial literature of marginalized Christians in the Third World and then drawing practical lessons from this testimony for our taking more seriously our interdependency with such peoples in any future intercultural dialogue.

John Kelsay (Chapter 9) probes the resonances and differences between Islam and reformed Christianity in their respective teachings on war and statecraft as well as contemporary religious critiques from both traditions of the secular state. Ronald M. Green (Chapter 10), in the particular case of Japanese business practices (influenced, e.g., by Confucianism and Ch'an Buddhism), shows how Japanese values interact transformatively with an emerging global business ethic in such a way as to make the former values increasingly inclusive and the latter ethic more responsive to needed intercultural nuance and structural change. Kusumita P. Pedersen (Chapter 11) probes how a wide variety of Western, Eastern, and indigenous religious traditions might be constructively related to attempts to solve environmental problems, especially through a cross-cultural approach to eco-justice on which they might agree. Darrell J. Fasching (Chapter 12) takes up the difficult and horrific issue of genocide, attempting to expose its underlying dynamic in Western and Eastern traditions and showing how that dynamic can be countervailed by narratives that inculcate respect for human rights. Dennis P. McCann (Chapter 13) concludes this series of essays by offering a set of reflections on their substantive arguments and common themes as well as their methodological implications for future ethical inquiry. Again, as with the commentary on Part 1, this concluding essay is intended to provide a critical sounding board that provokes the reader's own reflections.

It is hoped that the essays in this volume, taken as a whole, will assist readers in coming to grips with moral issues in our contemporary situation, which, unfortunately for us all, are likely to continue into the next century. The editors and authors share the belief that any effective effort to solve these problems will require, in the final analysis, intercultural exchange of the sort represented by this book's re-visioning of religious ethics. We the editors now invite you the readers to join us in the quest for better understanding of the moral traditions, problems, and prospects that confront us as we continue to live and work together in an increasingly complex world of global interaction, where "all is like an ocean, all is flowing and blending; a touch in one place sets up movement at the other end of the earth" (Dostoevsky 1976, 299).

Notes

1. The initial paragraphs of this introduction are drawn from our earlier publication, Twiss and Grelle 1995, 21–24.

References

Braybrooke, Marcus. 1992a. *Pilgrimage of Hope: One Hundred Years of Global Interfaith Dialogue*. New York: Crossroad.

_____. 1992b. *Stepping Stones to a Global Ethic*. London: SCM Press.

Dostoevsky, Fyodor. 1976. *The Brothers Karamazov*. Translated by Constance Garnett. Revised by Ralph E. Matlaw. New York: W. W. Norton.

George, William P. 1994. "The Promise of a Global Ethic." *Christian Century* (May 18-25):530–533.

Giroux, Henry A. 1988. *Teachers As Intellectuals: Toward a Critical Pedagogy of Learning*. New York: Bergin and Garvey.

Küng, Hans, and Karl-Josef Kuschel, eds. 1993. *A Global Ethic: The Declaration of the Parliament of the World's Religions*. New York: Continuum.

O'Connor, June. 1994. "Does a Global Village Warrant a Global Ethic?" *Religion* 24:155–164.

Outka, Gene and John P. Reeder Jr., eds. 1993. *Prospects for a Common Morality*. Princeton: Princeton University Press.

Twiss, Sumner B., and Bruce Grelle. 1995. "Human Rights and Comparative Religious Ethics: A New Venue." *The Annual of the Society of Christian Ethics*: 21–48.

Part One

Comparative Religious Ethics and Interreligious Dialogue

Chapter One

Four Paradigms in Teaching Comparative Religious Ethics

SUMNER B. TWISS
Brown University

It is well known that comparative religious ethics is a field with a number of alternative paradigms for scholarly inquiry. Indeed, a modest literature has appeared in recent years attempting not only to typologize and characterize these paradigms—in terms of aims, methods, and presuppositions—but also to assess their hermeneutical and epistemological strengths and weaknesses (see especially Lovin and Reynolds 1985; Green and Reynolds 1986; Sizemore 1990; Yearley 1990a; and Schweiker 1992). What is considerably less well known are the curricular paradigms and experimentation for instruction in the field.

This situation needs to be redressed for a number of reasons. First, we need to gain a better sense of how the field's scholarship stands up to scrutiny in the classroom where strengths and inadequacies of goal and method are often revealed when exposed to the probative questions of students. Second, ongoing curricular experiments may themselves yield new guidance for doing work in the field—for example, in identifying objectives, critiquing cultural presuppositions, designing useful hermeneutical strategies, forging insightful cross-traditional comparisons, and identifying needs for texts, anthologies, and other course materials. Third, we need to construct a way for teachers in the field to become more aware of what their colleagues are doing in the classroom—in order to share the successes

This essay was originally published, without the afterword, as "Curricular Perspectives in Comparative Religious Ethics: A Critical Examination of Four Paradigms" in *The Annual of the Society of Christian Ethics* (1993):249–269. It is reprinted with the permission of *The Annual*'s editors. The title and references have been changed to conform with the requirements of the present book.

and failures of curricular experiments and help one another to avoid blind alleys, meet challenges, and capitalize on successful pedagogical strategies and course designs. Fourth, we need to become more aware of curricular strategies in the field in order to assess them in light of published discussions of curricula in religious studies concerned with cross-traditional inquiry. Not only would our teaching be likely to benefit from such a broader assessment but also our curricular designs and experiments might themselves advantage that broader context of discussion.

This chapter aims to describe, interpret, and assess the range of curricular paradigms in comparative religious ethics, with an eye to the above four considerations. It uses three types of materials: (1) solicited course syllabi as well as answers to questions designed to make these syllabi and their instructors' thinking as perspicuous as possible; (2) published discussions of aims and methods of inquiry in comparative religious ethics; and (3) published discussions of curricula in comparative religious ethics and, to a lesser extent, comparative religious inquiry and teaching more generally (see, e.g., Yearley 1990b, 1991; Lovin and Reynolds 1991; and Juergensmeyer 1991).[1] While the latter two bodies of material serve as the initial basis for reviewing, interpreting, and evaluating the first, I believe that the data of the first generates an insightful angle of vision on the published discussions of the other two.

Four Curricular Paradigms

From the data available to me, I discern four basic curricular paradigms, which, adapting some of the field's methodological language, I label as follows: (1) formalist-conceptual comparison, (2) historical comparison, (3) hermeneutical-dialogical comparison, and (4) comparative methods and theory. I will specify each paradigm in terms of its typical goals, focal questions, method of inquiry, presuppositions, range of comparison, course materials, pedagogical strategies, levels of instruction, and institutional contexts.

The first curricular paradigm I call formalist-conceptual because its courses use Western moral theory and conceptual analysis to sort out and critique modes of moral reasoning and argument, moral principles and doctrines, and sources of authority and appeal in Western theistic traditions. Courses within this paradigm apply the standard types of moral theory (e.g., deontological, consequentialist) and moral doctrine (e.g., double effect, moral rights, just war) to religious ethical reflection about such matters as war and pacifism, sexual ethics, and social justice in Western moral traditions (e.g., secular, Christian, Jewish, Islamic). By and large these are courses in moral problems (or applied ethics) similar to analogous courses in philosophy departments but distinguished from the latter by serious attention to traditions other than secular moral philosophy.

The goals of these courses, similar to their philosophy department counterparts, include developing students' cognitive skills in moral analysis and argument—clarifying the conceptual underpinnings of positions, assessing the cogency of moral arguments, and enabling students to construct their own moral positions on important moral issues, concepts, and themes. The dominant focal questions are either (1) how does this or that tradition reason about selected practical moral issues, how does this reasoning compare with contemporary secular moral thought, and what position do you (the student) take on these issues? or (2) how are we to best understand philosophical and theological accounts of, for example, justice and/or love, what are their strengths and weaknesses, and what do they have to teach us about how to conceive of the relationship between love and justice and the nature of moral agency?

The presuppositions of these courses include the following (see Lovin and Reynolds 1985, 12–18; Sizemore 1990, 88–94; and Schweiker 1992, 266–267).[2] Moral traditions are conceived as expressions of patterns of moral rationality identified in the light of Western philosophical reflection. Moral reasoning is the most accessible and important phenomenon in moral life, and that life is conceived as being concerned with principles, rules, and justifications of decisions and actions. Moral thought is defined initially by paradigms of Western moral rationality, though these may be refined in dialectical interaction with the ethical reflection of religious traditions. Facts and values are distinguishable, though they can be related through processes of practical moral reasoning. Moral rationality is often regarded as epistemically autonomous from religious beliefs, though these can be related in practical moral reasoning. Moral theory is important for reflecting on practical problems. There is nothing wrong with ethnocentricity, especially if patterns of moral reasoning are shared across cultural traditions and if one focuses on Western traditions or those traditions (e.g., Hinduism, Gandhi's thought) informed by contact with the West.

The method of inquiry in these courses corresponds quite well to Russell Sizemore's observation that work within the formalist approach to comparative religious ethics conceives of both method and field as concerned with distinguishing and relating "faith and reason" (Sizemore 1990, 91). Put succinctly, the method of these courses involves using Western moral theory to clarify, analyze, and assess the reasoning of religious ethical traditions about practical moral issues or philosophical and theological accounts of significant principles or virtues. This procedure involves identifying the role and effects of religious premises in moral arguments and is more open than secular moral philosophy courses to seeing significant conceptual nuance introduced by religious beliefs. Proper use of the method includes some historical contextualization of materials studied, though this is not the dominant concern of these courses.

The range of comparison for these courses is focused on Western moral traditions, including, for example, classical Greek philosophy; biblical traditions; Christian, Judaic, and Islamic traditions; secular moral philosophy in the modern period; and occasional outreach beyond the West to traditions informed by dialogue with the West. Because the range of comparison is Western yet also open to different moral traditions in the West, I characterize it as both intracultural and cross-traditional. As might be expected, course materials include both classical and modern texts and/or works by thinkers from Western traditions embodying philosophical and theological reflection on practical moral issues or accounts of principles and virtues. I do not perceive any significant commitment to employing comparative religious ethics literature, though the instructors are surely aware of this literature (this is not a criticism but rather an observation). As mentioned earlier, these courses do assign some materials that historically contextualize issues and arguments.

These courses are typically taught by a single ethicist-instructor, sometimes enriched with guest lecturers from other relevant disciplines, in a standard lecture-discussion section format. The courses employ the pedagogical strategy of having students write short interpretive, analytical, or constructive papers focusing on moral arguments about topical issues or concepts. These papers may be supplemented by midterm and final exams as well as longer term papers on such topics as consequentialist moral theory, natural law, criteria for just war, the morality of abortion, justice as fairness, and the varieties of love and their interrelation. The courses are taught at the introductory or intermediate level, requiring no prerequisites other than some degree of conceptual sophistication for the intermediate level. In my small sample of syllabi, all of these courses are taught within university (private and public) religious studies departments, though there is no need for such restriction; so this observation is probably an artifact of the sample size.

The second curricular paradigm is what I call historical-comparative, though some within the field might epistemologize it as "ethical naturalism" (e.g., Lovin and Reynolds 1985, 29–30; and Lovin and Reynolds 1991, 251); I think, however, that this latter label may be too limiting. These courses aim to effect a historically and culturally contextualized empathetic understanding and appreciation of the diversity of religious ethical traditions, and to that end they are informed by work in comparative religious ethics and the history of religions. By and large, these courses attempt to characterize the nature of whole traditions while at the same time using sociomoral problems as points of contact between, and modes of access to, the traditions' fundamental beliefs and modes of thought.

Although these courses are concerned with modes of moral reasoning, their principal aim is to develop students' empathetic comprehension of similarities and differences in moral and religious thought among traditions. Their emphasis is not so much on developing cognitive and conceptual skills in moral argument as to develop a way for students to deeply understand "the other," so that they might subsequently in their lives be in a stronger position to deal with moral and religious pluralism. A subsidiary goal involves assessing approaches to comparative religious ethics with an eye to advocating the superiority of a historical framework.

The focal question for those courses is encapsulated in the question: How do beliefs about human nature, salvation, evil, the good life, and the order of the world affect the way that traditions conceive of the spheres of personal and social life and how they reason about or otherwise deal with sociomoral issues (e.g., war, poverty, economic injustice, sexual relations)? Clearly, there is some similarity here with courses in the previous paradigm but with this difference: The historical courses put a premium on describing with empathy the whole worldview of the traditions being studied rather than tending, as the formalist courses do, to isolate out in analytical fashion moral concepts, principles, and doctrines. This observation introduces the presuppositions of the historical courses.

For these courses, persons and groups are conceived as so intimately shaped by cultural and historical forces that modes of reasoning can only be understood and assessed within the holistic system of moral, religious, empirical, economic, political, and other beliefs constituting a tradition (see Lovin and Reynolds 1985, 18–20; Sizemore 1990, 88–94; and Schweiker 1992, 268). Thus, for this paradigm, comparative moral inquiry requires helping students gain a participant-observer view of traditions so that their integrity is respected rather than distorted while being studied. This perspective, then, devalues ethnocentrism and even fights against it by being somewhat antitheoretical because of the perceived biasing effects of Western-derived categories of moral analysis. Moreover, these courses presuppose that, in addition to contextually shaped reasoning, moral thought is crucially informed by the moral imagination—for example, imaginative empathetic insight into "the other." And further, moral judgments and positions are conceived as complex equilibrations of fact, principle, and emotion.

As a result of such presuppositions, these courses employ a method of inquiry that is (broadly) phenomenological—attempting to bracket students' cultural beliefs so that they might enter into the worldviews of other traditions and describe what they find with a second naïveté, in the hope of enabling them to understand and appreciate the diversity of moral beliefs and reasoning practiced in those traditions (see, e.g., Twiss and Conser 1992, 1–74). The technique of systematic empathy is so important to these courses' method of inquiry that it comes as no surprise that their method is informed by historical and social anthropological methods and data.

In order to teach their lesson of sensitive understanding and appreciation of "the other," these courses tend to compare only two or three traditions in depth. Often these traditions are drawn from radically different cultures—for example, one Western tradition and one Eastern—but other variations are also taught (the intracultural study of two traditions such as Christianity and Judaism, or even the intratraditional study of, for example, Protestant and Roman Catholic moral thought). The latter variations do not undercut the courses' attempt to reach beyond the categories of Western moral philosophy because each tradition is still treated as an integral unity with its distinctive modes of rationality studied in epistemic context. The materials studied in these courses are quite extensive in terms of genre and historical spread—for example, classical and modern primary texts and thinkers, treatises and myths, ritual activity and ethnographically recorded ways of life, interpretive overviews of entire traditions, case studies from comparative religious ethics, and history of religions materials. Clearly, this range of material differs considerably from the more limited philosophical and theological texts studied by formalist courses. This difference is surely explained by this paradigm's distinctive aims, methods, and presuppositions.

Also different from the formalist courses are the historical paradigm's preferred pedagogical strategies. Though the standard lecture-discussion section format is occasionally used, more typical is the seminar requiring students' prior study in the field of religion. Team teaching—usually combining one ethicist with one historian of religion or religious thought—emerges as a significant pedagogical strategy, presumably to ensure depth of understanding of, and control over, the diverse course materials. When there is only one instructor, he or she is often a historically oriented ethicist or a historian of religion or religious thought with considerable competence in ethics. Course requirements range from short interpretive papers to quizzes and exams to final research papers, though significantly they emphasize informed student discussion and seminar presentations. Paper topics focus on interpreting an aspect or theme in two traditions, with comparison and contrast of similarities and differences between the traditions' handling of a moral issue or concept. The level of these courses, as might be expected, ranges from the undergraduate intermediate course to the graduate seminar. A few introductory-level versions are also taught, and these typically have more inventive requirements beyond the usual papers and exams—for example, preparation of assigned study questions, or one- or two-page weekly responses to interpretive questions—in order to ensure students' ongoing absorption of the course materials. Most of these courses are taught at universities, private and public. A few are taught in private colleges, but in these cases team teaching may require special resources, such as an external grant to hire a visiting specialist in comparative religious ethics or a tradition of special interest.

The third curricular paradigm—what I call the hermeneutical-dialogical—appears to be a recent development, at least as a distinctive type of course in comparative religious ethics. These courses seem to synthesize some elements from the two preceding paradigms, while at the same time going a step further. They self-consciously start with the fact that we live in a morally and religiously pluralistic world and attempt to design a method of study that can be conceived along the lines of William Schweiker's recent proposal of comparative religious ethics as a type of moral praxis involving the construction of a common moral world (fusion of horizons) between the scholar's own moral tradition on the one hand, and the moral tradition(s) of particular interest on the other (Schweiker 1992). This praxis, according to Schweiker, involves a dialectic of translation from one moral world to another (the other to ours), of receptivity to the other (insight into the other's moral world), and, through continuous dialogue between our world and the other's, a constructive effort to answer the question of how we (ourselves and the other) should live (a distinctive good of this praxis). This proposal for re-visioning comparative religious ethics captures quite well the design of courses within the hermeneutical-dialogical paradigm.

The aims of these courses include the goal of developing empathetic understanding and appreciation of religious ethical traditions (similar to the historical paradigm) as the basis for the more primary goal of developing students' disciplined thinking about a topic of existential or practical moral significance (similar to the formalist paradigm) that encourages students' normative appropriation (transformation of view) of aspects of the traditions in working out a new moral self-understanding or practical policy that might be acceptable to, and combine important insights from, those traditions (this is the new contribution of the hermeneutical paradigm) (see, e.g., Yearley 1990b and 1991).[3] The basic focal question of these courses is encapsulated in the formulation: in a pluralist world, how are we to think about moral problems of global or intracultural significance and/or philosophical-existential issues of selfhood and society? The global problems of choice include such issues as ethnic violence, structural evil, the environment, and inequity of material goods among nations. Intracultural problems include racism, attitudes toward women and gays, and poverty and homelessness. And philosophical-existential issues range from how to understand the self to questions of how to understand and respond to the human capacity for evil, how to envision a just and good society, and how to conceive of the relation between transcendence and the unity of persons.

The presuppositions of these courses are similar to those of the historical paradigm but include others that appear to be variations on certain presuppositions of the formalist paradigm (see Schweiker 1992). For example, the hermeneutical courses agree with the historical paradigm that persons and groups are shaped by historical, social, and cultural contexts to the extent of yielding seemingly different context-bound patterns of rationality. At the same time, however, despite the acknowledged diversity of beliefs, the hermeneutical courses, like the formalist, appear to presuppose that people and groups share similar sorts of practical moral problems and tasks as well as rough similarities of thought and experience sufficient to gain access to one another across cultural boundaries. In light of presuppositions such as these, these courses advocate that students employ empathetic understanding to enter imaginatively the context and worldview of other traditions and, further, that after taking up these standpoints of "the other" they enter into a respectful dialogue of equals where each exposes his or her own cultural assumptions to the standpoint of "the other" and works to solve shared sociomoral problems through the fusion of moral horizons and the forging of practical agreements. Students are encouraged to become co-participants in a dialogue where they represent imaginatively the "voices" of other traditions.

The method of inquiry, then, for these courses is best conceived as hermeneutical dialogue. This dialogical method takes two alternative forms. One is conceived as interreligious dialogue about moral issues, and there appear to be two subtypes here: (1) the students are prepared through extensive reading to take part in a mini-parliament of world religions where teams of students each represent a different tradition in the dialogue; and (2) the instructors themselves as scholar-advocates represent the traditions and invite students to participate in a dialogue guided by their expert voices. The other form of dialogue appears to be an exercise in comparative hermeneutics wherein students, guided by expert instructors, expose and assess the deep assumptions of the traditions (including the students' own) in a seminar format. Both forms of hermeneutical dialogue aim at insider-participant comprehension, normative appropriation (fusion of horizons), and disciplined thinking about topics of existential or practical moral concern.

The range of comparison in these courses is typically rather broad, involving two or more traditions. Some courses focus on dialogue among intracultural moral traditions (e.g., Western religions, American moral traditions), and others are cross-cultural (e.g., major world religions, East and West). As might be expected, course materials are quite diverse, including classical texts, works by thinkers from religious ethical traditions, modern interpretive overviews of traditions, studies from historical sociology and the history of religions, Western philosophical studies of pertinent concepts and issues, historicist (including feminist) critiques, studies in comparative religious ethics, and instructor-designed "moral problems" readings (e.g., on global issues, futurist predictions).

The pedagogical strategies of these courses can be quite innovative—for example, the mini-parliament of world religions. Team teaching and the use of guest lecturers are prevalent. And, though some lecture-discussion may take place, the usual pedagogical format is the seminar. Course assignments, while including brief and longer interpretive papers, are often quite inventive: for example, group project teams meeting independently to formulate working papers subsequently presented to the whole class, students writing original policy proposals on sociomoral issues, and each student preparing weekly short papers (one to two pages) and oral comments. Often in this format, student contributions to class discussion are explicitly graded. Although the level of instruction for these courses ranges from introductory undergraduate to advanced graduate, the intermediate and advanced levels (with prerequisites) are more typical. Such courses are taught within both colleges and universities, public and private.

The fourth curricular paradigm is what I call comparative methods and theory. Courses within this paradigm critically examine the major scholarly approaches to comparative religious ethics as well as interpretive and theoretical issues raised by these approaches. The aims of these courses include: (1) careful examination of alternative methods in comparative religious ethics including attention to presuppositions, sources, cross-cultural categories of analysis, conceptions of moral rationality, methodological practices, and hermeneutical and epistemological dimensions; (2) usually the advocacy of one method as being superior on hermeneutical, epistemic, or pragmatic grounds; (3) assessment of such metatheoretical issues as the possibility of cross-cultural generalization, debates over moral relativism and universalism, and problems of disciplinary ethnocentric bias; and (4) clarification of the moral teachings of various traditions, either those examined by the comparative methods being studied and/or others introduced as further tests for the adequacy of those methods. As might be expected, the focal questions of these courses are: What are the major approaches in comparative religious ethics? Is any one more adequate than the others, and for what purposes? What do these methods say or imply about such issues as moral relativism, moral universalism, prospects for a common morality, and ethnocentric bias?

Presuppositions of these courses concern the significance of (meta)theoretical reflection for comparative religious ethics. Such reflection is assumed to constitute a necessary condition for adequate descriptive and normative work in the field and is conceived to combat ethnocentric and disciplinary bias. In addition, these courses presuppose that theory and data significantly interact. Such presuppositions, then, inform the courses' method of inquiry, which involves a close examination and assessment of both the theoretical underpinnings and the case studies of alternative approaches in comparative religious ethics. Criteria of assessment are introduced or forged in the course examination and include such things as testing methods and results against careful reading of primary materials, determining the degree of ethnocentric distortion in case studies, and comparing the hermeneutical and epistemological adequacy of alternative methods.

The range of comparison for these courses has two dimensions: method and tradition. In the first dimension, the methods compared are typically historical sociology, formalist and quasi-formalist approaches, ethical naturalism, and historicist critique.[4] The range of methodological comparison has not yet included (but certainly could include) what I have called the hermeneutical-dialogical. In this respect perhaps, it could be said that the curricular paradigms are ahead of scholarship in the field—at least to the extent that the hermeneutical-dialogical paradigm seems to have been around longer in comparative religious ethics' instructional context than its scholarship. Regarding the second dimension of comparative range, the traditions studied by these courses are often the same as those studied by extant scholarship and therefore are characterizable as cross-cultural and cross-traditional. This is not to say that these courses preclude studying other traditions and genres of materials, for these provide important learning experiences as well as excellent test cases for assessing the adequacy of methods. Course materials, then, include methodological and theoretical work in comparative religious ethics, moral philosophy, and history of religions, as well as existing case studies and primary texts and thinkers from religious ethical traditions.

Given the theoretical emphasis of these courses, they are typically taught at the advanced level to both undergraduates and graduate students who are prepared by prior course work in ethics, history of religions, or philosophy of religion. The format is invariably the traditional seminar, and the courses are taught either by individual scholars in comparative religious ethics or by a team of two instructors (one ethicist and one historian of religions). Course requirements include oral and written seminar papers and a longer research paper on a methodological or theoretical issue. The institutional context for these courses is, from my sample, invariably the private or public university (usually with doctoral programs). This restriction is no doubt due to the fact that these courses lend themselves to preprofessional training for potential scholars of ethics and religion, though occasionally they are taught to advanced undergraduates (usually majors in religious studies).

Assessment of the Paradigms

I now turn to a tentative assessment of these four paradigms, sketching briefly my perception of each paradigm's principal strengths and weaknesses and then concluding with my view of which curricular paradigm appears particularly persuasive.

The formalist-conceptual courses have a number of important strengths, not least of which is the intensive development of students' cognitive moral skills and critical reasoning capacities, useful for living a moral life in our complex society and culture. Moreover, the fact that these courses encourage students to develop their own reflective moral positions on sociomoral problems of major and continuing significance clearly helps prepare them to (re)enter society with a critical moral stance. Furthermore, the fact that these courses expose students to some of the major religious ethical traditions significant in American culture helps put them in a position to appreciate the moral thought and experience of subpopulations in the culture.

Despite these clear strengths, the formalist courses appear also to suffer (at least potentially) from distinct weaknesses. Studying moral thought in light of Western paradigms of rationality may reinforce a tendency toward ethnocentric bias precisely because the courses provide little exposure to cultural-moral alternatives outside the West. The assumption that cogent reasoning is the most significant aspect of a moral life is problematic, for it leaves unaddressed the gap between cognition and behavior, a gap that might be closed by greater emphasis on developing students' empathetic and imaginative skills, self-criticalness about deep presuppositions and biases, and interpersonal group decisionmaking skills and virtues. In failing to acknowledge fully the great diversity of moral worlds across cultures and in de-emphasizing the historical-cultural embeddedness of students' thinking, these courses may encourage students to adopt an uncritical moral universalism and a certain degree of ahistoricity in their moral thought. Finally, though these courses examine how to relate fact and value as well as moral and religious belief in practical moral argument, they nonetheless may encourage some naïveté about these relationships, inasmuch as they de-emphasize significant dialectical interaction and interpenetration of such dichotomous categories and, further, may project the idea that moral reasoning is epistemically autonomous. In citing these potential weaknesses, I am not questioning the competence or sophistication of the instructors of these courses but rather am concerned about certain emphases or tendencies within course design that may be misunderstood or misappropriated by less sophisticated students.

The strengths of the historical-comparative courses are equally impressive, though of a different character than the formalist. One evident strength is the development of students' empathetic understanding and appreciation of cultural-moral differences and similarities. Such understanding and appreciation provide a necessary condition for subsequent constructive life encounters with radically different moral traditions. Related to this strength is the development of students' respect for different moral standpoints (countervailing ethnocentric bias) as well as development of their imaginative and historical skills, which are important to a moral life in a pluralistic society and an increasingly global culture. Moreover, these courses countervail dichotomous thinking about fact and value and religion and morality inasmuch as they encourage sensitivity to the close relationships and influences among moral, factual, and religious beliefs in a complex but integrated web of belief. This perspective introduces a healthy realism about how people ordinarily reason about practical moral matters.

Noting these strengths is not to say that these courses have no potential weaknesses. For one thing, their emphasis on empathetic understanding and appreciation of moral diversity, while important, can lead to an imbalanced lack of appreciation for the equally important role of critical reasoning in moral life. Moreover, in emphasizing the radical diversity in moral, religious, and even factual belief, these courses may run the danger of students' being so impressed by diversity that they slip into an uncritical stance of moral relativism, or even subjectivism. As two commentators have suggested about the scholarly approach of ethical naturalism, these courses might be perceived by students as providing only cabinets of curiosities (Lovin and Reynolds 1985, 28), undercutting the important notion that moral traditions constitute ways of meeting common tasks and challenges in life. The holistic tendency underlying these courses' method of inquiry can be taken by students as denying that there is any way to adjudicate cultural-moral differences over shared problems. Furthermore, this tendency may have the unfortunate effect of producing an antitheoretical bias in students, blinding them to the interaction between theory and data and to the possibility that some theorizing may be inescapable for understanding traditions and constructing cogent moral positions.

Related to this problem may be a resulting lack of appreciation for the power of alternative methods in comparative religious ethics as well as for the value of careful reasoning in articulating and defending moral positions. Finally, as observed by Schweiker in regard to ethical naturalism, these courses may fail to acknowledge sufficiently that any interpretive understanding enacts its own world of moral meaning as a condition for understanding others (Schweiker 1992, 268–269, 284). Students need to be made aware of the hermeneutical problems and responsibilities posed by this condition of interpretive understanding if other traditions are to be properly comprehended. Again, in citing these potential weaknesses, I am speaking of the dangers of student misunderstanding and/or misappropriation, not of instructor competence.

Hermeneutical-dialogical courses also have their distinctive strengths and weaknesses. Their most significant strength is that they aim to develop in students a balanced range of moral skills and virtues—an empathetic understanding and appreciation of difference and similarity, a deep self-criticalness about cultural bias, disciplined thinking about significant beliefs and issues, and interpersonal skills in dealing with peers about controversial moral problems. These courses also provide students with a clear vision of moral and religious pluralism in the contemporary world, balanced by an equally important awareness that moral cultures and traditions often share common problems of personal and social life at the practical level (a sort of problem-oriented unity amid diversity of view). The dialogical approach of these courses encourages respect and appreciation for different others as moral equals in a conversation about shared problems and concerns, even to the point (as noted by Yearley 1990a, 100–101) that students are enabled to express a distinctive virtue of regret that they are barred from full existential embrace of other cultural-moral ideals.

By the same token, however, these courses provide considerable resources from other cultural-moral traditions for students' re-visioning of self and society, and the dialogical approach to shared problems—directed toward re-visionment of policy and concept—helps to counteract an uncritical slip into extreme moral relativism or subjectivism. Additional strengths of these courses noted by their instructors include confronting students' ignorance about their own cultural-moral heritage, self-consciously addressing a culturally diverse student population, and developing a course pedagogy that attracts students' existential involvement.

Again, citing these strengths is not to imply that courses within this paradigm lack their share of distinctive problems. To begin with, inasmuch as these courses are taught to students blessed and burdened with a relative lack of life experience, the hermeneutical-dialogical approach could encourage a premature fusion of moral horizons before differences among moral cultures are fully appreciated. Inasmuch as instructors report that some students are woefully ignorant of their own moral heritage, this observation raises the question of whether students are in a strong enough position to appropriate responsibly other moral horizons. Moreover, to the extent that a number of these courses aim at having students achieve practical working agreements about how to approach and solve global problems, the time constraints of such a semester course might well encourage students to take premature leaps to moral compromise; in the real world of geopolitics these are complex problems about which compromise and agreement may best be forged slowly and incrementally.

In a related vein, the ambition of some of these courses to provide exposure to many different traditions may result in a superficial understanding of cultural-moral similarities and differences. A single course can only do so much in the limited time available: To learn about traditions in depth; to master the complexities of, for example, global sociomoral issues; and then to forge solutions to these problems seems a lot to achieve in twelve or thirteen weeks. This is not to suggest that the courses should not be attempted but rather to caution against overloading students to the point of permitting them to attain only superficial comprehension. Finally, on a practical note, it appears that many of these courses require a rather high level of faculty and library resources that may not be available in all institutional contexts. This resource demand could, on the one hand, work against the development and proliferation of these courses and, on the other, encourage cutting corners, again leading to a superficial educational product.

The strengths of the comparative methods and theory courses are, like with the other paradigms, distinctive and considerable. These courses are notable for their encouragement of critical reflection about the relationship between theory and data and about the distortive effects of deep assumptions that result in ethnographic and disciplinary biases. Moreover, they provide students with a broad and deep comprehension of research programs in comparative religious ethics, as well as compelling them to articulate and apply criteria of assessment to these programs. In effect, these courses provide students with a solid training ground for scholarly inquiry in comparative religious ethics. Furthermore, students are compelled to grapple in a sophisticated way with some major questions in the field of ethics—for example, whether there is a common morality across cultures, whether the categories of Western ethics distort other cultural-moral traditions, and whether the specter of moral relativism is a real worry. Finally, students are exposed in a sophisticated way to considerable cross-traditional moral and religious data, presumably resulting in a deep appreciation of the similarities and differences among cultural-moral traditions.

These courses also have their share of distinctive weaknesses. To begin with, by their very nature, they appear to be largely oriented to preprofessional training in the field and thus may have a limited audience. Moreover, they seem most appropriate for students who have already done work in ethics or at least one religious tradition and again attain a limited audience. Their focus on current scholarly approaches in comparative religious ethics may result in students gaining a somewhat myopic view of possible methods for the field—for example, it may be no accident that these courses tend to overlook the scholarly significance of the curricular paradigm of hermeneutical dialogue. By the same token, however, it can also be argued that having a strong training in current dominant methods may provide a powerful basis and motivation for seeking other new, more adequate approaches. Finally, the (meta)theoretical perspective of these courses appears somewhat abstract and removed from practical and existential moral topics, thereby providing students with a possibly distorted view of what morality is all about.

With the strengths and weaknesses of each paradigm now identified, the time has come to articulate my own view of which curricular paradigm appears particularly persuasive for instruction in the field. This view is shaped by an inductive observation concerning the emphases of the four paradigms—namely, each type represents a different leitmotif for our study of others. The formalist paradigm studies ourselves (and others); the historical paradigm studies others (and ourselves); the hermeneutical-dialogical paradigm studies others and ourselves as equals; and the comparative methods and theory paradigm studies how we ought to study others and ourselves. The parentheses and lack of parentheses are meant to capture the nuance of how "the other" is approached—in the formalist, through ourselves and our cultural lens; in the historical, more directly, bracketing ourselves and our cultural lens; in the hermeneutical, through an open dialogue between others and ourselves as equal co-participants; and in the comparative methods and theory, from a metaperspective standing above others and ourselves.

Now I want to make some hermeneutical-methodological observations about these leitmotifs. With regard to the formalist, our cultural lens can easily distort the other, though this may be mitigated by the extent to which we study others within our culture. With regard to the historical, it may be problematic that we can successfully bracket ourselves and approach the other directly. With regard to comparative methods and theory, it may be problematic that we can escape our own and others' cultural and social location in a metaperspective (are not all perspectives located?). And with regard to the hermeneutical-dialogical, we seem to encounter an approach that may avoid cultural distortion and the problematics of bracketing and metatheoretical perspective, because of its ongoing acknowledgment of "the other," resulting in continuing checks on bias and distortion as well as temptation to a God's-eye point of view. These observations suggest to me that the hermeneutical-dialogical courses incorporate the most adequate presuppositions and method of inquiry.

The presuppositions of the hermeneutical-dialogical courses strike just the right balance with respect to how moral thought is shaped by diverse cultural and historical context while simultaneously recognizing that cultural groups and traditions share similar sorts of tasks and have similarities of thought amid differences sufficient to ground dialogue across cultural boundaries. And these presuppositions strike just the right balance with regard to the equal significance in the moral life of cognitive moral skills, empathetic understanding, respect for the other, and interpersonal skills for engaging in constructive moral dialogue. Furthermore, these courses' method of inquiry—a hermeneutical dialogue conceived as a type of moral praxis aimed at constructing a common moral world enabling translation between cultures as well as practical accommodation to shared tasks and problems—appears to do justice to the plurality of moral and religious thought in a situation where it is far from evident that any tradition is superior to the others.

Also important to my preference for this paradigm are pedagogical considerations. These courses incorporate and address many of the aims of the other paradigms—for example, empathetic understanding in historical and cultural context, development of critical reasoning capacities along with imaginative and interpersonal skills, and clear awareness about the effects of culturally biasing categories and the need to use a nondistortive method. In addition, the innovative pedagogical strategies of hermeneutical and interreligious dialogue about important sociomoral problems and philosophical-existential themes are both existentially engaging and adaptable to a variety of instructional levels and institutional contexts. The pedagogical problems posed by these courses appear surmountable, though I concede that this point might be argued with respect to the other curricular paradigms as well. Nonetheless, I hasten to add that if these other paradigms were to address their problems effectively, then in all likelihood they would be drawn closer to the hermeneutical-dialogical paradigm, thus indicating the latter's greater adequacy.[5] Therefore, it seems to me that the hermeneutical-dialogical curricular paradigm is the most promising for future instruction in the field, though I also believe there is a role for the other paradigms as well, given the fact that they meet important needs and that hermeneutical-dialogical courses tend to put strains on faculty and library resources not be easily resolvable in all institutional contexts.

To conclude, I think that the present study, despite its limitations of sample size as well as the limitations of its author, suggests the importance of our becoming more continuously aware of experimental curricular strategies in the field, thereby enabling us to be more cognizant of the strengths and limitations of the courses we teach. I believe that this discussion indicates the value of institutionalizing a mechanism for collegial sharing of course designs and evaluations, and I invite all to reflect on how this might best be accomplished.

Afterword

In reviewing this paper, my colleague John Reeder raised a number of such important and insightful issues that I believe they—and my responses to them—warrant the broader audience of this afterword. Since his perceptions and criticisms may well anticipate those of others, it may be expeditious to get them on the table.

Reeder begins his critical comments by suggesting that a Western-oriented moral problems course need not assume a reasoning/principle model of morality, nor does it need to assume an autonomy thesis about morality and ethics. He further suggests that a historical course may adopt a hermeneutical stance in its methodology for studying other religious ethical traditions. I accept both of these points. With respect to the first, I need only note that a number of the historical and hermeneutical-dialogical courses in the sample are precisely moral problems courses that avoid making the assumptions identified with the formalist paradigm. And, with regard to the second point, I am quite willing to concede that historical courses may be (re)designed with a hermeneutical aim and dimension. But, then, I need to go on to reiterate the larger lesson here. Taken together, both of these points tend to support my earlier critical observation about the formalist and historical courses—namely, that in redressing certain of their weaknesses in presupposition and method, the resultingly modified courses come, by reason of these changes, ever closer to the hermeneutical-dialogical paradigm. Reeder also suggests that the extreme methodological positions represented by the formalist and historical paradigms—roughly, universalism versus particularism—are no longer regarded as viable in their extreme versions. Rather, he contends, awareness of theoretical debate about the diversity of moral paradigms in the West (e.g., neo-Kantianism, neo-Aristotelianism, benevolence-sympathy views), combined with a more sophisticated historical view of how to approach similarity/dissimilarity among moral traditions, has led to the emergence of a consensus about method in comparative religious ethics that is explicitly hermeneutical and that leads to courses which examine closer-to-home (Western) traditions, contexts, and materials. I agree in part with this observation, especially since I have cited evidence indicating that even formalist courses are concerned to some extent with matters of historical contextualization and explicitly confine their attention to principally Western traditions. Nonetheless, except perhaps for those dealing explicitly with themes of benevolence and virtue in Western traditions, the courses within the formalist-conceptual paradigm still appear largely oriented to more standard types of Western moral theory, and it remains true that they are much less concerned with historical context than courses in the other paradigms. Moreover, regarding the historical paradigm, although I agree that some of its courses may have a hermeneutical dimension and focus on closer-to-home traditions, they cannot be properly characterized as openly hermeneutical-dialogical, nor do they tend to restrict their comparative focus to Western moral traditions.

Reeder further suggests that I ought to argue that: (1) the formalist and historical paradigms are reflections of earlier traditions of teaching and scholarship (resting on opposed methodological assumptions); (2) these paradigms are still evidenced in some courses, and, in any case, students could perceive courses as expressive of those paradigms; (3) methodologically speaking, many courses end up somewhere in the middle between these paradigms due to the aforementioned advances in theory and historical understanding; and (4) a hermeneutically oriented method could be employed in a variety of courses with differing aims and foci (e.g., a limited comparison between traditions and a focus on sociomoral problems; an uncovering of whole traditions that contrast significantly with Western traditions; a controlled comparison of only two traditions from different cultural contexts; and comparative method and theory).

In responding to this plausible alternative vision of curricula in comparative religious ethics, I should perhaps begin by emphasizing that the typology of curricular paradigms developed in this chapter is by no means the only possible lens for viewing and examining the courses within the sample. As a consequence, I am open to alternative typologies, including the one suggested in (4), and I had even entertained developing a similar typology with species and varieties of intracultural versus cross-cultural comparison, extensive versus limited comparison, "moral problems" versus "general moral-religious existential themes" orientation, explicitly versus implicitly (or even non-) theoretical orientation, and the like. I came to the conclusion that such an alternative typology might tend to obscure rather than illuminate genuine differences in presupposition and method among courses in the sample and, furthermore, that such a typology might make it harder to relate this study to current methodological discussions in the field. For these two reasons, then, among others, I selected a strategy of methodological typologization (the four paradigms)—precisely in order to ferret out and highlight differences in presupposition and method and to engage the extant methodological literature. I hasten to add that these alternative visions for examining the curriculum in the field are not mutually exclusive, and I welcome the insights generated by visions other than my own. Reeder has made a very fine start in this respect.

With respect to the other points in Reeder's alternative vision, I can be reasonably brief. I agree with the basic thrust of (1)—about the formalist and historical paradigms being reflections of earlier traditions. Indeed, in arguing for the greater adequacy of the hermeneutical-dialogical paradigm, I was suggesting that the other two paradigms ought eventually to be left behind. I certainly agree with (2)—about the continuing presence of these paradigms—since the evidence of the sample clearly indicates that they are still operative. I am sympathetic with the basic thrust of (3)—about many courses falling in between the paradigms—but I am inclined to think that a category such as "somewhere in the middle" obscures more than it illuminates genuine differences among these courses, differences that may be more vividly brought out by the contrasts among the first three paradigms as I have outlined them. Perhaps I have created some misleading straw persons (so to speak), but ideal types or paradigms often clarify reality as well as generate illuminating debate, and this has been my intention. I do not deny that the dividing lines among the paradigms can be breached and that they are breaking down—this is why I thought it might be significant to point out that the majority of courses in the sample are located in the historical and hermeneutical paradigms, with an ever increasing number in the latter. The basic claim of (4)—about the hermeneutical method being adaptable to a variety of courses—is undeniably true, as is clearly indicated by the fact that courses within the hermeneutical paradigm of the sample range across the spectrum of aims and foci cited by Reeder and by this chapter.

I conclude this brief excursus with an acknowledgment of gratitude to Reeder for raising these points and compelling me to attend to them. Without such conversation partners we cannot learn.

Notes

1. Taken together with a few published course descriptions and pedagogical discussions, the database for this study included thirty-five course descriptions/syllabi. I am grateful to the following colleagues for sharing with me their course descriptions and pedagogical reflections: Diana Cates (Iowa), Anthony Cua (Catholic University), Darrell Fasching (South Florida), Joel Gereboff (Arizona State), Bruce Grelle (California State, Chico), Roderick Hindery (California State, Northridge), Timothy Jackson (Stanford), William Jennings (Muhlenberg), John Kelsay (Florida State), Robert McKim (Illinois), Susan Niditch (Amherst), Gene Outka (Yale), John Reeder (Brown), Frank Reynolds (Chicago), Henry Rosemont (St. Mary's, Maryland), James Smurl (Indiana, Indianapolis), Jeffrey Stout (Princeton), Douglas Sturm (Bucknell), and Tod Swanson (Arizona State).

2. In private correspondence, both John Kelsay and John Reeder have taken exception to my articulation of some of these presuppositions, contending, for example, that they are too realist in orientation and too focused on a reasoning/principle model of morality, that they overstate the commitment to the autonomy of ethics thesis, and that they reflect a now outmoded scholarly approach. I concede that I may state a bit too starkly some of the presuppositions, but my intention in so doing is to highlight tendencies and images projected by these courses as well as to relate them to current methodological paradigms in the scholarship of the field. Some of these criticisms and my response to them are discussed in the afterword.

3. The alternative formulations of "fusion of horizons," "normative appropriation," and "transformation of view" were suggested to me by John Reeder in private correspondence.

4. Illustrative works include, for historical sociology, the writings of Max Weber; for formalist and quasi-formalist approaches, Green 1988 and Little and Twiss 1978; for ethical naturalism, Lovin and Reynolds 1985; and for historicist critique, Stout 1988.

5. Perhaps this is the place to note that the majority of courses in my sample fall within either the historical or the hermeneutical paradigm. Moreover, there is evidence to suggest that the dividing lines among the paradigms may be breaking down—in the direction of the hermeneutical-dialogical paradigm.

References

Green, Ronald M. 1988. *Religion and Moral Reason.* New York: Oxford University Press.

Green, Ronald M., and Charles H. Reynolds. 1986. "Cosmogony and the 'Questions of Ethics.'" *Journal of Religious Ethics* 14, 1 (Spring):139–155.

Juergensmeyer, Mark. 1991. "Comparative Ethics." In *Tracing Common Themes,* edited by John B. Carman and Steven P. Hopkins, 263–272. Atlanta: Scholars Press.

Little, David, and Sumner B. Twiss. 1978. *Comparative Religious Ethics: A New Method.* New York: Harper and Row.

Lovin, Robin W., and Frank E. Reynolds. 1985. "In the Beginning." In *Cosmogony and Ethical Order: New Studies in Comparative Ethics,* edited by Robin W. Lovin and Frank E. Reynolds, 1–35. Chicago: University of Chicago Press.

_____. 1991. "Teaching Comparative Religious Ethics." In *Tracing Common Themes,* edited by John B. Carman and Steven P. Hopkins, 249–261. Atlanta: Scholars Press.

Schweiker, William. 1992. "The Drama of Interpretation and the Philosophy of Religions: An Essay on Understanding in Comparative Religious Ethics." In *Discourse and Practice,* edited by Frank E. Reynolds and David Tracy, 263–294. Albany: State University of New York Press.

Sizemore, Russell F. 1990. "Comparative Religious Ethics As a Field: Faith Culture and Reason in Ethics." In *Ethics, Wealth, and Salvation,* edited by Russell F. Sizemore and Donald K Swearer, 87–89; nn. 260, 261. Columbia: University of South Carolina Press.

Stout, Jeffrey. 1988. *Ethics After Babel.* Boston: Beacon Press.

Twiss, Sumner B., and Walter H. Conser Jr., eds. 1992. *Experience of the Sacred: Readings in the Phenomenology of Religion.* Hanover, N.H., and London: Brown University Press/University Press of New England.

Yearley, Lee H. 1990a. *Mencius and Aquinas.* Albany: State University of New York Press.

_____. 1990b. "Education and the Intellectual Virtues." In *Beyond the Classics? Essays in Religious Studies and Liberal Education,* edited by Frank E. Reynolds and Sheryl L. Burkhalter, 89–105. Atlanta: Scholars Press.

_____. 1991. "Bourgeois Relativism and the Comparative Study of the Self." In *Tracing Common Themes: Comparative Courses in the Study of Religion,* edited by John B. Carman and Steven P. Hopkins, 165–178. Atlanta: Scholars Press.

Appendix: Four Illustrative Course Descriptions

Formalist-Conceptual Comparative Paradigm

"Religious Ethics and Moral Problems"
(Introductory Undergraduate Level)
John Kelsay, Florida State University

Is it ever right to lie? Should capital punishment be abolished? Is the use of animals in scientific research justifiable? This course focuses on the ways that Jews, Christians, and Muslims analyze and make judgments about these and other issues. Students will learn about the various methods of reasoning, sources of authority, and possible arguments characteristic of ethics in the major religious traditions of Western culture, and will be challenged to develop their own skills in moral argument. Illustrative course topics and readings from the course syllabus: Theories of Ethics (Macquarrie, Childress, Hare); Religion and Morality (Frankena, Kelsay, Jacobs); Lying and Moral Argument (Bok, Herring, Kant); Friendship (C. S. Lewis); Sexual Ethics (Wasserstrom, O'Connell, Nelson, Noval, Fyzee); Legal Enforcement of Morality (*Bowers v. Hard-*

wick, Hart, Little, MacKinnon); Abortion (*Roe* v. *Wade,* Harrison, *Humanae Vitae,* Herring, Hathout); Capital Punishment (van den Haag, Yoder, Kelsay); Citizenship and Social Justice (Kotb, M. L. King, Cuomo, Henry); Use of Animals by Humans (Singer, Linzey, Bleich, Masri); Environmental Ethics (White, Gore, Berry); Practices of Piety (Guroian, Johnson, Kelsay, Wouk, Malcolm X).

Historical Comparative Paradigm

"Ethics of World Religions" (Intermediate Undergraduate Level)
James Smurl, Indiana University at Indianapolis

The religious beliefs and values of the world's religions often are compared. This seems inevitable; indeed, when done well, it can be intellectually and socially profitable. Not all such comparisons are "odious"—at least not if they are made with empathy and with concern for accuracy in one's facts, for clarity in one's concepts, and for the verifiability of one's judgments.

This course aims to show how comparisons between the moral values and the social-ethical positions of religious traditions can be accomplished with accuracy and empathy, clarity and reasonableness. In order to succeed we first shall need to ask open-ended, rather than prejudicial, questions. Second, we shall need to restrict our questions to those that are possible to answer. And, finally, attending to what may be one of the most important factors in comparisons, we shall need to make certain that the things compared are roughly equal—heeding the well-known caution about comparing "apples and oranges." If all of these activities are carried forward with the kind of empathy recommended by the Native American who invited people to "walk around in his moccasins for a while," then a rich and rewarding learning experience is what we can expect.

In order to achieve our goals we first shall become acquainted with several different traditions of moral values rooted in the religious beliefs and practices of Asian and Western cultures. We shall learn the basic facts about those traditions of religious ethics by asking factual questions (who? what? when? where? and why?). In the process we shall become acquainted with the basic moral concepts and with the moral standards these traditions endorse for both personal and social life in the family, at work, in the natural environment, and in social institutions. Next, we shall compare the patterns of moral belief, practice, and teaching in these traditions in order to determine in which ways they are similar and in which ways they differ. Finally, we shall determine whether or not there are any generalizations that can be made about general, human considerations entailed in the ethics of world religions.

Course units include: Introduction—Course Goals and Methodology, Nature of Ethics, Relationship of Religion and Ethics, Nature of Comparative Religious Ethics (as an intracultural as well as a cross-cultural study); Ethics in Asian Religions—Chinese, Hindu, Buddhist, and Japanese Traditions (including foundations and ethics in different spheres of life); Ethics in Western Religions—Jewish, Christian, and Muslim (including foundations and ethics in different spheres of life); and Comparative Religious Ethics (including foundations, applications, and topics for debate—e.g., universal moral principles, experiences of transcendence, myth and ritual, hope, and moral virtue). Basic course readings are drawn from Carmody and Carmody, Smart and Hect, Smurl, and encyclopedias and dictionaries of religion and ethics, supplemented by specially prepared readings and handouts.

Hermeneutical-Dialogical Comparative Paradigm

"Religious Perspectives and the Twenty-First Century"
(Senior Seminar for Undergraduate Majors)
Douglas Sturm, Bucknell University

The idea for this course arose from the "Critical Issues" segment of the projected Parliament of the World's Religions for 1993. The seminar is designed to encourage thinking about the long-range future—what it might be and what it should be— from the perspective of divergent religious communities. I have isolated four areas in which we are confronting social-cultural issues of a long-range character: (1) Earth, (2) Gender, (3) Wealth, and (4) Violence. During the initial portion of the seminar, we shall engage in working sessions attempting to design more precisely the actual questions that arise in each of these four areas. Among other things, we shall, for the purposes of stimulating our minds, read W. Warren Wagner's *The Next Three Futures* . . . which develops a set of alternative projections ("ideal types") of the future—liberal, radical, and countercultural. I intend this set of projections as a heuristic device for comparative purposes as we proceed to unfold the central (social) ethical orientation of selected religious communities: (1) Christianity, (2) Buddhism, and (3) Primal Religions . . . We shall use the book of writings— past and present—from the world's religions developed by the DePaul faculty (edited by Crossan) as a common base for our consideration. Against that background, we shall then engage in a more specialized study of each of the segments in the resultant twelve-part grid (four areas/three religious communities). So, for instance, in the area of (2) Gender, we shall explore such sources as (a) Uta Ranke Heinnemann, *Eunuchs for the Kingdom of Heaven,* (b) Jose Ignacio Cabezon (ed.), *Buddhism, Sexuality, Gender,* and (c) Paula Gunn Allen, *The Sacred Hoop.* I intend, as we proceed through each of these parts, to have different subsets of students adopt a perspective for purposes of our deliberations. The seminar assumes that religious communities are not merely "traditions"; that they are living communities engaged in responding to the challenges of history; that they are not single-voiced; that they have been influenced by each other in their encounters with each other and most likely shall continue to do so; that they are not all "ultimately" the same, but that they are not necessarily diametrically in opposition to each other either; that each conceives itself as providing authentic means of dealing with the issues of the world; and that each contains critics who, although emerging from the same history, nonetheless seek to press the community into alternative directions. At the heart of the seminar resides the "idea of interreligious dialogue" as a need of our times given current conditions of human history. . . . The central idea of the seminar is to form a kind of mini–Parliament of the World's Religions through which we can represent a group of religiously minded persons from divergent backgrounds and communities reflecting about our common future.

Comparative Methods and Theory Paradigm

"Seminar in Religion and Culture: Comparative Religious Ethics"
(Seminar for M. A. and Upper-Level Undergraduate Students)
John Kelsay, Florida State University

This seminar will acquaint the student with certain basic ideas in the comparative study of religious ethics. The focus is on understanding the questions and assumptions that inform the major approaches to such study; the method will be to analyze portions of the work of scholars who illustrate these approaches and to ask about the philosophical point of view on which they draw. Along the way, students will also learn a good bit about the moral teaching of several religious traditions and about the general questions of ethics. Illustrative course topics and readings from the syllabus: Introduction (Geertz); Religion and Society—Max Weber's Contribution (Weber, Runciman, Zeitlin, Little), Ernst Troeltsch (Troeltsch, Little); Religion and Morality—Ron Green (Green, Kant, Lauritzen, Stendahl, Schechter, Zaehner, Weber), Little and Twiss (Little and Twiss, essays from Outka and Reeder, Gerhardsson, Bornkamm, Ladd, Rahula, *JRE* articles), Islam (Kelsay, Hodgson, Rahman, Hourani), Human Rights (Little et al.). Background reading for those with little previous work in ethics (P. Taylor, Broad) or in world religions (Bush et al., Streng's series).

Chapter Two

Scholarship and Citizenship: Comparative Religious Ethicists as Public Intellectuals

BRUCE GRELLE
California State University, Chico

Writers and scholars are citizens. It is therefore obvious that they have a strict duty to participate in public life. It remains to be seen in what form and to what extent.
Emile Durkheim ([1904] 1973, 58)

How might comparative religious ethicists bring their theoretical, historical, and philosophical concerns to bear upon the moral lives and struggles of their fellow citizens outside the academy? To what extent might their work contribute not only to an understanding of this wider public world but also, perhaps, to its transformation?

I have argued elsewhere that comparative religious ethics can be understood as a form of critical-constructive inquiry that seeks to clarify and respond to the struggles and wishes of the age (Grelle 1993a, 1993b, 1995). Many of the struggles and wishes of *our age* have found expression in the movement for interfaith dialogue. In this chapter I will propose that one of the main ways that comparative religious ethicists might pursue a vocation as public intellectuals is to relate their work to interreligious dialogues on practical moral issues.

We live in a world that is characterized by persistent abuses of human rights, by vast disparities of wealth and power between individuals and nations, by the degradation of the environment, and by seemingly unending religious, racial, and ethnic conflict and violence. These and other practical moral issues have increasingly been the focus of dialogue between representatives of diverse religious communities.

Interreligious moral dialogues seek to address the question of how we are to think about and respond to moral problems such as these in a religiously and culturally pluralistic world. These dialogues typically call upon the religions of the world, and upon all people of good will, to share responsibility for the creation of a more just and peaceful order at local, regional, and global levels. Most participants entertain the hope that such dialogues can lead to new moral self-understandings and practical policies that might be acceptable to, and combine important insights from, different religious and cultural traditions. It is believed that this would be an important if not indispensable first step toward joint action aimed at alleviating if not resolving the sort of moral problems mentioned above (see Küng and Kuschel 1995; Twiss 1993, 256–258).

There are a number of good reasons why comparative religious ethicists, as *scholars*, should be interested in interreligious moral dialogues. As Peggy Morgan (1995) has reminded us, religious believers, as well as texts and history, are the raw material, the research field, for academics. Interfaith gatherings that promote dialogue give scholars the opportunity to meet a considerable number and variety of believers, including religious leaders, who are not normally gathered together in one place. Many academics also teach courses that analyze the phenomenon of dialogue itself and, in their case, such gatherings provide ready-made case studies about which to teach and write. There is every reason to believe that the method of participant-observation pioneered by some sociologists, anthropologists, and phenomenologists might be profitably employed at interfaith gatherings by comparative religious ethicists as they seek to extend their understanding of religion and morality in the contemporary world (Morgan 1995, 158).

But for comparative religious ethicists as *public intellectuals* who seek to link scholarship with *citizenship,* interreligious dialogues are—or can be—more than raw material for teaching and research. Such dialogues can themselves provide an effective vehicle for addressing issues of public importance and for efforts to bring about the sort of personal and social transformation that will be required if we are to address many of the social and moral problems we are facing.

Of course, many comparative religious ethicists are themselves members of faith communities, and they may participate directly in interfaith activities primarily as people of faith and as representatives of particular religious and moral traditions. But in this chapter I will be interested in whether and how comparative religious ethicists might play a role in interreligious moral dialogue, not primarily as people of faith who also happen to be scholars of religion, and not primarily as scholars of religion who happen to view interfaith activity as an interesting topic of teaching and research, but as public intellectuals who bring a distinctive perspective and set of goals and values to bear upon the activity of moral dialogue.

Comparative Religious Ethicists as Public Intellectuals

Public intellectuals seek to unite—in their thinking, speaking, and writing—the tasks and virtues of scholarship with the tasks and virtues of citizenship. More specifically, a public intellectual seeks to balance the *scholar's* critical distance from taken-for-granted assumptions and institutions with the *citizen's* commitment to a shared moral life.[1]

Public intellectuals may be *social critics* who focus on political and material culture. They may be *cultural critics* who discuss a peoples' aesthetic and artistic heritage and identity. Or they may be *religious critics* who focus on spiritual questions regarding the ultimate meaning and purpose of a people's life together (Dean 1994, xiv). But what unites these various forms of intellectual activity and what makes them public is their effort to relate the stories scholars tell to the stories current in the society at large, to expose them both to mutual discussion and criticism, thereby getting the story right for scholarship but also for popular consciousness (Bellah et al. 1985, 302). Such intellectual activity is public not just in the sense that its findings are publicly available or useful to some group or institution outside the academic world. Rather, it is public by virtue of its effort to engage citizens in dialogue about matters of common interest and the common good (Bellah et al. 1985, 303–304; Dean 1994, xvii, 153–172).

But in recent years a growing number of observers have noticed a decline in the number and influence of public intellectuals and a dissolution of the unity between the tasks and virtues of scholarship and citizenship. Several of these observers have argued that this decline and dissolution is especially apparent in the work of many *academic* intellectuals—those scholars, teachers, and writers who earn their livings in institutions of higher education.

Russell Jacoby has provided one of the most provocative accounts of intellectual life in the "age of academe." According to Jacoby, "the habitat, manners, and idiom of intellectuals have been transformed within the past fifty years."

> Campuses are their homes; colleagues their audience; monographs and specialized journals their media. . . . Academics write for professional journals, that . . . create insular societies. . . . The professors share an idiom and a discipline. Gathering in annual conferences to compare notes, they constitute their own universe. . . . As intellectuals became academics, they had no need to write in a public prose; they did not, and finally they could not. (Jacoby 1987, 6–7)

This failure to employ a vernacular language that encourages and enables public dialogue about matters of common interest is closely related to another troubling feature of much academic discourse: its fragmentation and apparent loss of a larger critical vision of how scholarship might contribute to that "sense of the whole" without which public life cannot be sustained (see Dean 1994, especially xxii, 3–18, 153–180). In this connection, Jacoby laments the prevalence in academic culture of a kind of conformism, caution, and lack of utopian vision (1987, 117). And Mark Krupnick observes that the extreme sophistication of much of academic scholarship has not protected it, in many cases, from a "preening triviality." Far from striving for a holistic view, "advanced academic theory has disintegrated—without much sign of regret—into myriad 'fields' and sects" (Krupnick 1986, 3). Despite its many individual triumphs, much of contemporary scholarship amounts to little more than a series of isolated activities that is lacking in interest or usefulness even for other scholars, let alone for educated members of the general public. Although academic scholarship has become more and more refined at the level of theory and method, it has become less and less consequential for public life (Graff and Gibbons 1985, 9).

A number of intellectual and institutional factors have contributed to the decline of public intellectual activity among academics. Certainly, the vogue enjoyed by poststructuralism, an intellectual movement that eschews all efforts to achieve a larger "sense of the whole" or to think and talk about a "common culture" or a "common good," has encouraged a tendency among many academic intellectuals to adopt a style of "endless refinement, esoteric jargon, romantic posturing, and fierce intramural polemic" (Michael Walzer, cited in Dean 1994, xix).[2] But even more significant are such factors as the professionalization of the academy and increasing disciplinary specialization.

Along with the emergence of industrial-corporate society came the rise of the research university, which quickly replaced the college as the model for higher education. Although the goals of the college had been the integration of various fields of knowledge and the cultivation of educated citizens capable of "an uplifting and unifying influence on society" (Bellah et al. 1985, 298), the hallmarks of the new universities were disciplinary autonomy, the production of specialized knowledge, and the preparation of a corps of scientific and technical experts, specialists, and professionals capable of managing the complex workings of the government and economy.[3]

Of course, this transformation brought about many positive achievements. The new educational system included students who had previously been excluded from higher education because of their class, gender, or race. It prepared larger numbers of people for employment in industrial society. And it generated the kind of specialized knowledge that is necessary in an increasingly complex technological economy and society (Bellah et al. 1985, 299–300).

But the professionalization and specialization of academic life also contributed to an erosion of the bond between scholarship and citizenship (Bellah et al. 1985, 299). Rather than thinking of themselves as public intellectuals who might shed light upon a common life they shared with their fellow citizens, academic intellectuals came increasingly to think of themselves in terms of their disciplines—as physicists, philosophers, literary critics, political scientists, and so on—each of which could boast its own professional associations, journals, and criteria for membership.

This is not necessarily to say that individual scholars have always had much choice in the matter. A scholar's job, salary, and opportunities for advancement depend on the evaluation of specialists, and this inevitably affects the issues discussed and the language employed (Jacoby 1987, 6). Universities reward faculty who can establish their own prestige through specialized publication directed toward and recognized by highly specialized expert publics or elites rather than through popular or practical action in the community or influence on public opinion and social change (Everett 1977, 99).

Thus, the professional has largely exchanged general citizenship in society for membership in the "community of the competent" (Thomas Haskell, cited in Bellah et al. 1985, 299). Within this world of specialized professional expertise, the worth of opinions is judged not by open competition with the opinions of one's fellow citizens but rather by the close evaluation of one's professional colleagues. And the professional's loyalties are not to some nebulous public realm but to that scholar's discipline and professional colleagues (Bellah et al. 1985, 299; Dean 1994, 20–23).

Indeed, the very notion of a shared *public* realm of common interests has been undermined by the ethos of professionalism and specialization. For it is the nature of each specialized discipline to disavow knowledge of the whole or of any part of the whole that lies beyond its own strictly defined domain. It would be "unprofessional" to claim knowledge or expertise outside one's specialty. Consequently, it became more and more difficult to think about public life as anything other than an arena in which disparate individuals and groups compete in the pursuit of their own private interests. That larger "sense of the whole" upon which a sense of the common good depends all but disappeared from academic intellectual discourse and from much of public life (Bellah et al. 1985, 299–307; Dean 1994, 6–39).

The emergence of religious studies departments in the 1960s and 1970s was due in large part to these same processes of professionalization and specialization. The more traditional theological approach to the study of religion, which had once dominated higher education, had begun to appear unprofessional to many academic intellectuals because it was too personally engaged, too preoccupied with "big issues" rather than sharply focused specialized studies. The religious studies approach, by contrast, was appropriately detached, scientific, and neutral (Dean 1994, 22–27). Indeed, the pressure to establish professional credentials and academic legitimacy by appealing to a spirit of scientific detachment was felt in an especially acute form by religious studies scholars. For despite the increasing acceptance of religious studies as part of the curriculum in many secular educational institutions, there remained a trace of the suspicion that "religion is caught, not taught" (Kitagawa 1959, 8).

In view of the problematic and unclear status of religion in the life of the contemporary university and contemporary intellectuals (see Bellah 1983b, ix), religious studies scholars have often gone even farther than other academic intellectuals in their insistence that scholarship should be characterized by a posture of "disinterested objectivity," "personal detachment," "disinterested irreverence," and "the perspective of the outsider" (Conrad Cherry, cited in Dean 1994, 25–26). Religious studies scholars have been anxious to assure all concerned that, just as in any other field of professional scholarship, they "would gauge their work . . . by how well it conformed to the acceptable specialties in the contemporary American university" (Cherry, cited in Dean 1994, 26). As was the case in other academic disciplines, "the politics of peer approval took precedence over the politics of public persuasion" (Dean 1994, 26).[4]

But what about religious ethics? Surely those engaged in the academic study of religious ethics have been forced by their subject matter itself to maintain a close connection between their scholarship and the larger social and moral issues that are of concern to the wider public.

It is true that many religious ethicists have established reputations as experts in technical areas of applied biomedical ethics, or business ethics, or legal ethics (see Dean 1994, 26). But very often, ethicists working in these areas are involved in highly specialized theoretical debates among themselves, or they are called in as technical experts to advise their professional counterparts in medicine, business, or law. Although such activities are valuable in themselves, the discourses that accompany them are frequently so technical or so sharply focused on the details of specific ethical decisions or policies that they are difficult to translate into a more generally public discourse on the moral dimensions of policymaking and the professions.

As for the field of *comparative religious ethics* more specifically, the literature to date has been remarkable for its preoccupation with issues of theory and method and for its lack of attention to substantive issues of practical moral concern. While there have been significant historical studies of particular traditions, this early literature has been characterized above all by ongoing debates among partisans of alternative methods and approaches to this new field of study.[5]

This tension between the *academic intellectual's agenda* of shaping a discipline and the *public intellectual's agenda* of shaping public discourse and opinion might lead one to conclude that, in this age of professionalism and disciplinary specialization, the university can no longer serve as an effective venue and vehicle for the work of public intellectuals. William Dean, for example, has argued forcefully that public intellectuals are more likely to be socially effective if they give their loyalties to virtually any other institution in the society's third (nongovernment, not-for-profit, voluntary) sector *except* the university.

According to Dean, third-sector institutions—churches, political movements, social action agencies, gender- and race-based rights and consciousness raising groups, environmental organizations, arts organizations, charitable foundations, and so on—offer public intellectuals a better venue or psychological home and a better vehicle or instrument for shaping public life than do universities. Furthermore, he believes that there is a simple reason for this:

> The professed norms of the nonuniversity third sector tend to pertain more directly to questions of the public good than do the norms of the university, let alone the norms of the first or second sectors. In the government sector, civil order is the highest norm, and, in the market sector, profit is the highest norm; whereas, in the third sector, some vision of a common good is the highest order. Social concerns are not only legitimate motivators in the third sector, but they are meant to be, however much they fail to be, the overriding motivators. In this respect, I believe the university is no longer a typical third sector organization; it is increasingly dedicated to professional activities that have little to do with the common good. (1994, 161)

Dean is not arguing that academic intellectuals should resign their professorships and seek work in the third sector. When he says that third-sector institutions are more suitable venues and vehicles for the work of public intellectuals than is the university, he is not talking about a place of employment but about a place where certain ideas and attitudes can be openly and critically fostered (1994, 160). Neither is he claiming that all academic intellectuals should be public intellectuals nor that all intellectuals teaching in universities or colleges fail to function as public intellectuals even within their universities and colleges. He argues only that academic intellectuals seldom become public intellectuals, that this is not accidental, and that it is a serious problem for public life when scholarship and citizenship become disconnected (1994, 157).[6]

And yet, Dean acknowledges that there are occasions, however rare, when the academic intellectual's professional agenda and the public agenda happen to coincide. This occurs most obviously in what he describes as the *new, socially responsive fields* like environmental studies, women's studies, and African-American studies (1994, 157–158). What I want to argue at this point is that, insofar as it addresses itself to the practical task of inter-religious dialogue on contemporary moral issues, *comparative religious ethics may itself be viewed as just such a new, socially responsive field where academic and public agendas intersect.*

As we begin to explore this relationship between comparative religious ethics and interreligious dialogue, it is important to recognize that the potential for such dialogue is present not only in the context of the interfaith movement as such but in numerous other social and institutional settings where representatives of different faith traditions and moral orientations encounter one another, including universities, public schools, and a whole range of civic and cultural organizations. I believe that there are a variety of opportunities for comparative religious ethicists to play a role as public intellectuals linking scholarship and citizenship in each of these settings.

I will first consider the comparative religious ethicist's own *primary* institutional setting, namely, the university. For I remain somewhat more optimistic than William Dean that it is possible for academics to play a role as genuinely public intellectuals even while remaining within and identifying with the university and even while utilizing their conventional vehicles of teaching and writing.[7] I will then sketch some possible roles for comparative religious ethicists in other civic and cultural settings, especially in the interfaith movement and in the public schools, both of which constitute important *secondary* locations for the work of comparative religious ethicists as public intellectuals. My discussion of each of these venues will be based largely on my own experiments with linking scholarship and citizenship at the local level in northern California over the course of the past several years.

Comparative Religious Ethics and
Interreligious Dialogue in the University

How might the activities of teaching and writing be enlisted in the search for practical strategies for addressing moral issues in the contemporary world? Might the institution of the university itself be utilized to facilitate dialogue between representatives of disparate religious and philosophical traditions? A consideration of these questions will help us assess the extent to which comparative religious ethics might be or become a new, socially responsive discipline where academic and public agendas intersect.

Teaching

Despite the many well-founded criticisms of intellectual life in the "age of academe," I continue to believe that university teaching can make a significant contribution to public life. My call for comparative religious ethicists to think and act more self-consciously as public intellectuals does not mean that they should give up what they have been doing in order to do something entirely different. But it does mean that they should think more explicitly about how the content and style of their teaching is related to their own and their students' responsibilities as citizens. By keeping the relationship between the classroom and public life in the foreground, teachers can help to cultivate a larger "sense of the whole" and a greater self-awareness on the part of their students and themselves that they are participants in cultural struggles over whether and how to reform society.

A particularly promising way of bringing comparative religious ethics to bear on the task of interreligious moral dialogue is offered by what Sumner B. Twiss (1993) has described as the "hermeneutical-dialogical" approach to teaching. This approach starts with the recognition that we live in a morally and religiously pluralistic world but that all people and groups share similar sorts of practical moral problems. It then seeks to construct a common moral world (a fusion of horizons) between one's own moral tradition, on the one hand, and the moral traditions(s) being studied, on the other. Such an approach itself constitutes a "moral praxis" that involves "a dialectic of translation from one moral world to another (the other to ours), of receptivity to the other (insight into the other's moral world), and, through continuous dialogue between our world and the other's, a constructive effort to answer the question of how we (ourselves and the other) should live (a distinctive good of this praxis)" (Twiss 1993, 256).[8]

A brief description of a course I have taught for several years may serve to illustrate this approach to teaching comparative religious ethics. "Cross-Cultural Environmental Ethics" is a course that involves an analysis and critique of the variety of ways in which religious and secular worldviews and ethics influence attitudes, behaviors, and policies toward the environment. It is part of the general education curriculum at a medium-sized state university and enrolls approximately eighty to a hundred students in two sections per semester.

The course begins with a presentation of the environmental problems that face us as we stand on the verge of the twenty-first century: the ongoing pollution of water and air, the accelerating human population growth, the depletion of natural resources (fossil fuels, forests, fisheries), the extinction of plant and animal species, and so on.[9]

In keeping with the model outlined by Twiss, the course then turns to a consideration of the structure and limitations of "our" intellectual and moral tradition, namely, the "secular" worldview and ethos of "modernity," which has not only shaped the outlook and aspirations of most North Americans and Europeans (including those of most American university students), but those of an increasingly large number of non-Western people around the world as well. This portion of the course identifies the typical patterns of thought and values (for example, materialism, mechanism, dualism, scientism, individualism, anthropocentrism) and institutional forms (for example, industrial economies, nation-states) that are definitive of modernity (see Bowman 1990, 7–23; Kinsley 1995, 125–140). The major focus of this portion of the course is not only upon the environmental impact of modern technological civilization but also upon the consumer lifestyle that it encourages and enables and upon the ethical, political, and spiritual impact of this ethos of consumerism. The variety of environmental problems that we face are presented not as a series of isolated technical problems but as an inevitable consequence of our form of life—our outlooks, behaviors, and institutional arrangements. The environmental crisis is thus seen as a reflection of a deeper crisis of culture and character that cannot be resolved by scientific or technological means alone but only by a profound intellectual, moral, institutional, and spiritual transformation.

Having defined the environmental crisis as a crisis of character, the course then brings this worldview and ethos of modernity into dialogue with a range of alternative intellectual and moral traditions. The particular traditions that are discussed vary from semester to semester but typically include some combination of Native American, biblical, Buddhist, Confucian, and Taoist traditions as well as such contemporary movements as ecofeminism, social ecology, and deep ecology. Through a critical reading and discussion of texts and videos and through formal and informal writing exercises, students become familiar with the key assumptions of each of these perspectives and reflect upon their implications for the students' own assumptions, values, and lifestyles. Such an encounter contributes to the creation of a "common moral world" and helps fuel the fire of the students' own ecological and moral imaginations—their creative abilities to picture a proper place for human beings in the natural world and to envision personal and societal ways of life that might correspond to that place.

In the third and final section of the course, students are asked to bring their ecological and moral imaginations to bear upon several contemporary policy issues involving questions about land use (multiple use versus permanent wilderness designations), air quality (the emission of "greenhouse gases" and the problems of ozone depletion and global warming), and the politics of financial aid and technology transfers from rich to poor countries. This section of the course draws attention to the diverse religious, philosophical, and moral assumptions about the relationship between humans and the earth, air, water, plants, animals, and God(s)—assumptions that are often at the root of ideological, economic, and political conflicts surrounding particular environmental issues. Students learn that questions about whether certain technologies should be employed or about whether certain environmental policies ought to be adopted are not only scientific, economic, and political questions; they are moral, philosophical, and religious questions as well.

Thus, the overall aim of such a course is threefold: to help students learn to appreciate the ambiguous moral and environmental implications of deep-seated religious and philosophical assumptions; to draw on diverse re-

ligious and secular worldviews as resources for our own moral imaginations and for the creation of a viable cross-cultural environmental ethic;
and to develop some skills for analyzing the ideological and ethical conflicts
surrounding selected environmental issues.

Many students seem to welcome and feel empowered by their discovery
of moral languages that provide alternatives to the dominant languages of
individualism and materialism. In both formal and informal feedback on
the course, many students have indicated that their encounter with alternative spiritualities and ethics has prompted them to greater self-awareness of
their own often unexamined assumptions about the meaning and goals of
human life and about the relationship of human beings to one another and
to the natural world. A considerable number report that they have been led
to reconsider their lifestyles or career goals as a result of their engagement
with the ecological and moral visions of the diverse figures and traditions
encountered in the course.

Of course, the personal transformations reported by students as the result of a single college course are often quite ephemeral. But unless we are
prepared to abandon all hope in the efficacy of education and adopt an
across-the-board cynicism about the ability of education to change attitudes and convictions, there is no good reason to assume that the student
outcomes of a course in comparative religious ethics are any more fleeting
than outcomes produced by other courses in the university curriculum. At
the very least, such a course introduces students to the simple fact that
there are serious and compelling alternatives to the worldview and ethos of
individualism and consumerism.

Obviously, the environment is only one of the issues that might be addressed by a hermeneutical-dialogical approach to teaching comparative religious ethics. Other issues might include such global problems as ethnic violence, human rights, or the imbalance of wealth and power between rich
and poor nations. Or such a course might focus on intracultural problems
such as racism, sexism, homophobia, poverty, and homelessness. Or it
might address existential questions of how to understand self and other,
how to respond to the human capacity for evil, or how to envision a just
and good society (Twiss 1993, 257).

Regardless of the particular issues selected for discussion, this approach
to teaching comparative religious ethics shares one of the basic presuppositions of most interreligious dialogues, namely, that people and groups share
similar sorts of practical moral problems and tasks as well as similarities of
thought and experience sufficient to gain access to one another across cultural boundaries (Twiss 1993, 265). Courses taught from this perspective

> advocate that students employ empathetic understanding to enter imagina-
> tively the context and worldview of other traditions and, further, that after

taking up these standpoints of "the other," they enter into a respectful dialogue of equals where each exposes his or her own cultural assumptions to the
standpoint of "the other" and works to solve shared socio-moral problems
through the fusion of moral horizons and the forging of practical agreements.
Students are encouraged to become co-participants in a dialogue where they
represent imaginatively the "voices" of other traditions. (Twiss 1993, 257)

This type of teaching provides important intellectual and moral background and context for many of the issues and controversies that arise in
other courses in the university curriculum and in civic life. Moreover, the
employment of a cross-cultural approach stresses the need to transcend the
parochialism that often characterizes discussions of morality and policy in
the United States. Many contemporary issues require an international response, and a sympathetic awareness of diverse worldviews and values is a
first step toward building the understanding, cooperation, and larger
"sense of the whole" that will be required in order to address many of the
global issues that students will be facing as citizens in the next several
decades.[10]

When measured according to the public intellectual's project of linking
scholarship to citizenship, the strengths of the hermeneutical-dialogical approach are considerable. It seeks to cultivate an accurate and empathetic
understanding and appreciation of religious ethical traditions as the basis
for the more primary goal of developing students' disciplined thinking
about a topic of existential or *practical moral significance*. It encourages
students' normative appropriation (transformation of view) of aspects of
the traditions in working out a new moral self-understanding or practical
policy that might be acceptable to, and combine important insights from,
these traditions (Twiss 1993, 256).

Research and Writing

The ethos of specialization and professionalism has had an even more significant impact on academic research and writing than it has had on teaching, thus making the linkage of scholarship and citizenship in scholarly
writing all the more challenging. As we have seen, the incentive and reward
structures for faculty in institutions of higher education tend to devalue and
discourage research and writing that is aimed toward an audience outside a
scholar's discipline. Colleges and universities reward those who can establish their own and their institution's prestige through publication directed
toward and recognized by highly specialized expert publics rather than
through popular, practical, or religious action or influence on public opinion or social change (Everett 1977, 99). Not surprisingly, most research and
writing in comparative religious ethics and other academic fields does not

reach the public. Scholars who do seek to address a larger public beyond the circle of their professional peers are often dismissed as mere "popularizers" who have somehow compromised or betrayed the professional standards of their disciplines and who do not contribute to the advancement of true scholarship.

To be sure, some academic writers do achieve a degree of influence and recognition beyond their disciplines, and a few even beyond the academy. But for the most part, Russell Jacoby is right when he states: "A 'famous' sociologist or art historian means famous to other sociologists or art historians, not to anyone else" (1987, 7). The point is not that scholars should be striving to become celebrities. It is simply to observe that most of them (most of us) work within self-enclosed esoteric cultures of experts that are disconnected from the popular culture and generally out of touch with any existing or emergent mass social movement (Everett 1977, 99).

Thus a major task confronting anyone interested in reconciling scholarship and citizenship is to rethink the goals of and the audiences for academic research and writing. This will involve resistance to the disciplinary notion that research has other experts in the field as its only legitimate audience and promotion of the idea that reviews, articles, books, and editorials for the general public are legitimate vehicles for academic writing.

Having said this, however, I should make clear that I do not believe that public intellectuals must entirely abandon specialized research nor that every piece of scholarship must exhibit an overriding public or cultural concern and pass some kind of civic litmus test. Obviously I am not arguing that scholars should be "unprofessional" and forsake accepted canons of research in favor of an ethos of amateurism. Nor do I imagine that the contemporary world is such that we can do without a significant degree of specialization in our intellectual and social lives.

But I do mean to suggest that we need to resist and rethink the part of the professional ethos that implies that one must exchange general citizenship in society for membership in the community of the competent (Bellah et al. 1985, 300). Moreover, to assume that there is a degree of specialization that is proper is, at the same time, to assume that there is a degree that is improper (Berry 1985, 207). And the impropriety begins precisely when specialists lose the ability, and perhaps even more importantly when they lose the will, to speak, at least from time to time, in a language that is intelligible to scholars in other disciplines and to their fellow citizens.

In *Habits of the Heart* (1985), one of the best recent examples of how scholarship can be brought to bear on matters of public concern, Robert Bellah and his colleagues described how the concept of a profession was once connected to the idea of a "calling" to serve one's community. Over time, however, professionalism became increasingly identified with the concept of a personal career—"a course of professional life or employment, that offers advancement or honor" (119). The goal of professionalism has thus come to be understood less and less in terms of contributing to the sustenance of a common form of life and more and more in terms of one's own individual "success" defined in terms of the enhanced status and material wealth that accompany advancement within one's profession.

In order to reconnect the tasks and virtues of scholarship with those of citizenship, it will be necessary to reappropriate the ethical meaning of professionalism itself, seeing it not only in terms of technical skill but in terms of the moral contributions that professionals make to a complex society. Scholarship would then become a profession in the older sense of the word, involving not merely standards of technical competence but standards of public obligation (Bellah et al. 1985, 211, 290).

What Bellah and his colleagues have said about the need to transform a narrowly professional social science applies to much of the rest of professional scholarship as well, including comparative religious ethics.

> Specialization requires integration; they are not mutually exclusive. A professional social science that loses concern for the larger society cannot do even its professional job, for there is too much of reality with which it cannot deal. And if we remember that "calling" or "vocation," with the implication of public responsibility, is the older meaning of "profession," then we would see that a really "professional social scientist" could never be only a specialist. He would also see social science as, in part, public philosophy. (1985, 300)

As Gerald Graff has argued, the university has a special obligation to help the public understand the meaning and significance of academic work in an era when this work has become increasingly complex and has increasingly challenged conventionally accepted forms of thinking (1992, 35). Yet, according to Graff, the university has been disastrously inept at this crucial task of popularization, which it has disdained as beneath its dignity. The bad press and widespread public criticism directed toward institutions of higher education in recent years should thus come as no surprise. "Having treated mere image making as beneath its dignity, the academy has left it to its detractors to construct its public image for it" (Graff 1992, 35). If the university and the professoriat have become easy prey for ignorant or malicious misrepresentations in recent years, they have largely themselves to blame.

Thus, far from sacrificing scholarship, it would be in the best interest of both the public and the academic profession itself for academics to attend more seriously to the task of clarifying their concerns to their fellow citizens. Writing for this audience would help to clear up misapprehensions about the values of research. But it would also require academics to speak more clearly and to respect the objections of those whose minds they presumably hope to change (Graff 1992, 36). The point is not to rule out spe-

cialized study but to ask that it participate in the creation of a larger sense
of the context of contemporary intellectual and social life, which encourages and enables us to see how the sum of what academics do can add up to
more than an inconsequential series of isolated activities (Graff and Gibbons 1985, 10). The present volume's effort to bring scholarship in comparative religious ethics to bear on the practical tasks of interreligious
moral dialogue is a modest but not insignificant step in this direction.

The University As Host Site for Interreligious Moral Dialogue

Finally, it is worth considering innovative efforts by some religion scholars
to utilize the institution of the university itself as a vehicle for facilitating
interreligious dialogues. One outstanding example of this can be seen at
California State University, Fullerton, where Benjamin Hubbard and his
colleagues in the Department of Religious Studies have established a Center
for the Study of Religious Diversity.

Hubbard (1996) notes that southern California, like most large urban areas, is the home to every one of the world's major religious traditions. Yet,
while the religious leaders of these various faith communities are steeped in
the knowledge of their own traditions, they often know very little about
one another. Among many laypeople and clergy alike, there are widespread
misconceptions and stereotypes of other people's faiths. Needless to say,
this kind of ignorance is responsible for a great deal of misunderstanding,
prejudice, and sometimes outright hostility and conflict between local religious groups.

Among the most significant tensions Hubbard sees in southern California
are those between Roman Catholics and evangelical Protestants over the
evangelicals' conversionary tactics among Latino Catholics. Another source
of tension is the view among some evangelicals that the Church of Jesus
Christ of Latter-day Saints (Mormons) is a "cult." A third is the tension between the Jewish community and such African-American religious groups
as the Nation of Islam. Obviously, other tensions between other groups
predominate in other locales.

The purpose of C.S.U., Fullerton's Center for the Study of Religious Diversity is to enable clergy and scholars of various faiths to meet one another
and discuss their beliefs, customs, and concerns on the relatively neutral
ground of the academy. The emphasis has not been on the task of healing
misunderstandings, building friendships, or developing programs of collaborative action to help the homeless or the hungry. Rather, the emphasis has
been on the more fundamental task of exchanging accurate information.
Such a goal is clearly within the purview of a public university and may
provide the matrix out of which these other commendable projects may
eventually flow.

Accurate information about those who are different from oneself makes an important contribution to cultural literacy and to religious and cultural tolerance. The popular media, when they deal with religion at all, tend to sensationalize and accentuate points of disagreement and controversy within and between religions rather than providing coverage that is balanced and fair to the self-understandings of religious communities. Despite the well-known antipathy toward religion that is widespread among many members of university faculties and administrations, the university may be one of the few institutions in American society that can provide the sort of relatively neutral setting that encourages open dialogue and conversation between disparate individuals and groups.[11]

Beyond the University: Secondary Venues and Vehicles for Comparative Religious Ethicists

Although I am more optimistic than some about the ability of academics to play a role as public intellectuals while remaining in the university, I nonetheless agree with such writers as William Dean (1994), William Everett (1977), and Nancy Fraser (1989), who argue that, ultimately, the pursuit of a vocation as a public intellectual will require scholar-teachers to move beyond their relative seclusion in universities, academic disciplines, and professional mind-sets (see Dean 1994, xviii).

Some scholars of religion have taken important first steps in this direction. They have spoken to local civic groups and service organizations, they have written editorials for local newspapers, and they have appeared on television news broadcasts and radio talk shows where they have acquired a measure of public prominence as experts who possess specialized knowledge about matters that require a degree of technical expertise. Religious ethicists are occasionally called upon to comment on abortion, AIDS, or other questions of medical ethics. Experts in world religions or religious history might be queried about the power of religion in the politics of Iran, Algeria, or Northern Ireland. Scholars in the field of American religious history might be interviewed about the rise of religious cults, or they may comment on the strength of fundamentalists in politics (Dean 1994, 26).

But all too often, this amounts to little more than a "sound-bite" approach to public intellectual activity. Scholars' expert voices and their civic voices remain disconnected from one another and from the institutions and movements that provide vehicles for the enactment of the ideas and values they articulate as scholars. The effectiveness of public intellectuals will depend largely on their ability to link their scholarship to those institutions and movements that constitute a "third sector" of social life which is distinct from the economy (the first sector) and the government (the second sector). In order to do so, they will have to develop "bridge discourses" (see Fraser

1989, 11, 1–13) that enable them to assume a role as mediators, facilitators, and translators between disparate publics within the various institutions that constitute civil society—schools, churches, labor unions, professional associations, political parties, civic and cultural organizations, media organizations, and so on. In the remainder of this chapter, I will focus on two such settings in which I have had some local and limited experience, namely, the interfaith movement and the public schools in northern California.

Comparative Religious Ethics and the Interfaith Movement

There are a variety of ways in which academics might be involved in interfaith work. Comparative religious ethicists and other religion scholars are often invited to participate in consultations that bring academics, religious leaders, and representatives from various nongovernmental organizations together to study and develop policy recommendations on such topics as human rights, population growth, and religious liberty (see Kelsay and Twiss 1994; Battaglia 1996). Religion scholars also often serve on the advisory boards of interfaith organizations and as members of various project- or issue-oriented working committees for interfaith groups at local, regional, and international levels. And finally, academics are often featured on the programs of interfaith conferences where they make presentations on the religious dimensions of contemporary issues or on the role of religions in history and society. For example, the program of the 1993 Parliament of the World's Religions in Chicago featured a section entitled "The Academy" in its table of contents, which listed a series of colloquia, panel discussions, and presentations by nearly sixty representatives of the world academic community (Council for a Parliament of the World's Religions 1993, 125–132). Academics also figured prominently among the presenters on most of the other topics addressed by the Parliament, including religious pluralism, the relationship between religion and science, religion and violence, spirituality and ethics in the workplace, and religion and the media.

Most of my own experience with the interfaith movement has been at the local level in Chico, California. Interfaith work at the local level, "on the ground" and "in the trenches," so to speak, is not nearly so exotic and spectacular as what one finds when one attends international interfaith conferences such as the one held in Chicago in 1993. Nor is it so momentous as consulting in policy groups with religious leaders and diplomats from around the world. But local interfaith groups illustrate quite well, in microcosmic fashion, many of the problems and possibilities inherent in interreligious efforts to address practical social and moral issues. My own experience at this level has helped me to appreciate the difficulty of such undertakings, and it has helped me to see a variety of ways in which comparative religious ethicists might collaborate with such groups in the development of strategies for addressing problems facing their communities.

The initial obstacle that local interfaith groups must overcome is the temptation to avoid addressing difficult and potentially controversial moral and social issues in the first place. Most interfaith organizations are, by their very nature, anxious to establish a spirit of unity and cooperation. Their understandable desire for conciliation and compromise can lead them to shy away from issues that might prove to be controversial and divisive. Pressure to avoid such issues is both internal and external. *Internal* pressure often comes from within the particular congregations and communities of faith that constitute the membership of interfaith groups. Leaders of these particular congregations naturally want to avoid affiliation with an inter-faith group that may say or do things that members of their own congregations might disapprove of. *External* pressures come from those civic leaders and members of the general public who may oppose what they perceive to be the liberal, "globalist," or "one world" political agenda of the interfaith movement or from those who simply feel that religion is a private matter and that religious organizations overstep their bounds when they meddle in community affairs by speaking out on controversial issues.

I have recently seen both of these pressures illustrated by the experience of a local interfaith group in my own community as it has struggled with the question of whether and how to respond to the challenge presented by the Christian Coalition and other groups and figures affiliated with the religious right. Over the course of several months in 1995 and on a few occasions since that time, the Chico Area Interfaith Council (CAIC) has wrestled with this question. Some participants in this discussion have vigorously supported a proposal for the CAIC to take a public stand opposing the Christian Coalition for its alleged extremism, intolerance, and lack of respect for America's religious diversity. Many of these same individuals have also urged the local group to affiliate with the Interfaith Alliance, a national organization formed to promote the "positive role of religion" in civil discourse and to provide people of faith with an alternative voice to that of the radical religious right.[12]

But others have argued that taking such a stand would be inconsistent with the CAIC's hard-won reputation as a nonpartisan organization. It was feared by some clergy and lay leaders alike that such an initiative would run the risk of alienating conservative members of their own congregations and that it might even undermine their congregations' support for and participation in the local Interfaith Council and its projects. Still others pointed to the likelihood that the adoption of such a stance would preclude the possibility of eventually opening dialogue and collaborating with more conservative religious groups in the community.

The question facing the group was thus a very practical one: whether to demonstrate moral courage by taking a clear stand on a current ethical-political issue even at the risk splitting the group, or to set this issue aside in order to preserve unity and to remain open to the future possibility of dialogue and cooperation with conservative religious groups, including those that may advocate or sympathize with the agenda of such organizations as the Christian Coalition.

While the group was still in the process of considering how to resolve this question, another series of events transpired that served to bring external pressure, in the form of negative media coverage, to bear upon the council's eventual decision.

In the wake of the Oklahoma City bombing, and in response to a rash of local incidents including several violent interracial and interethnic conflicts and attacks on a gay bar and on the local Planned Parenthood clinic, the CAIC sponsored a series of five community forums entitled "Violence in the Community: A Time for Change, A Call for Action." The first forum gathered a group of local clergy to discuss the role of faith communities in responding to what was characterized as a widespread societal "climate of violence." Subsequent forums featured the local police chief discussing intolerance and hate crimes; the county school superintendent explaining how societal violence impacts the schools; and the news director of a local television station addressing the topic "Distortion, Anger, and the Media." The final forum, entitled "Creating a Peaceable Community: How to Get Involved," consisted of concurrent workshops conducted by representatives from a range of social service and community organizations.

A recurrent theme throughout the series was a recognition of the role played by the words and images broadcast by radio and television in the creation of a climate of intolerance, hatred, and violence in the local and national communities. It was against this background that the board of directors of the Interfaith Council voted to send a letter to the management of a local radio station voicing concern about its decision to begin airing a program by radio talk-show host G. Gordon Liddy, which had recently gained notoriety for its mean-spirited and violent rhetoric.

The local daily newspaper responded to this gesture by attacking the CAIC. A bold headline and front-page story in the *Chico Enterprise-Record* (June 10, 1995) reported the council's action and raised questions about the political agenda it was seeking to promote. The story prompted a flurry of letters to the editor describing the members of the Interfaith Council as "poor deluded liberals" and criticizing them for putting politics before people's souls and for advocating censorship. A few days after the initial story ran, the newspaper published a lead editorial entitled "The Cultural War Continues," which charged that the real agenda of these local religious leaders "appears to be what is tantamount to a political action committee" to alert local citizens about the menace of conservative Christians. According to the editor, this agenda was revealed when the Interfaith Council's board of directors "admitted . . . discussing . . . the possibility of affiliating with the national Interfaith Alliance." The editorial characterized the Interfaith Alliance as a part of the "religious left—with its 1960s liberation theology use of the rhetoric of class struggle to promote dubious political causes . . ." and went on to chastise the local interfaith group for failing to endorse the agenda of the Christian right.

> Certainly conservative Christians have an agenda—it is to return this country to what it was intended to be, a God-fearing nation. They want to promote traditional bedrock moral, cultural, biblical and constitutional values. One would think the Interfaith Alliance would applaud that goal. And that the local Interfaith Council would join in that endeavor. (*Chico Enterprise-Record*, June 15, 1995)

What is at stake here, concluded the editorial, is "not a disagreement over fundamental principles of Christian doctrine. It is a battle in the ongoing cultural war for the soul of this country."[13]

As might be imagined, all of this media attention exacerbated the dilemma facing the local Interfaith Council. More leaders reported that members of their congregations had begun to raise questions, in light of the recent newspaper coverage, about whether their churches should continue to be affiliated with such an apparently liberal and controversial organization as the Interfaith Council. This fueled the concerns of those who were worried about undermining the Interfaith Council's base of support among local congregations as well as its reputation as a nonpartisan organization. In the end, to the chagrin of some and the relief of others, the board of directors of the CAIC decided not to take a public stand opposing the Christian Coalition and not to join the national Interfaith Alliance, but rather to refer these issues to the council's constituent members for their individual decisions.[14]

It would be easy enough to argue that, in this case, the CAIC simply lost its nerve and sacrificed moral relevance and courage for the sake of maintaining a vague and ineffective sense of unity and goodwill. And to the extent that the council's decision was motivated by a desire to avoid any more negative media coverage, such a judgment would be justified.

But I believe that it would be a mistake to dismiss this case so quickly. Such an easy dismissal would overlook the extent to which this example illustrates several of the *tactical challenges* facing both comparative religious ethics and the project of interreligious moral dialogue as they seek to bring religious perspectives to bear upon contemporary social and moral issues and the task of social change. All ecumenical and interfaith organizations confront dilemmas such as this one on a more or less routine basis, though the resolution of such dilemmas is rarely an easy or routine matter.

The first and most basic challenge is simply to demonstrate that the world's religious traditions have the obligation and ability to play a constructive role in addressing contemporary social and moral issues. This should be obvious. But as our brief example illustrates, there are people, both within and outside religious communities, who, for different reasons, seem not to realize or accept this.

Actually, it is not that hard to appreciate why many people think the world would be better off if religion simply kept to itself and did not get involved in controversial social and moral issues. So many of the images and experiences of religion in the contemporary world confirm the impression that religion is a chief source of intolerance, hatred, conflict, and violence within and between communities. And it is true that much misunderstanding and hostility can be traced to the words and works of religious leaders, movements, and institutions.

But, as Gerald Barney made clear in his address to the 1993 Parliament of the World's Religions, the religions of the world exercise an important influence on the conduct of millions of people. To exclude them in an analysis of social, economic, and ecological problems, as is often done by scholars and policymakers, is to ignore a decisive factor (see Kuschel 1995, 99). And indeed, much of the significance of the interfaith movement, whether at the local, national, or international level, resides in its vision that the religions of the world—through their spiritual and ethical values, their institutions, and their vast influence—can and must play a major and positive role in shaping life on our planet as we move into the twenty-first century (Beversluis 1994, 69).

The *obligation* of religious traditions to play a constructive ethical-political role needs to be stressed to religious leaders and to religious communities themselves. The *ability* of religions to play such a role is what needs to be stressed to a secular public, which often sees religion as part of the problem rather than part of the solution. As Barney noted in Chicago:

> There are about forty wars in progress around the world, and the hostilities inspired by religions are major factors in virtually every one of these wars. Religious beliefs also stand in the way of attention to a number of critical issues. The best known of many examples is the attitude of various faiths to family planning, but equally important are teachings concerning "progress" and the difference between needs and wants. For these reasons it is critically important that the leaders of the world's religions be engaged in a dialogue on the critical issues of the future. (Gerald Barney, cited in Kuschel 1995, 100)

Scholarship in comparative religious ethics can encourage and support those members of faith communities who do seek to draw their communities' attention to pressing moral issues, and it can help demonstrate to a skeptical secular public that the words and works of religious people can be a great resource in the struggle for a more compassionate, just, and peaceful world. While not ignoring the crimes that have been committed in the names of all the world's religions or the role that religions have undeniably played in the creation or exacerbation of many contemporary world problems, comparative religious ethicists can help interfaith groups make the case that religions have always been and must continue to be involved in efforts to ameliorate these problems. Comparative religious ethics can help shed light on the complex and ambiguous role of religions in history and society, both as sources of conflict and as spiritual and moral resources in the struggle for reconciliation, peace, and justice. Simply demonstrating the relevance of the world's religious traditions for addressing contemporary moral issues is one of the main ways that comparative religious ethicists can make common cause with the interfaith movement.

A second, more important and difficult challenge facing the interfaith movement is to find a way to unite rather than polarize constituencies from diverse religious traditions as well as conservatives and liberals within the same tradition. As my example of the CAIC's dilemma about how to respond to the Christian Coalition illustrates, this is not an easy task. It requires pragmatic judgments about how best to balance the interfaith movement's goal of being inclusive of the widest possible range of religious and moral voices and perspectives while, at the same time, seeking to provide a critical perspective on the status quo and to become an effective agent of social and moral transformation.

It is not too difficult, in most communities, for people from diverse faith perspectives and political orientations to identify such issues as poverty, hunger, homelessness, and violence as moral problems that deserve attention, even though these same people may have very different views of the causes and cures for such problems. Local interfaith groups often take a lead in addressing these problems by organizing educational forums, fundraisers, soup kitchens, shelters, and so on. Initiatives like these foster the spirit of unity and cooperation that most interfaith organizations seek to cultivate (although questions about exactly where to locate soup kitchens and shelters for the homeless can often prove to be quite divisive!). The material and symbolic significance of such projects is limited, but it should not be minimized. Such projects make important contributions to the welfare of local communities, and they demonstrate the ability of religious communities to be positive forces rather than sources of conflict and division.

But what about those issues on which there is no such consensus? Religious communities fiercely disagree about such issues as the full human rights of women and children, homosexuality, structural injustice, and the proper relation between religious and secular law and institutions. It is often difficult to frame these issues in such a way that it is even possible to begin dialogue, let alone reach agreement about a course of collective action. How might interfaith groups develop a moral language capable of framing issues in a way that unites disparate groups in the pursuit of a common project of social change? I believe that the comparative study of religious ethics can help shed light on the ethical-political contexts within which such questions must be addressed.

The moral discourse of the interfaith movement, like all moral discourse, takes place in the context of a struggle for intellectual and moral leadership or *hegemony* in the wider society. In this respect at least, our local editorial writer in Chico was correct to view the confrontation between the Christian Coalition and the Interfaith Alliance as an episode in the so-called "cultural war." The interfaith movement, like every other religious or social movement that seeks to bring about social and moral change, is a participant in the ongoing struggle over whose moral vision will set the terms of ethical-political debate in the wider society.

But to leave the matter here, as just one more example of the inevitable confrontation between alternative worldviews and ethics, is too simple. It tends to encourage an already widespread suspicion that religious-moral discourses are unable to transcend the narrow self-interest of the particular social groups that espouse them. Public discourse about the common good becomes virtually impossible in such an intellectual climate.

One of the interfaith movement's great contributions to public life is its affirmation that, through dialogue and negotiation, it is sometimes possible to identify common interests that are, or that can be, shared by disparate groups with alternative religious and moral orientations and languages. Indeed, this is what makes the movement such a promising vehicle for the work of comparative religious ethicists as public intellectuals. The interfaith movement is one of the few places in contemporary society where it is possible to employ a moral language of universal interests and the common good while recognizing and even celebrating the irreducible plurality of religious, social, and cultural life.

It is true that religious and moral ideas and discourses are always the ideas and discourses of particular groups in particular times and places. And the comparative study of religious ethics confirms that, all too frequently, these ideas and discourses simply reflect or rationalize the narrow sectional interests of the particular groups that espouse them.

But the existence of a connection between moral discourses and sectional interests does not necessarily mean that all claims to religious or moral universality are a mere pretense or form of deception. On the contrary, there are many instances in which religious-moral discourses do succeed, at least *to some degree,* in going beyond the simple expression and defense of a group's own narrow self-interests. The ruling ideas of every age may be the ideas of the ruling group, but they are typically something more than mere rationalizations of that group's narrow self-interest (Walzer 1988, 447).[15]

A truly hegemonic social group—one that is able to "rule" through intellectual and moral leadership as opposed to one that simply "dominates" through force and coercion—must be willing and able to present itself plausibly as the representative of the interests that are shared in common by disparate groups in society. This means that the ethical-political ascendance of a group will ultimately depend to a great extent upon its ability to represent the "universal interests" of the widest possible number of groups in society.

To be sure, when we speak about the ability of religious-moral discourses to "transcend" the narrow self-interest of particular social groups, we must not make the mistake of believing that it is ever possible to completely sever the link between interests and discourse in any absolute sense. On the contrary, we must always remain aware of the importance of the relationship between a group's interests and the ideas and values it espouses.

Moreover, we can only talk about the *degrees* of "universality" that are embodied in particular religious-moral languages, because hegemony is never total or complete. No moral discourse can ever be fully or perfectly representative or expressive of the aspirations and interests of all the disparate groups in society because of the irreducibly pluralistic nature of social, cultural, and religious life.

The hegemony of a social group is thus best understood as a relationship of compromises. The struggle for and exercise of intellectual and moral leadership involves a continuous process of forming and re-forming an equilibrium between the interests of the leading group and those of other groups in society. The extent of a group's intellectual and moral influence will always be qualified by its ever-changing relations to other groups in society and by the compromises that it must constantly make if it is to retain its legitimacy in the eyes of those allied groups whose interests it seeks and claims to represent.

One of the main tasks of comparative religious ethicists as public intellectuals is to assess and compare the *degrees of universality* that are embodied in the moral discourses of particular religious groups or traditions in specific times and places. To what extent do these discourses reflect or rationalize the narrow sectional interests of a particular social group? To what extent do they succeed in identifying or creating and expressing what might be regarded as "universal human interests" that are shared by disparate groups in a given society or historical epoch? Which discourses are more and which are less inclusive of the interests of the widest number of human beings—regardless of religion, race, class, gender, ethnicity, sexual orientation, and so on?

Similarly, comparative religious ethicists can assess the *degrees of compromise* and the balance between compromise and conviction that are exhibited by the moral discourses of particular groups. Too much compromise and a group loses its critical power and prophetic vision. Too little compromise and a group is relegated to the margins of public discourse, just one more sectarian interest group among others. Although it is true that such sectarian groups are occasionally able to exercise a considerable

amount of influence on the direction of ethical-political debate on particular issues, they are rarely able to bring about and sustain far-reaching
changes in the prevailing worldview and ethos. Considerations such as
these have a direct bearing on the tactical challenges facing the interfaith
movement as it seeks to balance its goal of being inclusive with its goal of
being an effective agent of social and moral change.

If we bear these sorts of considerations in mind as we assess the CAIC's
refusal to publicly condemn the Christian Coalition and affiliate with the
Interfaith Alliance, we may conclude that this was not simply a capitulation
to internal and external pressures to avoid taking a stand on divisive issues.
Rather, *given the particular circumstances* in which it found itself, the local
council's decision may well be viewed as a legitimate pragmatic judgment
about how it could be most effective in achieving its goal of promoting solidarity among disparate local groups while maintaining the reputation for
nonpartisanship that allows it to play a unique and potentially transformative role in the community.

As is the case in many communities, the CAIC finds itself in a situation
where religious and political discourse is often polarized. There are any
number of issue-oriented organizations across the religious and political
spectrum that stake out a position on most controversial topics, including
school prayer, abortion, gay rights, and many of the other issues addressed
by the agenda of the Christian Coalition. But there are few organizations—
religious or secular—whose overriding purpose is to cultivate understanding and cooperation between people from diverse backgrounds and faith
perspectives.

Over the nearly fifty years of its existence, first as a council of churches
and now as an interfaith council, the CAIC has frequently seen its members
disagree about theology and politics, but the members have found numerous ways of responding positively to the needs and aspirations of the local
community through both education and practical action. Because of its reputation for nonpartisanship and inclusivity, the Interfaith Council has often
been enlisted by numerous civic groups and social service agencies as a
partner in joint efforts to improve the lives of local citizens regardless of
their religious faith or political affiliation. The council has regularly acted
as a clearinghouse for community information and as a liaison between
hospitals, convalescent homes, agencies of city and county government,
and issue-oriented citizens' groups.

Moreover, despite the impression that may have been given by the present discussion, the CAIC has not typically shied away from controversial issues. Rather, it has provided one of only a handful of regular forums for the
open discussion of a whole range of issues that are of interest to the local
community, including many controversial issues ranging from homosexuality in the church to the question of Christian complicity in the Holocaust

and the role of the media in fostering a climate of violence and consumerism. Although the CAIC has typically sought to facilitate dialogue and discussion rather than to advocate a particular position, this has not prevented many of its critics from charging that its willingness to even provide a public forum for the consideration of some of these issues demonstrates the council's partisan nature.

The CAIC's refusal to adopt a language of confrontation and condemnation was consistent with its history and its own understanding of its mission to encourage open, inclusive, and ongoing dialogue on all matters of interest to the local religious community. To have acted otherwise may well have undermined its reputation for nonpartisanship and may thereby have threatened its effectiveness and perhaps even its continued existence.

In cases where the climate of debate is already polarized and divisive, a moral language of conciliation and compromise may actually be more prophetic and potentially transformative than the more apparently prophetic rhetoric of confrontation and condemnation. Of course, in other circumstances, and for other types of interfaith organizations such as the Interfaith Alliance, a moral language of confrontation and condemnation is precisely what is needed to address pressing social and moral issues. My point is not that interfaith groups, including the CAIC, never can or should play a more partisan role. Social and moral relevance and effectiveness should never be sacrificed simply for the sake of maintaining a vague and ineffective spirit of unity and cooperation. But judgments about which language *actually is* more or less relevant and effective must always be based on a reading of the ethical-political circumstances in which one finds oneself. Within the interfaith movement as a whole, there is a role for groups like the CAIC as well as for groups like the Interfaith Alliance. There is a need for both a language of conciliation and a language of confrontation. And there is a need for those within the movement to be able to make pragmatic judgments about the circumstances in which one is appropriate and the other is not.

Comparative Religious Ethics and Interreligious Dialogue in the Public Schools

Perhaps more than in any other single American institution, the public schools are places where people of all different faiths and those of no faith come together on a regular and sustained basis. And yet, until quite recently, religion has been all but absent from the public school curriculum, and most public school teachers and administrators have little or no acquaintance with the academic study of the world's religions. The public schools are an extremely significant, though largely neglected, venue for the work of comparative religious ethicists as public intellectuals.

Most people are aware that the courts have found public school sponsorship of religious practices to be inconsistent with the First Amendment to the Constitution of the United States, and many mistakenly and resentfully believe that this means religion has been banished from the public schools. These people are often not aware that *teaching about* religion in the public schools is perfectly consistent with constitutional principles. Indeed, as Justice Tom Clark wrote in *Abington School District* v. *Schempp* (1963), "it might well be said that one's education is not complete without a study of comparative religion or the history of religion and its relationship to the advancement of civilization."

The academic study of religion makes an indispensable contribution to historical and cultural literacy through its analysis and interpretation of the religious experiences, stories, symbols, rituals, doctrines, values, and institutions of human beings in different times and places. It is impossible to achieve an adequate understanding of human history and culture (literature, art, music, philosophy, law, ethics, politics) without knowing the role that religious beliefs, practices, and communities have played and continue to play in human life. Put simply, we learn a lot about human beings (ourselves and others) by studying their religions.

The cross-cultural and historical study of religion is also an integral part of education for citizenship in a pluralistic society. A basic requirement of citizenship in American society is respect for religious liberty and freedom of conscience. As guaranteed by the religious liberty clause of the First Amendment, this respect must be extended to members of all religious communities as well as to those who are members of none. Yet such respect is difficult to sustain without some objective knowledge of the histories, beliefs, and customs of the diverse peoples and traditions of the world. Without such knowledge, it is all too easy to caricature and trivialize the religious beliefs and practices of our fellow citizens, especially if they happen to be from a religious, racial, or ethnic community that is different from our own. A civil society cannot long survive in such a climate of ignorance and misunderstanding.

After years of either ignoring or actively avoiding religion, there are signs that public school systems in several parts of the country are beginning to recognize the importance of the academic study of religion. In California, for example, the State Board of Education has adopted a history–social science curriculum that explicitly calls for more attention to be given to the study of religion and ethics. This document stresses the importance of religion in human history and states that "students must become familiar with the basic ideas of the major religions and the ethical traditions of each time and place" (California State Department of Education 1988, 7).

To understand why individuals and groups acted as they did, we must see what values and assumptions they held, what they honored, what they sought and what they feared. By studying a people's religion and philosophy as well as their folkways and traditions, we gain an understanding of their ethical and moral commitments. By reading the texts that people revere, we gain important insights into their thinking. The study of religious beliefs and other ideological commitments helps explain both cultural continuity and cultural conflict. (California State Department of Education 1988, 13)[16]

Of course it is one thing to say that more attention should be given to the topics of religion and ethics in the public schools. It is another thing to prepare teachers and administrators to deal knowledgeably and responsibly with the range of legal and pedagogical questions that arise in connection with the topic of religion and public education. Public schools have increasingly turned to comparative religious ethicists and other religion scholars for assistance in addressing these issues.

There are three main ways that religion scholars can contribute to the responsible integration of the academic study of religion into the public schools. The first is to help familiarize teachers, administrators, school boards, parents, and, ultimately, the students themselves with the historical background and constitutional principles that provide the framework for thinking about religion and public education. Perhaps the most useful approach to this task has been developed by Charles Haynes, a religion scholar, and his colleague, attorney Oliver Thomas, in the book *Finding Common Ground* (1994).

Building upon the broad consensus represented by the Williamsburg Charter,[17] Haynes and Thomas call for a "return to first principles," arguing that the religious liberty clauses of the First Amendment provide the civic framework within which it is possible to find common ground on many of the issues that divide Americans. In many places around the United States, public school students and teachers have found themselves caught up in clashes and controversies over religious holidays, equal access to school facilities by religious groups, religion in the curriculum, and religious practices. Haynes and Thomas argue that the key to resolving these controversies "is for all sides to step back from the debate and to give fresh consideration to the democratic first principles that bind us together as a people. Then, in light of our shared civic commitments, we can work for policies and practices in public education that best protect the conscience of every student and parent in our schools" (1994, 1.1).

Haynes and Thomas have traveled to school districts throughout the United States helping to mediate disputes about religion and public education. In every case they insist that the starting point for local communities must be an agreement that the ground rules of the debate will be the "three Rs" of religious liberty: rights, responsibilities, and respect. "Within this framework, all perspectives have a right to be heard, and each citizen has an obligation to protect the freedom of conscience of all others. Agreeing on civic principles allows the dialogue to begin and enables people of all faiths or none to work toward consensus on the proper role of religion in the public schools" (Haynes and Thomas 1994, 1.6). What is being sought is not agreement over religious beliefs or political policies, but rather "a shared commitment to the religious liberty principles by which citizens with deep religious differences can negotiate their differences with civility and respect." Such a commitment can provide the basis for reforging "a common vision for the common good in public education" (1994, 1.7, 1.8).

With the support of the Freedom Forum First Amendment Center at Vanderbilt University, and in collaboration with local school districts, "Three Rs" projects have been launched in Utah, Georgia, Maryland, Tennessee, and California. The California Three Rs Project—Rights, Responsibilities, Respect: Educating for Citizenship in a Diverse Society—is directed by Nicholas Piediscalzi and has a statewide organization with a well-developed agenda for working with public school teachers and administrators. One of the central aims of the project is to establish a network of resource teachers throughout California who can provide schools with expertise in First Amendment principles and in appropriate ways to teach about religions and cultures in the classroom.

Typically, teams from the public schools—consisting of community representatives, teachers, administrators, and school board members—attend a seminar on the First Amendment and the history of Supreme Court decisions regarding religion and public education. Participants become acquainted with the Court's distinction in *Schempp* (1963) between the school-sponsored *practice* of religion on the one hand and the *academic study* of religion on the other. They learn about the principle of government neutrality toward religion set forth in *Lemon* v. *Kurtzman* (1971), about the principles of nondiscrimination and the protection of students' religious speech as legislated by the Equal Access Act (1984), and so on. Through case studies and role playing, participants learn how to use constitutional principles to negotiate conflicts and to work toward consensus on issues of religious and ethnic diversity confronting schools and local communities. These teams then provide leadership in their local school districts. The seminar is followed up by a series of meetings during the year to reinforce what was learned and to provide collegial support. Religion scholars from several universities in California have been actively involved in this project (Hatfield 1996, 7–8).

But familiarity with the constitutional principles that set the terms for discussing religion and public education is only the first step. The responsible integration of the study of religion into the public school curriculum also requires teachers to have content knowledge of the religious histories and traditions about which they are now expected to teach. In California, the world history curriculum for the sixth, seventh, and tenth grades deals explicitly with the religions of India, China, and the Middle East. Other grade levels deal with the role of religion in American history and society. And some general knowledge of world religions is also a necessary background for understanding many of the "current events" that are discussed throughout the K–12 curriculum. Yet the fact is that most teachers have never had even a basic introductory course on the world's religions as a part of their professional preparation.

Not only are most teachers unprepared to deal with religion as it arises in the curriculum, they are also ill-equipped to understand the role of religion as it arises in the lives of many of the students in their classrooms. I have spoken with many teachers who are anxious to learn more about religion not only because it will help them to teach more effectively about ancient civilizations or the history of the United States but also because it will help them to better understand and communicate with students and parents who may be Jehovah's Witnesses, or Sikhs, or Muslims, or traditional Hmong. Teaching teachers about the world's religions is a second way that comparative religious ethicists can contribute to dialogue about religion in the public schools.

Increasingly, public schools have begun to call upon religion scholars to conduct in-service workshops as part of teachers' ongoing professional development. These workshops focus on providing knowledge about the structure and history of various religious traditions. Over the past several years, my colleagues and I have worked with curriculum specialists in the public schools in organizing and presenting workshops on Hinduism, Buddhism, Judaism, Christianity, and Islam, as well as on such topics as religion and values in American history and society and the religions of the Hmong and other Southeast Asian immigrants.

In addition to their focus on content, these workshops must also respond to teachers' practical questions about appropriate and effective techniques for teaching about religions. Is role playing an appropriate way to teach about diverse religious practices? Should teachers allow or encourage students to share their own religious beliefs, practices, and customs? Are teachers allowed to illustrate points by reference to their own religious practices? Should they respond to students' questions about their own religious affiliations or beliefs? Although these sorts of pedagogical questions are not entirely different from those faced by religious studies professors in state universities, they arise in a particularly sensitive way in the public schools. For this reason, it is usually a good idea for religion scholars to work as part of a team with master teachers and curriculum specialists as they seek to address such questions together.

Obviously, in addition to this piecemeal approach to what amounts to remedial education for in-service teachers, a longer-term approach to this problem is to integrate the academic study of religions into teacher preparation and credentialing programs. There are any number of institutional and political obstacles that will likely need to be overcome in order to bring about such a reform. But here again, recent developments in California may indicate a move in this direction. As of January 1998, all persons applying for a social science teaching credential must satisfy Standard Nine of the California Department of Education's standards for Social Science Teacher Preparation. This standard requires each prospective social science teacher to demonstrate knowledge of the impact of religious ideals, beliefs, and values on human history and society. At my own university, the Department of Religious Studies has designed a new course entitled "Teaching About Religions in American Public Schools," which will help prepare pre-service teachers to approach the study of religion in an academically and constitutionally appropriate fashion.

Finally, a third way that religion scholars can help to facilitate the public schools' contribution to advancing interreligious understanding is through the development of curriculum materials. In addition to introductory textbooks on world religions and audiovisual resources that are accessible to elementary and secondary school students, there is a special need for lesson plans that can be integrated into other larger units in the curriculum. Even in those schools that are committed to introducing the academic study of religion, only a relatively small amount of time and space in the curriculum as a whole will ever be given over to the explicit discussion of religion. There is simply too much other material that has to be covered. Despite the rhetoric of the state-mandated curriculum, religion is usually only addressed, if at all, in those areas of the history, social science, or literature curriculum where it naturally arises from time to time. Brief, relatively self-contained lesson plans that can be used to supplement passing references to religion in these areas of the curriculum are much needed. Scholars of religion, working closely with teachers and curriculum coordinators, can assist in the design and review of materials suitable for use in such settings.

The area of religion and public education is perhaps the most obvious and significant area in which the academic and public agendas of comparative religious ethicists intersect. There is enormous opportunity for religion scholars to contribute to the education of their fellow citizens outside the university and, thereby, to the consolidation of the standing of religious studies as an academic discipline. By helping to dispel our ignorance of one another's most sacred values and traditions, the academic study of religions in public schools plays a crucial role in helping us "learn to live with our deepest differences" (First Liberty Institute 1990).

Conclusion: Reconciling Scholarship and Citizenship

This chapter began with an epigram from Emile Durkheim. A key figure in the professionalization of modern academic life, Durkheim was also a public intellectual whose numerous practical interventions in the social, political, moral, and educational life of his age were not extraneous to his conception of the scholarly enterprise but rather flowed directly from it (Bellah 1983a, 366). He recognized, far more than many contemporary scholars, that coherence and continuity in disciplined intellectual inquiry do not stem from consensus around a theoretical or methodological paradigm so much as from concern for practical problems in the world (Bellah 1983a, 377). One does not need to endorse Durkheim's theories of religion and ethics to recognize his life and work as exemplary embodiments of the unity between scholarship and citizenship.

Durkheim viewed his own discipline of social science as a continuing reflection on the contradictions and paradoxes of modern society, on the dilemmas for action these create, and on *the practical question of what must be done* to address these contradictions and dilemmas (Bellah 1983a, 377–378). Durkheim did not urge scholars to aspire to become politicians or policymakers, much less ideologues: "What I mean is that above all our action must be exerted through books, seminars, and popular education. Above all, we must be *advisers, educators*. It is our function to help our contemporaries know themselves in their ideas and in their feelings, far more than to govern them" (Durkheim 1973, 59; cited in Bellah 1983a, 366; italics in original).

As comparative religious ethicists assume mediating positions between disparate publics both within and beyond the university, they do not abandon their primary and more traditional role as *educators*. But they extend this role into new venues, serving as *translators, critics,* and *creators* of alternative moral visions and languages.

As *translators,* they seek to interpret and communicate the underlying assumptions of alternative worldviews and ethics in terms that are intelligible to those who do not share those same assumptions. In this way they help to facilitate interreligious understanding and dialogue in the universities, in the interfaith movement, in public schools, and in other civic and cultural settings and organizations where people from diverse backgrounds come into contact with one another. This type of public intellectual activity preserves comparative scholarship's traditional emphasis on a "dispassionate capacity to comprehend and explain other people's experience of their worlds without interjecting one's own preferences" (Paden 1992, 73–74). But such impartiality is now conceived not in terms of scientific or professional detachment, but rather in terms of *engagement* in a practical moral project of dialogue and mutual understanding.

But inquiry in comparative ethics involves more than interpretation and understanding of the arguments on various sides of controversial moral issues. It also sets these arguments in a broader context and shows how they are embedded in complicated struggles for power between competing groups. As *critics,* comparative religious ethicists must involve themselves in "clarifying—if not exposing—the social uses of morality, and in particular religiously inspired public morality" (Smurl 1976, 51).

Comparative ethicists must be especially alert to the tendency of interreligious dialogues to accept at face value the dominant voices in religious traditions while overlooking the more muted voices of minorities and oppressed groups. Not all social hierarchies are morally illegitimate, and not all minorities are oppressed. But all too often, religious and moral discourses falsely portray the sectional interests of dominant groups as the universal interests of all human beings. They also frequently reify or "naturalize" contingent social relationships as biologically or divinely sanctioned, thereby legitimating the status quo and the continued dominance of the present ruling groups. Yet the moral languages of religious traditions can also provide powerful tools for criticism of the status quo and for the expression and defense of the dignity of all individual human beings (Grelle 1995, 530–535; Stalnaker 1996, 4). One of the main critical tasks of comparative religious ethics is to keep this ambiguous role of religious and moral languages in full view of those who observe or participate in interreligious moral dialogues.

Finally, comparative religious ethicists are *creators* as well as translators and critics of religious and moral visions and languages. As scholars and citizens, they are participants in contemporary religious and cultural conflicts and struggles over the definition of moral ideals and values and over the selection of which ideals and values will set the terms for debate in the wider society. As a form of *creative cultural activity* (see Everett 1977, 97–108), comparative religious ethics can assist the interfaith movement's efforts to create and articulate alternatives to the dominant moral languages of our time: a *discourse of wisdom* to counterbalance the *discourse of science* and to help prevent the misuse of scientific research; a *discourse of spirituality* to counterbalance the *discourse of technology* and to help keep the risks of highly efficient but morally ambiguous technologies under control; a *discourse of ecology* to counterbalance the *discourse of industry* and to help place limits on an ever-expanding economy and consumer lifestyle; and a *discourse of justice* to complement a *discourse of freedom and democracy* that too often masks the concentration of power and wealth in the hands of fewer and fewer people (see Kuschel 1995, 98).

As public intellectuals, comparative religious ethicists do not abandon scholarship in favor of activism. But they do resist the notion that scholarship consists simply in the accumulation and distribution of knowledge, and they work against the impression that traditions and cultures have a permanent character, that they have already been formed rather than being in the process of transformation. Instead, they promote the alternative view that the proper study of cultures and traditions is "intrinsically involved with *that which has to be done*" (Giroux 1988, 150–151).

To listen, to reflect, to criticize, to respond—these are the tasks of social inquiry today, as they always have been. They are not tasks that will yield to cleverness. . . . They require our full personhood. To accept these tasks is itself a form of moral discipline. (Bellah 1983a, 380)

Notes

1. See Walzer 1988 for a fascinating study of this balance between distance and commitment in the lives of public intellectuals in the twentieth century.

2. This is not the place to debate the strengths and weaknesses of poststructuralism, deconstructionism, and postmodernism. See Spretnak 1991 (especially 1–32 and 233–234) for a brief and lively critique of deconstructive postmodernism. Both Spretnak (1991) and Dean (1994) offer lengthy discussions of how public intellectual activity and a discourse of the common good remain possible even in the wake of deconstructive postmodernism.

3. This account is drawn from Bellah et al. 1985 (297–307) and Dean 1994 (19–39). For representative accounts of the emergence of a culture of professionalism and its relationship to the specialization of academic disciplines, see Bender 1993, Bledstein 1976, and Kimball 1992.

4. I am not arguing for an abandonment of the "religious studies" approach in favor of a return to the "theological" approach. Neither am I suggesting that objectivity, properly understood, should cease to be viewed as a vital norm for the conduct of religious studies (see Bird 1998). I only want to point out that the new religious studies departments have been no more conducive to the development of public intellectuals than have other academic departments.

5. For overviews of some of these debates, see Grelle 1993b (1–64), Lovin and Reynolds 1985 (1–35), and Twiss 1993. Issues of theory and method are not without their own intrinsic interest and significance, but all the attention devoted to efforts to define the specialized subject matter of religious ethics might be read as a symptom of religious ethicists' professional anxiety to carve out an intellectual and institutional niche for themselves in the disciplinary structure of the contemporary research university. Indeed, Jeffrey Stout has argued that Little and Twiss's pioneering work, *Comparative Religious Ethics: A New Method* (1978), is best read as a response to the crisis of professional identity confronting scholars of religion in secular institutions. Stout notes that we find the words "religious" and "comparative" where the words "Christian" and "theological" used to be, and he goes on to discuss the difficulties that religious ethicists have faced in their attempt to establish and maintain their standing in the secular academy "without giving up either the profoundly historical character of [their] topic or [their] reasons for being interested (be they theological or not)" (Stout 1980, 294).

6. When he nominates the third sector, but not the third sector's universities, as the best home for public intellectuals, Dean recognizes that the university seems to offer the obvious place and instrument for religious critics. After all, academic intellectuals are already located in universities and colleges and have, it would seem, only to use their occupational resources for public work. But Dean is convinced that the prevailing ethos of professionalism and specialization undermine the university's

potential to serve as a primary venue for the work of genuinely public intellectuals (1994, 157). Thus, even though the university is the customary, expected, and preferred home and instrument of intellectuals in American society, it is the nonuniversity, voluntary organizations within the third sector that offer "religious" critics the better home and the better instrument (154).

7. Here I use "university" as a shorthand for institutions of higher education. See Everett 1977 for a discussion of religious ethicists' *locations* and *vehicles* and for a discussion of the significance of and distinctions between university, college, and seminary settings. See Dean 1994 for a parallel discussion of the *venues* and *vehicles* of public intellectuals.

8. Twiss acknowledges a significant debt to Schweiker (1992) and Yearley (1991) for this formulation of the hermeneutical-dialogical approach to teaching comparative religious ethics. See Chapter 1 in the present volume for an expanded version of this article by Twiss.

9. For representative summaries of these and other environmental problems, see Brown et al. 1996 and Kennedy 1993.

10. Of course, there are potential problems with the hermeneutical-dialogical approach to teaching comparative religious ethics. One such problem is that this approach might encourage a "premature fusion of moral horizons" (Twiss 1993, 263). A relative lack of life experience, along with a widespread ignorance of their own religious and moral heritages, raises the question of whether most students are "in a strong enough position to appropriate responsibly other moral horizons" (Twiss 1993, 263). Another potential problem is the danger of oversimplifying both the traditions and the moral problems that are being studied. Teachers who employ the hermeneutical-dialogical approach must always be on guard against facile comparisons between very complex traditions of thought and practice and very different cultural-historical contexts, and they must discourage naive or simplistic analyses of and solutions to complex moral problems. But of course these two problems must be faced by every pedagogical and curricular approach to the subject of comparative religious ethics.

A third potential problem is that the hermeneutical-dialogical approach might encourage an overly romantic conception of religions and cultures as whole-ways-of-life and thereby fail to fully appreciate the fact that religious and cultural traditions do not speak in a single voice, that they encompass disparate religious-ethical expressions and are typically characterized by political struggles between dominant and oppositional groups (see Grelle 1993a). Similarly, the metaphor of a "fusion of horizons," which is at the heart of this approach, may encourage an apolitical and overly optimistic conception of dialogue that fails to fully account for the social-historical factors and institutional forces that can hinder, constrain, and distort conversation and dialogue. But these potential weaknesses can be overcome by frequent and explicit attention to the variety of ways in which individuals and groups employ religious and moral discourses *both* in order to legitimate *and* in order to critique particular lifestyles, policies, and institutions. I am indebted to Aaron Stalnaker (1996) for helping me to see that my earlier criticism (Grelle 1993a) misses the main point of the metaphor of a "fusion of horizons" and that such a criticism really only applies as a critique of the naïveté of the practitioner of the hermeneutical-dialogical approach and fails to indict the approach as such.

11. For other experiments with using the university as a host site for interreligious dialogue, see Morgan 1995 (169, note 2) on the International Interfaith Centre, Westminster College, Oxford, which has been set up jointly with the World Congress of Faiths and the International Association for Religious Freedom. This center is intended to provide Westminster College with a research resource as well as to facilitate dialogue between religious leaders and academics. Beversluis (1994, 70) provides another example of the university as host site for interreligious dialogue, namely, a 1994 conference in Grand Rapids, Michigan, cosponsored by a grassroots interfaith association in collaboration with Calvin, Aquinas, and Grand Valley Colleges, which brought together academics, clergy, and laity.

12. According to its mission statement, The Interfaith Alliance "offers Americans a mainstream faith-based agenda committed to the positive role of religion as a healing and constructive force in public life. The Interfaith Alliance draws on shared religious principles to challenge those who manipulate religion to promote an extreme political agenda based on a false gospel of irresponsible individualism" (see the Interfaith Alliance's site on the World Wide Web). The Interfaith Alliance's board of directors is comprised of clergy and lay leaders from mainstream Protestant, Catholic, and Jewish organizations. The organization is headquartered in Washington, D.C., and has chapters in thirty-three states.

13. Many of these same themes appeared in the religiously and politically conservative press's coverage of the 1993 Parliament of the World's Religions. See, for example, John Zipperer 1993 and "Supermarket of the Gods," editorial, *Christianity Today*, September 13, 1993.

14. To date, the Congregational Church of Chico (United Church of Christ) is the only one of the constituent members of the CAIC that has decided on its own to affiliate with the Interfaith Alliance.

15. Elsewhere (Grelle 1995) I support this claim with the historical examples of the moral discourses of "freedom" and "democracy," which originated as expressions of the sectional interests of the bourgeoisie in its struggle against the economic and political restrictions of feudalism but which have since that time been appropriated by and extended to other social groups in different times and places to the point where they have assumed the status of what might well be described as "universal" human interests. See also Twiss et al. 1994 and Twiss and Grelle 1995 for the application of a similar perspective to the evolution of the moral discourse of human rights.

16. Similarly, the California history–social science curriculum emphasizes the "importance of the application of ethical understanding and civic virtue to public affairs. At each grade level the teacher of history and the social sciences will encourage students to reflect on the individual responsibility and behavior that create a good society, to consider the individual's role in how a society governs itself, and to examine the role of law in society. The curriculum provides numerous opportunities to discuss the ethical implications of how societies are organized and governed, what the state owes to its citizens, and what citizens owe to the state. Major historical controversies and events offer an appropriate forum for discussing the ethics of political decisions and for reflecting on individual and social responsibility for civic welfare in the world today" (California State Department of Education 1988, 6).

17. The Williamsburg Charter (reprinted in Haynes and Thomas 1994, A.1–A.14) was signed by representatives of many faiths, by former Presidents Ger-

ald Ford and Jimmy Carter, and by some two hundred other national leaders. It argues that the religious liberty principles of the First Amendment provide a shared space in which people who disagree can meet to negotiate their differences with civility and respect.

References

Battaglia, Tony. 1996. "Religious Studies and Contemporary Moral Issues." *Exchanges: Newsletter of the California State University System Institute for Teaching and Learning* 7, 1 (Winter):7.

Bellah, Robert N. 1983a. "The Ethical Aims of Social Inquiry." In *Social Science As Moral Inquiry*, edited by Norma Hann, Robert N. Bellah, Paul Rabinow, and William M. Sullivan, 360–381. New York: Columbia University Press.

_____. 1983b. Introduction to *Religion and America: Spirituality in a Secular Age*, edited by Mary Douglas and Steven M. Tipton, ix–xiii. Boston: Beacon Press.

Bellah, Robert N., Richard Madsen, William M. Sullivan, Ann Swidler, and Steven M. Tipton. 1985. *Habits of the Heart: Individualism and Commitment in American Life*. Berkeley: University of California Press.

Bender, Thomas. 1993. *Intellect and Public Life: Essays on the Social History of Academic Intellectuals in the United States*. Baltimore: The Johns Hopkins University Press.

Berry, Wendell. 1985. "The Loss of the University." In *Criticism in the University*, edited by Gerald Graff and Reginald Gibbons, 207–218. Triquarterly Series on Criticism and Culture, No. 1. Evanston, Ill.: Northwestern University Press.

Beversluis, Joel. 1994. "Bringing the Parliament into Academia." *Bulletin of the Council of Societies for the Study of Religion* 23, 3 (September):69–72.

Bird, Frederick. 1998. "A Defense of Objectivity in the Social Sciences, Rightly Understood." Paper presented to the Comparative Religious Ethics Interest Group at the Society of Christian Ethics Annual Meeting, Atlanta, January 9, 1998.

Bledstein, Burton. 1976. *The Culture of Professionalism: The Middle Class and the Development of Higher Education in America*. New York: W. W. Norton.

Bowman, Douglas. 1990. *Beyond the Modern Mind: The Spiritual and Ethical Challenge of the Environmental Crisis*. New York: The Pilgrim Press.

Brown, Lester R., et al. 1996. *State of the World 1996*. New York: W. W. Norton.

California State Department of Education. 1988. *History–Social Science Framework for California Public Schools Kindergarten Through Grade Twelve*. Sacramento: California State Department of Education.

Council for a Parliament of the World's Religions. 1993. *The Parliament of the World's Religions*. Chicago: Council for a Parliament of the World's Religions.

Dean, William. 1994. *The Religious Critic in American Culture*. Albany: State University of New York Press.

Durkheim, Emile. [1904] 1973. "The Intellectual Elite and Democracy." Translated by Mark Traugott. In *Emile Durkheim on Morality and Society*, edited by Robert N. Bellah, 58–60. Chicago: University of Chicago Press.

Everett, William. 1977. "Vocation and Location: An Exploration in the Ethics of Ethics." *Journal of Religious Ethics* 5, 1:91–114.

First Liberty Institute. 1990. *Living with Our Deepest Differences: Religious Liberty in a Pluralistic Society*. Senior High School Edition. Boston: Learning Connections Publishers.

Fraser, Nancy. 1989. *Unruly Practices: Power, Discourse, and Gender in Contemporary Social Theory*. Minneapolis: University of Minnesota Press.

Giroux, Henry A. 1988. *Teachers As Intellectuals: Toward a Critical Pedagogy of Learning*. Critical Studies in Education Series, edited by Paula Freire and Henry A. Giroux. New York: Bergin and Garvey.

Graff, Gerald. 1992. *Beyond the Culture Wars: How Teaching the Conflicts Can Revitalize American Education*. New York: W. W. Norton.

Graff, Gerald, and Reginald Gibbons. 1985. Preface to *Criticism in the University*, edited by Gerald Graff and Reginald Gibbons, 7–12. Triquarterly Series on Criticism and Culture, No. 1. Evanston, Ill.: Northwestern University Press.

Grelle, Bruce. 1993a. "Comparative Religious Ethics As a Form of Critical Inquiry." *The Annual of the Society of Christian Ethics*:271–281.

_____. 1993b. "Politics, Hegemony, and the Comparative Study of Religious Ethics." Ph.D. diss., University of Chicago Divinity School.

_____. 1995. "Hegemony and the 'Universalization' of Moral Ideas: Gramsci's Importance for Comparative Religious Ethics." *Soundings* 78, 3-4 (Fall-Winter):519–540.

Hatfield, John. 1996. "Assisting Public School Instructors in Teaching about Religion." *Exchanges: Newsletter of the California State University System Institute for Teaching and Learning* 7, 1 (Winter):7–8.

Haynes, Charles C., and Oliver Thomas, eds. 1994. *Finding Common Ground: A First Amendment Guide to Religion and Public Education*. Nashville, Tenn.: The Freedom Forum First Amendment Center.

Hubbard, Benjamin. 1996. "Facilitating Dialogue Between Religious Leaders in a Public University." *Exchanges: Newsletter of the California State University System Institute for Teaching and Learning* 7, 1 (Winter):6.

Jacoby, Russell. 1987. *The Last Intellectuals: American Culture in the Age of Academe*. New York: The Noonday Press.

Jameson, Fredric R. 1988. "On *Habits of the Heart*." In *Community in America: The Challenge of "Habits of the Heart,"* edited and introduced by Charles H. Reynolds and Ralph V. Norman, 97–112. Berkeley: University of California Press.

Kelsay, John, and Sumner B. Twiss, eds. 1994. *Religion and Human Rights*. New York: The Project on Religion and Human Rights.

Kennedy, Paul. 1993. *Preparing for the Twenty-First Century*. New York: Random House.

Kimball, Bruce A. 1992. *The "True Professional Ideal" in America*. Cambridge, Mass: Blackwell Publishers.

Kinsley, David. 1995. *Ecology and Religion: Ecological Spirituality in Cross-Cultural Perspective*. Englewood Cliffs, N.J.: Prentice-Hall.

Kitagawa, Joseph M. 1959. "The History of Religions in America." In *The History of Religions*, edited by Mircea Eliade and Joseph M. Kitagawa, 1–30. Chicago: University of Chicago Press.

Krupnick, Mark. 1986. *Lionel Trilling and the Fate of Cultural Criticism*. Evanston, Ill.: Northwestern University Press.

Küng, Hans, and Karl-Josef Kuschel, eds. 1995. *A Global Ethic: The Declaration of the Parliament of the World's Religions.* New York: Continuum.

Kuschel, Karl-Josef. 1995. "The Parliament of the World's Religions, 1893–1993." In *A Global Ethic: The Declaration of the Parliament of the World's Religions,* edited by Hans Küng and Karl-Josef Kuschel, 77–105. New York: Continuum.

Little, David, and Sumner B. Twiss. 1978. *Comparative Religious Ethics: A New Method.* New York: Harper and Row.

Lovin, Robin W., and Frank E. Reynolds. 1985. *Cosmogony and Ethical Order: New Studies in Comparative Ethics.* Chicago: University of Chicago Press.

Morgan, Peggy. 1995. "The Study of Religions and Interfaith Encounter." *Numen* 42, 2 (May):156–171.

Paden, William E. 1992. *Interpreting the Sacred: Ways of Viewing Religion.* Boston: Beacon Press.

Schweiker, William. 1992. "The Drama of Interpretation and the Philosophy of Religions: An Essay on Understanding in Comparative Religious Ethics." In *Discourse and Practice,* edited by Frank E. Reynolds and David Tracy, 263–294. Albany: State University of New York Press.

Smurl, James F. 1976. "Cross-Cultural Comparisons in Ethics: A Critical Response to Sally Wang." *Journal of Religious Ethics* 4, 1:47–55.

Spretnak, Charlene. 1991. *States of Grace: The Recovery of Meaning in the Postmodern Age.* San Francisco: HarperCollins Publishers.

Stalnaker, Aaron. 1996. "Comparative Religious Ethics and Contemporary Critique." Paper presented at the New England–Maritime Regional Meeting of the American Academy of Religion, Harvard Divinity School, Cambridge, March 29.

Stout, Jeffrey. 1980. "Weber's Progeny Once Removed." *Religious Studies Review* 6, 4:289–295.

Twiss, Sumner B. 1993. "Curricular Perspectives in Comparative Religious Ethics: A Critical Examination of Four Paradigms." *The Annual of the Society of Christian Ethics*:249–269.

Twiss, Sumner B., Abdullahi A. An-Na'im, Ann Elizabeth Mayer, and William Wipfler. 1994. "Universality vs. Relativism in Human Rights." In *Religion and Human Rights,* edited by John Kelsay and Sumner B. Twiss, 30–59. New York: The Project on Religion and Human Rights.

Twiss, Sumner B., and Bruce Grelle. 1995. "Human Rights and Comparative Religious Ethics: A New Venue." *The Annual of the Society of Christian Ethics*:21–48.

Walzer, Michael. 1988. *The Company of Critics: Social Criticism and Political Commitment in the Twentieth Century.* New York: Basic Books.

Yearley, Lee H. 1990. "Education and the Intellectual Virtues." In *Beyond the Classics? Essays in Religious Studies and Liberal Education,* edited by Frank E. Reynolds and Sheryl L. Burkhalter, 89–105. Atlanta: Scholars Press.

———. 1991. "Bourgeois Relativism and the Comparative Study of the Self." In *Tracing Common Themes: Comparative Courses in the Study of Religion,* edited by John B. Carmen and Steven P. Hopkins, 165–178. Atlanta: Scholars Press.

Zipperer, John. 1993. "The Elusive Quest for Religious Harmony." *Christianity Today* 37, 11:42–44.

Chapter Three

Reckoning with Religious Difference: Models of Interreligious Moral Dialogue

KATE McCARTHY

California State University, Chico

In an effort to take the pulse of contemporary Christian attitudes toward non-Christian religions, I recently visited two Christian-identified bookstores in California. The first, located in the small town where I live, is a large store that sells—in addition to books—Christian art, T-shirts, gifts, music, and videos. Searching the many aisles of books, I did not find a section on world religions. Instead, books with information about other religions were found in two sections labeled "Cults/New Age" and "Apologetics." These labels indicate two things about one common Christian approach to other religions: Non-Christian religions do not share the same categorical status as Christianity but are rather seen as "cults," and consequently the primary goal in understanding them is to develop more effective methods of evangelism or apologetics. In both of these sections, the books had a clearly defensive tenor—subtitles like "Fast Facts on False Teachings," "the Christian Versus Demon Activity," and "Defending the Christian Faith to Non-Believers" were typical.

In the second store, which is affiliated with a major consortium of seminaries and which sells texts for a wide array of graduate courses, books on other religions abounded, organized in several large sections labeled "Ecumenism," "Interreligious Dialogue," and separate sections for many individual non-Christian religions. Materials in this store seemed to share a comparably univocal message about the meaning and value of dialogue:

"Foundations for a Global Theology," "Death or Dialogue," and "The Dialogical Future of Religious Reflection" were typical subtitles. This array represents another common but very different premise for interreligious dialogue: Other religions are legitimate vehicles of salvation, parallel and comparable to Christianity, and dialogue with representatives of these traditions is vital to Christian self-understanding. Shoppers at these two stores, it occurred to me, have far less common ground, in spite of shared Christian identity, than the Christians who shop at the seminary bookstore have with the non-Christians with whom they might take classes, or than the evangelical shoppers at the first store might have with their conservative counterparts in certain branches of Judaism, Hinduism, or Islam.

It seems, then, that religious pluralism, so often analyzed as a problem of interreligious relations, is more properly understood as a problem of individual religions themselves. It is becoming clear that there is not a "Buddhist approach" and a "Muslim approach" to dialogue that must be reconciled with a "Hindu approach" and a "Jewish approach," but rather that there are a variety of models of understanding religious difference that may be found across religious boundaries, and these models point to some of the most critical areas of internal religious tension. In that light, this chapter will examine three alternative models of understanding religious pluralism that have emerged out of one tradition, Roman Catholic and Protestant Christianity, but that find parallels in other traditions. I focus on the Christian tradition not only because it is my own and the one I know best but also because this is a tradition that, for a variety of reasons, has devoted a great deal of theological attention to the question of religious pluralism and has worked out thorough systematic responses to the issue.

These models of religious difference are complex and often ambiguous, dealing as they do with three intricate issues: (1) soteriology—notions of what one must do to be saved, enlightened, redeemed, and so on; (2) concepts of ultimate reality—the nature of God, Brahman, *sunyata,* and so on, and whether or not these are names for the same thing; and (3) interreligious dialogue itself—perspectives on how and why participants in various religions ought to talk with one another. Frustratingly, responses to these issues do not neatly line up with each other; one may be convinced of the worthlessness of dialogue but completely affirming of salvation outside one's own tradition, or one may reject that possibility while at the same time asserting the oneness of all conceptions of ultimate reality. In what follows I hope to elucidate some of this complexity.

Examples of these approaches among Jewish, Hindu, Buddhist, and Muslim individuals and institutions suggest the cross-cultural validity of these models and the universality of *intra*religious pluralism, which adds layers to the challenge of interreligious relations but also offers resources for responding to that challenge. It will be vital to confront and understand this rich but often painful internal diversity if interreligious dialogue is to proceed with clarity and achieve substantive ends.

Exclusivism, Inclusivism, and Pluralism Revisited

Contemporary Christian theological approaches to other religions—two extremes of which are represented at the two bookstores discussed previously—are many and often fiercely divided. In most treatments of this issue, these positions are sorted into a now widely recognized typology of exclusivist, inclusivist, and pluralist models (Race 1983; D'Costa 1986; Knitter 1990; and so on). These models continue to serve as a helpful organizational device and facilitate illuminating comparison with non-Christian approaches. But three-part typologies, although a delight to the systematician, are rarely adequate to the reality they hope to characterize, as is increasingly apparent in this case (see, for example, Markham 1993). Too easily these models serve as straw men for the polemics of those with opposing views, and rigid schematization often obscures consideration of some of the most interesting aspects of the issue, which appear where the exclusivist, inclusivist, and pluralist positions intersect, overlap, and blur. In exploring these three models, then, I hope not only to elucidate the positions as they have developed among Christian thinkers and their parallels in other traditions but also to examine the subtle nuances of some new approaches that press beyond these categories. Finally, I will offer a critical assessment of each approach in light of its implications for interreligious dialogue on contemporary moral issues.

Christian Exclusivism

On the surface, exclusivism is the approach to understanding religious difference that is least conducive to interreligious dialogue and cooperation. In Christianity, this model begins with the assertion of a radical disjunction between Christian revelation and all other forms of religion and identifies Christianity as the exclusive source of human salvation. For the exclusivist, explicit affirmation of belief in Christ, if not affiliation with a Christian institution, is required of all people, and thus evangelism forms a central part of Christian life.

Exclusivist theology has venerable roots in the Christian tradition, drawing on a particular set of biblical texts (especially Matt. 11:27; John 14:6; Acts 4:12; Phil. 2:10–11) so often cited that it can be difficult to recall that the New Testament has anything else to say on the subject. The exclusivist position is also linked with a particular Christological orientation, one that was canonized amid great controversy in the creeds of the early Christian centuries. This view proclaims a highly divinized understanding of Jesus as the unique and preexistent Christ, the son of God who was ordained from all time to die for the sins of, and thereby redeem, the world. Affirmation of the universal saving significance of Christ for all peoples and all times invited an antagonistic posture toward other religions that, although rarely surfacing in official church proclamations, was nonetheless a powerful undercurrent in much premodern Christian theology.[1]

Over the centuries, the exclusivist position was strengthened by the social and political pressures faced by the growing Church. The combination of the consolidation of the Church's political power and the hostility of its contacts with non-Christian peoples as the Roman Empire disintegrated, especially as Islam emerged as a powerful rival missionary religion in the seventh century, fostered a Church-centered, institutional understanding of salvation that further justified intolerance of non-Christian religions. Once explicit Christian affiliation was established as requisite for salvation, it followed that all other outward forms of religious expression were to be rejected. The formula promulgated by Cyprian, bishop of Carthage in the third century, that "outside the Church there is no salvation" was affirmed by popes and theologians until well into the modern period. Although this was certainly not the only approach taken by medieval Christian thinkers (as will be shown below), underlying confidence in the absolute supremacy of Christianity remained intact throughout most of Christian history, until it faced the impact of the Enlightenment's intellectual revolution and the nineteenth-century explosion of information about, and consequent fascination with, non-Christian religions.

Although the official positions of most mainstream Christian churches and the majority of academic theologians today reject the exclusivist position, it remains widely represented in popular Christianity and in some sophisticated evangelical theology. The most important figure in the emergence of modern forms of exclusivism is Swiss Reformed theologian Karl Barth (1886–1968). The cornerstone of Barth's theological project, a reaction against nineteenth-century liberalism, is the argument that the human being is constitutionally incapable of coming to know God through any "natural" human activity—rational, affective, or ethical. God is knowable only insofar as God freely chooses to make Godself known. Thus Christian theology cannot begin with abstract speculation about general revelation, or common ethical imperatives in all religions, or universal religious impulses, but only with the event in which God has chosen to be revealed, the revelation in Christ as witnessed by the Bible. All the speculation and institutional constructs of human religion, including those of Christianity, stand under the decisive judgment of this revelation, which according to Barth's neoorthodoxy reveals them to be human-centered contrivances that lead us nowhere but back to ourselves. It is precisely the Christocentrism of the neoorthodox approach that, while it militates against ecclesiocentric triumphalism, stimulates a more subtle form of exclusivism. The Christian message is seen as self-reflexive: What Christ proclaims is not primarily a moral or eschatological vision but Christ himself, and thus it is through Christ alone that humanity is to find salvation.

Although the position was developed more fully among his followers, Barth himself asserted the decisiveness and uniqueness of God's self-revelation in Jesus Christ in relation with other religions, arguing that by God's grace, Christianity is endowed with its "character as the religion of truth over against the religions of error" (Barth 1956, 344). Hendrik Kraemer, a disciple of Barth who more explicitly took up the question of Christian relations with non-Christians, concludes his massive study of Christian mission with the clearly exclusivist affirmation that "the core of the Christian revelation is that Jesus Christ is the sole legitimate Lord of all human lives and that the failure to recognize this is the deepest religious error of mankind" (Kraemer 1938, 433).

That Christianity's status as the one true religion derives from no inherent quality of its own but rather comes entirely from without in the radical act of God's grace exhorts Christians to great humility but also great confidence in their encounters with non-Christians. This attitude is the hallmark of the contemporary evangelical approach to non-Christian religions. The triumphalism one hears in the proclamations of the first World Missionary Conference held in Edinburgh in 1910, for instance, is not ecclesial but Christological; it is Christ, not the assembled (Protestant) Christian churches, who will soon win victory over the non-Christian world.

In the contemporary theological world, the exclusivist position no longer holds sway as it did under the influence of Barth and Kraemer earlier in the twentieth century. Most mainstream churches, Protestant and Catholic, and most academic theologians have rejected exclusivism in favor of various forms of inclusivism and pluralism, as will be described below. But the exclusivist position cannot be dismissed as easily as some of its critics would like. For one thing, it remains the official position of most evangelical denominations, including the powerful Southern Baptist Convention in the United States, which are growing rapidly even as mainstream churches continue to decline in membership.

Evangelical Christians who are critical of the ecumenical efforts of the World Council of Churches have formed their own para-church networks for the explicit purpose of resisting the perceived humanistic tendencies of such liberal bodies and reasserting the exclusivity of the Christian message. Such was the purpose of the Frankfurt Declaration approved by an evangelical convention in 1970. This document, which clearly reflects the three-part Barthian premise of an exclusively biblical frame of reference, a Christocentric view of salvation, and the categorical difference between Christian revelation and other religions, concludes that the only legitimate form of Christian participation in interreligious "dialogue" is "a proclamation of the gospel that aims at conversion." (Frankfurt Declaration 1970, 846). Today, a similarly ecumenical effort is under way under the rubric of "AD 2000," a massive evangelical crusade bringing together Christians (now including Catholics) whose doctrinal divisions might be sharply divisive but who share this conviction of the need to evangelize non-Christians.

Exclusivism is also defended by a number of academic theologians who see in contemporary pluralistic proposals the same dangers Barth saw in the liberal theology of his day. Perhaps most notable among these is Lutheran theologian Carl Braaten, who vehemently rejects generic conceptions of religious salvation and calls for a biblically based affirmation of Christ as the only source of salvation; "and by Christ we do not mean some anonymous Christ principle but the concrete reality and historical person of Jesus as the Christ" (Braaten 1992, 78). Of particular concern to many of these scholars is the loss of the particularity and uniqueness of Christianity seen to result from the acceptance of religion as a generic category in which there are multiple expressions. Exclusivist theologians argue that religious pluralism is "the result of the disintegrating effects of sin rather than the flowering of creativity" (VanderWerff 1992, 113), and insist that only the act of God in Christ, not any human efforts at religious reunion, can reconcile that division.

The exclusivist position is often understood to reject the value of interreligious dialogue. In fact, exclusivists are often eager participants in interfaith exchanges, though they define the goals of such encounters differently from their liberal counterparts. The 1993 Parliament of the World's Religions, commemorating the centennial of the 1893 World's Parliament of Religions, offered an opportunity for reflection on dialogue among evangelicals, who were a prominent presence at the 1893 event but almost invisible in 1993. Evangelicals were divided over whether or not to endorse this interfaith event, and those who did participate in it had diverse interpretations of its value. For some, the existence of such an event implied a quest for religious unity, understood as a syncretism that is anathema to traditional Christian faith. For others, it offered an opportunity for valuable dialogue with non-Christians who are increasingly encountered as neighbors, coworkers, even friends. As Canadian evangelical theologian Clark Pinnock argues, if the event gave Christians the chance to "actually present their view of the world and salvation in the presence of others in the hope of perhaps communicating to them and learning from them, then there could be no objection to that, since our love for people requires us to do that" (cited in Zipperer 1993, 44).[2] In his reflections on the parliament, David Neff insists that such dialogue is a necessary good neighbor policy:

> In recent years, we have encountered Buddhists, animists, Hindus, and Muslims in dominantly white middle-class suburbs. Some run donut shops, some

are accountants, some are research chemists and physicists. All of those we
have observed demonstrate stronger family structures than many of the Christian families we know. Not interacting with them would be a personal loss and
a failure to live up to our calling as Christians. (Zipperer 1993, 20)

But understanding and neighborliness do not for the evangelical exclusivist
obviate the need for conversion. Acknowledging the growing debate in
evangelical circles about the need for explicit affirmation of Christian faith,
Neff's conclusion affirms the common denominator of exclusivist positions:
"No one should teach that non-Christians will be saved because of good
works or noble intentions. All God saves will be saved through the atoning
death of Jesus Christ" (Zipperer 1993, 21).[3]

Ironically, as many evangelical critics have noted, there are often limits to
dialogue at events like the 1993 parliament, imposed precisely by those
who champion the most pluralistic worldviews. Representatives of Wicca,
the Nation of Islam, and a huge variety of non-Western traditions are welcomed at the dialogue table, but Christians holding fast to traditional exclusivist truth claims find few willing dialogue partners. An evangelical pastor reports being frightened by the steamrollering pluralism he encountered
at the parliament: "These people are dead serious about solving the problems of the world through religious unity, and woe to those who stand in
their way" (Erwin W. Lutzer, cited in Zipperer 1993, 43). Christian exclusivists, these evangelicals would remind us, are not *anti*dialogue, as is often
assumed; they simply define the goals of dialogue differently and reserve
the right to bring uncompromising truth claims to the dialogue table.

These various scholarly and popular expressions of Christian exclusivism
together suggest the defining features of this approach to religious difference, which can now be summarized. First, it affirms a discontinuous relationship between Christianity and all other religions. The revelation of God
in Christ is not simply superior to other revelations, it is categorically different from them and therefore incommensurate. Second, it builds upon
foundations of biblical authority, which may, but do not necessarily, involve biblical literalism. For the exclusivist, the biblical statements of the
uniqueness of Christ and the universal significance of his life, death, and
resurrection cannot be relativized by new interpretations, however attractive contemporary circumstances may make such readings. Third, it draws
upon a particularly Christocentric understanding of salvation. All salvation
is achieved in and through the work of Christ, not by a God so generically
conceived as to be found present in non-Christian traditions. To be saved,
according to the exclusivist position, one must explicitly affirm this Christological source of redemption. Finally, exclusivism defines the goals and
method of interreligious dialogue in relation to its central concern for evangelism. Although the Christian cannot learn anything of soteriological sig-

nificance from these encounters, dialogue is valuable insofar as it helps the Christian better understand and therefore more effectively evangelize the non-Christian. This last point is worthy of emphasis. Christian exclusivism looks not only inward but outward; it not only makes affirmative claims about the uniqueness of Christianity's worldview, it also makes negative claims about all competing visions (Eck 1993, 174).

Non-Christian Exclusivism

The exclusivist-inclusivist-pluralist typology was developed by Christian scholars to describe Christian ideas. It should not be surprising, then, to find that these categories account awkwardly at best for the data of other religions and their approaches to religious difference. This poor cross-cultural fit is the most serious limitation of this paradigm as a universal model. Still, there are parallels. To the extent that they share Christianity's monotheism and its unitary conception of truth, Judaism and Islam articulate exclusive claims comparable to those of Christianity. For all three monotheistic traditions, there can be no compromise on the oneness of the divine, and all three make claims that link this one God to the particularity of their own tradition in ways that are at least normative if not exclusive. The *shema,* the daily prayer of Jews, proclaims the particularity and universality of the God of Israel: "Hear O Israel, the Lord our God, the Lord is one"; and the Muslim *shahadah,* or creed, one of the five essential "pillars" of Islam, uses similar one-and-only language: "There is no God but Allah, and Muhammad is the prophet of God."

But confidence in the unique and normative status of their own God and God's revelation to them has not resulted in full-blown exclusivist theology for the majority of Jews and Muslims. This difference may be attributed to several factors. Judaism's minority status and relative lack of political power throughout history have certainly inhibited its tendency to develop an outward-looking exclusivism. For much of its history, Christianity has been associated with the world's dominant economic and political powers, fostering the development of a kind of religious colonialism not possible for Jewish theologians. Even Islam, which for many centuries was the leading economic, cultural, and political force of half the world, did not develop the equivalent of Christian exclusivism. In this case the explanation may be more purely religious. Both Judaism and Islam can be characterized as *orthopractic* rather than *orthodox* religions; proper ethical and ritual conduct is emphasized more than assent to propositional truths. This orientation tends to limit the kind of oppositional self-definition characteristic of Christian exclusivism, which has insisted that belief in Jesus as the Christ, rightly formulated, is requisite for salvation.

Finally, institutional differences between Christianity and the other two Western religions may contribute to their distinct approaches to other religions. Islam, like Judaism, lacks the overarching institutional structures (the papacy, the magisterium, denominational institutions) that have facilitated Christianity's concern for pure and uniform religious worldviews (Lewis 1993, 178). In both these traditions, then, although internal matters of faith and practice may be hotly, even violently, debated, there is not the same kind of urgency about achieving a unitary system of belief, and therefore there is also not the same pattern of conceptually opposing that system to all others. Certainly Jews and Muslims have made negative assessments of other religious positions, especially Christian claims about the divinity of Jesus. But their mainstream theology, for these and other complex reasons, has tended to look inward more than outward, to work out the particularity of their own religious visions without systematic efforts to correlate or contend with alternative worldviews.

If Jews and Muslims have not developed the kind of outward-looking exclusivism typical of evangelical Christianity, neither have they universally championed dialogue of the sort promoted by liberal Christians. Jewish interest in interreligious dialogue is limited, most Jewish theologians tending to believe that the goal of mutual agreement or even full mutual understanding on matters of ultimate truth is fundamentally wrongheaded. As the Orthodox Rabbinical Council of America states in its guidelines on dialogue, "There cannot be mutual understanding concerning these topics, for Jews and Christians will employ different categories and move within incommensurate frames of reference and evaluation" (cited in Braybrooke 1992, 196).

On matters of practical concern, however, Jewish interest in interfaith work is keen. Coordinated by the International Jewish Committee on Inter-Religious Consultations, Jewish groups active in interreligious dialogue tend to bring a pragmatic and often political perspective to these exchanges. For many Jews, self-preservation serves as the primary motive for interreligious dialogue. Having experienced the lethal impact of Christian triumphalism, Jews seek in dialogue to preserve the distinctness of their own faith and to "help Christians become aware of the deep-rooted anti-Judaism of traditional church teaching" (Braybrooke 1992, 196). Blu Greenburg summarizes well a widespread Jewish sense of Christian history: "I know this general truth: whenever the Good News was combined with power, it became the bad news for Jews. In every era in Christian Europe, the closer Christians got to their sacred texts, the more painful things became for Jews. The more strongly Jesus was believed to have atoned for human sin, the more sins were committed against the Jews" (1984, 229). The most widely held Jewish position may thus better be characterized as a kind of separatism rather than exclusivism, for it lacks the Christian exclusivists' interest in conversion yet also resists the pluralists' effort to correlate all religious truth claims in a universally intelligible system.

Historically, Islam has come closer than any other major world religion to espousing an exclusivism equivalent to that of traditional Christianity.

Like Christianity, traditional Islam claims that its revelation is not only universally but also exclusively true; the revelation to Muhammad is not only relevant to all peoples of all times, it is the only revelation to hold that status (Lewis 1993, 175). Although Muhammad is not understood as divine by Muslims, his designation as the "Seal of the Prophets" reflects the Islamic conviction that their revelation is unique and unsurpassable. What's more, Islam's central belief in the oneness and transcendence of Allah makes the problem of idolatry, of revering as God that which is not, a central concern. This concern is easily focused on those of other religious traditions, which are seen as either willfully rejecting or ignorantly misperceiving this single essential truth of the universe. Conversion of others to the straight path of Islam is thus often seen as a Muslim duty, and one can discern a kind of Muslim exclusivism in the tradition's adamant rejections of truth claims that might compromise the unity and omnipotence of Allah.

Most notable of these, of course, is the Christian claim to the divinity of Christ. The doctrine of the Trinity is understood by Muslims as the fundamental error of Christianity, which corrupts the great truths taught by Jesus the prophet (Qur'an 5:73–79, 6:101).[4] But Islam's emphasis on orthopraxis, its conviction that final judgment will be based on deeds rather than beliefs, and its self-understanding not as the replacement but the fulfillment of the essential truths of Judaism and Christianity, work against a fully exclusivist theology. Although mainstream Muslim theology comes closer than traditional Jewish thought to an exclusivism like that of Christianity, it lacks the sense of radical disjunction between its own and other religious paths. For the Muslim, other religions, particularly Judaism and Christianity, are limited and/or distorted versions of a truth that is clarified and perfected in Islam (Waardenburg 1979, 246–247). This, as I will suggest below, is the defining trait of inclusivist, not exclusivist, thinking.

Exclusivism and Fundamentalism

We are all too aware, however, of forms of religious resurgence in the contemporary world that display the ugliest face of exclusivism. In the tense, often violent, relationships between Tamil Hindus and Sinhalese Buddhists in Sri Lanka, between Orthodox Jews and Muslims in Israel, between Sikh separatists and Hindu nationalists in India, between conservative Christians and secularists in the United States, the rhetoric of exclusivism is used to support a variety of fundamentalist positions. Although it would be naive to claim that these conflicts are driven solely by social and political issues, it must be made clear that they do not derive directly from theological positions. Claims to universally normative religious truth do not in all or even most cases lead to hostility toward those with differing views.

It seems that there are particular circumstances that make the language of religious fidelity in a given community more oppositional and antagonistic toward outsiders. Fundamentalisms emerging in a variety of religious communities can be distinguished from traditionalist or conservative expressions of those traditions in that fundamentalisms are decidedly modern responses to uniquely modern crises (Lawrence 1989, 100–101). These extreme expressions of exclusivism can be seen as efforts to define and defend personal and communal identity in a social and political context in which such identity is lost or threatened. In an effort to clarify the "family resemblances" of fundamentalist movements worldwide, Martin E. Marty and R. Scott Appleby point to this common context:

> Fundamentalisms arise or come to prominence in times of crisis, actual or perceived. The sense of danger may be keyed to oppressive and threatening social, economic, or political conditions, but the ensuing crisis is perceived as a *crisis of identity* by those who fear extinction as a people or absorption into an overarching syncretistic culture to such a degree that their distinctiveness is undermined in the rush to homogeneity. (1991, 822–823)

What this context suggests is that, in spite of the religious character of fundamentalist exclusivisms, they must be understood in broader cultural terms and distinguished from the more carefully nuanced and traditionally supported claims of the kind of theological exclusivism sketched above.

Indeed, the theology articulated by fundamentalist groups is often derived only through selective, narrow, and rationalized readings of their religious traditions (Marty and Appleby 1991, 836–837). The "family values" championed by Christian fundamentalists in the United States, for instance, are often quite alien to the New Testament gospels (in which Jesus defines family, for instance, in terms of the community of those pursuing a common social and spiritual vision, and in which he says absolutely nothing about homosexuality) but reflect the search for a clearly defined and cohesive core philosophy to help reorient a society that is perceived to have lost its way. Similarly, Donald Swearer argues that the Buddhism championed by the Sinhalese extremists in their opposition to separatist Tamil Hindus in Sri Lanka is based on an "absolutistic, moralistic, and nationalistic ideology ostensibly Buddhist but in fact an innovative departure from the religious system of classical Sinhalese Buddhism" (Swearer 1991, 639; see also Tambiah 1986, 139).

In the case of militant Islam of both Sunni and Shi'i varieties, fundamentalist claims can be seen as a response to the "social and economic disequilibrium . . . opposition to state authority, the experience of colonialism . . . the weight of dependency in the world economic system" and "the failure of leaders—religious as well as political—to deal with these failures" (Piscatori 1994, 361). For many in these groups, the "other" that looms as a threat to identity or even survival is the juggernaut of Western secular and capitalist culture and the local elites who would compromise or cooperate with it. Interethnic conflict is also a powerful catalyst to fundamentalist exclusivism. In the many new nations created in the post–World War II realignment, national elites were unable to articulate the basis for a national identity that could allow rival ethnic blocs to coexist peacefully, allowing animosities to fester and fostering the ideological use of religious claims (Marty and Appleby 1991, 824). In this kind of postcolonial context, the reassertion of traditional religious truth claims in exclusivist modes is seen as a matter of survival, part of the effort to shape an authentic identity (Griffiths 1990, 70).

In the case of North American Christian fundamentalism, the perceived threat driving exclusivist claims is somewhat different. This type of exclusivism must be seen as a defensive reaction not to an encroaching cultural monolith but to the bewildering pluralism of contemporary society itself. The speed of technological change and the breakdown of the illusion of cultural homogeneity leave many in North American society with a deep need for firm moorings, readily available in the unambiguous doctrines and strict moral codes of fundamentalist Christianity.

In addition to its unique cultural context and its idiosyncratic use of tradition, the fundamentalist approach to religious difference must also be distinguished from traditional exclusivism in its assessment of the value of interreligious dialogue. Although they, like exclusivists, reject the possibility of saving truth outside their own tradition, fundamentalist groups are not necessarily motivated by an effort to convert and thereby save those outside their community. Rather, they seek to delineate and defend an absolute truth that provides a sense of identity and that must be protected from all compromise. For the fundamentalist, the primary target of proselytism is often not the religious "other" but the lax member of one's own religious community (Marty and Appleby 1991, 822). For this reason, the logic of interreligious dialogue is not as finely developed among fundamentalists as it is among exclusivists like Barth and Braaten. The project is either rejected out of hand or entered into as a simple confrontation of truth against falsehood.

The point to be made about all these fundamentalisms is simply this: Their expressions of religious exclusivism are not strictly religiously determined but derive in large part from contextual cultural and political factors. Understanding and responding to this kind of exclusivism, therefore, requires attention to more than theology. Until the wider anxieties that inform fundamentalist exclusivism are addressed, attacks on it will only increase its vehemence.

The exclusivist model of interreligious relations, then, is found across religious boundaries, and with significant variants within a single tradition. Its common claim is the uniqueness of its own revelation and the inadequacy of all other religious paths, but this claim can derive from secular as well as theological premises and may or may not involve active efforts at conversion or the rejection of interreligious dialogue.

Christian Inclusivism

The middle part of the twentieth century saw the transformation of Western perspectives on world religions from an abstract curiosity about exotic foreign peoples to a living encounter with people whose traditions were increasingly recognized as genuinely faithful. This period also saw the deepening of these traditions' own self-consciousness and assertiveness with regard to Christianity in the struggle against the heritage of colonialism. A new generation of Christian theologians endeavored to reconcile the mentality of this new world with a continued affirmation of the normative status of Christian revelation. Inclusivism, the most widely held Christian approach to religious difference, grows out of that effort.

Inclusivism's fundamental assertion is that salvation is available outside of the Christian religion, but only because of the grace of God in Christ, which is universally efficacious. In this sense, non-Christian religious paths are affirmed as good and true by being *included* in the Christian economy of salvation. For the inclusivist, salvation is still Christological, but in an ontological, not epistemological, sense. For the *exclusivist,* we recall, one must not only receive the grace of God made available through Christ but know of and explicitly acknowledge that grace. For the *inclusivist,* the epistemological affirmation is not necessary; one can be saved without ever knowing of the work of Christ at all. Christian inclusivism builds upon an optimistic assessment of the traditional theological concept of general revelation, the knowledge of God made possible to human beings through their natural capacities. For exclusivists, general revelation, if acknowledged at all, is valued as a point of contact that can facilitate evangelism; for the inclusivist, it is the vital bridge that makes interreligious dialogue possible.

This approach, too, draws on long Church tradition. Biblically, it emphasizes the wisdom and Logos traditions that interpret Jesus as the manifestation of God's creative-redemptive activity in the world. In the works of patristic theologians like Justin Martyr, Irenaeus, and Origen, Jesus is identified with the divine Logos, a concept that fused the Jewish understanding of the Word as the messenger of God's wisdom with the Stoic notion of the pervasive rational principle of the universe. Unlike a theology of outright hostility to non- or pre-Christian wisdom, a theology built on Logos Christology could acknowledge the godliness of such wisdom and incorporate it into a single universal scheme of salvation. Having included other wisdom traditions, this theology could then stake out the highest point in the scheme for the revelation in Jesus Christ.

In the medieval period, another form of inclusivist theology developed in the work of Thomas Aquinas, achieving prominence in Catholic thought. In his effort to bring an Aristotelian philosophical framework into harmony with Christian theology, Aquinas discerned in non-Christian religions a natural revelation rooted in the universal human capacity for reason. Although dialogue with Muslims and pagans on the basis of shared revelation was impossible, dialogue on the basis of reason alone was not only possible but imperative (Aquinas 1955, 61). This natural reasoning capacity, however, needs to be clarified and amplified by divine revelation, according to Aquinas, who claims that it is in the Christian faith alone that this critical elucidation is made. This early formulation of the inclusivist position makes clear its guiding principle: confidence in the continuity between Christian and non-Christian revelation premised on the pervasiveness and perfection of the former. In other words, the inclusivist posture makes possible a genuine appreciation of non-Christian religions in a way that was not possible for Barth and Kraemer, but does so in Christian terms.

Classic formulations of the inclusivist model in the modern period are found in the work of Protestant theologian Paul Tillich (1886–1965), whose work draws heavily on existential philosophy,[5] and Catholic theologian Karl Rahner (1904–1984),[6] whose famous designation of "anonymous Christians" expresses well the genuine but derivative value of non-Christian traditions in the inclusivist model. If, within their own cultural systems, people practice neighborly love, live in a state of radical hope, and face the challenge of death as a surrender to life, Rahner argues, those people reveal an implicit Christian faith and may legitimately be called "anonymous Christians" (1978, 311–321). This anonymity, however, is not finally adequate for Rahner. Explicit preaching of the Christian message remains a vital missionary task because in the self-realization of their Christian faith, previously "anonymous" Christians grasp their relation to God more clearly and purely and are thus more open to salvation (1980, 76).

Rahner's version of the inclusivist position has become the norm for contemporary Catholic theology. Rahner was instrumental in the drafting of Vatican II documents on the subject, which clearly reject the fortress mentality that had characterized the Catholic Church's perspective on modernity and its attendant concerns for religious pluralism. In the important Vatican II document "Declaration on the Relation of the Church to Non-Christian Religions" *(Nostra aetate)*, Rahner's inclusivism comes through with striking clarity. It begins with an affirmation of God's universal plan for human salvation and the corresponding unity of all peoples, and goes on to affirm the Church's respect for the religions and the real truths they reveal and promote, but concludes with an assertion of the normativity of Christian revelation and the consequent ongoing importance of Christian missionary work.[7] The dominant Catholic model as represented by this text continues to assert the uniqueness and normativity of Christian revelation, but like Barth's approach it shifts the locus of that uniqueness from the historical Christian tradition and the institutional Church to the Christ event itself. Unlike that of Barth and the exclusivists, however, the Catholic approach expresses the normativity of Christ in inclusive terms that draw all religions into the light of the ontologically necessary salvific act of God in Christ.

Most of the mainstream Protestant churches, too, present forms of inclusivism as their official positions on the question of other religions. It is difficult to judge, however, how widely inclusivism is accepted in the popular Christian community; the gap between the piety of those in the pews and the statements of their denominational leaders is often quite wide. In the United States, the rapid growth of evangelical churches and the continuing membership decline in mainstream churches may suggest that the straightforward exclusivist approach has greater appeal than more ambiguous inclusivist theologies.

When Tillich and Rahner developed their positions on this issue, they were among the most progressive on the Christian theological scene. Since that time, however, a variety of more thoroughgoing affirmations of religious pluralism have developed among Christian theologians, as I will sketch below. In response, a number of Christian theologians have recently worked out more sophisticated versions of the inclusivist model that seek to preserve its most essential claim but avoid some of the obvious cultural insensitivities and presumptions involved in such concepts as anonymous Christianity. Among these thinkers, many of whom have made career-long studies of non-Christian religions, the other religions are taken more seriously on their own terms, not just as pale reflections of Christian truths but as spiritual systems with their own integrity from which Christians themselves can learn a great deal. Nonetheless, these inclusivists continue to assert, in defense against the pluralist position, that Christians cannot renounce the traditional claim to uniqueness. A significant shift has been made by some of these contemporary figures[8] from a constitutive to a representative or paradigmatic understanding of the Christ event (Knitter 1995a, 27–28). That is, the Christ event *represents* in the clearest way possible the universal saving will of God; it does not in itself *constitute* that saving action for all of humanity.

Christian inclusivists tend to be eager champions of interreligious dialogue. Indeed, many Christians come to the inclusivist position, as Tillich in part did, out of the experience of dialogue with others, the authenticity of whose faith and spiritual practice could then no longer be denied. For the inclusivist, true two-way dialogue is mandated in a way that can never be the case for the exclusivist, whose primary concern remains evangelical.

The Christian inclusivist, while believing that Christian revelation is normative, also affirms the real and different insights of non-Christian traditions and is prepared to be enlightened by them. In the modern period, very
successful interreligious exchanges have been sustained on inclusivist
premises. Indeed, most of the Christian organizers of and participants in
the 1893 World's Parliament of Religions, the event often used to mark the
beginning of the interfaith movement (Braybrooke 1992, 1), shared inclusivist beliefs. This view was clearly expressed by Reverend John Henry Barrows, chairman of the parliament's general committee, who asked, in the
face of sharp criticism of the event from more conservative Christians,
"Why should not Christians be glad to learn what God has wrought
through Buddha and Zoroaster—through the sage of China, and the
prophets of India and the prophet of Islam" (Barrows 1893, 75). But Barrows's review of the parliament also makes clear that for the inclusivist,
there are real limits to dialogue: "The non-Christian world may give us
valuable criticism and confirm scriptural truths and make excellent suggestions as to Christian improvement, but it has nothing to add to the Christian creed" (1551).

Many contemporary theologians might not express the finality of Christianity so categorically, but they are equally convinced that authentic dialogue can be sustained on the premise of Christianity's normative status. Indeed, they argue, without such a premise dialogue remains shallow and
inconsequential. Gavin D'Costa, an Indian Roman Catholic theologian, for
instance, argues that commitment to the doctrine of the Trinity forms a better basis for interreligious dialogue than does any affirmation of the truth
of all religions.[9]

There are important differences among inclusivist theologians, to be
sure, especially with regard to the status of Jesus Christ as the paradigmatic
representation or constitutive source of all salvation, but what continues to
unite inclusivists is a three-part conviction. First, God and human faith are
generic realities. That is, there is a single divine reality, which Christians
call God, but which is genuinely encountered in the spiritual experiences of
people of all faiths. Second, God's saving will for humanity is universal and
pervasive among all the peoples of the earth; no one is left out of the economy of salvation. Finally, however, inclusivists insist that God's saving will
is expressed normatively and unsurpassably in the life, death, and resurrection of Jesus Christ.

Non-Christian Inclusivism

It is not surprising that Christianity, as a world-dominant religion often allied with colonialist powers, should have developed this kind of theology as
a template for its interaction with others. But inclusivist thinking is by no

means limited to Christianity. One also finds a striking version of inclusivism in Muslim theology. Islam's relationship with other religions is unique in that its scripture, which is understood as revelation in a more absolute sense than in any other tradition, makes explicit assessments of two other major world religions, Christianity and Judaism. These predecessor monotheistic traditions are seen as limited and distorted, requiring correction and fulfillment in the final revelation given in the Qur'an, but also as essentially holy, revealed by God, and therefore containing truth and deserving of respect (see especially suras 3, 5, and 6). According to Muslim doctrine, the monotheistic "religions of the book" have a unique status warranting their recognition and protection whenever under Muslim rule. Just as inclusivist Christians recognize the possibility of salvation among those non-Christians who sincerely practice their faith, it is a commonly held Muslim view that Christians and Jews can be saved in and though righteous pursuit of their own faiths (Nasr 1990, 130).

The theological bases of Muslim and Christian inclusivism are significantly different, however. Whereas the Christian inclusivist doctrine is built on the foundation of the universal impact of the Christ event, radiating both backward and forward in time, Muslim inclusivism is founded on a sequentialist understanding of revelation: Islam completes and perfects what was only partially revealed to (and subsequently misunderstood by) Christians and Jews. Thus one does not see an inclusivist interpretation so prominent in Muslim assessments of religious developments subsequent to its own emergence (Lewis 1993, 176).

A second example of non-Christian inclusivism can be seen in the Buddhist traditions of Asia. Buddhism is noted for its generally open and tolerant attitudes and for its reticence on the kinds of doctrinal matters that typically lead to inter- and intrareligious conflict. The central concern of Buddhism is the alleviation of suffering, its "gospel" message that suffering has a source that can, through spiritual discipline, be cut off. In a famous parable, the Buddha is said to have compared the concern for metaphysical particulars with a man shot by a poisoned arrow who refuses treatment of the wound until he can establish the name, caste, and physical features of the arrow's shooter. Given this pragmatic orientation, it is no surprise that Buddhists have historically been quite accommodating to those whose religious beliefs differ. Yet the predominant Buddhist approach to religious difference can still be characterized as inclusivist, for these alternative religious systems are incorporated into the universal and normative truth claims of orthodox Buddhism.

The essential religious concept underlying Buddhist inclusivism is the paradox of ultimate and relative truths. Reality can be understood in two ways, according to Buddhist teaching: as it "really is," that is, how it would appear to us if we were completely freed from ignorance and delusion; and as it appears in our conventional perception. It is the goal of Buddhist discipline to realize the ultimate oneness of these levels of perception; apprehension of this paradox is vital to Buddhist spiritual progress. Those truth claims that seem to conflict in the conventional realm can on this premise be recognized as ultimately harmonious.

The two-truths doctrine works out in Buddhist encounters with non-Buddhists in a pattern of accommodation facilitated by the doctrine of *upaya,* or skillful means. According to this concept, truth "must be apprehended and communicated in relation to the abilities and capacities of the individuals being taught" (Ingram 1988, 95); any means may be skillfully employed by the Buddhist teacher to lead non-Buddhists to specifically Buddhist truths. Other religious ideas and practices are thus not rejected but appropriated as partial truths valuable for the cultivation of the full truth of Buddhist enlightenment. On this premise, many ideas and practices not found in the earliest Buddhist tradition (at least at the canonical level), including devotionalism and divinities like the Chinese goddess of compassion Kwan-Yin, have been incorporated into mainstream Buddhism.

Contemporary Buddhist scholars employ the theme of the ultimate identity between mundane and supramundane realms as the foundation for interreligious dialogue. Shohei Ichimura, for instance, develops the Mahayana Buddhist notion of *sunyata,* or emptiness, in this regard (Ichimura 1986). The concept of *sunyata* insists on the insubstantiality of all of reality to the point that ultimately there can be no distinction between the realm of suffering and rebirth (samsara) and the realm of release from it (nirvana). Yet on the practical, conventional level, such contrasts meaningfully persist. On the foundation of this paradox, Buddhists can affirm and incorporate into their worldview apparently contradictory truths, all of which are ultimately *sunya,* void of substantial, independent reality.

These assimilationist and accommodationist concepts do not, however, diminish the universalist claims of the Buddhist tradition or its historic commitment to the unique perfection of its own religious insight. The Four Noble Truths taught by the Buddha are not seen as four among many but as *the* essential truths requisite for human enlightenment. The *upaya* doctrine permits the employment of any spiritual concept or practice for the purpose of leading seekers to these truths, but the means can never surpass the end, which remains Buddhist. Indeed, the Buddhist process of accommodation and incorporation of non-Buddhist themes has been highly selective. "In spite of its philosophy of assimilation, the Buddhist teaching remains as categorical in its rejection of anything compromising faith in the Three Jewels as Christian theology is in its rejection of anything compromising faith in Jesus Christ" (Ingram 1988, 108).

These examples suggest that the inclusivist approach to religious difference is diverse but also that it, like the exclusivist response, constitutes a consistent cross-cultural pattern of religious encounter. Inclusivists are authentically open to the truth of other religious claims, believe in the possibility of salvation outside their own religion, and support interreligious dialogue as a mutually enriching enterprise. What distinguishes them from pluralists, however, is the inclusivists' commitment to their own tradition as universally normative—because it is the constitutive source of all human salvation, or the fulfillment of divine revelation in history, or the paradigmatic representation of a universally available spiritual transformation. For the inclusivist, the truth and value of all other religious paths remain in these important ways derivative.

Christian Pluralism

The last of the three major approaches to religious difference worked out in Christian theology is a somewhat looser class of positions commonly referred to as "pluralist" for their thoroughgoing endorsement of religious diversity. Broadly conceived, pluralist responses to the question of religious diversity are united in a fourfold affirmation, the first three of which address the issue of religion as a generic category in asserting: (1) that religious diversity is permanent, that the multiplicity of religions will not be superseded or fulfilled by any one single religion; (2) that there is a possible, though not necessarily actual, parity of validity among the religions; and (3) that there can be no final or absolute and universal expression of truth in any one religion (Wiles 1992; Race 1983; Knitter 1990). Finally, Christian pluralist theologies are united in their endorsement of scaled-down doctrines of Jesus Christ. Pluralists in various ways argue for a humble Christology that affirms (4) that Jesus may indeed be unique, but that uniqueness is to be expressed in terms other than those of finality or unsurpassability.

For some, the pluralist move emerges from the very practical effort to develop more adequate models for interreligious understanding and cooperation. Representatives of this ethical-dialogical case for pluralism include Leonard Swidler, Rosemary Ruether, Donald Swearer, David Lochhead, Tom Driver, and Paul Knitter. These very different theologians are united in their argument that to maintain absolute, universal religious truth claims in a world that is so thoroughly pluralistic is both unethical and inimical to the dialogical process that is so vital to meaning-making in that world. History has demonstrated the practical effects of Christologies that absolutize the relation between God and Christ in such a way as to define those who are outside of Christ as subnormal. Christian anti-Semitism; the patriarchal subjugation of women; and insensitive, sometimes brutal, religious colonialism are cited as the ethical fruits that demonstrate the inadequacy of exclusive and inclusive theologies, however much these effects may be distortions of the intent of the theologies' formulators (Ruether 1974, 1987). To

preserve any vestige of Christian supremacy is to maintain the universaliz-
ing habit that has been manifested in the domination and even annihilation
of the non-Christian other and the exclusion and subjugation of women[10]
throughout Christian history.

Further, these scholars argue, such absolutist claims doom from the outset the project of genuinely open interreligious dialogue, a project that is vital to Christian theology because of its roots in both the relational mission
of Jesus Christ and the contemporary global context in which it must make
meaning (Driver 1981). For a pluralist, the very question of Christianity's
relation with non-Christian traditions is permanently and self-consciously
open-ended. No a priori schemes for relating different religions, however
soteriologically generous to the non-Christian, will be employed by the pluralist, who opts instead for the ongoing process of interaction, mutual discovery, and redefinition.

Deeply attuned to the pluralism and politicization of the contemporary
scene, these thinkers highlight the importance of theological accountability
to those who have been exploited by or left out of traditional theological
schemes. Indeed, some of the best pluralist theology is emerging from postcolonial contexts where Christians experience their faith in multicultural,
multireligious environments and where triumphalist versions of Christian
doctrine are extremely unpalatable (see, for example, Balasuriya 1984;
Pieris 1988; Song 1991; Chung 1990). The imperative of listening to those
voices in a real dialogue and reformulating theological statements to redress their ethical inadequacies makes an important argument for the pluralist move.

It is one thing to reject all expressions of Christian absoluteness on the
grounds of moral imperatives; it is another to adjudicate among claims
about the nature of ultimate reality made by these traditions. A second case
for a pluralist Christian theology has emerged among philosophy of religion scholars who address this problem of the conflicting truth claims of
the various religions. Two ways of understanding these conflicts have
emerged among pluralists, which might be called convergent and nonconvergent models of religious difference. In the convergent model, the varied
and apparently contradictory religious explanations of reality are seen as
diverse responses to a single ineffable ultimate; in the nonconvergent
model, ultimate reality itself is conceived as pluralistic.

The most important representative of the convergent hypothesis is the
British philosopher and theologian John Hick. At the heart of Hick's thinking is a vision of God as the transcendent center of the universe of human
religiousness, around which the various faith traditions revolve. This is the
theocentric shift that is often identified as the hallmark of pluralist theologies. Instead of imagining the universe of faith as revolving around a Christological center, Hick argues for a God-centered or, more recently, a reality-

centered perspective in which each of the world's religions is seen to revolve around the one ultimate reality. In *An Interpretation of Religion* (1989), Hick's fullest exposition of his philosophy, his hypothesis is put forth clearly: The different religions are to be seen as "different ways of experiencing, conceiving and living in right relation to an ultimate reality which transcends all our varied visions of it" (1989, 235–236).[11] For some, the phenomenological encounter with the Real occurs in personal terms; for others, in nonpersonal terms, in forms that Hick calls the divine *personae* and *impersonae* (1989, 248; 1990, 190–191; 1993, 164–179). Following Kant, Hick posits a real *an sich* behind the diversity of religious phenomena, and he is thus able to affirm the pluralism of religions without affirming ultimate metaphysical pluralism and the relativism he seems to fear that would entail (1995, 27–30). Differences among truth claims across religions, then, must be understood as diverse cultural expressions, rich in meaning and not to be diluted or superseded, deriving from the same root experience of encounter with the Real.

The nonconvergent pluralist hypothesis is developed in the work of Indian Catholic philosopher and theologian Raimon Panikkar. Panikkar insists that pluralism must be more than sheer acknowledgment of plurality and wishful thinking about unity, and that unity is not an indispensable ideal and need not be the theologian's eschatological expectation (1987, 109). In an affirmation that goes beyond Hick and beyond the general pluralist position that religious diversity is permanent, Panikkar argues that the religious pluralism that is permanent as a historical phenomenon is not something laid over a single numinous Real but rather represents the structure of ultimate reality itself (1984, 110; 1993, 121). Apparently in direct response to Hick, Panikkar reproaches the pluralist view that would affirm the ultimate unity of religions as different paths to the same summit: "It is not simply that there are different ways leading to the peak, but that the summit itself would collapse if all the paths disappeared. The peak is in a certain sense the result of the slopes leading to it. . . . It is not that this reality *has* many names as if there were a reality outside the name. The reality *is* the many names and each name is a new aspect" (1981, 24, 29). For Hick, all subjective religious experiences converge in a single ineffable Real, while for Panikkar, this variety points to the irreducible metaphysical pluralism of ultimate reality itself.[12]

The terrain that forms common ground for Hick and Panikkar, however, is finally much larger than that on which they differ. For both, pluralist views emerge out of studies of religion as a generic category of human existence and their efforts to make sense of that category with philosophical tools. Any interpretation of religion that takes seriously the data of its expressions across time and continents and that reflects upon the structures of human consciousness, Hick and Panikkar are agreed, cannot defend the ultimate unity of religions. Such a unity may characterize ultimate reality, and may perhaps be glimpsed in the mystical experience, but cannot be imposed on the diverse range of human religious phenomena. The transcendent mystery of Hick's Real _an sich_ and Panikkar's _advaitin_ "cosmotheandric" conception of reality do not merely tolerate but in fact _depend upon_ a great diversity of images, experiences, and doctrinal systems for their disclosure.

There may also be compelling reasons arising from Christian commitment itself for moving away from the exclusivist and inclusivist positions that have in large part defined Christian history. These theological reasons are developed most clearly by those whose pluralist orientation is informed by Christological investigation. Spurred by the lively Anglican debates of the past several decades and the increasingly public work of critical New Testament scholars like those represented by the Jesus Seminar, there is now a third important stream of pluralist thinking emerging from contemporary Christology, where the question of the nature and validity of the classical Christian doctrine of the incarnation and its implications for Christian relations with non-Christians is being interrogated. Drawing on a long tradition of critical biblical studies, many of these scholars distance the Jesus of history from later Christological elevations of him, drawing some striking conclusions like "the full coequal deity of Jesus is nowhere taught in the New Testament" and "the very few texts in which Jesus seems to be designated 'God' are almost all of them disputable" (Cupitt 1979, 108).[13] The "myth" of the complete ontological unity of God and Jesus was both believable and necessary in the years of the Church's establishment, most of these pluralists will concede, but it is simply not believable today and in fact contributes to a catalogue of theological and ethical problems.

For pluralists, there may be a unique interaction of the divine and human in Christ, but this uniqueness does not imply finality and exclusiveness, as the new pluralist Christologies try to show. Whereas inclusivists affirm a uniqueness of Jesus that is final and unsurpassable, "pluralists view Jesus' uniqueness as a statement of the universality and indispensability of His message and mission" (Knitter 1990, 97), comparable to the similarly indispensable uniqueness of other wisdom traditions.

In many ways this Christological discussion gets at the most important aspect of the case for a pluralist theology of religions. It speaks out of the heart of Christian doctrine rather than from any cultural considerations that might be deemed historically contingent and extrinsic to Christian confession. Traditionally, Christology has served as the linchpin of arguments against making the pluralist move. That argument goes as follows: It might be good to engage in dialogue with our non-Christian neighbors for a variety of practical reasons, and we certainly ought to improve our record of treatment of them, but at the bottom we must confess Jesus the Christ, the uniquely full revelation of God in human affairs, by which all other religions are to be judged or fulfilled. If this Christology can be shown on the basis of historical and textual study to be itself contingent and unnecessary, and more importantly if authentically Christian faith can be shown to survive, even thrive, with an alternative, nonnormative Christology, then a critical step will be taken toward the legitimation of a *Christian* theology of religious pluralism. Whether or not the case made so far achieves that is, of course, an open question, which will be addressed below.

Interreligious dialogue is clearly a vital enterprise for theological pluralists. Their perspective makes interreligious dialogue a necessary tool for introducing others to this unique expression of the divine, but, unlike the exclusivist or inclusivist approaches, it presents Jesus in that dialogue not as the only path to salvation but as one manifestation of the mysterious divine that must be complemented by other analogously unique revelations (Knitter 1990, 97; Wiles 1992, 77). Of particular interest to pluralists is the ethical imperative of dialogue. Pluralist theology is linked with global perspectives on social issues and with the conviction that religious cooperation on these issues is vital for global survival. Indeed, as noted above, it is this sense of urgency on practical matters that has prompted many to shift to a pluralist theological model.

It must be acknowledged that the pluralist approach is not only a minority position within Christianity today, it is also largely confined to academic circles. No major Christian denomination endorses a pluralist theology, and it does not appear widely represented at the popular level. While the gap between the theological thinking of the academy and that of Christian churches and communities is notoriously wide, it is particularly striking in this case. Scholarly challenges to the unique divinity of Christ send shock waves through popular American culture, for all its secularization, as evidenced by recent treatments of this issue in the mainstream press. Pluralist theology rests on a relatively sophisticated interpretation of Christian scripture and doctrine, one that clergy may encounter in seminaries but rarely preach from pulpits, in part because it is still difficult to reconcile with the worship traditions of Christian communities.

Non-Christian Pluralism

Of all of these models for understanding religious difference, the pluralist option is most narrowly associated with Western intellectual developments and is therefore least widely represented outside Christian theology. The postmodern turn in Western intellectual endeavors has left no area untouched, and its impact is especially great in religious discourse. To the historical-critical study of biblical texts, which reveals their complex and culturally conditioned origins, are added critiques of ideology exposing the distortions within the texts and traditions made in the interests of the pow-

ers behind them and a thoroughgoing insistence that both "text" and inter-
preter are shifting pieces of an always changing puzzle of interpretation in
which fixed meanings are neither possible nor desirable.

It is out of this intellectual context that the pluralist movement in Christian theologies of religion has emerged. The particularity of this cultural
perspective means that we should not be surprised to find only a very few
expressions of pluralist religious thinking outside of Western intellectual
circles. Indeed, many critics of pluralism argue that it is precisely the cultural particularity of the pluralist approach that makes it an inappropriate
model for global religious interaction. Its dethroning of traditional truth
claims and insistence on the multiplicity of authentic religious paths are un-
intelligible or anathema to the vast majority of the world's faithful, including the Christian faithful.

We can, however, find rough parallels to the kind of pluralism espoused
by Hick and Panikkar outside of Christian theological circles. The clearest
of these is the traditional Hindu perspective on religious truth, expressed by
Swami Vivekenanda at the 1893 parliament and later by Sarvepalli Radhakrishnan and by Gandhi. As part of the Hindu renaissance of the late
nineteenth century, Vivekenanda came to Chicago as an emissary of an enlightened, tolerant Hinduism that could be harmonized with the wisdom of
all the great religions. Hinduism's well-known inclusive spirit and its ability
to incorporate infinite images of the divine and multiple spiritual paths
were turned outward by Vivekenanda to encompass the non-Hindu traditions as well. "'All religions,' he said [at the parliament], 'from the lowest
fetishism to the highest absolutism' are so many attempts of the human
soul to grasp and realize the Infinite, 'as determined by the condition of
birth and association'" (Braybrooke 1992, 33). This Hindu version of
Hick's theocentric pluralism would later be expressed also by Radhakrishnan in his exposition of Hindu philosophy: "If religion is the awareness of
our real nature in God, it makes for a union of all mankind based on communion with the Eternal. . . . The different religions take their source in the
aspiration of man toward an unseen world, though the forms in which this
aspiration is couched are determined by the environment and climate of
thought" (Radhakrishnan 1963, 134).

Gandhi took this endorsement of pluralism a step further in his insistence
that all people of faith not only should tolerate but have a sacred duty to
study and learn from the wisdom of other traditions, based on the conviction that ultimate truth is too vast and mysterious to be adequately grasped
by any one approach. In his declaration that "all religions are true," Gandhi
states: "I do not aim at any fusion. Each religion has its own contribution to
make to human evolution. I regard the great faiths of the world as so many
branches of a tree, each distinct from the other, though having the same
source" (Gandhi 1962, 8–9). One hears in all of these statements clear par-

allels to Hick's convergent model of pluralism; confidence in the ultimate oneness of the mystery that stands as the goal and center of all religions serves as the basis for a celebration of religious pluralism. It is important to note, however, that Hick and his Indian counterparts all represent the elite philosophical strands of their traditions. Radhakrishnan's Vedantic vision of religious unity is as far removed from village-level Hindu worship as Hick's neo-Kantian account is from an evangelical camp meeting.

But there is another interesting pluralist parallel found outside of Christianity, among non-Christians who see in their own traditions patterns of marginalization and oppression resulting from the religious conviction that one's own truth is higher or better than another's. It is telling, I think, that feminists in the world's religions—who have felt the brunt of religious institutions' tendency to define orthodoxy and punish "otherness"—should be the ones at the forefront of pluralist developments. The Jewish feminist Judith Plaskow, for instance, critiques the Jewish concept of "chosenness" in order to liberate Jewish spirituality from its connection with hierarchical dualisms. "So long as the Jewish people holds onto a self-understanding that perpetuates graded distinctions within the community, Jewish spirituality will be defined by and limited to a small proportion of Jews. Women, the unlearned ... and others will be excluded from the relationship with God that comes through full participation in community" (Plaskow 1990, 104). Although her concern is for a Judaism that is more inclusive of different kinds of *Jews,* Plaskow is aligned with those Christians who link a pluralist theology with the effort to overcome a legacy of "otherness" in their own tradition. Parallel with the pluralist Christians' recasting of Jesus' uniqueness, Plaskow opts to replace the concept of chosenness with that of "distinctness": "The Jewish community and the subcommunities within it, like all human communities, are distinct and distinctive. ... The term distinctness suggests, however, that the relation between these various communities—Jewish to non-Jewish, Jewish to Jewish—should be understood not in terms of hierarchical differentiation but in terms of part and whole" (1990, 105).

As with the other two models of understanding religious difference, then, pluralism is an approach that can be found in various forms within and across various religious traditions. Common to these positions is an assessment of one's own religious position as nonabsolute and a corresponding affirmation of the possibility of salvation or its equivalent among those of other faiths. Pluralists may understand the diversity with which ultimate reality is perceived as convergent or nonconvergent, but they are agreed that interreligious dialogue is vital, not in order to evangelize more effectively, or even to enhance with new insights and spiritual practices the essential truth that one already possesses in one's own religious tradition, but rather in order to arrive at religious truth, which is itself understood by pluralists as dialogical. It is important to emphasize the uniquely modern or post-modern character of pluralist positions. Their self-conscious and self-critical reckoning with religious diversity is only made possible by the modern fact of widespread interreligious encounter, and their endorsement of this pluralism often relies on sophisticated modern (if not postmodern) intellectual schemes. For this reason, pluralist approaches to religious difference remain largely the purview of educated elites in the religious traditions in which they are represented. Defenders of pluralism, it seems to me, have not adequately attended to this gap between their own theologies and those of their fellow religionists; doing so will be critical to the prospects for widespread endorsement of pluralist thinking.

Assessment

The Current Crisis

Religious pluralism is a fact that will not go away. After many centuries of confident missionary proclamations of the coming triumph of one or another religious vision, and one century of liberal championing of a coming unity of world religions, it appears clear at the turn of this millennium that religious difference is a feature of our human situation with which we will be reckoning for a long time. The efforts of individual traditions to come to terms with this pluralism have been a perennial challenge for most of the world's religious communities. What is new at this point in the modern history of interreligious dialogue is not pluralism itself or even the awareness of it, but the degree to which interfaith exchanges are linked with the global effort to address problems of human suffering and injustice.

It has been widely argued that the contemporary global scene makes interreligious cooperation imperative as never before. The interconnectedness of the world's peoples environmentally, technologically, economically, and politically is increasingly real, and we are increasingly aware of how fraught with conflict these interconnections are. The cooperative global village once imagined so hopefully is, we are discovering, not the automatic result of technologically empowered cultural encounter. Rather, we are witnessing as concomitant to our interconnection the resurgence of violent nationalism, massive environmental degradation, international systems of labor exploitation, and a widening gap between the world's haves and have-nots.

Today's crises are unique. Although Cold War fears of nuclear annihilation may have abated, increasing environmental degradation presents a common threat from which no nation can hide and which no single nation can solve. Similarly, the internationalization of economies has meant that political borders are no guarantee of protection against exploitation, and often that national sovereignty is no match for the power of multinational businesses. Culturally, the exchange of information and commodities made possible by technology threatens the survival of nondominant cultures and calls into radical question the very notion of individual cultures.

The role of religion in this situation is critical. Far from slipping into anachronism as many once predicted, religion is alive and well, for better or worse, in the postmodern world that has simultaneously thrown us together and robbed our individual cultural narratives of their self-evident truth status. Religious language is often employed in the sometimes desperate efforts of contemporary groups to reestablish identity and community in the face of postmodern loss of moorings, making clear that religion has not lost its potential for exacerbating cultural conflict. At the same time, many representatives of religious communities are calling attention to the unique potential of the world's religious traditions to address these profound global crises, reminding us that religious traditions can be great resources for thinking about the proper humble role of self in the larger contexts of community, world, and cosmos. This is the premise of recent efforts to establish a common global ethic endorsed by the world's major religious communities (see Küng and Kuschel 1993). The task of reconciling conflicting truth claims—of finding ways for those of diverse religious perspectives to cooperate with one another without sacrificing the life-sustaining particularity of their own faith commitments—has thus become, in the present context, not a matter of intellectual speculation but one of planetary survival.

In this regard, we can now briefly review the three broad models of interreligious understanding sketched above in terms of their value to such a project. If it is true that religious identity has the potential both to fuel and to heal intercultural conflict, and I believe we have plenty of evidence that it does, then the question is not whether religion will be brought to bear on matters of global concern but rather *how* it will be brought to bear. Each of the three approaches considered here—exclusivism, inclusivism, and pluralism—brings strengths and weaknesses to the dialogue table. An assessment of these lays the groundwork, I believe, for some tentative conclusions about religious difference and moral cooperation.

Exclusivism: The Value of Commitment

As indicated above, the caricature of exclusivism as inimical to interreligious dialogue is one that should be viewed with suspicion. It is an unfortunate myth that those who maintain commitment to absolute formulations of religious truth necessarily seek to repress religious diversity. In some cases, exclusivists are precisely those who, from an experience of marginality and alienation, seek to defend minority religious positions against a more powerful cultural force. In the United States, we must acknowledge that those conservative Christians who seek to establish a Christian presence on local school boards and in village square holiday displays are not *necessarily* doing so out of a desire to eradicate the religious and secular identities of their neighbors, but rather out of a very real felt experience of having their own religious identity dismissed from public discourse. Thus, in the effort to achieve practical interreligious cooperation, it is important to distinguish between the strong assertion of one's own identity, and even the effort to make that identity a viable force in public discourse, from the denial (that may or may not accompany these) of the legitimacy of other religious identities.

What's more, it cannot be said that all exclusivist religious positions are hostile to the project of interreligious cooperation on ethical issues. Indeed, recent joint efforts of conservative Protestants, Catholics, and Jews in the United States, under the auspices of such groups as the Christian Coalition and Focus on the Family,[14] attest to the possibility of those with very different faith commitments coming together where their social and political agendas overlap. Political liberals may decry the policy goals of such interfaith efforts, but it cannot be denied that these are in fact examples of interfaith cooperation on moral issues that surmount theological differences, and that they are capable of producing very tangible results. Indeed, it is these groups, to the chagrin of religious liberals, who are making the most headway in reintroducing religious values into U.S. public policy discourse.

The great strength of the exclusivist approach to religious difference is precisely its profound commitment to its own vision. As critics of pluralist theologies have noted, it is often those with the most absolutist theologies who bring the most substantive resources to the dialogue table (Placher 1989, 147). In the present context of global ethical crisis, these are not resources that we can afford to dismiss. Affirmations of pluralism are too often made at the expense of particular religious commitments. When that happens, we may find our mutual tolerance a poor substitute for actual beliefs on which to base cooperative efforts on behalf of the environment, the poor, or the culturally marginalized. To illustrate by way of example, if I as a Christian give up the claim to Jesus' unique divinity, I may find it conceptually easier to collaborate with Buddhists and Muslims, but on what will we collaborate, and why? If, on the other hand, I believe that the word and example of Jesus Christ, the only Son of God, mandate my responsibility to "the least of these" and to the inviolable dignity of creation, then I have a profound motivation to work with my Buddhist and Muslim colleagues, who are differently motivated by ethics of compassion and obedience on particular areas of overlapping concern.

Of course, the exclusivist position also brings undeniable liabilities to interfaith cooperative efforts. Christian exclusivism remains associated with a premodern Christian worldview whose viability for interreligious collaboration is highly dubious. Non-Christians the world over recall the degree to which Christian missionary work and economic and political colonialism have been linked, and they are rightly suspicious of the invitation to work with those who still unabashedly seek to convert them. This tension is illustrated in the current relationship between evangelical Christians and Jews in the United States, in which two trends are observable. Some Jewish groups are actively collaborating with evangelicals and Catholics on common political agendas and social welfare projects, as symbolized by the presence of two rabbis on the program of a recent Christian Coalition convention. A clear example of this phenomenon is the current collaboration between the Catholics, "modern" Orthodox Jews, and conservative Christians in the home school movement on the issue of government vouchers for private religious schooling.

At the same time, the Southern Baptist Convention outraged many Jews with the resolution adopted at their annual meeting in June 1996 to direct their "energies and resources toward the proclamation of the Gospel to the Jews." Strong reactions from B'nai B'rith, the Anti-Defamation League, and the World Jewish Congress indicate that this conversionary push will be a setback to Jewish-Christian dialogue on matters of common social and political concern.

Although exclusivism brings the invaluable resource of uncompromising commitment to just those ethical principles on which solutions to the enormous crises the world faces may depend, this resource will inevitably be wasted if that commitment is not dissevered from the conversionary push that denies the comparable commitments of others. To see how this might be done, we must turn to inclusivists and pluralists.

Inclusivism: The Value of Integration

The great strength of inclusivist thinking for interfaith ethical cooperation is its vision of the religious universe as a coherent whole. To the inclusivist, whether Christian, Hindu, or Buddhist, various human descriptions of the cosmos are integrated into a single system. From this perspective, there is a natural foundation for dialogue and collaboration because there is an underlying confidence that those who might appear so religiously alien are really not so different at all. In their own albeit limited ways, each of these other traditions are recognized by the inclusivist as continuous with one's own; the sense of danger and threat that characterizes much of the exclusivist's interreligious encounters is thus avoided.

The success of interreligious ventures made on inclusivist premises is well demonstrated by post–Vatican II Roman Catholic initiatives. Since the Declaration on the Relationship of the Church to Non-Christian Religions (1965) reoriented the Catholic view of other faiths, the Church has initiated a variety of interfaith encounters, coordinated by the Vatican Secretariat for Non-Christians established by Pope Paul VI in 1964. The secretariat coordinates visits with world religious leaders, publishes texts designed to clarify the teachings of non-Christian religions and their relation to Catholic teaching, and maintains an active Catholic presence in worldwide interreligious dialogue meetings.

An illustrative example of Catholic interfaith activity based on inclusivist premises was the interreligious World Day of Prayer for Peace held in October 1985, initiated by Pope John Paul II. At this event, held in Assisi, Italy, representatives of all major religions participated in a day of fasting and prayer. Although the representatives offered prayers from their own traditions in the presence of the others, no common prayers were said, and there was "no intention of seeking a religious consensus" (Braybrooke 1992, 253). The pope made clear that he participated as a follower of Jesus Christ and in obedience to the Church's task of being an "effective sign" of the unity of the human family.

Catholic leadership of such an event was made possible by the inclusivist conviction, rooted in Natural Law theory, that there are common roots uniting all human religious endeavors and that dialogue with others can be an enhancement to faith. But inclusivism also assumes that the fullness of religious life is found only in one's own tradition, and thus Catholic interfaith efforts continue to have a missionary element. This goal was expressed by the secretariat in one of its early statements. Its task, the first secretary stated, "is to prepare the ground, in order to make capable of receiving the seed, and then to leave it to germinate quietly and peacefully" (cited in Braybrooke 1992, 249). This "quiet and peaceful" strategy has resulted in a somewhat ambiguous role for Catholic missionaries, who are seen much more today in social service than proselytizing roles.

This ambiguity—genuine respect and interest in dialogue coupled with an ongoing, if subtle, interest in conversion—is the greatest problem with the inclusivist approach when it comes to practical interfaith efforts. The willingness of other groups to cooperate with inclusivists on ethical imperatives will always be circumscribed by those groups' anxiety about being proselytized or co-opted. To the extent that inclusivists resist their missionary impulses, however, they risk compromising the vision of the world that makes their interfaith cooperation possible in the first place.

The problem with inclusivist interfaith action can also be expressed in terms of the very problems it will take on. For the inclusivist, the only projects worthy of interfaith effort are those that conform to the preestablished norms of one's own tradition. When these norms overlap, as they do, for instance, between Catholics and Buddhists on opposition to the death penalty, then formidable coalitions can be formed. But the Catholic inclusivist model, which only grants divine status to those Buddhist principles also found in Catholic teaching, blinds it from considering the possible moral imperative of, for instance, the rights of nonhuman species.

And while inclusivists may thus close off opportunities to discover new moral imperatives and joint action, they may also, conversely, make unwarranted assumptions about what appear to them to be universal norms but are in fact quite specific to their own tradition. Theologically, inclusivists assume that what they see in other religions is a distorted or undeveloped version of their own religious truth, which is precisely what makes genuine appreciation of these others possible. Ethically, inclusivists find their own values reflected, however dimly, in the behavioral codes of other religions. It must be recognized that this kind of self-reflexive vision, both ethically and theologically, is highly prone to distortion. Nirvana is *not* heaven, and tribal respect for the environment is *not* a pale version of the Christian doctrine of stewardship, however tempting the commonalities may be. Interfaith cooperation on ethical issues requires real openness to the very different ways the world's religions conceive of the problems of the world, let alone their varying ethical responses to these crises. This openness remains a serious challenge to the inclusivist way of thinking about religious difference.

Pluralism: The Value of Openness

In their commitment to this kind of openness as a first principle, pluralist models of understanding religious difference offer their greatest strength to interfaith collaboration on ethical matters. Because they believe that religious truth is not and cannot be the sole province of any one religious group, pluralists in whatever religious tradition are, at least in principle, eager participants in interfaith projects. Indeed, many pluralists find themselves more at home in these interfaith groups than in their own congregations, where pluralist thinking remains marginal.

There are several reasons why a pluralist approach seems to make the most sense for interfaith dialogue and cooperation. From a pluralist perspective, there is every reason to find areas of overlapping concern and work with members of other religious communities on particular global problems. Of the three major models of understanding religious difference, pluralists have taken most seriously the postmodern recognition that religious statements are inevitably textured by the cultural and sociopolitical location of their formulators. Pluralists thus insist that responsible religious statements will not claim the falsely universal status that has historically wrought so much misunderstanding and oppression. This humility goes far in overcoming the perceived arrogance of exclusivist models and the subtle religious imperialism of inclusivism. Pluralists are not only open to the possibility that others may have comparable spiritual resources for addressing vital issues; they are also, again in principle, open to the possibility that others may identify other and equally important issues to address. This, of course, is a vital resource for interfaith action on such issues as poverty, the environment, race, gender, class oppression, and violence.

The strength of the pluralist position for interfaith work being relatively self-evident, I think it is perhaps more important here than in the other cases to pay careful attention to the less obvious liabilities of such an approach. Criticisms of Christian pluralism have been swift in coming and sharp in impact.[15] Grounds for this criticism are not only theological and institutional (denying the unique divinity of Christ violates the essential truth of the gospel and breaks with the historical identity of the churches) but also, surprisingly enough, dialogical. According to many critics, pluralism offers in fact a weaker foundation for interreligious cooperation than other more traditional approaches.

It is sensitivity to the problem of defining the other in terms of oneself that prompted the pluralist rejection of inclusivism. In renouncing that approach, however, there is a tendency to name an alternative organizing structure that, while perhaps not particular to any one religious tradition, is nonetheless alien to those with whom the pluralist would like to converse. The nonexclusive frameworks put forward by pluralists as the foundations for interreligious dialogue, whether they reflect convergent or nonconvergent visions of ultimate reality, are themselves, critics remind us, shaped by particular historical settings and religious orientations, and are therefore open to the same critique as traditional truth claims (see, for example, Heim 1995, 117–124). "Such moves are in danger," Christoph Schwöbel observes, "of replacing one set of culturally conditioned attitudes of superiority with another equally conditioned set of attitudes which are, at least implicitly, characterized by similar assumptions of superiority and therefore potentially as 'imperialistic' as the attitudes they attempt to replace" (1990, 42–43).

The interpretation of religion as a generic category, however widely conceived, can result in one dialogue partner's entering into the conversation with an understanding of the other that is not only unrecognizable to that other but that excludes from the outset any self-understanding of the other that involves particular truth claims (DiNoia 1990, 13). In other words, the pluralist might be heard saying: "We welcome everyone to the dialogue table. Except of course those who actually *believe* the claims of their tradition."

This critique gets at the most serious problem underlying pluralist thought: its inability to reckon adequately with the particularity of its own and other traditions. As William Placher has noted, the most interesting conversation partners are often those who have entered most deeply into the particularities of their own traditions, and thus to base dialogue or interfaith collaboration exclusively on a pluralistic understanding of reality is to cheat the dialogue of some of its richest resources. "Therefore, view with grave suspicion any proposed rules for interreligious dialogue that rule the

Hasidic Jew, the conservative Roman Catholic, the Tibetan Buddhist, or the Sufi mystic out of the conversation in advance and admit only those whose worldviews have been in particular ways shaped by the assumptions of Western modernity" (Placher 1989, 147).

This problem with the pluralist approach can be illustrated, I believe, with reference to the so-called "culture wars" currently being waged in the United States. The Constitution's commitment to a pluralist society and consequent separation of church and state would seem to lay the foundation for a kind of neutral religious interchange much like that envisioned by pluralists in the interfaith movement. Unfortunately, Americans' efforts to protect religious neutrality at the level of the state have fostered a kind of religious vacuity in the culture. In the attempt to prevent any one religious group's particular vision from threatening those of others, America has for all practical purposes barred religious ideas from public discourse, and the country is the worse for it. Because whether we acknowledge it or not, vacuums always get filled, and in this case the vacuum of American religion has been filled by a worldview particularly suitable to the interests of economic elites, a worldview that is consumerist, individualist, overtly secular but deeply steeped in Protestant Christianity. Like the pluralist model, this default "religion" that has arisen in the absence of the excluded traditional worldviews sees itself as open to all but in fact leaves many groups—from conservative white Christians to black Muslims to Native Americans—profoundly alienated. The powerful political force of the religious right now demonstrates how serious the backlash against that situation can be, as a threat has arisen to the American experiment in pluralism that is greater than has been faced in a long while.

In the area of interfaith dialogue, recent responses to the Global Ethic Declaration of the 1993 Parliament of the World's Religions offer a more direct illustration of the potential pitfalls of a pluralist approach to ethical cooperation. This document, drafted by Hans Küng and approved by the representatives at the parliament, has been widely circulated among religious studies scholars and others involved in interreligious dialogue. The Global Ethic is intended, Küng insists, neither as "a global ideology, nor a single unified global religion transcending all existing religions, nor a mixture of all religions" (Küng and Kuschel 1993, 7). Rather, it seeks to articulate a kind of lowest common denominator of ethical principles from all the religions, "the minimum of what the religions of the world already have in common now in the ethical sphere" (8). Although general support for the motivation behind and goals of the document has been widespread, a number of criticisms have also arisen that reflect just the kinds of problems pluralist initiatives can fall prey to.

The two kinds of criticisms that have been raised indicate the rock and the hard place between which pluralists find themselves. On the one hand, the declaration has been chastened for a kind of crypto-Christian and even imperialist orientation. In spite of its universal language, critics like Sallie King have argued, what is really being presented is "an unabashedly Christian document attempting to speak for the religions of the world" (King 1995, 213).[16] King bases this accusation on the central role played the Golden Rule in the document, as well as the decidedly First World flavor of its pronouncements on, say, private property.[17] Others have called attention to the privileging of humanist principles that the documents' efforts to speak "from below" without recourse to sacred texts might indicate. Although I do not find the force of these criticisms sustained by the actual text of the Global Ethic documents, I do think the fact of these responses is telling. For a Buddhist like King, one more universal proclamation from a First World Christian source, however well intentioned, is inevitably, and rightly, to be viewed with great suspicion. This, then, is the first kind of challenge pluralists face: In their effort to speak without privileging their own religious tradition over others, their inevitable reflection of that tradition, or of the secularist culture in which it now lives, becomes a more invidious, because dishonest, version of older kinds of religious chauvinism.

On the other hand—and this is the flip-side risk of pluralist thinking—when the Global Ethic does succeed in avoiding the privileging of Western, Christian principles, it speaks in such generalities as to be void of meaningful ethical content. What does it mean to declare that "every human being must be treated humanely" (Küng and Kuschel 1993, 21), for instance, when the religions' definition of what it is that constitutes a human being, let alone humane treatment, cannot be agreed upon? The kinds of generalities one can speak from a truly pluralist position are often unhelpful and can also serve as masks for the power interests that go unnamed and therefore unchallenged in such rhetoric.[18]

It is important to emphasize that these risks of pluralist thinking are just that. There is nothing inherent to a pluralist approach that dooms it to either subtle imperialism or worthless platitudes. The dangers of this and the other two models remind us how complicated and thorny religious difference is, but if we take them seriously they can also begin to point the way toward an authentic and fruitful interreligious encounter that preserves the strengths of each approach.

Pointers Toward a Viable Interfaith Moral Dialogue

It is time to acknowledge that just as no single religion is likely to replace the pluralism we now experience, so no one model of how to understand that difference is likely to emerge within or among the religions. For that reason, we would do better, I believe, to strategize about how those of us who are pluralists, whether we are Christian, Buddhist, Pagan, or Jewish, might better learn to understand and collaborate on actual social problems with inclusivists and exclusivists, whether they are Muslim, Hindu, Confucian, or secular. Given the dimensions of exclusivism, inclusivism, and pluralism as sketched above, four observations strike me as central to that effort.

The Dialogue Is Not Even-Handed

First, we must do a historical reality check. The language of interreligious initiatives, from the 1893 parliament to the 1993 Global Ethic Declaration, is the language of openness, inclusiveness, and equality. It must be acknowledged, however, that it has overwhelmingly been North American and European Christians who have formulated those initiatives and championed interreligious dialogue. The language of equality belies the very real power imbalances that in fact continue to privilege First World Christian peoples and make real dialogue impossible (Knitter 1995a, 85–86). Christian advocates of dialogue, I believe, have not yet adequately reckoned with the profound culpability of their churches and societies in the historical and contemporary suffering of nondominant peoples. Both numerically and in terms of its association with economic and political power, Christianity overwhelmingly remains the world-dominant religion. The suspicion or lack of interest with which many calls to interfaith cooperation are still met must be understood in this light. What may sound like an invitation to dialogue among equals is actually more like a "dialogue" between an elephant and a mouse. Indeed for many, as indicated above, entry into dialogue is more a survival strategy than a means of gaining religious enrichment. Those who would invite others to give up their absolutist claims as a prerequisite for dialogue do not have an adequate grasp of what those claims have meant to those in positions of historical powerlessness.

Honest interreligious encounter must take seriously these present and historical power arrangements. This means that Christians in particular must bring an extra dose of humility to the table and take extra pains to examine the assumptions that undergird their interreligious proposals. More specifically, it means that priority in defining and designing interreligious projects must be given to the historically voiceless. This is not to grant absolute status to the truth claims of history's victims, but to give "hermeneutical privilege" to those who are uniquely capable of smelling out the dangers of co-optation and distortion to which dialogue is so prone. Paul Knitter makes this case well:

> We can prevent—or at least defend ourselves against—the co-optation of dialogue by making sure that in *all* of our interfaith encounters the poor and suffering and those caring for the suffering Earth will be *present* and will have a *privileged place* in our conversations. In other words, we will recognize and insist not simply that "each voice contributes equally" but that some of us have a more urgent and a more helpful word to speak—namely, those who in the past have not spoken and who in the present are victims. If dialogue must al-

ways be *"par cum pari"* (equal with equal), there are also those who are *"primi inter pares"* (first among equals). (1995a, 95)

This call for an affirmative action in interfaith dialogue will no doubt prove controversial. If it serves only to promote a little more humility among some of us, though, it will have served the dialogue well.

Commitment Precedes Openness

A second foundational lesson for interfaith ethical cooperation is that universal truth claims are the stuff of religions, and that the resources for collaboration on social and environmental issues are dangerously depleted when we attempt to bracket these in the quest for common cause. As a Christian, I do not participate in interfaith efforts because of my commitment to interreligious dialogue but because of my commitment to the Gospel. This recognition does nothing to compromise the imperatives of interfaith work; it simply grants the particular religious identities of participants a logical priority over dialogue, which is more effectively a second or, as I will suggest next, third act. Such an arrangement makes it easier for exclusivists and pluralists to work together without having first resolved their religious differences or even their motivations for participation in the joint project. Interreligious ethical efforts must rest content with the fact that some participants will seek the conversion of others (though restraints on how that occurs can and must be clarified), and the fact that all will bring different ultimate goals to the penultimate tasks at hand.

The amount that could be accomplished before such ultimacies would clash is vast. Whereas the fundamentalist insists that the only universal truth is his own, and the "postmodern fundamentalist" (Knitter 1995a, 77) insists that there are no universal truths, the person of faith in interreligious dialogue can find more humble bases for cross-cultural cooperation. Yes, we are all circumscribed by our own religious and social locations, and no, we cannot impose our own truths on those of others, however absolutely true we believe them to be. We can, however, by turning to the practical problems before us, break out of the nihilistic isolation of either of the fundamentalist options. Charlene Spretnak tells a good story of this discovery. From an encounter with a young devotee of postmodernism, she reports the following exchange:

> "So you would say that our perceptions are not only culturally informed but culturally invented?"
> "Absolutely." . . .
> "And we, all of us, have, according to your perception, no real connectedness?"
> "That's what discourse is for."

"Is it sufficient?"

"Must be. Here we are."

"Here we are on a planet, a unique habitat, it seems. Let's think about
 . . . say, *water* on this planet. Every individual manifestation of every
 life-form, animal or plant, needs water to exist. We have that in
 common. We are all in relationship through our mutual need for water. There may be other aspects of our existence as well by which we
 are in relationship—but would you agree at least that we all share in
 this one undeniable, irrefutable desire, no matter what discourse
 about it might be invented?"

The young man nodded warily.

I smiled. "Good. Let's start there." (1991, 17)

The point here is that while metanarratives remain elusive and dangerous, and our own individual narratives cannot be the basis for dialogue,
our shared relationship with the earth and its resources can be; and we
need not, cannot, and should not sacrifice particular religious beliefs to engage in such dialogue.

Action Precedes Consensus

Spretnak's invitation "Let's start there" gets at the third premise I would
lay down for successful interreligious moral dialogue. The twin threats of
relativism, to which the critics of the pluralist position point, and absolutism, which the pluralists themselves are determined to resist, define the
narrow path successful dialogue must negotiate. Important openings in this
path are made by the recognition, brought to theological prominence by
liberation theology, that committed action can and should precede intellectual formulations of the meaning of such action. Christian liberation theologians have argued that the truth of religious statements resides in their
enactment (see, for example, Gutiérrez 1973, 3–19; 1983, 59), and thus
that what is important is not so much that we *believe* correctly as that we
follow the path of justice and love modeled by Jesus Christ. As Jon Sobrino
has said: "It is more important for Christianity that the Christian reality
take place than that it be correctly understood, and that what is most fundamental for Christians is that love happen in this world" (1988, 170).

This is powerful insight for those who seek to collaborate with the religious "other" but who are concerned not to compromise their own religious identity. With a praxis-based approach, and with the "privilege" of
the voiceless as a guide, people of diverse faith traditions can meet on the
common ground of human suffering and liberation from suffering.[19] If the
liberationists are right, and I am convinced that they are, then interreligious
dialogue is appropriately understood not as a second but as a third act. The
first step must be our individual and communal discoveries of the meaning

of our own faith in the context of shared praxis. That is, I learn what it means to be Christian by attempting to follow Christ in concrete acts of love and justice in the world. Second, we engage the religious "other" in actual ethical projects that, out of our varied commitments, are recognized as religiously mandated. Finally, only after these two acts, we might engage in dialogue about the meaning of our shared action. Of course, each step in the process informs the next in an ongoing cycle of meaning-making. Who I am will increasingly be determined by whom I have discovered you to be in the process of liberative praxis.

The value of this approach for *intra-* as well as interreligious dialogue was recently brought home to me in my own work with a local chapter of Habitat for Humanity, an ecumenical Christian organization (made famous by the participation of former president Jimmy Carter) that builds and renovates homes in partnership with low-income families. I have discovered that those of us who participate in this group are very diverse ideologically and theologically. What brings my evangelical Protestant neighbor to the building site is quite different from my own motivation, which is shaped by the progressive Catholic tradition. But the work is profoundly meaningful to both of us, and so we work together, with a valuable double effect: The project is enriched by both our efforts, and we are both brought into contact with another dimension of what it means to be Christian by being brought into dialogue with each other.

The fact that this dialogue occurs while painting a wall together rather than across a conference table is significant. The evangelical Protestant and I are not likely to bring the other to new theology or new political positions. But when I see her across the aisle at a highly charged political debate in our community, I am no longer able to dismiss her as the "other," as I might have a short time ago. After several months of working together, she no longer *is* other, and, by extension, neither are those who pray and vote like she does. In my experience, and there is evidence to suggest that this model works in the wider context of what Knitter calls "globally responsible dialogue,"[20] joint action on behalf of and in partnership with the world's voiceless can precede and make possible the kind of conceptual exchange that has thus far characterized interreligious dialogue but not borne much ethical fruit. The rush to consensus, for which projects like the Global Ethic have been criticized (King 1995), can be avoided if participants can shift from anxiety about the *premises* to trust in the *process* of interfaith encounter.

The Most Important Dialogue Is Intrareligious

My final observation takes me back to where I began. Religious difference is not a problem *out there* to be solved through negotiation between the re-

ligions. Rather it involves the internal structure of our own religious traditions. There is a diversity among Christians that rivals anything demonstrated at either of the parliaments, and there is comparable variety in every
tradition that we wrongly refer to as a "religion" in the singular. Acknowledgment of this intrareligious diversity is critical for two reasons.

First, it makes us aware that in dealing with matters of faith we are dealing first and foremost with human beings and communities, not with
monolithic ideologies. All religion, like all politics, it seems, is local. When
that is recognized, the problem of reconciling "Christianity" with "Judaism" or "Hinduism" is reconfigured. The task now becomes one of clarifying and addressing the difficult particular issues that arise where our
communities intersect, as they increasingly do.

Second, I am increasingly convinced that good intrareligious dialogue is
more important for planetary health than interreligious dialogue.[21] There
are in all religious traditions, in addition to profound and vital resources,
real obstacles to dealing with the world's social, political, and environmental crises, but these obstacles cannot be dismantled by outsiders. It is the
job of Christians to convince Christians that the Bible does not justify the
exploitation of the environment. Muslims must persuade Muslims that the
Qur'an mandates no sexual hierarchy. Hindus must show Hindus that
dharma cannot be instituted by violence. These are no small tasks, but they
are among the most pressing. The real face of the "other" is, if we are honest, often our neighbor in the pew or across the fence; in encountering him
or her, we gain the most useful practice for more dramatic global encounters with religious difference.

Notes

1. Tertullian's "The Prescriptions Against the Heretics" offers an early and clear
example of this polemical approach (Greenslade 1956, 31–32).

2. Pinnock represents the more liberal evangelical view that repentant non-Christians can be saved by the grace of Christ without explicit knowledge of that grace (a
position that approaches the inclusivist model described below), while the majority
of evangelicals hold fast to the position that only those who explicitly affirm personal faith in Jesus Christ will be saved.

3. Colin Chapman attempts to sort out these evangelical positions and offer a
foundational set of principles on which evangelicals of various perspectives might
agree. He reflects the mainstream evangelical attitude in his exhortation to Christians to go to evangelize with boldness, "a boldness that will drive us to our neighborhoods, communities, countries, and the ends of the earth with the good news,
shared compassionately, and shared earnestly" (1990, 22). Evangelical positions on
pluralism are also critically assessed in Phillips 1992. Phillips argues that evangelicals can at most adopt an agnostic position toward the possibility that one can be
saved by Jesus without knowing Jesus. For another evangelical critique of Pinnock's
position, see Demarest 1992.

4. A polemical example of the Muslim critique of the distortions of Christianity is Sayyid Qutb, "That Hideous Schizophrenia," in Griffiths 1990, 73–81.

5. Tillich defines faith generically as the state of being grasped by ultimate concern (1963, 4; 1957, 1). While revelation has an objective component determined by God's initiative, the subjective human aspect of the religious experience is vitally important for Tillich, who recognizes it in all religions. Tillich can thus affirm (as Barth could not) the occurrence of revelation throughout the broad history of religions. The criterion for determining the finality of revelation, Tillich argues, is the degree to which the medium of revelation is able to become fully transparent to the Ground of Being it reveals. In Jesus Christ, Tillich finds this criterion uniquely met, and he identifies Christ as "a symbol which stands for the decisive self-manifestation in human history of the source and aim of all being" (1963, 79). For Tillich, the revelation of God in the historical person of Jesus is normative in both a paradigmatic and an ontological sense: Jesus not only models but also makes possible the New Being of life in the Spirit in which all humans, even non-Christians, can now participate (Newport 1984, 119–120). Tillich's position is thus inclusivist in that other religions are deemed authentically revelatory, but what they reveal can never surpass—because they have no reality apart from—the revelation of Jesus of Nazareth. But two important elements of Tillich's analysis militate against too strict a reading of this claim of Christian finality. First, it is precisely the sacrifice of the particular for the sake of the universal that gives the Christian revelation its status; Tillich believed that Christians must be willing to abandon all triumphalist postures if they were to plumb the truth of their own tradition and its significance. Second, Tillich, more than many theologians of his day, actually participated in living encounters with non-Christians, especially Buddhists and Jews, an experience that lends authenticity and depth to his appreciation of non-Christian revelation. It was an experience with Buddhists in Japan that led to the publication of Tillich's *Christianity and the Encounter of the World Religions* (1963), and he is reported to have commented that such encounters prompted him to want to rewrite his entire *Systematic Theology* "oriented toward, and in dialogue with, the whole history of religions" (Dillenberger and Welch, 1988, 331).

6. Rahner begins with the premise of a universal aspect of the human condition, a fundamental openness to transcendence that he calls the "supernatural existential." He understands God as that which reaches out and meets this condition, drawing the human being out in perpetual self-transcendence. Genuine revelation outside of Christianity can then be deduced on the premise of this universal phenomenon. Many Catholic theologians before Rahner, building on the premise of God's desire that all should be saved, had acknowledged that those outside of Christianity could truly encounter God. Rahner moves beyond his predecessors in insisting that God's grace meets these individuals not in spite of but *in and through* the historical structures of their religious lives, that is, through the non-Christian religions. Rahner's theology affirms, for the first time in modern Christian theology, that non-Christian religions are "positive means of gaining right relationship to God, and thus for the attaining of salvation" (1966, 125). But for Rahner, as for Tillich, the normativity of Christian revelation is maintained alongside this open affirmation. Rahner makes clear his conviction that salvation is won for the non-Christian by Jesus Christ, and that it is better, though not necessary, that this source be explicitly recognized.

7. A few widely quoted statements from this document sum up the mainstream Catholic position. Referring to non-Christian religions, it insists: "The Catholic Church rejects nothing of what is true and holy in these religions. She has a high regard for the manner of life and conduct, the precepts and doctrines which, although differing in many ways from her own teaching, nevertheless often reflect a ray of that truth which enlightens all men" (Vatican II 1965, 739). Following this statement of openness and affirmation, however, the declaration goes on to apply a fulfillment model of the religious life of humanity in which Christian revelation is presented as final and definitive: "Yet she proclaims and is in duty bound to proclaim without fail, Christ who is the way, the truth and the life (Jn. 1:6). In him, in whom God reconciled all things to himself (2 Cor. 5:18–19), men find the fullness of their religious life" (739).

8. This is the position Hans Küng takes in *On Being a Christian* (1976), where he sharply criticizes the notion of anonymous Christianity. More recently, Küng's work has moved closer to the pluralist position, though he has resisted making that shift explicit (see also Goulder 1977).

9. According to this doctrine, D'Costa argues, God is always making Godself known in new and particular ways, and is therefore never fully, exhaustively revealed. Trinitarian Christians ought thus be open to the truth of other religions, "for the activity of the spirit cannot be confined to Christianity." Yet this inexhaustible mystery "is known through Christ and the Spirit, and it is only on the basis of this particularity that we are able to affirm the universal agency of God's redeeming activity, for the God who redeems is always and everywhere the triune God revealed in Christ" (1990, 17). The word "only" in the previous sentence is what makes D'Costa's position distinctly inclusivist; the value and truth of other religions can only be affirmed by the inclusivist on the basis of the normative truth revealed in his or her own religion.

10. Marjorie Hewitt Suchocki (1987), for instance, makes a compelling case for the correlation between religious exclusivism and sexism.

11. Hick summarizes and defends his pluralist hypothesis against critics in *A Christian Theology of Religions* (1995).

12. Heim 1995, part 2, offers a more explicitly theological expression of this view.

13. Current Jesus scholarship might not go this far, but it does suggest a decisive distinction between the historical Jesus as understood by himself and his immediate followers and later canonical credal statements (see, for example, Borg 1994; Crossan 1991, 1994).

14. See also the declaration "Evangelicals and Catholics Together" appearing in the journal *First Things* (May 1994), in which a group of evangelicals and Catholics commit to common cause on, among other things, abortion, euthanasia, eugenics, and population control.

15. D'Costa 1990 offers a good summary of these criticisms.

16. King is responding to a related document written by Leonard Swidler entitled "Toward A Universal Declaration of a Global Ethic," which was presented at the 1993 American Academy of Religion Annual Meeting. Swidler, who has worked closely with Küng on the Global Ethic project, wrote this text in wording intended to represent both religious and nonreligious groups, while Küng's text is more explicitly tied to the world's religions.

17. In fairness, it should be noted that the document ratified by the parliament goes much farther than Swidler's in condemning the unjust distribution of global wealth.

18. This criticism is made forcefully by Paul Knitter (1995b).

19. It must be made clear that this is not a proposal for a common essence of all religions. It is rather, as Paul Knitter has repeatedly argued, a common *context* in which dialogue might begin to take place (see especially Knitter 1995a, 54–72).

20. Knitter offers several examples from India and Sri Lanka (1995a, 157–180).

21. Sallie King (1995) has expressed a similar view in her insistence that dialogue between liberals and conservatives in the individual traditions must precede interfaith efforts to articulate a global ethic.

References

Aquinas, Thomas. 1955. *On the Truth of the Catholic Faith: Summa Contra Gentiles*. Translated by Anton C. Pegis. New York: Doubleday.

Balasuriya, Tissa. 1984. *Planetary Theology*. Maryknoll, N.Y.: Orbis Books.

Barrows, John Henry, ed. 1893. *The World's Parliament of Religions*. Chicago: Parliament Publishing Company.

Barth, Karl. 1956. *Church Dogmatics*. Volume 1, book 2. Translated by G. T. Thompson and Harold Knight. Edinburgh: T. & T. Clark.

Borg, Marcus J. 1994. *Jesus in Contemporary Scholarship*. Valley Forge, Pa.: Trinity Press International.

Braaten, Carl. 1992. *No Other Gospel! Christianity Among the World's Religions*. Minneapolis: Fortress Press.

Braybrooke, Marcus. 1992. *Pilgrimage of Hope: One Hundred Years of Global Interfaith Dialogue*. New York: Crossroad.

Chapman, Colin. 1990. "The Riddle of Religions." *Christianity Today* 34, 8:16–22.

Chung, Hyun Kyung. 1990. *Struggle to Be the Sun Again: Introducing Asian Women's Theology*. Maryknoll, N.Y.: Orbis Books.

Crossan, John Dominic. 1991. *The Historical Jesus: The Life of a Mediterranean Jewish Peasant*. San Francisco: HarperSanFrancisco.

_____. 1994. *The Essential Jesus: Original Sayings and Earliest Images*. San Francisco: HarperSanFrancisco.

Cupitt, Don. 1979. *The Debate About Christ*. London: SCM Press.

D'Costa, Gavin. 1986. *Theology and Religious Pluralism*. Oxford: Basil Blackwell.

D'Costa, Gavin, ed. 1990. *Christian Uniqueness Reconsidered: The Myth of a Pluralistic Theology of Religions*. Maryknoll, N.Y.: Orbis Books.

Demarest, Bruce A. 1992. "General and Specific Revelation: Epistemological Foundations for Religious Pluralism." In *One God, One Lord: Christianity in a World of Religious Pluralism*, edited by Andrew D. Clark and Bruce W. Winters, 189–206. Grand Rapids, Mich.: Baker Book House.

Dillenberger, John, and Claude Welch. 1988. *Protestant Christianity Interpreted Through Its Development*. New York: Macmillan.

DiNoia, J. A., O.P. 1990. "Pluralist Theology of Religions: Pluralistic or Non-Pluralistic?" In *Christian Uniqueness Reconsidered: The Myth of a Pluralistic Theology of Religions,* edited by Gavin D'Costa, 119–134. Maryknoll, N.Y.: Orbis Books.

Driver, Tom. 1981. *Christ in a Changing World: Toward an Ethical Christology.* New York: Crossroad.

Eck, Diana L. 1993. *Encountering God: A Spiritual Journey from Bozeman to Benares.* Boston: Beacon Press.

Frankfurt Declaration. 1970. *Christianity Today* 14, 19:843–846.

Gandhi, Mohandas K. 1962. *All Religions Are True.* Edited by Anand T. Hingorani. Bombay: Bharatiya Vidya Bhavan.

Goulder, Michael. 1977. "Jesus, the Man of Universal Destiny." In *The Myth of God Incarnate,* edited by John Hick, 48–63. Philadelphia: Westminster Press.

Greenburg, Blu. 1984. "Mission, Witness, and Proselytism." In *Evangelicals and Jews in an Age of Pluralism,* edited by Marc H. Tanenbaum, Marvin R. Wilson, and James Rudin, 226–239. Grand Rapids, Mich.: Baker Book House.

Greenslade, S. L., trans. 1956. *Early Latin Theology.* Philadelphia: Westminster Press.

Griffiths, Paul J., ed. 1990. *Christianity Through Non-Christian Eyes.* Maryknoll, N.Y.: Orbis Books.

Gutiérrez, Gustavo. 1973. *A Theology of Liberation: History, Politics, and Salvation.* Maryknoll, N.Y.: Orbis Books.

_____. 1983. *The Power of the Poor in History.* Maryknoll, N.Y.: Orbis Books.

Heim, S. Mark. 1995. *Salvations: Truth and Difference in Religion.* Maryknoll, N.Y.: Orbis Books.

Hick, John. 1989. *An Interpretation of Religion: Human Responses to the Transcendent.* New Haven: Yale University Press.

_____. 1990. "Straightening the Record: Some Responses to Critics." *Modern Theology* 6:187–195.

_____. 1993. *Disputed Questions in the Theology and Philosophy of Religion.* New Haven: Yale University Press.

_____. 1995. *A Christian Theology of Religions: The Rainbow of Faiths.* Louisville, Ky.: Westminster John Knox Press.

Ichimura, Shohei. 1986. "*Sunyata* and Religious Pluralism." In *Buddhist-Christian Dialogue: Mutual Renewal and Transformation,* edited by Paul O. Ingram and Frederick J. Streng. Honolulu: University of Hawaii Press.

Ingram, Paul O. 1988. *The Modern Buddhist-Christian Dialogue: Two Universalistic Religions in Transformation.* Lewiston, Maine: The Edwin Mellen Press.

King, Sallie B. 1995. "It's a Long Way to a Global Ethic: A Response to Leonard Swidler." *Buddhist-Christian Studies* 15:213–219.

Knitter, Paul F. 1990. "Key Questions for a Theology of Religions." *Horizons* 17, 1:92–102.

_____. 1995a. *One Earth, Many Religions: Multifaith Dialogue and Global Responsibility.* Maryknoll, N.Y.: Orbis Books.

_____. 1995b. "Pitfalls and Promises for a Global Ethics." *Buddhist-Christian Studies* 15:221–229.

Kraemer, Hendrik. 1938. *The Christian Message in a Non-Christian World.* New York: Harper and Brothers.

Küng, Hans. 1976. *On Being a Christian.* Translated by Edward Quinn. Garden City, N.Y.: Doubleday.

Küng, Hans, and Karl-Josef Kuschel, eds. 1993. *A Global Ethic: The Declaration of the Parliament of the World's Religions.* New York: Continuum.

Lawrence, Bruce B. 1989. *Defenders of God: The Fundamentalist Revolt Against the Modern Age.* San Francisco: Harper and Row.

Lewis, Bernard. 1993. *Islam and the West.* New York: Oxford University Press.

Markham, Ian. 1993. "Creating Options: Shattering the 'Exclusivist, Inclusivist, and Pluralist' Paradigm." *New Blackfriars* 74:33–41.

Marty, Martin E., and R. Scott Appleby. 1991. "Conclusion: An Interim Report on a Hypothetical Family." In *Fundamentalisms Observed,* edited by Martin E. Marty and R. Scott Appleby, 814–842. Chicago: University of Chicago Press.

Nasr, Seyyed Hossein. 1990. "The Islamic View of Christianity." In *Christianity Through Non-Christian Eyes,* edited by Paul J. Griffiths, 126–134. Maryknoll, N.Y.: Orbis Books.

Newport, John P. 1984. *Makers of the Modern Theological Mind: Paul Tillich.* Waco, Tex.: Word Books.

Panikkar, Raimon. 1981. *The Unknown Christ of Hinduism.* Revised Edition. Maryknoll, N.Y.: Orbis Books.

_____. 1984. "Religious Pluralism: The Metaphysical Challenge." In *Religious Pluralism,* edited by Leroy Rouner, 97–115. Notre Dame, Ind.: University of Notre Dame Press.

_____. 1987. "The Jordan, the Tiber, and Ganges: Three Kairological Moments of Christic Self-Consciousness." In *The Myth of Christian Uniqueness: Toward a Pluralistic Theology of Religions,* edited by John Hick and Paul F. Knitter, 89–116. Maryknoll, N.Y.: Orbis Books.

_____. 1993. *The Cosmotheandric Experience: Emerging Religious Consciousness.* Maryknoll, N.Y.: Orbis Books.

Phillips, W. Gary. 1992. "Evangelicals and Religious Pluralism: Current Options." In *The Challenge of Religious Pluralism: An Evangelical Analysis and Response,* 174–189. Proceedings of the Wheaton Theology Conference, volume 1. Wheaton, Ill.: Wheaton Theology Conference.

Pieris, Aloysius J. 1988. *An Asian Theology of Liberation.* Maryknoll, N.Y.: Orbis Books.

Piscatori, James. 1994. "Accounting for Islamic Fundamentalisms." In *Accounting for Fundamentalisms,* edited by Martin E. Marty and R. Scott Appleby, 361–373. Chicago: University of Chicago Press.

Placher, William. 1989. *Unapologetic Theology: A Christian Voice in a Pluralistic Conversation.* Louisville, Ky.: Westminster John Knox Press.

Plaskow, Judith. 1990. *Standing Again at Sinai: Judaism from a Feminist Perspective.* San Francisco: HarperSanFrancisco.

Race, Alan. 1983. *Christians and Religious Pluralism: Patterns in the Christian Theology of Religions.* Maryknoll, N.Y.: Orbis Books.

Radhakrishnan, Sarvepalli. 1963. "Religion and Religions." In *Relations Among Religions Today,* edited by Moses Jung, Swami Nikhilananda, and Herbert W. Schneider, 131–136. Leiden, Netherlands: E. J. Brill.

Rahner, Karl. 1966. *Theological Investigations V.* Translated by Karl H. Kruger. Baltimore: Helicon Press.

_____. 1978. *Foundations of the Christian Faith.* Translated by William V. Dych. New York: The Seabury Press.

_____. 1980. "Christianity and the Non-Christian Religions." In *Christianity and Other Religions,* edited by John Hick and Brian Hebblethwaite, 52–79. Philadelphia: Fortress Press.

Ruether, Rosemary Radford. 1974. *Faith and Fratricide: The Theological Roots of Anti-Semitism.* Minneapolis: The Seabury Press.

_____. 1987. "Feminism and Jewish-Christian Dialogue: Particularism and Universalism in the Search for Religious Truth." In *The Myth of Christian Uniqueness: Toward a Pluralistic Theology of Religions,* edited by John Hick and Paul F. Knitter, 137–148. Maryknoll, N.Y.: Orbis Books.

Schwöbel, Christoph. 1990. "Particularity, Universality, and the Religions: Toward a Christian Theology of Religions." In *Christian Uniqueness Reconsidered: The Myth of a Pluralistic Theology of Religions,* ed. Gavin D'Costa, 30–46. Maryknoll, N.Y.: Orbis Books.

Smart, Ninian. 1992. "Pluralism." In *New Handbook of Christian Theology,* edited by Donald Musser and Joseph L. Price, 360–365. Nashville, Tenn.: Abingdon Press.

Sobrino, Jon. 1988. "Theology in a Suffering World: Theology as *Intellectus Amoris.*" In *Pluralism and Oppression: Theology in World Perspective,* edited by Paul F. Knitter, 153–177. Annual publication of the College Theological Society, vol. 34. Lanham, Md.: University Press of America.

Song, Choan-Seng. 1991. *Third Eye Theology.* Revised edition. Maryknoll, N.Y.: Orbis Books

Spretnak, Charlene. 1991. *States of Grace: The Recovery of Meaning in the Postmodern Age.* New York: HarperCollins.

Suchocki, Marjorie Hewitt. 1987. "In Search of Justice: Religious Pluralism from a Feminist Perspective." In *The Myth of Christian Uniqueness: Toward a Pluralistic Theology of Religions,* edited by John Hick and Paul F. Knitter, 149–161. Maryknoll, N.Y.: Orbis Books.

Swearer, Donald K. 1991. "Fundamentalistic Movements in Theravada Buddhism." In *Fundamentalisms Observed,* edited by Martin E. Marty and R. Scott Appleby, 628–690. Chicago: University of Chicago Press.

Tambiah, S. J. 1986. *Sri Lanka: Ethnic Fratricide and the Dismantling of Democracy.* Chicago: University of Chicago Press.

Tillich, Paul. 1957. *Dynamics of Faith.* New York: Harper and Row.

_____. 1963. *Christianity and the Encounter of the World Religions.* New York: Columbia University Press.

VanderWerff, Lyle. 1992. "Religious Pluralism and the Uniqueness of Christ." In *The Challenge of Religious Pluralism: An Evangelical Analysis and Response,* 111–118. Proceedings of the Wheaton Theology Conference, volume 1. Wheaton, Ill.: Wheaton Theology Conference.

Vatican II. 1965. "Declaration on the Relation of the Church to Non-Christian Religions *(Nostra aetate).*" In *Vatican Council II: The Conciliar and Post Conciliar Documents,* edited by Austin Flannery, O.P. Revised edition, 1988, 738–742. Grand Rapids, Mich.: William B. Eerdmans Publishing Co.

Waardenburg, Jacques. 1979. "World Religions As Seen in Light of Islam." In *Islam: Past Influence and Present Challenge,* edited by Alford T. Welch and Pierre Cachia, 245–275. Albany: State University of New York Press.

Wiles, Maurice. 1992. *Christian Theology and Inter-religious Dialogue.* Philadelphia: Trinity Press International.

Zipperer, John. 1993. "The Elusive Quest for Religious Harmony." *Christianity Today* 37, 11:42–44.

Chapter Four

A Global Ethic in the Light of Comparative Religious Ethics

SALLIE KING

James Madison University

The "Global Ethic" is a proposed consensus statement on ethics from the world's religions that is emerging from the community of persons engaged in interreligious dialogue, most prominently from the Parliament of the World's Religions held in 1993. Although it has engendered considerable interest among those engaged in dialogue, heretofore it has received little attention from comparative ethicists.

In this chapter I will briefly describe the Global Ethic and then introduce themes in comparative ethics that are inherent to a discussion of this Ethic. I will devote the greatest part of the chapter to an examination of specific concerns about and potential uses of the Global Ethic.

Proposals for a Global Ethic

There are two main proposals before the international community for instituting a global ethic. The better-known and more important proposal was initially elaborated by theologian Hans Küng of Tübingen, Germany, and then amended and subsequently issued by the Parliament of the World's Religions.[1] The second was composed by Leonard Swidler of the Department of Religion at Temple University in Philadelphia; it is discussed at conferences and on the Internet by way of Swidler's Center for Global Ethics. I shall briefly describe each proposal in turn.

Parliament of the World's Religions

By a global ethic we do not mean a global ideology or a single unified religion beyond all existing religions, and certainly not the domination of one religion

118

over all others. By a global ethic we mean a fundamental consensus on binding
values, irrevocable standards, and personal attitudes (Küng and Kuschel 1993,
21; emphasis in original removed).

We know that our various religious and ethical traditions often offer very different bases of what is helpful and what is unhelpful for men and women, what is
right and what is wrong, what is good and what is evil. We do not wish to gloss
over or ignore the serious differences among the individual religions. However,
they should not hinder us from proclaiming publicly *those things which we already hold in common* and which we jointly affirm, each on the basis of our
own religious or ethical grounds (Küng and Kuschel 1993, 22).

In early 1992, as preparations for the 1993 Parliament of the World's Religions went forward, the parliament's council sent Daniel Gómez-Ibáñez to
ask Hans Küng to compose a draft of a global ethic, which, the council
hoped, could be endorsed by the parliament. Küng agreed and after extensive
interreligious debate and consultation produced the draft, which, after further consultation and with numerous changes, was issued by the parliament.
Küng reports that he consulted with over a hundred scholars and representatives of world religions. Gómez-Ibáñez states that the parliament's consulting
network was "equally large" (Küng 1993; Gómez-Ibáñez 1996).

The Global Ethic is intended as a consensus statement of the world's religions of that core area of their various ethical affirmations that they all
hold in common. At the same time, it should not exclude the ethical values
of the nonreligious. The Ethic declares: "We confirm that there is already a
consensus among the religions which can be the basis for a global ethic—a
minimal fundamental consensus concerning binding values, irrevocable
standards, and fundamental moral attitudes" (Küng and Kuschel 1993, 18;
emphasis removed). Thus, while claiming to represent absolute norms, the
Ethic attempts to be no more than "minimal," allowing individual religions
to express their own full ethical visions, as has always been the case.

What, then, does the Ethic affirm? It is based upon "a fundamental demand: Every human being must be treated humanely." Human rights are
expressly affirmed ("Every human being without distinction . . . possesses
an inalienable and untouchable dignity. And everyone, the individual as
well as the state, is therefore obliged to honour this dignity and protect it.
Humans must always be the subjects of rights.") The Ethic also affirms
beneficence ("Possessed of reason and conscience, every human is obliged
to behave in a genuinely human fashion, to do good and avoid evil!"), as
well as positive and negative forms of the Golden Rule, of which, in his
commentary, Küng cites versions from many religions:

There is a principle which is found and has persisted in many religious and ethical traditions of humankind for thousands of years: What you do not wish done

to yourself, do not do to others! Or in positive terms: What you wish done to yourself, do to others! This should be the irrevocable, unconditional norm for all areas of life (Küng and Kuschel 1993, 23–24, 71–72; emphasis removed).

These fundamental principles then issue in the affirmation of "four irrevocable directives" that serve as "broad . . . guidelines for human behaviour." An obvious effort has been made to ground the four directives in the ancient ethical codes found in the world's religions. They are presented as follows.

1. "Commitment to a culture of non-violence and respect for life." Based upon ethical traditions found in the ancient codes of many religions that declare: "You shall not kill!" (or, in positive terms: "Have respect for life!"), this directive enjoins behavior that respects the human rights to "life, safety, and the free development of personality," declaring that conflicts "should be resolved without violence within a framework of justice" and that we should work "within an international order of peace which itself has need of protection and defence against perpetrators of violence." It further declares: "Armament is a mistaken path. . . . There is no survival for humanity without global peace!" and commends the development of a "culture of non-violence," extending to the protection of animals, plants, and the Earth.

2. "Commitment to a culture of solidarity and a just economic order." Based upon ancient religious codes that state: "You shall not steal! (or, in positive terms: "Deal honestly and fairly!"), this directive states: "No one has the right to rob or dispossess in any way whatsoever any other person or the commonweal. Further, no one has the right to use her or his possessions without concern for the needs of society and Earth." Emphasizing that there will never be peace without a just economic order, it declares: "Wherever might oppresses right, we have an obligation to resist—whenever possible, non-violently." It advocates "a sense of moderation and modesty" instead of unbridled consumption.

3. "Commitment to a culture of tolerance and a life of truthfulness." Based upon ancient religious codes that declare: "You shall not lie!" (or, in positive terms: "Speak and act truthfully!"), this directive applies to everyone, but it singles out as bearing especially great responsibility for truthfulness persons who work for the mass media; artists, writers, and scientists; the leaders of countries; politicians and political parties; and representatives of religion.

4. "Commitment to a culture of equal rights and partnership between men and women." Although this directive seems to point in an-

other direction, it is based upon the ancient religious codes' insistence: "You shall not commit sexual immorality!" (or, in positive terms: "Respect and love one another!"). The directive condemns all forms of sexual exploitation and sexual discrimination, including "patriarchal domination and degradation, which are expressions of violence." It endorses both celibacy and marriage; the latter "should guarantee security and mutual support to husband, wife, and child. It should secure the rights of all family members" (Küng and Kuschel 1993, 24–34; emphasis removed).

Finally, the Ethic put forth by the parliament concludes with an appeal for a "transformation of consciousness" and a "conversion of the heart" to change life on Earth for the better (Küng and Kuschel 1993, 35–36; emphasis removed). It is followed by a list of signatories from religious leaders at the Parliament, who included Baha'is, Brahma Kumaris, Buddhists, Christians, practitioners of native religions, Hindus, Jains, Jews, Muslims, neo-pagans, Sikhs, Taoists, Theosophists, Zoroastrians, and members of inter-religious organizations (Küng and Kuschel 1993, 37–39).

Swidler's Proposal

Leonard Swidler's "Universal Declaration of a Global Ethic" grew out of his long commitment to ecumenism. In 1991, he and Hans Küng jointly published "Editorial: Toward a 'Universal Declaration of Global Ethos'" in the *Journal of Ecumenical Studies,* calling for the composition of a global ethic. The draft that resulted is especially well known in ecumenical circles.

Swidler's Universal Declaration is conceived as the same sort of document as that issued by the parliament: a consensus statement of the world's religions and a declaration of the shared core area of ethical commitment, conceived as "the fundamental attitude toward good and evil, and the basic and middle principles needed to put it into action." It finds in each religious tradition, "grounds in support of universal human rights, . . . a call to work for justice and peace, and . . . concern for conservation of the earth" (Swidler 1996b, 1). Like the parliament's Ethic, Swidler's declaration cites the Golden Rule as a fundamental principle that "has been affirmed in many religious and ethical traditions" (Swidler 1996b, 2).

The Universal Declaration affirms eight basic principles:

(1) Because freedom is of the essence of being human, every person is free to exercise and develop every capacity, so long as it does not infringe on the rights of other persons. . . . (2) Because of their inherent equal dignity, all humans should always be treated as ends, never as mere means. . . . (3) Although humans have greater intrinsic value than non-humans, all such things, living and non-living, do possess intrinsic value simply because of their existence and, as such, are to

be treated with due respect. . . . (4) Humans . . . seek to unite themselves, that is, their "selves," with what they perceive as the good: in brief, they love. . . . This loving/loved "self" needs to continue its natural expansion/transcendence to embrace the community, nation, world, and cosmos. (5) This expansive and inclusive nature of love should be recognized as an active principle in personal and global interaction. (6) Those who hold responsibility for others are obliged to help those for whom they hold responsibility. (7) Every human's religion or belief should be granted its due freedom and respect. (8) Dialogue . . . is a necessary means . . . whereby men and women can live together on this globe in an authentically human manner. (Swidler 1996b, 2–3)

The final level of articulation is made up of ten "middle principles" that are said to be "those which underlie the 1948 United Nations Universal Declaration of Human Rights," recast in the language of rights and responsibilities. These are: (1) equal treatment and protection by the law and the responsibility to follow all just laws; (2) the rights to "freedom of thought, speech, conscience and religion or belief" and the responsibility to exercise these rights in ways that respect all and produce maximum benefit to all; (3) "the right and the responsibility . . . to learn the truth and express it honestly"; (4) "the right to a voice . . . in all decisions that affect" oneself and the responsibility "to participate in self-governance as to produce maximum benefit" for all; (5) equal rights for all women and men and the responsibility to act in ways respectful of the other; (6) "the right to own property of various sorts" and the responsibility to use it to produce maximum benefit for all; (7) the expectation that "all humans should normally have both meaningful work and recreative leisure" and "an obligation to work appropriately for their recompense"; (8) the responsibility to provide "the most humane care possible," falling first on parents and then on the larger community; children and adults must also be educated for "the full development of the human person"; (9) the responsibility to "strive constantly to further the growth of peace on all levels . . . granting that a) the necessary basis of peace is justice for all concerned; b) violence is to be vigorously avoided, being resorted to only when its absence would cause a greater evil; [and] c) when peace is ruptured, all efforts should be bent to its rapid restoration—on the necessary basis of justice for all"; and (10) the responsibility to protect the environment and to destroy plants and animals "only for some greater good," such as food (Swidler 1996b, 3–6). Here the Universal Declaration ends.

Comments and Preliminary Remarks

As can readily be seen, there is considerable difference in content between the two proposed systems of global ethics. However, a detailed comparison would leave us no time to consider the larger issues implicit in both. I limit myself to the following brief comments.

On my reading, Swidler's version is much more "Western" than the parliament's. The identification of freedom as "the essence of being human," the assumption that humans have "greater intrinsic value" than nonhumans, the language of "selves" uniting in love, and the use of utilitarian language throughout the middle principles are all instances of concepts and language that would be quite alien to many Asian perspectives. In addition, Swidler's language on property rights also seems to reflect a much more First World perspective than the parliament's discussion of economic justice. I am therefore inclined to believe that the parliament's Global Ethic Declaration relied much more on interreligious and international consultation than Swidler's Universal Declaration.

With regard to the fact that two proposals for establishing a system of global ethics have been independently propagated, the obvious must be stated: It is scandalous that two versions exist and in a sense are vying against each other, especially when one considers that they both were drafted by white, prosperous, Catholic men who are from the dominant world culture (one German, one American). If these two scholars from closely related backgrounds cannot reconcile their differences and produce a single draft, then how can anyone expect people from other religious, national, and ethnic backgrounds to agree to either proposal? This dilemma recalls the era of great Christian missionary work in Asia; it was one thing to harangue Asian people to convert to the "only truth," Christianity, but quite another to maintain credibility as the many Christian sects with missions in Asia quarreled among themselves.

If I do not specify otherwise, in the following discussion the word "Ethic" and the phrase "Global Ethic" refer to the parliament's version. With the endorsement of the Parliament of the World's Religions, this version must be regarded as preeminent. Swidler's proposal will be referred to as the "Universal Declaration."

Themes in Comparative Religious Ethics

Relativism Versus Absolutism

The Global Ethic is one chapter, now in the forefront, of the larger discussion in comparative ethics on the possibility of a common morality. Robert Merrihew Adams defines "common morality" as "the large area of overlap of the diverse moralities of different people and groups of people" (Adams 1993, 99). This is precisely how the Global Ethic is conceived, with the focus in its case upon the morality shared by the different religions of the world. As the common morality discussion immediately raises all the issues associated with the debate between relativism and absolutism, so does the Global Ethic discussion.

There is no question that the Global Ethic supports a version of absolutism. The document's introduction states, "We affirm that there is an irrevocable, unconditional norm for all areas of life" (Küng and Kuschel 1993, 15). The question, then, is: Does the Ethic affirm absolutism in a way that is acceptable or unacceptable?

The Global Ethic seems to be uniquely constructed to address this challenge. On the one hand, it claims to be the common ground that *already exists* among the world's religions—the overlapping, shared area among the various particular ethical systems of the religions. It "represents the minimum of what the religions of the world already have in common now in the ethical sphere" (Küng and Kuschel 1993, 8). Thus, if this is correct, the Ethic does not impose anything on anyone but merely points to what is already there; it is "not a new invention but only a new discovery" (Küng and Kuschel 1993, 71; emphasis removed). On the other hand, its framers insist that while the Global Ethic is necessary, it is not sufficient; it serves as a minimal base that the various particular ethical systems must elaborate and supplement. As Küng writes in his commentary:

> I should make it clear that even in the future, the global ethic cannot replace, say, the Torah of the Jews, the Christian Sermon on the Mount, the Muslim Qur'an, the Hindu Bhagavadgita, the Discourses of Buddha or the Sayings of Confucius. How could anyone come to think that the different religions wanted to avoid the foundation for their faith and life, thought and actions? These sacred scriptures offer as it were a maximal ethic, compared with which the Declaration Toward a Global Ethic can offer only a minimal ethic. (Küng and Kuschel 1993, 73)

Thus, the Global Ethic claims not to be in a *position* to displace any religion's ethical system. It is supplemental, not alternative. Each particular religion's ethical system is preserved inviolate. The only thing the Global Ethic aspires to negate and displace is ethical relativism.

In its negation of relativism, does the Global Ethic constitute a pernicious form of absolutism? There are three parts to the answer. First, if (and only if) the world's various religions are able to freely embrace the Ethic as representing a view consonant with their own can accusations of imperialism be avoided. Second, to the extent that the Global Ethic permits genuine diversity in those areas beyond the minimal common ground of shared ethical commitment that it declares inviolate, it again avoids imperialism. We will return to these two issues below.

The third issue involves whether it can be considered "pernicious absolutism" to declare inviolate the core area of commitment to nonviolence, justice, truthfulness, and the avoidance of sexual immorality. David Little provides a framework for discussing this issue by arguing in favor of an intuitionism in which human beings immediately know that certain things (his example is gratuitous torture) are "simply and transparently wrong in themselves." For Little, the recognition of such intuitions is a measure of both the mental and spiritual health of individuals and the viability of moral theories (1993, 80, 81). (Persons who violate them may be regarded, following Ronald Dworkin, as "criminals against humanity.") If we follow this approach, the question of whether the Ethic's declaration that nonviolence, justice, truthfulness, and sexual morality are absolute moral norms constitutes a pernicious form of absolutism hinges upon whether these values represent the fundamental ethical intuitions of humankind. Such a way of considering the issue seems to be very much in harmony with the thinking of the framers of both versions of the Ethic.

Ethical Theory Versus Normative Ethics

Gene Outka and John Reeder, the editors of *Prospects for a Common Morality,* conclude their sketch of their contributing authors' views of the philosophical issues involved in the idea of a common morality with the statement, "At the end of the day, there is more normative than theoretical agreement, a fact that is significant in itself" (Outka and Reeder 1993, 27). The experience thus far of interreligious discussions on the Global Ethic tends to support this judgment. Significantly, the normative territory generally affirmed by the contributors to *Prospects for a Common Morality* seems to overlap significantly with the normative territory affirmed by the Global Ethic: human rights, nonviolence, truthfulness, and the like. The question of epistemic hubris may be raised in this connection. "To aspire to a 'God's eye' vantage point, or to suppose that our certainties will survive later scrutiny when so many of our forebears' certainties look quaint or false to us now, arrogates arbitrarily to ourselves a sense of validity no mortals enjoy" (25). It is indeed an odd expression of modernity to issue an absolutist statement such as the Global Ethic. How can such a thing be justified in the modern world?

It can only be said that this question lies outside the domain of the Global Ethic itself. The Ethic limits itself to reporting what amounts to an empirical claim: that persons throughout the world affirm a certain set of moral values. An explanation of how and why such cross-cultural unity might exist lies beyond its purview. No doubt religious people will look to their own faiths for explanation. (Muslims can turn to the statement that "Allah has sent messengers to all peoples"; Christians can refer to "general revelation," and Jews to the seven Noahide laws. I suspect that all religions can find their own explanations.) Of course, religious explanations will not satisfy moral philosophers. If the empirical observation of shared moral ground passes the test of time, moral philosophers will either have to come up with their own theory or declare the matter insoluble by their methods.

Concerns Regarding a Global Ethic

Process

Concerns about the process by which the Global Ethic has been composed and affirmed have been well explored by Paul Knitter and June O'Connor; these concerns generally amount to worries about control. O'Connor eloquently sums up the issue with the simple question, "Whose consensus?" (O'Connor 1994, 161).

Knitter, for his part, worries that neither the parliament nor Swidler are paying attention to the fact that "our language and our truth claims are not only *culturally* conditioned, but they are also *economically* and *politically* conditioned. . . . Our interpretations and our language . . . can . . . *oppress* the ability of others to assert and live their own truths" (Knitter 1995, 222). This is not a problem particular to the parliament and Swidler but a "systemic distortion," a pervasive tendency "within all use of language." However, the parliament and Swidler do need to take particular note, because:

> Whenever the language of civil discourse and religious dialogue comes forth from those who are in political or economic power, such language can all too easily be a ploy to maintain the structures of power. The discourse becomes "managerial"—it manages what will be discussed, the method for discussion, and the goals of the discussion; what does not fit these determinations is judged, in the political discourse, as a disruptive "interest group"; in the religious dialogue it might be called a *closed* or *primitive* or *fundamentalist* or *polytheistic* or *feminist* perspective (Knitter 1995, 222–225).

This raises three important issues.

First, are the Parliament of the World's Religions and/or Swidler guilty of employing a "managerial" process in composing and revising their documents? Observe the following constellation of concerns articulated by O'Connor:

> Given the great historical influence and cross-cultural presence of the Christian tradition, given its expansionist role in the world, and given its complicity with the educated elites who introduced or co-operated with colonialism in the past and who benefit from neocolonialism today, it should not be surprising that some invited signatories received or approached Hans Küng draft of the *Declaration Toward a Global Ethic* with frowned wonder and some measure of reluctance. These facts, together with the one-week time frame for on-site revisions—together with the decision by the parliament leadership to make the signing of the declaration not only a parliament event, but also a media event—hint at some of the pressures that faced the signatories and those who chose not to sign. (O'Connor 1994, 162)

In fact, only one revision was allowed on-site, the decision to change the title of the document from "Declaration of a Global Ethic" to "Toward a Global Ethic (An Initial Declaration)" (Gómez-Ibáñez 1996, 10). Of course, the key fact is that the document was already the product of extensive discussions among representatives of world religions before it ever reached the parliament. Moreover, anyone who has ever served on a committee can understand the impossibility of working in a milieu such as the parliament, with hundreds of participants attempting to revise a single document. Nevertheless, this process of consultation was not widely understood at the parliament, and the proceedings appeared to some to be quite "managerial" indeed (the drafting of the Ethic is discussed at length in Gómez-Ibáñez 1996 and Küng 1993).

Difficulties with the parliament's handling of the "Initial Declaration" of the Ethic may be compounded by its inability to facilitate further discussion of the issue. Lacking staff, funding, and facilities, the parliament has no means to carry forward the discussion of the Global Ethic, though it is certainly possible that the Ethic will be discussed at future meetings of the parliament.

Thus it seems that the task of continuing this discussion must, in large part, fall to others. It should be mentioned in this regard that Hans Küng has recently published *Yes to a Global Ethic,* which, as can be readily apprehended from the title, is not a free and open discussion of the strengths and weaknesses of the Ethic but is very much a "managed" show of support from political and religious leaders.[2]

Swidler is working actively to forward the discussion of both his and the parliament's versions of the Ethic. Swidler's Center for Global Ethics has posted on the Internet a call for responses to his proposed Ethic. In this discussion, the theologian John Hick has had this to say in response to Swidler's draft:

In this first stage of the search for a global ethic, rather than getting the peoples of other cultures to debate our Western draft, agreeing or disagreeing with it as the only document on the table, we should say: "Here is the kind of draft that comes naturally to us in the industrialized West. What kind of draft comes naturally to you, and to you, and to you?" And then the next stage beyond this should be to bring a plurality of drafts together and see what comes out of the interaction between them. . . . So long as we only have a modern Western draft there will be the danger of the whole project looking like an act of Western cultural imperialism. This has never been the intention. And the danger can be avoided by directing every effort to get people from within the other great cultural streams of human life to participate in the search from their own independent points of view.

It cannot count as a legitimate criticism that the search for a global ethic has originated in the West; for it had to originate somewhere! . . . But it would be a

ground for legitimate criticism if the search remained concentrated around our
Western contribution to it. (Hick 1996, 3)

Perhaps heeding this comment, Swidler's Center for Global Ethics declares:

> Additional versions of "A Universal Declaration of a Global Ethic" from vari-
> ous geographical regions, as well as diverse religious and ethical traditions are
> also being encouraged. . . . [I]t is vital that as many different groups as possi-
> ble work through the issues (perhaps using the two present drafts as starting
> points) and express their ideas in precise written words, thereby both con-
> tributing to the final draft, and taking ownership of it (Swidler 1996a).

In fact, Swidler's Internet discussion group has elicited a variety of responses to his draft.[3] However, to my knowledge, no major alternative
draft has yet been generated by any group.[4]

Fear that the powerful will use a Global Ethic against the less powerful
follows directly from the above concern about managerial process. Margaret Farley expresses this concern succinctly:

> Feminists resist theories of common morality primarily because they have been
> harmful to women (and to some men). In the name of universality, of a total
> view of human nature and society, such theories have in fact been exclusive, op-
> pressive, and repressive of women and of men who do not belong to a dominant
> group. Whether consciously or unconsciously, the formulators of such theories
> have inaccurately universalized a particular perspective; as a result, the needs
> and moral claims of some groups and individuals have been left out, their roles
> and duties distorted, and their full voices silenced. (Farley 1993, 171)

In short, history gives ample evidence that when a powerful group manages
a discussion in such a way that they declare their perspective to be the universally correct one, the less powerful may well suffer the consequences:
Women and minorities may be forced to "be" what hegemonic men think
they are.

How would this concern play out in the context of the Global Ethic? We
must look at both the political and religious contexts. As we shall see in the
next section, from a political point of view the Global Ethic is seen to support the UN Universal Declaration of Human Rights and so far has been
generally welcomed by politically oppressed groups. It is those who oppose
international monitoring of human rights abuses who have reason to fear
whatever power this document may someday wield. Thus, the initial assessment indicates that politically the Global Ethic will not prove to be a tool
of oppression.

However, the implications of the document in the religious context may
well be different. Here, the managerial concerns arise with a vengeance.

The Global Ethic potentially says: "We all share a core of the same morality." If this statement is true, then there will be no problem. If the statement is false, however, then two unpleasant possibilities may ensue. Either a group with a differing moral vision would be labeled "immoral" by the rest of the world, with the consequence of exacerbating hatred and the potential for aggression against that group; or the divergent group would feel compelled to abandon their own moral vision in order to avoid hatred and aggression. Either way, they lose. It is therefore *essential,* if the Global Ethic or its successor is interreligiously and internationally accepted, when it states "We all share a core of the same morality," that that statement be true.

Finally, in response to the "Whose consensus?" question, it must be said that the Global Ethic is clearly at best a consensus of the mainstream and the liberal or progressive wings of the various world religions. As Karl-Josef Kuschel reports: "Even at the planning stage, evangelical and fundamentalist church groups refused to collaborate in the Parliament" (Küng and Kuschel 1993, 95). Participants in interreligious dialogue know how difficult it can be to get evangelicals and fundamentalists to participate. We should be mindful of this and nuance Knitter's concern about managerial discourse that marginalizes groups including, as he specifies, "fundamentalists." For surely it is one thing to be pushed to the margins by a powerful group and another to refuse to participate in discussions when repeatedly invited.

Khalid Duran, a Muslim and a historian of religion, has written an interesting response to Swidler's version of the Ethic, which focuses upon this point. He emphasizes the differences among Muslims with respect to a proposal of this sort and stresses that while the great majority of Muslims "are especially receptive to universalistic undertakings," the framers and proponents of a Global Ethic should beware of fundamentalists. He declares: "I know that there are Islamists around who just wait for someone like Leonard Swidler to hijack his global ethics. No one has proclaimed in words so loudly in favor of the emancipation of women as the mullahcracy in Iran. . . . There in the name of the Islamic Republic and its emancipation of women women are sprayed with acid because a single lock of hair slipped out a little from under the required head covering (Duran 1996, 4–5). To combat this proclivity among fundamentalists, he advocates "conceptually specifying the general principles [of a Global Ethic] and thereby going somewhat into detail" (4) to prevent signatories from agreeing to abstract language that they can then freely interpret in any way their authoritarian politics and narrowly prescriptive religious views indicate.

Duran goes so far as to suggest that fundamentalists be left on the sidelines: "How, then, can one work out in detail such a global ethic and be just to all sides—I do not mean here to Islamists or similar Fundamentalists among Jews, Christians, Buddhists, Hindus and others. Let us leave that marginal group on the side, for it is already extraordinarily difficult to reach a consensus among the majority streams" (Duran 1996, 5–6). Duran's suggestion raises an important issue: Would it be "fair" in drafting a document that calls itself "global" to leave out some voices? In particular, would it be "fair" to leave out those who refuse to participate in the discussions, or those whose frequent public pronouncements leave no doubt that they are opposed to the very intention of the project, or those who covertly attempt to derail the project, or those—shall we make it difficult?—whose values are precisely the values that the framers and supporters of the document are intentionally trying to challenge and ultimately displace? The Global Ethic cannot be other than a proponent for sincere tolerance and acceptance of religious diversity. It is clear that it has been composed in order to contribute to the bringing into being of a world based upon this value. How could those whose values are based upon strict exclusivism possibly be party to it?

Here, David Little's argument in support of ethical intuitionism (discussed previously) could play an important role. Should fundamentalists be left out of the effort to articulate and affirm a "global" ethic? His argument would seem to indicate that leaving them out could be justified if, but only if, they violate or advocate violating what are perceived as fundamental moral intuitions. Thus, extremists who utilize fundamentalistic ideology to justify state, group, or individual violence or oppression could be regarded as "criminals against humanity" and thus outside the pale of cooperative international discourse. Those who simply believe in the inerrancy of, for example, the Bible or the Qur'an, could not be so regarded.

In sum, the Global Ethic is a liberal document, another piece of evidence that there is probably more unity among liberal adherents of a variety of the world's religions than there is between liberals and conservatives of the same religion. One might hope that fundamentalists in the many religions might be spurred on by the prospect of the Global Ethic to participate more readily in intrareligious dialogue. It is at least as likely, however, that this prospect will only further fortify resistance to such dialogue. Perhaps the Ethic is just one more stark reminder of the urgency and difficulty of intrareligious dialogue between liberals and conservatives. In the end, the identification of common ground between the latter seems a much more difficult task than the establishment of a Global Ethic that mainstream and liberal strands of the world's religions can endorse.

Content

1. Have the framers of the Global Ethic moved too quickly and facilely to pronouncements of moral similarity among the world's religions? O'Connor raises this issue in a way that will elicit sympathy from many scholars.

The accent on similarity is likely to trouble scholars and teachers of the world's religions. For professors rightly resist easy generalizations from students who exude enthusiastic claims that "all the religions are really saying the same thing, deep down" or that "the world's religions are simply different paths to the same reality." On the contrary, scholars and teachers invite students to enter the complexity of the religions, to explore the contradictions of the religions, and to study the cultural and historical specificity of religions. They tend to discourage the discovery of similarity as too easy for the new student, as premature in effort, and thus as superficial and inaccurate in conclusion. (O'Connor 1994, 161)

Although this statement is certainly true in itself, I doubt that it applies to the Global Ethic. The latter does not express a claim that "all the religions are really saying the same thing, deep down" or that "the world's religions are simply different paths to the same reality." Indeed, the strength of the Global Ethic is its ability to point to a small but important area of claimed overlap in the area of ethics only, while stressing the uniqueness of the various religions in other respects. It says nothing whatsoever about soteriology, to which the above claims probably refer. So while it is true that scholars of world religions are allergic to the kind of statement that O'Connor mentions, the appropriate scholarly response to the Global Ethic, it seems to me, is a more careful scrutiny of the particular claim that the Ethic *does* make.

2. *Is* there a consensus? The claim that the Ethic makes, of course, is that there is a particular area of unity among the world's religions constituted by a small set of normative ethical statements that they all affirm. The real issue, and one quite interesting and important for scholars to consider, is whether this claim is true. This, indeed, is the key to the entire Ethic.

Consider, for example, nonviolence, the first of the four "irrevocable directives" of the Global Ethic. Is it the case that Buddhism and Islam have the same view on nonviolence? How could it be said that they do? Nonharmfulness *(ahimsa)* is the first of the Buddhist lay precepts, regarded as essential behavior for all Buddhists. The paradigm behavioral examples are the Buddha, who spoke against war and intervened to stop a war; and King Aśoka, who gave up war when he converted to Buddhism. In the case of Islam, although peace is a central value, war is still regarded as acceptable and even a duty under certain circumstances. The paradigm example is Muhammad, who led the fighting in many battles. How can it be said that the views of these two religions on the use of violence are the same? They certainly are not the same in their fully developed forms.

However, this is not the entire issue. The framers of the Global Ethic are attempting to determine whether language on the subject of nonviolence can be found that both Buddhists and Muslims (as well as others) could jointly affirm. This is another matter. For example, the parliament's version of the

Ethic calls us to affirm a "commitment to a culture of non-violence and respect for life." This will satisfy Buddhists. On the other hand, the discussion of the directive states: "Persons who hold political power must . . . commit themselves to the most non-violent, peaceful solutions possible" (Küng and Kuschel 1993, 25). This allows considerably more maneuvering space and might make the Ethic acceptable to those who are not absolute pacifists but note that the use of violence is never directly condoned—this allows the Ethic to remain acceptable to pacifists. I have been told that Muslim representatives who have concerns over the nonviolence provisions of this version of the Ethic have said that they will be more ready to sign if language insisting upon the necessity of justice is tied to the language calling for nonviolence. In contrast, Swidler's version of the Ethic states directly: "Violence is to be vigorously avoided, being resorted to only when its absence would cause a greater evil" (1996b, 5). This statement directly condones the use of violence under some circumstances. It therefore might be more acceptable to nonpacifists, but Buddhists and other pacifists would likely be very reluctant to affirm it.

We know what it means if language cannot be found that all will affirm: it means there is no unity on this point of moral behavior. What, however, does it mean if the language can be carefully adjusted and nuanced until all major religions can affirm it? Does it mean that we have found the point of shared moral vision? Or does it mean only that we are benefiting from the abilities of some very skilled wordsmiths, or possibly very skilled scholars of comparative religious ethics? I think we need not be so cynical. The evidence of the Global Ethic seems to confirm Robert Merrihew Adams's assertion that there is a core of common morality (lying, stealing, and killing are generally held to be wrong) that shades off into areas that are morally less clear (white lies, property rights, and euthanasia are debated) (1993, 95). Assuming that this is the case, it would indeed require skilled wordsmiths and ethicists to carefully formulate just the right language, even given a true area of common morality.

3. The parliament's Global Ethic seems to have some difficulty with coherence. On the one hand, the Ethic fundamentally intends to represent "the minimum of what the religions of the world already have in common now in the ethical sphere" (Küng and Kuschel 1993, 8; emphasis removed). On the other hand, Gómez-Ibáñez relates that he and Küng agreed that "we must challenge the world with the ethic"; "the ethic should raise the level of ethical standards and expectations" (Gómez-Ibáñez 1996, 4, 5). In other words, there is an is/ought struggle being waged within the pages of the Ethic, an attempt to reflect what "already" is hand in hand with an attempt to raise standards beyond where they presently are. These are two quite different tasks!

This struggle can be exemplified by the Ethic's treatment of male-female equality. The fourth "irrevocable directive" asks us to affirm a "commitment to a culture of equal rights and partnership between men and women" and explicitly condemns "patriarchy, domination of one sex over the other, exploitation of women," and so on (Küng and Kuschel 1993, 32). Swidler's version states even more explicitly: "Women and men are inherently equal and all men and women have an equal right to the full development of all their talents" (Swidler 1996b, 4). These are well and good as "ought" statements, but surely no one could seriously propose that these statements accurately reflect "an ethic [that] already exists within the religious teachings of the world" (Küng and Kuschel 1993, 18)!

Needless to say, there is considerable resistance over this portion of the Ethic. This resistance simply reflects the incoherence between the two ambitions of the framers. All religions have their reformers, and it may be that this part of the Ethic reflects the direction in which the world's religions will inevitably evolve. It simply does not reflect what "already" is.

Potential Uses of a Global Ethic

One of the reasons comparative religious ethicists look with interest toward interreligious dialogue is that such dialogue constitutes an arena of conversation, which may result in practical efforts to address concrete human needs.

Indeed, the framers of the Global Ethic intend very consciously to make a real difference in the world. After sketching the all-too-familiar ills—economic, political, ecological, and social—that beset us, the text of the Ethic reads:

> On the basis of personal experiences and the burdensome history of our planet we have learned
>
> that a better global order cannot be created or enforced by laws, prescriptions, and conventions alone;
>
> that the realization of peace, justice, and the protection of earth depends on the insight and readiness of men and women to act justly;
>
> that action in favour of rights and freedoms presumes a consciousness of responsibility and duty, and that therefore both the minds and hearts of women and men must be addressed;
>
> that rights without morality cannot long endure, and that there will be *no better global order without a global ethic.* (Küng and Kuschel 1993, 20–21)

Thus, a global ethic, if it fulfills the intention of its creators, should contribute toward the development of a better global order.

Of what practical use could a global ethic be? I will discuss six such uses, which fall into the three categories of theoretical-educational-cultural, political, and religious.

Theoretical-Educational-Cultural

1. In direct proportion to the breadth of dissemination it receives, the Global Ethic will inevitably stimulate thought and discussion regarding the possibility of a common ethic and the similarity or uniqueness of ethical systems cross-culturally. Indeed, the Ethic may be the only document directed at a broad, popular audience to directly address this theme from the point of view of an affirmation of a common ethic. Given the pervasiveness in modern Western culture of both subliminal and overt messages espousing cultural and ethical relativism, this document has the potential to level the playing field somewhat, to give those wishing to resist relativism some materials to draw upon in the debate.

2. Marcus Braybrooke suggests that the Global Ethic "could play an important part in Values Education, perhaps particularly in Britain where there is widespread concern about moral standards" (1994, 101). The same could be said of the United States! Indeed, if broadly affirmed by groups representative of a diverse society, the Global Ethic could be used as the basis of ethical instruction in public schools within pluralistic societies such as the United States and Great Britain. We often hear America's public schools faulted for their failure to teach ethics; yet, given the currently predominant concern in the United States to respect diversity, what can the public schools do but respond, as they have, by asking: "Whose morality?" A Global Ethic affirmed by diverse groups representative of the major ethnic, religious, and socioeconomic groups making up American society could provide legitimacy to the teaching of ethics in public schools without compromising the essential respect due all these groups in their diversity.

3. As O'Connor points out, the Global Ethic helps "to highlight the important distinction between the ethical and the political-legal arenas of life." She elaborates upon the usefulness of this distinction:

> People who are not in touch with the moral and ethical heritages of human life and those who ignore, dismiss, or repudiate those heritages tend to rely on individual rights, contractual agreements, political arrangements, and cultural conventions for a sense of what is good. Yet history documents an enduring tension between the ethical and the legal, a tension that makes visible a difference between them. Resistance movements of diverse sorts (democratic, socialist, anarchic), civil rights and other human rights movements, ethnic pride movements, and women's liberation movements, for example, illustrate in multiple and various ways a single point: social and civil laws and cultural customs can be morally unjustifiable, ethically intolerable. (1994, 159)

Public schools, in the United States and other countries, have not been known for their readiness to teach materials potentially challenging to the political status quo. Nonetheless, given some of the values that American society publicly embraces, the schools need to be continually pressed on this point. Consideration of the Global Ethic with respect to the ethical-legal distinction would make a very appropriate activity for public school celebration of Martin Luther King Jr. Day, for example.

Thinking along the same lines as O'Connor, Khalid Duran states that in the Muslim world the Global Ethic could become a focal point for the "age-old conflict between the scholars of the law and the teachers of ethics who feel that stagnation of the law has led to what are, from an ethical point of view, absurdities. . . . Muslims who put ethics above and the law beneath will be thrilled to hear of this project. Those who take the shari'a [law] as their shield without understanding the difference between shari'a and akhl q [ethics] will be apprehensive" (1996, 3). It is clear that from Duran's perspective, the influence of the Global Ethic will be beneficial to this debate.

4. If (and only if) the Global Ethic were to be broadly embraced and affirmed, it would succeed in negating the specter of relativism without thereby establishing a pernicious absolutism. Indeed, the Global Ethic's primary usefulness comes from its ability to rein in both extreme reactions to pluralism. To relativists it says: "There is an absolute"; to exclusive absolutists it says: "The truth that you treasure is also found elsewhere, it is not your exclusive possession."

Political

5. The Global Ethic has an important affinity with the UN Universal Declaration of Human Rights. In places, the Ethic uses explicit "rights" language:

> All people have a right to life, safety, and the free development of personality in so far as they do not injure the rights of others. No one has the right physically or psychically to torture, injure, much less kill, any other human being. And no people, no state, no race, no religion has the right to hate, to discriminate against, to "cleanse," to exile, much less to liquidate a "foreign" minority which is different in behaviour or holds different beliefs (Küng and Kuschel 1993, 25).

Indeed, the Global Ethic is in part conceived as supporting the Universal Declaration of Human Rights; as Küng comments, "a declaration on a global ethic should provide ethical support for the UN Declaration on Human Rights, which is so often ignored, violated and evaded. Treaties, laws, agreements are observed only if there is an underlying ethical will really to observe them" (Küng and Kuschel 1993, 56).

The UN declaration on human rights, and associated international covenants, have already faced considerable scrutiny on the question of universality versus cultural relativism. Do international human rights covenants simply impose a particular, Western set of ethical and political views upon the world? The Consultation Group on Universality vs. Relativism in Human Rights, sponsored by the Project on Religion and Human Rights, studied this question and found the following:

> In analyzing the positions of speakers in the international debate about universality vs. relativism in human rights, it found that state actors often use the language of cultural particularity and relativism as a screen to perpetuate and defend human rights violations for self-interested political ends. It also found, by contrast, that nongovernmental organizations and individuals tend to use elements of local culture to translate human rights into cultural idioms so that they might be more effectively recognized and respected. . . . Moreover, the Group found that many oppressed people(s)—regardless of their cultural imbeddedness and differences—have little or no difficulty with the notion of universal human rights: the Group regarded this fact as one of the most decisive in the debate. (Twiss and Grelle 1995, 26–27)

These observations readily apply to the human rights aspects of the Global Ethic as well. Daniel Gómez-Ibáñez reports that shortly before the parliament met and issued the Global Ethic, he was approached by a diplomat in New York who asked him whether the text of the Global Ethic could be made public. Gómez-Ibáñez replied that it would not be made public for some months. The diplomat frowned and replied, "I wish we could take it to Vienna this week for the UN Conference on Human Rights. It would be so useful." Gómez-Ibáñez comments:

> You will recall that the Conference on Human Rights was nearly torn apart by disagreement between two points of view. Representatives of several countries argued that human rights are not absolute, but instead are conditioned by culture, and that the Western countries' assumption that there might be such a thing as universal human rights was just another example of neo-colonial domination. . . .
> "Toward A Global Ethic" clearly states that human rights are not relative, and that the requirement to treat all persons humanely, without exceptions, is fundamental to the religious faiths of all the world's peoples. The diplomat in New York knew that such an unequivocal statement might have been very helpful in the debates which opened the Vienna Conference on Human Rights (1996, 2).

Aung San Suu Kyi of Burma, as her response to the Global Ethic, sent a paper that echoes precisely these views.

> Many authoritarian governments wish to appear in the forefront of modern progress but are reluctant to institute genuine change. Such governments tend to claim that they are taking a uniquely national or indigenous path towards a political system in keeping with the times. . . . It is often in the name of cultural

integrity as well as social stability and national security that democratic reforms based on human rights are resisted by authoritarian governments.

. . . In fact the values that democracy and human rights seek to promote can
be found in many cultures. Human beings the world over need freedom and
security that they may be able to realize their full potential. The longing for a
form of governance that provides security without destroying freedom goes
back a long way. (1996, 227–229)

Similarly, Mutombo Nkulu states: "Africans are today very concerned with
the issue of human rights and cannot reject a project such as a 'Universal
Declaration of a Global Ethic' which helps to end the violation of human
rights in the world" (1996, 14).

Simply put, no one wants to be tortured, injured, killed, hated, discrimi-
nated against, "cleansed," exiled, or liquidated, and they do not want these
things done to others they care about. Whether, on this basis, they follow a
subliminal principle of universalization, or whether they are simply looking
at the situation pragmatically, the result is the same: People all over the
world recognize that if they don't want their own basic human rights violated, their best bet is to try to prevent all human rights violations. Hence,
the nearly universal acceptance of the principles and language of human
rights.

Those such as Aung San Suu Kyi, who are struggling for the well-being
of the oppressed, and those such as the diplomat in New York who spoke
with Gómez-Ibáñez, who work for the real enactment of human rights protections in the international arena, will readily and enthusiastically welcome and endorse the Global Ethic. The Ethic will be seen, as intended, as a
powerful tool capable of undercutting the claims of those authoritarian
"state actors" who would use the cry of protecting indigenous culture and
resisting Western imperialism to justify their violations of human rights.
Since religion permeates every corner of culture in a traditional society, if
representatives of the world's religions freely endorse the Global Ethic, this
will strongly demonstrate that traditional cultures do share basic human
rights commitments. Such broad endorsements will thereby expose claims
to the contrary made by authoritarian "state actors" as lies.

Religious

The Global Ethic could be useful for overcoming interreligious suspicion
and divisiveness, as follows.

6. On October 25, 1993, the Harrisonburg, Virginia, *Daily News Record*
carried a story on its (lower) front page under the headline "Girl Scouts
Vote to Allow Members to Drop God from Pledge." Part of the text read:
"Promising to serve Allah instead of God, or simply to serve, is now OK for
Girl Scouts, but the decision to allow the choice was not universally

cheered Sunday by people outside the scouts. 'This is one more organization that has become morally relativistic and that's deeply disappointing,' said Tom Minnery, a spokesman for Focus on the Family, an evangelical Christian organization based in Colorado Springs, Colo." (cited in King 1995b, 214).

This conservative Christian clearly believes that to serve Allah or "simply to serve" is less moral, in some sense, than to serve the Christian God. Thus, to him, and to those he represents, non-Christian morals are inferior to Christian morals. Indeed, the notion that those whose lives are based on other values and religions are moral at all seems alien to his way of thinking. This identifies a real problem: the inability of conservatives within every religion to recognize the morality of the other *as* morality.

The Global Ethic strikes directly at this point. If the more conservative followers of the world's religions came to see that the morality of the "other" shares significant moral ground with "my" or "our" morality, their automatic impulse to reject and often vilify what is different from "me" and what "we" believe would be undercut at the base. Thus, the Global Ethic could be a powerful teaching tool to convey the message that "my" morality overlaps in important ways with the morality of that "other" religion of which I am suspicious and mistrustful; my conclusion can only be that the "other" is not so entirely "other" as I had thought. Given the deep human tendency to fear and reject the "other," a foundational area of unity, publicly acknowledged by the world's major religious leaders and reiterated frequently in each religion's teachings, could be powerful medicine indeed.

Conclusion

We have seen throughout this chapter that the Global Ethic has the potential to constitute a breakthrough on the question of universality and relativism in ethics. In addition, it provides important support for international human rights; it is a highly useful tool for healing interreligious relations; and it may offer a way forward for establishing public school ethics education. However, none of this potential can be realized unless the Ethic is genuinely embraced by a great and diverse array of representatives of the world's religions after a period of careful scrutiny and consideration. On the contrary, if the Ethic is pushed forward by any of its composers, endorsers, or supporters without proper scrutiny and voluntary affirmation by the world's religions, its fundamental nature will be transformed, it will lose every shred of its efficacy, and it will become nothing but an expression of imperialism.

It is to be hoped that those now responsible for the Ethic will ensure that it receives the most open and transparent scrutiny possible, that both positive and negative responses receive wide circulation, and that alternative drafts from other religions be circulated as well; in short, that no one could have cause to complain of being railroaded into approving a document that might be difficult for them to accept on the basis of their own religious values. The Global Ethic is worthless if it is not genuinely embraced by all faiths. In the end, a rush to agreement that is not based upon the identification of true common ground could only lead to disappointments and feelings of betrayal. We would be much better off with no Global Ethic than with a false one. But we would also, I believe, be better off with a true Global Ethic than with none at all. And, indeed, a true Global Ethic does seem to be within reach.

Notes

1. The author wishes to express her very great appreciation to Jim Kenney and Daniel Gómez-Ibáñez for their separate and very helpful comments to her on the topic of the parliament and the resulting global ethic.

2. A collection of responses from scholars edited by Karl-Josef Kuschel, entitled *Scholars Reflect on a Global Ethic,* is expected to be published shortly. It is to be hoped that this will be a more balanced collection.

3. The Center for Global Ethics operates an Internet subscriber network. To subscribe, address an e-mail message to listserve@vm.temple.edu and in the message write "SUBSCRIBE G-ETHIC [your name]."

4. I have composed an alternative draft of "Principles of a Buddhist Proposal for a Global Ethic" based upon the Five Lay Precepts of Buddhism. This draft is remarkably close in content to Küng's draft; however, it represents no one but the author (see King 1995a).

References

Adams, Robert Merrihew. 1993. "Religious Ethics in a Pluralistic Society." In *Prospects for a Common Morality,* edited by Gene Outka and John P. Reeder Jr., 93–113. Princeton: Princeton University Press.

Braybrooke, Marcus. 1994. "Report on the Chicago Parliament of the World's Religions: Declaration Toward a Global Ethic." *Faith and Freedom* 47 (Autumn and Winter):91–102.

Duran, Khalid. 1996. "Leonard Swidler's Draft of a Global Ethic: A Muslim Perspective." On-line posting, http://rain.org/~origin/gethic/geth004.

Farley, Margaret A. 1993. "Feminism and Universal Morality." In *Prospects for a Common Morality,* edited by Gene Outka and John P. Reeder Jr., 170–190. Princeton: Princeton University Press.

Gómez-Ibáñez, Daniel. 1996. "Moving Towards a Global Ethic." On-line posting, http://www.silcom.com/~origin/sbcr/sbcr231.

Hick, John. 1996. "Towards a Universal Declaration of a Global Ethic: A Christian Comment." On line posting, http://rain.org/~origin/gethic/geth003.

King, Sallie B. 1995a. "A Buddhist Perspective on a Global Ethic and Human Rights." *Journal of Dharma* 20, 2 (April-June):122–136.

_____. 1995b. "It's a Long Way to a Global Ethic: A Response to Leonard Swidler." *Buddhist-Christian Studies* 15:213–219.

Knitter, Paul F. 1995. "Pitfalls and Promises for a Global Ethics." *Buddhist-Christian Studies* 15:222–229.

Küng, Hans. 1993. "The History, Significance, and Method of the Declaration Toward a Global Ethic." In *A Global Ethic: The Declaration of the Parliament of the World's Religions,* edited by Hans Küng and Karl-Josef Kuschel, 43–76. New York: Continuum.

Küng, Hans, ed. 1996. *Yes to a Global Ethic.* New York: Continuum.

Küng, Hans, and Karl-Josef Kuschel, eds. 1993. *A Global Ethic: The Declaration of the Parliament of the World's Religions.* New York: Continuum.

Little, David. 1993. "The Nature and Basis of Human Rights." In *Prospects for a Common Morality,* edited by Gene Outka and John P. Reeder Jr., 73–92. Princeton: Princeton University Press.

Mutombo, Nkulu. 1996. "The African Charter on Human and Peoples' Rights: An African Contribution to the Project of Global Ethic." On-line posting, http://astro.temple.edu/~dialogue/Center/mutombo.html.

O'Connor, June. 1994. "Does a Global Village Warrant a Global Ethic?" *Religion* 24:155–164.

Outka, Gene, and John P. Reeder Jr., eds. 1993. *Prospects for a Common Morality.* Princeton: Princeton University Press.

Suu Kyi, Aung San. 1996. "Towards a Culture of Peace and Development." In *Yes to a Global Ethic,* edited by Hans Küng, 222–236. New York: Continuum.

Swidler, Leonard. 1996a. "Center for Global Ethics." On-line posting, http://rain.org/~origin/gethic/geth022.

_____. 1996b. "Universal Declaration of a Global Ethic." On-line posting, http://astro.temple.edu/~dialogue/Center/declarel.html.

Swidler, Leonard, and Hans Küng. 1991. "Editorial: Toward a 'Universal Declaration of Global Ethos.'" *Journal of Ecumenical Studies* 28, 1 (Winter):123–125.

Twiss, Sumner B., and Bruce Grelle. 1995. "Human Rights and Comparative Religious Ethics: A New Venue." *The Annual of the Society of Christian Ethics*:21–48.

Chapter Five

*Commentary
on Part One*

MARCUS BRAYBROOKE
World Congress of Faiths

"We live in a world that is characterized by persistent abuses of human rights, by vast disparities of wealth and power between individuals and nations, by the degradation of the environment, and by seemingly unending religious, racial, and ethnic conflict and violence," writes Bruce Grelle. He speaks, I think, for many engaged in interfaith activity when he continues:

> Interreligious moral dialogues seek to address the question of how we are to think about and respond to moral problems . . . in a religiously and culturally pluralistic world. These dialogues typically call upon the religions of the world, and upon all people of good will, to share responsibility for the creation of a more just and peaceful order at local, regional, and global levels. Most participants entertain the hope that such dialogues can lead to new moral self-understandings and practical policies that might be acceptable to, and combine important insights from, different religious and cultural traditions. It is believed that this would be an important if not indispensable first step toward joint action aimed at alleviating if not resolving the sort of moral problems mentioned above.

The question that those who share this hope need to ask themselves is whether their work is effective or at least whether it could be more effective. A glance at a newspaper is enough to suggest that we have a long way to go to alleviate the problems that Grelle identifies. Recent conferences at the International Interfaith Centre at Oxford have focused on questions about the effectiveness of interfaith work. For example, the theme of the 1997 conference was "The Place of Dialogue in Halting and Healing Conflict," and speakers from Northern Ireland and Bosnia spoke of their achievements and disappointments.

The chapters in Part 1 suggest ways in which interfaith activity could be more effective. Such activity needs to involve a wider range of believers, especially traditionalists of different faiths. It should seek to clarify a method by which people of many traditions can engage each other in discussion of pressing moral problems. And public awareness of the importance of interfaith work should be increased by appropriate educational work and by engaging in public debate.

Broadening the Range of Participants

Is interfaith activity only for pluralists? When I helped to organize the Year of Interreligious Understanding and Cooperation, which marked the centenary of the 1893 World's Parliament of Religions, I made it clear that while I was personally sympathetic to a pluralist position, this could not be the basis of the centenary year. Such an approach would have made it difficult, if not impossible, for many members of mainstream religious traditions to take part. The cumbersome name for the year was deliberate. "The Year of Religious Unity" or "One Religion for One World" would have been more catchy titles, but it would have put off those who are suspicious of any sniff of syncretism. The United Religions Initiative has repeatedly had to counter the supposition that it intends to promote a "One World" religion; its title in reality is intended to mirror that of the United Nations—an organization that is clearly enough not trying to make everybody members of the same nation.

The phrase "Understanding and Cooperation" was designed to encourage as many people as possible to engage in interfaith activities. There are those who reject any meeting with members of another faith tradition, who are often labeled "extremists" or "fundamentalists," although the cause of their suspicion of and hostility to others may be primarily due to political and economic divisions. Many others, who perhaps are best described as "traditionalists," do not wish to give religious legitimacy to another faith tradition—or quite possibly have not thought about the matter—but do recognize that people of different faiths have to live together and need to understand something about each other. It may be quite simple information about diet—for example, what foods should not be served at a civic reception in a religiously plural city? It may be information about religious festivals. A pluralist society requires respect for those of other persuasions. Even societies where one religion is dominant may have to take account of significant religious minorities. Teddy Kollek, for example, when he was mayor of Jerusalem, tried to be sensitive to the religious concerns of Muslim and Christian minorities. Many Islamic states have to make allowance for significant minorities of other faiths. In Great Britain, the bishops of the established Church of England often now speak on behalf of all faith communities and, unlike their nineteenth-century predecessors, do not use their privileged position to encourage discrimination against other denominations or religions.

It has been encouraging that recently a growing number of leaders of large religious communities have endorsed the need for interreligious understanding and cooperation, but many would reject any idea of an emergent world faith, and some are hesitant about the universalism that they consider is inherent in the Global Ethic. Fifty years ago, Dr. Sarvepalli Radhakrishnan suggested that as each religion emphasized its universal elements, "the gradual assimilation of religions will function as a world faith" (Radhakrishnan 1947, 55). I sympathize with this and believe that dialogue is in part a theological and spiritual quest whereby we shall grow in understanding of the mystery of the Divine. I have written recently that the interfaith movement needs its mystics (Braybrooke 1997). Yet, if the universalist or pluralist approach is made a sine qua non for interfaith activity, then it will remain a minority concern, even being viewed by some as a substitute religion. The issues that face our world society, however, are too pressing for this, and it is urgent that people of faith should come together to try to reduce violence and poverty and to protect the planet.

Kate McCarthy shows that within most religious traditions there is debate about that religion's relationship to other faiths, suggesting that the three categories of "exclusive," "inclusive," and "pluralist" can be applied to different positions within those religions. She also argues that advocates of each position have a contribution to make to interfaith dialogue. This, I think, is very important if interfaith activity is to win the support of the majority of believers, who have a traditional faith. McCarthy recognizes the inadequacies of the threefold categorization. It is also questionable, as we see from the confusion caused by the widespread use of the term "fundamentalist," whether it is helpful to apply terms coined in one tradition to another. Nonetheless, by doing so, McCarthy has made clear the variety of approaches within different faith traditions. I recall at the opening meeting of a Jewish-Christian dialogue group that after the first session someone suggested that the Jews should go into one room and the Christians into another. When each had sorted out what they agreed upon, then, the speaker said, we should come back together. Any participant in dialogue and any student of religion recognizes that no faith is monolithic.

People from each of the three approaches, McCarthy argues, have significant contributions to make to interfaith activity. The "exclusivist" stresses commitment, and this is a welcome reminder that interfaith activity should not evade questions of truth. I have taken some part in Christian-Jewish dialogue, and in my *Time to Meet* (1990) I argue that much traditional Christian writing about Judaism has been theologically and historically wrong. There are those who have suggested that many Christian participants in

Jewish-Christian dialogue have changed their theology so as to avoid offending the Jews, but the issue is one of truth, not of accommodation. A new Christian theology of Judaism will only be convincing if it can be argued from biblical sources.

The particular faith commitment of participants helps to ensure that the dialogue is concerned with truth. I recall one insipid dialogue event, when everyone was so agreeable and universalist that after a short while there was nothing left to discuss. If we wish to engage with people of another faith, we need to meet those who are committed to that faith. We should, however, beware of thinking that only the traditionalist is committed. The struggle to reexpress a faith in contemporary thought forms may spring from a deep commitment to that faith and a longing that it should be more influential in the contemporary world. Equally, a commitment that does not allow for the commitment of others may allow for practical cooperation but not for deeper dialogue, because the central tenets of the religion are not open to question. There may be an explanation of the faith, and mutual clarification, but not alteration—although, of course, unchanging faiths are open to reinterpretation!

The "exclusivist," if belonging to a missionary religion, will not give up on mission. This need not inhibit practical cooperation. Christians and Muslims both belong to missionary religions but may find common cause, for example, in opposing racism. It is less clear whether the "inclusivist" retains the hope that others will be converted to his or her own faith, and this causes some ambiguity for the dialogue partner. Inclusivists seem at least implicitly to claim that their religion is the "best." Although this may be appropriate for a Christian or Muslim or Jewish theologian who seeks to evaluate other religions in the light of a particular revelation, it is inappropriate for the student of religions or the interfaith activist. The difficulty, as McCarthy says, is for inclusivists to acknowledge the "otherness" of the other, and not see the other in their own terms. As A. G. Hogg, professor of philosophy at Madras Christian College, said in criticism of J. N. Farquhar's claim that Christianity was the fulfillment of Hinduism, Christianity answers those questions that Hinduism was not asking (Hogg 1909; Braybrooke 1971).

I also find it difficult to see on what external grounds it is possible to argue that one religion is better than another. The inclusivist seems to me to try to give a false objectivity to a personal faith commitment. I am happy to affirm that it is in Jesus Christ that I have been grasped by the boundless love of God, and my response to other faith traditions is in the light of that encounter. I am glad to bear witness to that commitment, but see no value in a comparative evaluation of other religions. Their adherents will witness to the life-giving meaning that they have found in their own tradition. "Pluralism," therefore, is an acknowledgment that the richness of the Divine Mystery cannot be contained in one tradition. As Stanley Samartha has written, "A sense of Mystery provides a point of unity for all plurality. In a pluralistic world, the different responses of different religions to the Mystery of the Infinite or *Theos* or *Sat* need to be acknowledged as valid" (Samartha 1991, 4). Such a view acknowledges the otherness of the other and welcomes the richness of religious diversity. Pluralism, in this sense, is very different from a covert "universalism," which suggests that despite the apparent variety religions really all agree. As Raimundo Panikkar has said, "Pluralism means something more than sheer acknowledgment of plurality and the mere wishful thinking of unity. Pluralism does not consider unity an indispensable ideal . . . nor is it the eschatological expectation that in the end all shall be one" (Hick and Knitter 1987, 109).

I doubt if we can reach, at least in the immediate future, widespread agreement on the philosophical or theological basis for interfaith work. Perhaps rather than assuming that pluralism is the basis for interfaith dialogue, we should acknowledge a pluralism of dialogue. I think McCarthy is right when she says, "no one model of how to understand" the differences of religion "is likely to emerge within and among the religions." I wonder if even as individuals most of us operate with only one model. I recognize that in part I could fit under all the categories. I have a personal commitment as a disciple of Christ, and in my theological thinking I seek as a Christian to see God's purpose in the whole religious life of humanity; but as a student of religion and as an interfaith activist, I do not presume that any faith has a privileged position.

Practical Concerns As the Basis for Interfaith Activity

Because of this variety of models for interfaith activity, a "liberation/human rights" basis for interfaith cooperation, as Paul Knitter suggests, is most likely to enlist the greatest support and involve all people from the various categories to which McCarthy points. I hope, however, that this emphasis does not displace other forms of dialogue, especially "truth-seeking" dialogue and spiritual sharing (Braybrooke 1995, 81–95).

Certainly, since the 1993 Parliament of the World's Religions, practical concerns seem to have been uppermost in interfaith activity. Indeed, the parliament itself began with a presentation on the critical issues of the day, to which the Global Ethic was intended to be an answer, showing that religions need not be divisive but could agree on certain basic moral imperatives. The continuing Council for a Parliament of the World's Religions has directed its energies to metropolitan Chicago, to plans for a parliament in South Africa, and to encouraging discussion of a Global Ethic. The Peace Council has focused spiritual energy on the devastation caused by land mines and has sought to identify with oppressed people, such as those who live in the Chiapas region of Mexico. The United Religions Initiative hopes to unite religions against violence and war. The valuable work of existing bodies such as the World Conference on Religion and Peace has concentrated on the problems of specific regions.

Yet practical cooperation is not without its difficulties. Is it genuinely interreligious and international, or are certain groups recruiting support for their own agenda? Is talk of "global" concerns a polite term for a new Western attempt to impose its values on the rest of the world? Does the emphasis on religious consensus allow space for the voices of religious minorities and of those who have no formal religious commitment? Many of these questions about whether sufficient agreement exists for common action by members of the religions of the world have become focused on discussion of the Global Ethic.

Sallie King, in her valuable article, highlights many of these questions. It is helpful that she draws attention to the existence of a "Global Ethic According to Swidler" as well as discussing the better-known version "According to Küng." I do not myself see it as a scandal that two versions exist. Indeed, soon after the parliament, when I spoke to an interreligious group in South Korea, one participant produced a Korean version of the Global Ethic, which emphasized environmental issues. I doubt if we shall ever have or would want an infallible text of a Global Ethic. It is the affirmation of the possibility of ethical agreement, and the educational process involved in the negotiations, that seems to me of real value—not the specifics of the text. This is shown by the express statement that the Global Ethic is not intended to replace the ethical codes of particular religions. Its aim is to point to common threads.

The claim that King quotes that the ethic was "not a new invention but only a new discovery" is surprising. Charles Bonney, the president of the 1893 parliament, had hoped that gathering would unite all religions and make "the Golden Rule the basis of that union" (cited in Braybrooke 1992, 13). In my *Stepping Stones to a Global Ethic* (1992a), I collected a range of documents produced by interfaith conferences during the last fifty years showing that some members of almost all religions do agree on certain ethical issues. The Global Ethic and the subsequent discussion have greatly increased the number of those who recognize this agreement. That recognition is a new discovery for each person who makes it, but a further discovery is to find out that others have arrived there first.

As King rightly observes, the Global Ethic reports what amounts to being an empirical claim "that persons throughout the world affirm a certain set of moral values." It does seem to imply that these values have an absolute character, as the language of "irrevocable directives" suggests, but, although some who saw drafts of the declaration wanted a reference to God included in the document, no attempt was made to ground it in an appeal to the "Almighty." I think that King is right to reject suggestions that the

Global Ethic constitutes a pernicious form of absolutism. The references to David Little and to Gene Outka and John P. Reeder, the editors of *Prospects for a Common Morality,* are tantalizing, and I hope that this area of discussion will be developed.

King highlights many other issues. I think there is widespread agreement that the process of developing the Global Ethic was faulty. Not enough people were involved in the production of the text, and the manner in which the parliament's Assembly of Spiritual Leaders was structured precluded proper discussion of the text. The text, or "Introduction," was shaped too by the wish to address the media.

There are questions about how to ensure the participation of minorities and those who feel powerless. Many in America and Europe are ignorant of the considerable interfaith activity in India, Japan, and other parts of Asia, just as many there are unaware of developments in the West. Last year, at the inaugural meeting in Cochin, southern India, of the Society for Values in Education, I introduced members to the Global Ethic. This will be relevant to their work, and their discussion will equally enrich the debate about the Ethic. Too few voices from Africa are heard in any interfaith gathering.

Even more difficult are the disagreements within religious traditions. This is why there are interfaith coalitions supporting opposing options, as, for example, the pro-life and the pro-choice parties to the debate on abortion. It is here I think that a consensus document may be the greatest threat to minorities, especially to those whose religious identity is resented by the mainstream. Christian churches quite often used to object to the participation of Unitarians at interfaith gatherings, especially if they were labeled as "Christians," and now often object to the presence of Unificationists. Sikhs may in a similar way object to the participation of Namdharis, and Muslims may resent the presence of Ahmadiyyas.

King points to the question of whether the ethical teaching of a tradition can be isolated from that tradition without distorting it. I think she is right that those who drafted the Global Ethic were aware of this danger and tried to avoid it. Despite the rather aggressive language of "irrevocable directives," I see the Global Ethic more as a signpost than a new set of commandments. Indeed, the discovery of agreement must be made by each individual as he or she becomes committed to "the global ethic, to understanding one another and to socially-beneficial, peace-fostering, and nature-friendly ways of life." This is why I think the declaration has particular educational value.

A signpost points backward, reminding us of the distance we have come in discovering our agreements across cultures and religious traditions, but it also points forward to the great distance we have yet to cover before our agreement begins to have real influence in the world. In Great Britain, Peggy Morgan (of Westminster College, Oxford) and I, with the support of the

Global Ethic Foundation and the International Interfaith Centre, have drawn together a group of people from different faiths to work on a project entitled "Testing/Trialling the Global Ethic." Each participant has been asked to say what "being human" means in that participant's faith tradition and then, again from the perspective of that tradition, to comment on the four irrevocable directives. We will then attempt to see what areas of agreement and disagreement exist. The intention is to produce a book for use in secondary schools, inviting young people to give their own answers to the questions, and then to see where they agree or disagree with the various religious traditions. My guess is that, as at the parliament, all might oppose unnecessary violence, but not agree on what violence, if any, is necessary.

The Global Ethic's value to my mind lies in public education. As more and more people find that they can identify with the Ethic's essential points, so the voice for a new culture will become more insistent. The authority of the Ethic, which may be expressed in several modified forms, lies not with its author or even with the Assembly of Spiritual Leaders but with those who identify with it and try to live in tune with its principles. Part of the educational task, which is central to the continuing work of interfaith organizations, is to increase the circle of those engaged in dialogue with members of other faiths who, it may be hoped, will discover that there are many concerns on which they agree.

The Educational Task

Questions of how people are prepared for work in the field of comparative ethics, which are addressed by Sumner B. Twiss, and, perhaps even more difficult, of how this ethical concern begins to influence public life, which Bruce Grelle discusses, therefore become of great importance.

The clarity of Twiss's analysis of the various approaches to teaching comparative religious ethics is helpful, although I suspect that many working in this field tend to "pick 'n mix." He identifies four paradigms. The formalist-conceptual concentrates on developing students' cognitive skills in moral analysis and argument. The historical-comparative's primary aim is to develop students' empathetic comprehension of similarities and differences in moral and religious thought among traditions. The hermeneutical-dialogical approach focuses on questions of how, in a pluralist world, we are to think about moral problems of a global or intracultural significance. The fourth paradigm, which Twiss calls "comparative methods and theory," examines the different approaches to comparative religious ethics.

The third paradigm, which Twiss himself prefers, fits the approach adopted by the Global Ethic. It is significant that the example given of this paradigm is a course taught by Douglas Sturm of Bucknell University. The idea for this course was the "Critical Issues" segment of the Parliament of the World's Religions, which grappled with the long-range future of divergent religious communities. The central idea of the seminar was "to form a kind of mini–Parliament of the World's Religions through which we can represent a group of religiously minded persons from divergent backgrounds and communities reflecting about our common future."

This approach seems similar to that underlying the project led by Peggy Morgan that I mentioned above. One question that has been raised is whether students have enough knowledge of particular faith traditions to engage in a critical discussion of common ground and agreements between faith traditions. As Twiss remarks, "the hermeneutical-dialogical approach could encourage a premature fusion of moral horizons before differences among cultures are fully appreciated." It seems likely that some students will use our projected book to look up what Buddhists or Sikhs think about violence instead of using the book in the interactive way that is intended—although thereby they will avoid "premature fusion of moral horizons." In Great Britain, at least under the previous conservative government, the stress has been on teaching British values, so the global emphasis of this approach has not been particularly welcome. Yet the great problems that face human society are global concerns. It has also not been evident that "British values" adequately reflect the pluralist multiethnic and multifaith nature of parts of contemporary British society. Perhaps the assumption of members of the Parliament of the World's Religions and of those who prepared and endorsed the Global Ethic that our world already is, and is increasingly becoming, a pluralist and global society is not self-evident to many people, and those who have opted into interfaith work, especially if it has an international dimension, are unrepresentative. It may even be that the difference of experience, of whether one has friends in another part of the world or friends in one's neighborhood who belong to a faith other than one's own, is as important as the theological differences between "exclusivists," "inclusivists," and "pluralists."

Addressing a Wider Public

This is one reason why there is a need, as Grelle argues, for more people who are engaged in both interfaith activity and in comparative religious ethics to be "public intellectuals." In my *Pilgrimage of Hope,* I wrote that in the early years of the interfaith movement, "many scholars kept aloof from interfaith bodies for fear that they would be placed in a false position or that their scholarly reputation would be jeopardized" (Braybrooke 1992, 286). With the growing emphasis on a phenomenological approach to religions, this changed to some extent, but Grelle makes clear that the pressures of academic life tend to confine many scholars to the academic world and leave them little time to engage in wider public debate.

Grelle, however, makes important suggestions about ways in which scholars of comparative religious ethics could engage in public discourse. He suggests that the university itself might be utilized to facilitate dialogue between
representatives of disparate religious and philosophical traditions. They
could write on these matters in a way that would reach the educated, but
not specialist, public. Their academic discipline might bring a rigor to the attempt of interfaith groups to grapple with controversial issues and thereby
help them to show that "one of the interfaith movement's great contributions to public life is its affirmation that, through dialogue and negotiation,
it is sometimes possible to identify common interests that are, or that can be,
shared by disparate groups with alternative religious and moral orientations
and languages." Grelle further suggests that the interfaith movement is a
promising vehicle for the work of comparative religious ethicists as public
intellectuals: "The interfaith movement is one of the few places in contemporary society where it is possible to employ a moral language of universal
interests and the common good while recognizing and even celebrating the
irreducible plurality of religious, social, and cultural life."

If interfaith groups and organizations attempt to translate the irrevocable
directives of the Global Ethic into more specific agreement on moral issues
and into plans for common action, the participation of scholars in the field of
comparative religious ethics will be important. Such dialogue needs to be
multidisciplinary as well as multifaith. Experts in a whole range of disciplines
may themselves be committed members of a faith. This was made clear to me
when I spoke to the group Retired Generals for Peace about the Global Ethic
and the role of the military in international peacekeeping. Many of these
high-ranking officers were committed members of a faith. If interfaith dialogue is to deal with the vital issues that face human society, it should not be
confined to religious specialists or religious leaders; it needs to engage those
with expertise in all the relevant disciplines. Most particularly, there should
be an attempt to involve in this debate those with political and economic
power as well as those who control the media. They, however, will perhaps
not be interested until there has been far wider public education on the vital
importance of interfaith cooperation. Only when politically aware publics
demand that nations act in the interest of world society, and seek to shape its
life on the basis of ethical values upheld by the great spiritual and humanist
traditions of the world, will change begin to happen.

A Sheer Illusion?

Is this hope, as Hans Küng asks in his preface to *A Global Ethic,* a "sheer illusion?" In answer, he points to the worldwide universal change of awareness
about economics and ecology, about world peace and disarmament, and
about the partnership between men and women. He suggests that the "Dec-

laration Toward a Global Ethic" may equally inspire people to a life of mutual respect, understanding, and cooperation. If that is to happen, then traditional and progressive members of faith communities need to engage in the debate about ethics together with those with relevant specialist knowledge, while educators at all levels need to build public awareness of this work and its vital importance for the future of us all and of our children.

References

Braybrooke, Marcus. 1971. *Together to the Truth*. Madras: CLS.

_____. 1990. *Time to Meet*. London: SCM Press.

_____. 1992. *Pilgrimage of Hope: One Hundred Years of Global Interfaith Dialogue*. London: SCM Press.

_____. 1995. *Faith in a Global Age*. Oxford: Braybrooke Press.

_____. 1997. "Interfaith Work Needs Its Mystics." *World Faiths Encounter* 16 (March):36–42.

Braybrooke, Marcus, ed. 1992a. *Stepping Stones to a Global Ethic*. London: SCM Press.

Hick, John, and Paul F. Knitter, eds. 1987. *The Myth of Christian Uniqueness*. London: SCM Press.

Hogg, A. G. 1909. *Karma and Redemption*. Madras: CLS.

Radhakrishnan, Sarvepalli. 1947. *Religion and Society*. London: Allen and Unwin.

Samartha, Stanley. 1991. *One Christ—Many Religions*. Maryknoll, N.Y.: Orbis Books.

Part Two

Religious Perspectives in Dialogue on Global Moral Issues

Chapter Six

Religion and Human Rights: A Comparative Perspective

SUMNER B. TWISS
Brown University

In this chapter I will outline an approach to religion and human rights that I believe provides a constructive way to examine their connections. After a brief introduction laying out some problems on the topic, I will develop a particular understanding of human rights and then examine some religious traditions in light of that understanding.

Introduction

I will introduce my subject by briefly describing a set of issues framed by the Project on Religion and Human Rights, an independent research organization with which I am associated.[1] In 1993–1994, the project established a set of consultation groups, composed of both scholars of religion and human rights activists, to examine some of the problematic relationships between religion and human rights in the contemporary world—the role of religion in violent conflict resulting in human rights abuses, the phenomenon of religious fundamentalisms and their apparent resistance to human rights, and recent challenges made in the name of religion to the universality of human rights. Let me elaborate.

Anyone who reads the newspapers can hardly be unaware of the violent conflicts in the former Yugoslavia, Armenia, Sudan, Rwanda, and Sri Lanka (to name but a few) in which religion appears to be a major factor. Moreover, we are also aware of the structural violence and oppression inflicted on minority religious groups (e.g., indigenous peoples) located in so-

A shorter version of this essay was originally delivered as the B. Frank Hall Memorial Lecture at the University of North Carolina, Wilmington, in February 1996.

cieties dominated by different majority traditions. These circumstances are disturbing and puzzling, for we commonly think of religions as standing for ideals of love, justice, peace, and brotherhood as part of their respective paths to salvation and liberation. Nevertheless, the fact remains that these traditions also appear to be one factor, interacting with others, leading to violence and abuse; the question is, how can this apparent paradox exist?

Part of the answer is as follows (see Kelsay and Twiss 1994, 1–16, for a fuller statement). Religions provide individuals and groups with a sense of identity, a place in the universe, oriented to some notion of a special reality, truth, or authority considered ultimate in some sense. In so doing, they foster a sense of group feeling that motivates not only behavior important to personal and social integration (cooperation, sharing, mutual respect, altruism) but also behavior that draws lines between an "us" (the in-group), who have the truth, know the good, and live rightly; and "them" (the out-group), who do not share these characteristics, or at least not fully. Now add to this felt sense of group difference and superiority the fact that many religions' sense of place in the universe is also bound up with proprietary claims to a certain territory that they feel they ought to control according to their views of the world, and the result is a considerable potential for violence and abuse against any out-group that challenges the in-group about its worldview, territory, values, or way of life. The cognitive dissonance or social-psychological stress produced by the other's challenge often leads to attempts by the in-group to reduce that stress by, for example, attempting to convert the other to its worldview, or developing social policies reinforcing the out-group's less legitimate second-class status, or, if the challenge is threatening enough, resorting to more direct methods of violence against the out-group, perhaps by removing it entirely (through genocide). Needless to say, such a dynamic is only intensified by other factors such as ethnic and racial difference, overpopulation, scarce resources, and political rivalry.

Again, anyone who reads the newspapers or perhaps listens to CNN's interviews with the University of Chicago's Martin Marty is likely to be aware of the recent worldwide phenomenon of religious fundamentalisms—not only the radical Christian right in our own society but also, for example, the radical Zionists and the revolutionary Muslims in other parts of the world. Certain groups within religious traditions share similarities that add up to challenges and resistance to the values, practices, and ways of life associated with secular societies and cultures. Religious fundamentalists of many persuasions appeal to certain fundamentals defining their faith and lives (often associated with a restricted, literally interpreted scriptural canon), tend toward a dualistic worldview defining their struggle on behalf of the good against the powers of darkness (other values and ways of life), and zealously advance their own absolutist values (including patriarchy) against those of the permissive modern world (Marty 1995).

In offering their adherents a sense of identity anchored in history and a stable sense of communal solidarity in absolutist and exclusivist practices, religious fundamentalists tend to see the values and phenomena of modern life—pluralism, consumerism, materialism, individual liberation from tradition, democracy interpreted as rule by lowest common denominator—as misguided, evil, demonic, heretical, contaminating, inauthentically human, and stoutly to be resisted if not actively combated (see Kelsay and Twiss 1994, 19–28, for a fuller statement). Inasmuch as human rights are viewed as part of the modern secular demonic ethos, they may appear to these groups as no more than the insidious insinuation of liberal, individualist, lowest-common-denominator values, purveyors of all that is to be rejected in favor of their own versions of the sacred and absolute truth.

Also in our newspapers are articles and editorials reporting challenges to human rights advanced in the form of claims about the irreducible differences among the world's religious and cultural traditions, which it is sometimes said ought to be respected even if they reject universal human rights values. These challenges come from two sources. First are those governments—notably in Asia, Africa, and the Middle East—that contend human rights are simply part of the West's neocolonial attempt to ram its values down the throats of the non-Western world, whose cultures and religions are different but as persuasive and valid among their peoples as the West's are among its peoples(see Kelsay and Twiss 1994, 31–59, for a fuller statement). These governments further claim that such Western values are often not appropriate to their traditions and societies, which ought to be left alone to live by their own systems of values as they see fit.

From a second direction come those claims by well-intentioned scholars of non-Western traditions who appear to agree that human rights represent a Western moral ideology that is imperialistic and culturally insensitive to the moral values of non-Western traditions (Twiss and Grelle 1995, 36–39). These scholars also tend to highlight what they perceive as the moral fragmentation of Western societies, which they attribute to the West's rights-oriented, adversarial, market-dominated culture with its misguided conceptions of human nature, truncated notions of true community, and loveless visions of the world. These scholars contend that, inasmuch as human rights are a manifestation of this morally bankrupt culture, perhaps we ourselves ought to put them aside and gain fresh moral wisdom from those non-Western traditions in which human rights are alien.

These, then, are some of the problems, and as my own background and interests lend themselves best to the problem of universality, I will focus the remainder of this chapter on it. Since I was the principal author for the consultation group paper concerned with such challenges to the universality of human rights, I want now to offer a brief report on our findings, for they help establish my vision for how comparative ethics may contribute to solving a set of practical human problems.[2]

Unmasking the Problem

There is unquestionably a widespread perception that universal human rights are in significant tension with religious, moral, and cultural diversity in the world. The underlying problem is this: Ideally, human rights ought to be, by definition, universal—a set of moral and legal claims regarding such issues as physical security, liberty, and important material goods to which all human beings are entitled by virtue of their humanity and without distinction. Yet the meaning of specific human rights norms are, arguably, conditioned by the historical and cultural experiences of societies and traditions. Therefore, it would seem that the articulation and implementation of such norms in concrete situations would be specific to a given society and tradition in its own time and space. By the same token, a moral system appropriate to one society might not be entirely appropriate to others, which might need to elaborate their own systems for their respective historical and cultural circumstances. But then, recognizing this, it seems somewhat problematic to speak of the universal validity of any given set of human rights norms.

Despite the persistence of this tension, the group self-consciously chose not to interpret it as an invalidation of universal human rights but rather as a challenge calling for the development of creative moral strategies to promote the popular legitimacy of human rights in all social and cultural contexts. It did this for certain very important reasons. To begin with, no persuasive case has yet been made to show that the tension is not resolvable. Moreover, human rights set aspirational norms, and no persuasive case has been made to show that human rights conceived as a goal for all peoples is either illegitimate or unattainable. Furthermore, in analyzing the positions of speakers in the international debate about this problem, the consultation group found that repressive governments often use the language of cultural and religious particularity as a smoke screen to deflect attention away from the abuses they perpetrate on their own citizens for self-interested political ends—for example, to stay in power or to profit from corruption. The group also found, by contrast, that nongovernmental human rights organizations tend to use elements of local culture and religion to translate human rights into cultural idioms so that they might be more effectively recognized and respected—an effort significant for the feasibility of relating human rights to many traditions. Moreover, the group found that many oppressed peoples—regardless of their cultural locations and differences—have little difficulty accepting the idea of universal human rights—a most important fact in my view.

The group also found considerable evidence that, contrary to governments' attempts to speak on behalf of supposedly unified and monolithic cultures and traditions, every society and culture is composed of diverse views about human rights, many of which embrace all human rights as universal, and some of which see certain rights (but significantly not all of them) as contestable within their traditions—the rights of women are particularly controversial. Finally, the group found evidence that a gap appears to exist in many societies between, on the one hand, relatively secular professionals and intellectuals oriented to universal human rights, and on the other, clerics and religious leaders familiar with their own traditions but less familiar with human rights in the international arena. Putting this diagnosis together with the fact that concepts of human dignity and social justice have considerable moral appeal both within and across traditions, the group proposed that the problem might be most effectively addressed by internal and cross-cultural dialogues about human rights.

Now, what I contend—and what deeply motivates my work on religion and human rights—is that comparative ethics, the cross-cultural study of moral and religious traditions, has a role to play in maximizing opportunities for productive dialogues. I will develop this role from two directions, first establishing an accurate understanding of international human rights and moving toward a discussion of religious traditions, and then arguing from the perspective of those traditions back in the direction of human rights. Thus I will pull the two sides together, so to speak, in an attempt to explore their possible convergence. I begin with the first direction.

Human Rights

I stipulate that human rights are to be understood as the set of rights articulated in the 1948 UN Universal Declaration of Human Rights and in the two related covenants adopted in 1966, jointly known as the International Bill of Human Rights and supplemented by subsequent treaties and conventions.[3] The Covenant on Civil and Political Rights guarantees rights such as freedom of thought and expression, freedom from arbitrary arrest and torture, freedom of movement and peaceful assembly, and the right of political participation in one's society. The Covenant on Economic, Social, and Cultural Rights provides for rights such as the right to employment and fair wages; to protection of one's family; to adequate standards of living; to health care; to peoples' self-determination regarding their political system and economic, social, and cultural development; and to ethnic and religious minorities' enjoyment of their own culture, religion, and language. International human rights have been further expanded and elaborated by, for ex-

ample, treaties on the prevention of genocide (1948), the status and protection of refugees (1951, 1966), the elimination of racial discrimination
(1965), the elimination of discrimination against women (1979), the elimination of discrimination based on religion (1981), the rights of children
(1989), and the rights of indigenous peoples (1993 draft, pending action).

I have specified these agreements and their dates and used reasonably
precise language for a reason. The dates symbolize the fact that the modern
international recognition of human rights has a history, beginning with the
aftermath of World War II and continuing up into the present. The range of
agreements shows that there are different types or generations of human
rights, beginning with the civil-political rights of individuals, continuing
with their socioeconomic rights, and more recently emphasizing the collective and developmental rights of whole peoples and groups. All three of
these generations of agreements are simultaneously in force. Moreover, I
have used the terms "covenant" and "treaty" in order to highlight the fact
that the promulgation of human rights is the product of negotiations and
agreements among diverse nations, cultures, and peoples. This language
also indicates that human rights have the force of international law
whereby nation-states are held accountable for their fulfillment. Finally, it
must be observed that all of these rights identify social conditions crucial to
the subsistence and flourishing of individuals and communities. This is why
the language of rights—the language of entitlements and priority claims—is
used. Human rights are moral and legal claims with such high priority that
they are construed as entitlements to certain conditions and goods that
must be socially guaranteed by states, which have correlative duties to satisfy them. All of these observations are important for a proper understanding of international human rights. Now, in order to move further in the direction of religious and cultural traditions, I need to deepen our
understanding of certain of these points.

Contrary to the seemingly prevalent view that human rights are simply
the product of Western moral views, it is a fact that the UN universal declaration, for example, was reached through a pragmatic process of negotiation among representatives of different nations and cultural traditions, and
this process has continued to characterize the drafting and adoption of subsequent covenants, conventions, and treaties (see, e.g., Humphrey 1984;
Bori 1994, chap. 7). This approach starts with the facts of cultural, religious, and moral diversity and finds that in situations of crisis people of
quite different backgrounds and traditions are nonetheless able to acknowledge their mutual respect for certain basic human values. The universal declaration was the historical product of the crisis brought about by the genocide and brutalization of individuals and communities during World War II.
In the face of this crisis, representatives from many cultural traditions
around the world recognized their mutual agreement in the judgment that

such acts are antithetical to the moral sensibilities of each and all their traditions, and through a process of pragmatic negotiation they agreed to incorporate this judgment into the language of specific human rights. The fact that the language of rights was employed was doubtless due to the dominance of the Western legal tradition in the international arena, but the mutually agreed-upon judgment about the proscription of certain acts and the protection of certain values was not simply a Western moral judgment.

Similarly, the human rights covenants of the 1960s were born from the mutual recognition that the oppression and material disadvantages suffered especially by people in developing countries (many formerly under colonial rule) were incompatible with the moral sensibilities reiterated in many traditions. Significantly, the influence of non-Western (or at least non–First World) countries and traditions was more prominent here, accounting in part for negotiated agreements placing greater emphasis on socioeconomic rights as well as on the collective rights of self-determination and development. Similar observations could be made about the other human rights treaties. My point is that different traditions are able to recognize that they have a shared interest in the protection of certain values. Brutality, tyranny, starvation, discrimination, displacement, and the like are recognized by all traditions as their enemy. Specific expressions of human rights are products of successive recognitions by diverse peoples of a set of values simultaneously embraced by their own distinctive traditions. No one tradition is the sole source of human rights values, and these values are not exclusively Western. At least in certain critical moments, participants from otherwise diverse traditions find that they have a shared set of aspirations as well as a shared capacity to suffer at the hands of those who would violate the dignity and well-being of individuals and communities. Moreover, since there is as yet no end to the suffering that human beings and groups inflict on each other, we can expect to see new moments of recognition and the addition of new human rights to those already identified.

As I have indicated, the international recognition of human rights has a history marked by at least three distinctive generations—civil-political, socioeconomic, and collective (see, e.g., Weston 1992, 14–21). Each successive generation does not replace but rather adds to as well as nuances the earlier generations, so that they are properly conceived as interrelated and best pursued in a constructive balance or harmony. Later generations not only add new human rights emphases to, but also help clarify the significance of, the earlier generations. Let me give an example. Very often, civil-political rights, when considered as a separate class, are misconstrued as concerned mainly with protecting the privacy, autonomy, and self-interested activities of socially isolated individuals. However, a different picture of their role emerges when we view them in relation to socioeconomic rights, which, in attempting to mitigate the exploitation of certain classes and formerly colonial peoples, highlight the importance of certain material goods and services in allowing people to flourish as politically involved members of their societies. This, in turn, puts us in a better position to see that civil-political rights themselves identify enablements or enpowerments necessary for persons to function as effective members of a polity or community where they are free to work out with others how best to advance their lives together in their society (see, e.g., Hollenbach 1994, 127–150). And the impact goes in the other direction as well, because exercising civil-political rights is likely to result in pressures for change that will enhance the satisfaction of socioeconomic needs (see, e.g., Park 1987, 405–413). The two generations interact and reinforce one another.

A further point follows from this understanding of the interdependence of human rights. Human rights are intended to be compatible not only with traditions that emphasize the primacy of individuals within the community (true of many Western societies) but also with traditions that may emphasize the primacy of community and the way that individuals contribute to it (true of many non-Western societies). In effect, international human rights are intended to advance a balancing and integration of individual and community interests for both more individualistic and more communitarian societies, in an attempt to avoid the pathological extremes of individual freedom without communal solidarity and communal solidarity without individual freedom (Loewy 1993, 124–125, 139–140). There can be different viable social patterns between these two extremes.

An important consequence of this historical and pragmatic conception of human rights involves a revised understanding of their status and justification. Human rights identify a wide range of conditions crucially important for maintaining the well-being and dignity of persons and communities as negotiated and agreed upon by representatives from diverse nations and cultures from their varying points of view. In effect, they represent a shared vision of moral and social values compatible with a variety of religious and cultural worldviews—a unity within a diversity. Clearly, at the international level their justification depends on a practical moral consensus (legally enshrined) among diverse nations and traditions that have openly acknowledged their mutual recognition of the human importance of these values, a public recognition grounded in shared historical experience of what life can be like without these conditions fulfilled.

At a second level of consideration, however, each of these traditions may justify to itself and its adherents its participation in the international consensus by appealing to its own distinct beliefs, norms, and ways of thinking contained within its particular philosophical or religious vision of the world. Thus, depending on the nature of the tradition, the priority of the conditions and goods identified by human rights may be understood and justified internally by appeals to, for example, divine will, natural law, natural reason, a cosmology, cosmogonic myths, views of human nature, and conditions necessary for entering the path to enlightenment; the list is open-ended precisely because of the rich variety of religious and cultural traditions. My point in distinguishing these two levels is to suggest that a pragmatic consensus at the international level may be compatible with, as well as supported by, a wide diversity of moral and religious traditions. Recognition of this possibility may make it easier for scholars and less threatening for adherents to probe these traditions for analogues, parallels, and convergences about human rights values, thereby facilitating both internal and cross-cultural dialogues.

Moreover, I think that this can be done without requiring these traditions to internally employ the *language* of rights or human rights, which might be alien to some. What is more important, in my view, is whether they somehow give priority to and guarantee respect for the values represented by human rights. Finally, distinguishing these two levels may have another important benefit. It may allow us to see more clearly the unique or distinct contributions that certain traditions might have to offer to the international community by way of supporting new human rights norms or emphases. For example, Buddhist dependent co-origination; Confucian one-bodiedness with heaven, earth, and the myriad things; and the emphasis of indigenous religions on the interdependence of humanity and nature may help guide the international community in recognizing and developing what have been called "green" rights.

Some Traditions

So far I have been approaching the issue of the possible connections between religion and human rights from the direction of properly understanding international human rights, and I have found some reasons for their compatibility and convergence. Now I will approach the matter from the other direction by considering some examples of religious traditions. For strategic reasons I have selected examples that are non-Western, represent multitudes of people, illuminate some of my earlier points, present controversial issues, and may make useful contributions to attaining a more humane ethos in the contemporary world. My examples are Confucianism and the class of indigenous religious traditions. For obvious reasons my discussion of these traditions must be selective and partial and must make great use of generalizations.

The Confucian Tradition

Confucianism has shaped the lives and thought of a very large percentage of people who have lived on this planet, principally in China but also in other East Asian societies as well (e.g., Japan and Korea). Although its overt status and influence have been considerably muted in this century due to the revolution and reeducation pursued by Chinese Marxism, the fact remains that Confucianism continues to affect the Chinese people in significant ways, particularly with regard to family structure, family cohesiveness, and related moral values. Moreover, with the passing of Mao Zedong and the decreasing influence and effectiveness of communism in the world, Beijing is searching for an alternative or at least a supplementary worldview and political philosophy to facilitate its efforts at modernization and economic development and to shore up its political legitimacy (see, e.g., de Bary 1995). An obvious candidate for this position is the Confucian tradition, making it especially important to understand this tradition's possible relationship to human rights in the contemporary world.

One common perception of the Confucian tradition is that it is authoritarian, hierarchical, meritocratic, and intrinsically resistant to human rights of any sort. Indeed, it is claimed by some scholars of the tradition that at its deepest moral and conceptual level, Confucianism is simply incompatible with human rights (see, e.g., Rosemont 1988). I believe that some of these perceptions are shortsighted and should be countered in the strongest possible way, especially if it is likely that the Confucian tradition will reemerge as a stronger social and political force in China. Contrary to these views, I wish to propose that all three generations of human rights, with varying degrees of emphasis, are compatible with the Confucian tradition.[4] Let me begin by offering a brief characterization of the tradition that I believe many scholars and adherents would accept.

The Confucian tradition is communitarian in outlook. That is to say, it holds that persons are essentially socially interrelated beings, and it emphasizes duties that people must pursue toward the common good as well as virtues needed for the fulfillment of those duties. Furthermore, Confucianism holds that certain reciprocal role relationships (e.g., ruler-subject, parent-child, elder sibling–younger sibling) are crucial in achieving a flourishing community of basic trust among persons all working together in a mutually supportive way to achieve a good life for all. At the same time, the tradition also emphasizes for all its adherents, from ruler to commoner, the importance of personal moral self-cultivation in relationship with others— "a benevolent man helps others to take their stand in so far as he himself wishes to take his stand, and gets others there in so far as he himself wishes to get there." (Confucius, in Lau 1979, VI:30). This self-cultivation incorporates the view that all people have the moral potential to develop the interrelated virtues of benevolence (compassion), righteousness (justice), propriety (civility), and wisdom (moral discernment), particularly when they are guided by moral exemplars (sages) who are themselves guided by their discerning interpretations of the tradition's basic texts (revealing a deep orientation to history and collective memory). This strong emphasis on individuals interrelated in the community is further grounded in a cosmological-metaphysical vision of the interdependence of all beings in the universe, which in turn sustains and develops a basic human sympathy for the whole and its constituent parts. This ideal of sympathy is cast in the image of extending care from within family relationships into ever larger concentric circles of care for others.

As a consequence of this vision, the Confucian tradition is greatly concerned about all those conditions—for example, social, economic, and educational—that bear on people's ability to cultivate their moral potential to flourish as responsible members of an organically flourishing community in a harmoniously functioning universe. This is not an unattractive moral vision, even to Western sensibilities, and I believe that it may not only be compatible with human rights but also support the international understanding of them. Let me briefly indicate why.

The tradition has historically emphasized in both its classical and subsequent phases the benevolent responsibility of the ruler or state to ensure the material welfare of the people—providing, for example, subsistence, livelihood, education, and famine relief. Such benefits are conceived as conditions necessary for people's moral self-cultivation of their potential, and to deny them these benefits means denying them the opportunity to fulfill their human and cosmological destiny. This is a primary theme in both Confucius (fifth century B.C.E.) and Mencius (third century B.C.E.), whose works contain much advice to kings along these lines. The theme is even taken so far as to impose limits on political legitimacy. Mencius, for example, advances the notion of righteous revolt against an emperor who, in materially oppressing the people, loses the "Mandate of Heaven" (the ultimate source of political legitimacy) (Lau 1970, 1B:8, 1B:12, 1A:7, 7B:14). Now it seems to me a short step from this kind of argument to the contention that the tradition has the resources to appreciate the second generation of human rights, which concern matters of material welfare. In fact, we may see this compatibility working in the background in the openness of twentieth-century Chinese regimes to the idea of socioeconomic rights as well as in their efforts to better the material conditions of the Chinese people (see Kent 1993, chap. 2). Of course, Marxism remains in the foreground in China, but the Confucian background may help to explain why a Western political import such as the concept of human rights has had such an appeal among the Chinese people.

There is also reason to suggest that the Confucian tradition may be more open to civil-political rights than is usually perceived. Here I would begin by citing Mencius's ideas of the human moral potential that is shared equally by all human beings and of the "natural nobility" (or "nobility of Heaven") that is attainable by all who develop this potential self-con-

sciously (see Bloom 1998). These ideas clearly strike themes of egalitarian-
ism, human dignity, and voluntarism similar to those underlying the first
generation of human rights. Even more to the point are those later Neo-
Confucian thinkers (eleventh–seventeenth centuries C.E.) who, in building
on the ideas of Mencius, advanced strong claims about the moral nature of
humankind, individual perfectibility, and the autonomy of the moral mind
and individual conscience. They also advanced provocative proposals regarding the self-governance of local communities, a reformed conception of
the law as a necessary force to check the political abuse of the people, and
even a conception of public education as a means of enhancing people's political participation in their communities (de Bary 1983).

I believe that notions such as these tend to move in the direction of recognizing the civil-political rights of individuals as positive enpowerments
for their mutual involvement in social and political processes aimed at communal flourishing. Here I might also point out that some contemporary
scholars of Confucianism as well as Confucian human rights activists self-
consciously represent the tradition as incorporating a heritage of ideas open
to civil-political rights and democracy, contrary to the neoauthoritarian
and antidemocratic representations of some political leaders (e.g., Lee
Kwan Yew of Singapore) (see, e.g., Kim 1994).

I would also suggest that the Confucian worldview is open to collective
rights. This suggestion is supported in part by the notion of righteous rebellion by the people collectively against material oppression and by the Neo-
Confucian recognition of the importance of communal self-government,
both of which tend in the direction of collective rights to political self-determination and community development. This tendency may also be supported by that highest of Confucian ideals—"the unity of Man and
Heaven" or "one body with heaven, earth and the myriad things"—which
defines humankind not only in anthropological but also cosmological terms
(Tu 1985, 171–181). This ideal extends Confucian humanism and its sense
of moral responsibility to a planetary or even universal scale, recognizing
collective claims to peace, harmony, and the well-being of the entire holistic
community of interdependent beings.

There are, then, reasons for thinking that the Confucian tradition—contrary to some popular and even scholarly perceptions—has the resources to
recognize, appreciate, and accept the priority of values represented by international human rights. This remains true even if the tradition itself prefers
not to internally employ the language of rights or human rights. If Confucianism were to reemerge as an important influence in China, one could
imagine productive internal and cross-cultural dialogues resulting in the
tradition's more explicit self-understanding in terms of these rights.[5] Moreover, such dialogues could result in Confucian contributions to the international human rights consensus: for example, strengthening the understand-

ing of civil-political rights as enpowerments aimed at community involvement and flourishing; demonstrating how the virtues of benevolence, civility, and trust can contribute to an effective human rights ethos; and cooperating with other traditions in advancing the importance of protecting the ecosystem for the interdependent communities of beings on the planet.[6]

Indigenous Traditions

In discussing briefly indigenous traditions and peoples in relation to human rights, I am obviously taking up a class of traditions, not just one, and this I frankly concede runs the risk of doing any one or all of them the injustice of an inadequately nuanced explication. But there is some justification for this strategy, beyond economy of presentation. For example, in drafting their recent declaration on indigenous peoples' human rights, members of these traditions have themselves discerned commonalties in their belief, practice, and circumstance. Of course, political reasons may be uppermost in their minds in regarding themselves in this way, for by not being organized into nation-states they are, as separate peoples, relatively powerless in the international arena. So there are sound political reasons—along the lines of strength in numbers and unity—for indigenous peoples to regard themselves as a common class. Nevertheless, from my limited perspective they do appear to share enough similarities to warrant considering them as a group, and as we shall see there may be advantages in so doing.

Indigenous traditions and peoples are prevalent throughout the world—for example, in Asia, Africa, the Americas, and the Pacific islands. There are hundreds of such traditions, representing more than 300 million people, many of them oppressed by surrounding dominant cultures and societies. Despite their great variety in terms of language, culture, history, religion, and social organization, these peoples appear to share some significant features. For example, though their religious beliefs are quite diverse—incorporating various views of divine transcendence and immanence, the relationality of human beings and the cosmic life, the connection between the physical and spiritual realms, connections between ancestors and living persons and families—their worldviews tend to connect them spiritually to natural environments and bioregional locations crucial to their religious expression (e.g., sacred natural sites, rivers and lakes, flora and fauna) (see Grim 1995). This spiritual connection to a bioregion is also tightly bound with social and economic ties to the same location. To use another example, again despite their diverse worldviews, indigenous peoples have religious beliefs that tend to support a metaphysically grounded moral orientation to the idea of group solidarity and what is sometimes called a thick theory of the good, defined in terms of communal flourishing and involving an understanding of persons as fulfilled in community roles. Moreover, despite their variety of social structures and circumstances, many indigenous traditions follow patriarchal models of social organization in which women are subjugated to male authority. Finally, many of these peoples are reactive against the values and practices of modern secular life in the dominant culture, particularly when these threaten the environment and ecosystem, which are so important to their lives spiritually, socially, and economically.

A common perception of these traditions is that they are in considerable tension with human rights values, particularly with regard to their tendencies toward group primacy and patriarchy.[7] I will consider each of these tensions in turn, beginning with group primacy. It is true that one of the principal differences between the values of indigenous religions and human rights involves the balancing of individual and group interests, though we may also encounter some misperceptions here as well. The international human rights community has tended historically to focus on the importance of the rights of individuals, whereas the moral attitudes of indigenous traditions are largely focused on the importance of the community and internal subgroups (e.g., family or clan) (Zion 1992, 194–195). In the former case, while individuals are conceived as social beings located in the community, they can be perceived apart from the social context in order to be protected from its oppressive influence. In the latter case, the individual cannot be so easily separated from the group, for it is only there that the individual has identity and dignity (as a group member). As a consequence of this difference in understanding social reality, not only are indigenous traditions thought to be hostile to human rights but also indigenous peoples themselves often interpret human rights as dangerous to them. That is, these peoples often regard human rights oriented to the dignity and equality of individuals as a means for the outside world to further assimilate and destroy their communities and traditions—through the imposition of a set of values that would undermine and supplant their way of life (Zion 1992, 193). So when this deep orientation to group solidarity is brought into contact with human rights, indigenous people, according to one scholar, often tend to develop such rights in the direction of the idea that "dignity is achieved by fulfillment of understood roles, through community sharing, and by the espousal of group rights as paramount over individual aspirations" (McChesney 1992, 222).

In order to probe this tension more deeply, however, we need to press a few obvious questions. Is it true that human rights are resistant to the notion of communal rights? Is it true that the moral attitudes of indigenous traditions are thoroughly hostile to individual rights, or might there be a diversity of views or nuances on the relative importance of group and individual?

For one thing, we have already seen that it is a misunderstanding to think that human rights exclude the recognition of collective or group rights.

Both of the international covenants acknowledge that all peoples have collective rights of self-determination regarding their political status and their economic, social, and cultural development. Moreover, both covenants also acknowledge that all peoples have the collective right to use their natural resources as they see fit according to their circumstances. Although it may be true that there is as yet no procedure for effectively arbitrating claims about violations of these rights, especially in the case of nonstate entities such as indigenous groups, these acknowledgments clearly show that human rights are not opposed to the concept of group rights.

Moreover, coming at the issue from the other side, indigenous traditions are not universally and thoroughly opposed to the rights of individuals. Indeed, in the case of some—for example, the Iroquois or Six Nations Confederacies in North America—there are reasons for thinking that the rights of individuals can coexist with communal rights. In this particular case, according to a number of historians and political theorists, the laws of the Iroquois Confederacy, founded in the epic legend of the Great Peacemaker, tended as far back as the seventeenth and eighteenth centuries (if not earlier) to balance unity, brotherhood, and group solidarity against the "natural rights" of all group members and the necessity to share resources equitably (Grinde 1992; Lyons 1993). Furthermore, it has been claimed that these rights significantly parallel the "Four Freedoms" of Franklin D. Roosevelt: freedom from fear, freedom from want, freedom of speech, and freedom of religion (Wallace 1994, 67–89).

Or, to take an example from the other side of the world, the Akan tradition in Ghana explicitly balances a notion of equal human dignity—derived from each person's possession of an inherent divine element, *okra*—with the notion of intrinsic human sociality—orienting individuals to membership in the group (Ilesanmi 1995, 315–316). This is done in such a way as to maintain that all persons are entitled to, for example, assurance of self-actualization, financial security, health assistance, and intimate human relationship, within a society of mutual aid, support, and solidarity. This balancing is nicely symbolized by two Akan proverbs: "When a human being descends upon the earth from above, he lands in a town"; and "A human being needs help" (Ilesanmi 1995, 315). This sort of understanding of the person—as individual supported by community—may even be useful to us in thinking about our own views of the individual person.

Moreover, as with other traditions in the contemporary world, we need to be attentive to the fact that there is a diversity of views within particular indigenous cultures—they too have their dissidents, minority interests, and feminists who, while recognizing the importance of the group, are also deeply concerned to argue from within their traditions that their moral and religious attitudes support other values as well. Furthermore, and I will return to this point shortly, the UN Draft Declaration of Indigenous Peoples

Rights clearly intends to provide a viable balancing of individual and collective human rights.

Let us now turn to the other tension—patriarchy versus the rights of women—by first setting a realistic contemporary context for its consideration. I believe that special sensitivity to group rights is called for in the case of indigenous peoples and traditions because they are vulnerable and fragile in the contemporary world. They are vulnerable because they are not organized into states and are therefore largely unrepresented in international forums. They are fragile precisely because of their deep connections to natural environments over which they exercise little control, being subject to encroachment by insensitive modern societies. To preserve their traditions and cultures, therefore, indigenous peoples need to invoke strongly their collective rights. In so doing, however, they may infringe upon other sorts of human rights recognized by the international community. If an indigenous society is patriarchal, the interests of women within that society could be jeopardized. To insist that these peoples observe international standards of women's rights, however, could in some cases lead to the destruction of an already threatened social structure, thereby harming their collective rights. This is an agonizing dilemma to which there are no easy answers.

The situation could, however, be helped by encouraging and supporting internal and cross-cultural dialogues among the indigenous traditions themselves. In fact, dialogues exploring the reconciliation of respect for indigenous cultures with the rights of their individual members (including women) are now taking place in connection with drafting and fine-tuning a declaration for indigenous peoples' rights. This process has examined indigenous moral values in relation to the full array of human rights, resulting in a cross-traditional declaration that attempts to integrate these values with human rights in a manner appropriate to indigenous peoples' situation of common vulnerability. Beyond this negotiation among their traditions, these peoples have also been conducting dialogues within their respective communities in order to engage the diverse voices and perspectives within their own traditions. And so, in addition to finding claims seeking "respect for our rights to self-determination . . . to benefit from our resources . . . to self-government," we also find statements admitting that "we, the indigenous and tribal people, must also recognize our past mistakes. . . . Often we have not fully respected the rights of women in our cultures" (Ewen 1994, 41, 101).

The upshot of these dialogues is symbolized well in the balance between group and individual rights, including the rights of women and the disadvantaged, achieved by the draft declaration. While clearly emphasizing "the fundamental importance of the right of self-determination of all peoples," this document also explicitly states that "indigenous peoples have the right to the full and effective enjoyment of all human rights and fundamental freedoms"; that "they have the individual rights to life, physical and mental integrity, liberty, and security of person"; that "particular attention should be paid to the rights and special needs of indigenous elders, women, children, and disabled persons"; and that "all those rights and freedoms recognized herein are equally guaranteed to male and female individuals" (Ewen 1994, 159–174). Thus there is some reason to expect that these peoples and traditions, operating under this declaration, will themselves develop ways, if they do not have them already, to counteract patriarchy.

It is somewhat ironic, but entirely understandable, that some of the world's most oppressed peoples and traditions are among those that most effectively recognize the interdependent generations of human rights. Moreover, they appear to be positioned to make distinct contributions to the international human rights consensus, which may well resonate with the views of other religious traditions. For example, beyond showing us concretely that it is possible to integrate group rights with individual rights, indigenous peoples are also vigorously advancing fresh human rights emphases on the importance of protecting, for present and future generations, "the ecology and harmony of Mother Earth," respecting "the collective right to live in freedom, peace, and security *as distinct peoples,*" and respecting "the right of peoples to manifest, practice, and develop their spiritual and religious traditions" in such a way as "to have access to their religious and cultural sites" (Ewen 1994, 163, 165). Although such rights are being claimed by indigenous peoples on their own behalf, they are also clearly relevant to many other peoples and traditions as well.

Conclusion

I think it would be useful to return to the three problems about religion and human rights with which I began, to see whether anything I have said could shed some light on their resolution. With respect to recent challenges to the universality of human rights, I believe that I have shown that human rights are not simply a Western moral ideology inappropriate to the rest of the world's traditions and peoples. Far from it. These are moral priorities shared by many, if not all, religious and cultural traditions. We have investigated this matter from two angles of vision—first, by showing that international human rights are a result of international and intercultural agreements and are in principle compatible with a diversity of traditions; and second, by showing that certain non-Western traditions sometimes perceived as hostile to human rights have, upon further consideration, the resources to be open to them as well as to contribute to their constructive advance. If this is true in even the difficult cases, one suspects that it is true in many others as well.

Can my approach help ease the resistance of religious fundamentalisms to human rights? I think that it can, for I believe that I can find some grounds for comparison and dialogue. Although it is true that fundamentalist movements are generally suspicious of international human rights, which they tend to associate with the "demonic" secularism of the modern world, it is not entirely true to say that they lack values and commitments resonant with human rights (see Kelsay and Twiss 1994, 27–28). For example, many of these movements deplore war, torture, and genocide—attitudes clearly consistent with individual and collective rights to physical security and suggestive of some shared ground. Moreover, most of these movements are deeply and actively committed to advancing practical measures for adequate nutrition, housing, medical care, education, and other essential social services, positioning them positively in relation to second-generation human rights. To be sure, such matters as gender equality and freedom of thought and expression remain deeply contested issues for fundamentalists, but the approach I have been developing demonstrates at least some ground for comparison and dialogue of a constructive sort, keeping open the possibility that these movements may in the future find internal resources for accepting more fully and self-consciously the international consensus on human rights.

Finally, with respect to the role of religion in violent conflict, my approach may be helpful, if only in an indirect way, by identifying and affirming the positive resources in religious traditions for the recognition and support of human rights. It does this in two ways. First, by trying to explicitly link the moral values of these traditions to the international consensus on human rights, my approach may assist in strengthening a convergent coalition of human endeavor against violence in the world. Second, in trying to maximize opportunities for internal and cross-cultural human rights dialogues, this approach may help to make "the other" less alien and threatening and thereby assist in counteracting the behavior that draws lines between in-group and out-group and fuels intergroup conflict. In both of these ways, then, my approach may help foster an ethos oriented toward respect for the important moral values represented by international human rights and by the corresponding aspects of religious traditions supportive of peace, dignity, and justice for individuals as well as communities.

Notes

1. The Project on Religion and Human Rights, originally located at Human Rights Watch, New York City, is now housed by the Law and Religion Program, School of Law, Emory University, Atlanta, Georgia 30322-2770. Its first publication, *Religion and Human Rights* (Kelsay and Twiss 1994), is available from that address. My statement of the problems here draws freely from the consultation group papers published in that book. I wish to acknowledge my debt to the other principal authors of those papers, namely, John Kelsay (Florida State University) and Charles B. Strozier (John Jay College, City University of New York).

2. In the following section, I profit considerably from the work of my co-collaborators, Abdullahi A. An-Na'im (Emory University) and Ann Elizabeth Mayer (University of Pennsylvania). For an earlier and more extensive summary of these findings, see Twiss and Grelle 1995, 25–29.

3. This section draws heavily from three prior publications: Twiss and Grelle 1995, 29–35; Twiss 1996, 362–373; and Twiss 1998. The formulations of the issues in these publications are much more extensive and nuanced than in the present chapter.

4. The following discussion of Confucianism and human rights is drawn from Twiss 1997. This topic is extended and deepened considerably in my unpublished paper, "Confucianism, Humane Governance, and Human Rights," presented at the Conference on Confucianism and Humanism at the East-West Center, the University of Hawaii, in May 1996.

5. Such cross-cultural dialogues have been spearheaded by Wm. Theodore de Bary (Columbia University) and Tu Wei-ming (Harvard University) at two international conferences on Confucianism and human rights held at the East-West Center, the University of Hawaii, in August 1995 and May 1996.

6. This might be an apt place to remark that the Confucian tradition, as represented by a Chinese delegate, in fact influenced the formulation of the first article of the 1948 UN Universal Declaration of Human Rights. The first version of this article read: "All men are brothers. As human beings with the gift of reason and members of a single family, they are free and equal in dignity and rights." The Chinese delegate argued for the inclusion of "two-men-mindedness"—the Confucian idea of a fundamental sympathy, compassion, or benevolence built into human nature—in addition to "the gift of reason." The wording finally adopted included "conscience" in addition to "reason," with the understanding that "conscience" referred to the emotional and sympathetic basis of morality, a "germ" or potential present in all persons, which reason must cultivate. Not only does this suggest that the declaration is less ethnocentric than some have supposed but it also suggests that the Confucian tradition may have more to offer to the international consensus on human rights. This historical report is taken from Bori 1994, chap. 7.

7. The following discussion is drawn from two earlier publications, Kelsay and Twiss 1994, 54–59, and Twiss and Grelle 1995, 40–45. For some of the formulations of the issues that follow, I am deeply indebted to Ann Mayer and other participants in the Project on Religion and Human Rights, notably Bishop Paul Reeves (a Maori from New Zealand), Oren Lyons (a Faithkeeper of the Turtle Clan, Onondaga Nation; State University of New York, Buffalo), John Mohawk (Seneca Nation; State University of New York, Buffalo), and Kusumita Pedersen (St. Francis College, Brooklyn).

References

Bloom, Irene. 1998. "Fundamental Intuitions and Consensus Statements: Mencian Confucianism and Human Rights." In *Confucianism and Human Rights*, edited by Wm. Theodore de Bary. New York: Columbia University Press. In press.

Bori, Pier Cesare. 1994. *From Hermeneutics to Ethical Consensus Among Cultures*. Atlanta: Scholars Press.

de Bary, Wm. Theodore. 1983. *The Liberal Tradition in China*. Hong Kong and New York: Chinese University Press and Columbia University Press.

_____. 1995. "The New Confucianism in Beijing." *The American Scholar* 64, 2 (Spring):175–189.

Ewen, Alexander, ed. 1994. *Voice of Indigenous Peoples: Native People Address the United Nations*, with the United Nations Draft Declaration of Indigenous Peoples Rights. Santa Fe, N.Mex.: Clear Light Publishers.

Grim, John A. 1995. "Native American Religions." In *Encyclopedia of Bioethics*. Revised Edition, edited by Warren T. Reich. Vol. 4, 1799–1805. New York: Simon and Schuster Macmillan.

Grinde, Donald A. 1992. "Iroquois Political Theory and the Roots of American Democracy." In *Exiled in the Land of the Free: Democracy, Indian Nations, and the U. S. Constitution*, edited by Oren Lyons et al., 227–280, notes 378–394. Santa Fe, N.Mex.: Clear Light Publishers.

Hollenbach, David. 1994. "A Communitarian Reconstruction of Human Rights: Contributions From Catholic Tradition." In *Catholicism and Liberalism: Contributions to American Public Policy*, edited by R. Bruce Douglas and David Hollenbach, 125–150. Cambridge: Cambridge University Press.

Humphrey, John P. 1984. *Human Rights and the United Nations: A Great Adventure*. Dobbs Ferry, N.Y.: Transnational Publishers.

Ilesanmi, Simeon O. 1995. "Human Rights Discourse in Modern Africa: A Comparative Religious Ethical Perspective." *Journal of Religious Ethics* 23, 2 (Fall):293–322.

Kelsay, John, and Sumner B. Twiss, eds. 1994. *Religion and Human Rights*. New York: The Project on Religion and Human Rights.

Kent, Ann. 1993. *Between Freedom and Substance: China and Human Rights*. Hong Kong and New York: Oxford University Press.

Kim Dae Jung. 1994. "Is Culture Dying? The Myth of Asia's Anti-Democratic Values." *Foreign Affairs* 73, 6 (November-December):189–194.

Lau, D. C., trans. 1970. *Mencius*. London: Penguin Books.

_____. 1979. *The Analects*. London: Penguin Books.

Loewy, Erich H. 1993. *Freedom and Community: The Ethics of Interdependence*. Albany: State University of New York Press.

Lyons, Oren. 1993. *What They Never Told Us*. New York: American Indian Law Alliance.

Marty, Martin E. 1995. "Comparing Fundamentalisms." *Contention: Debates in Society, Culture, and Science* 4, 2 (Winter):19–39.

McChesney, Allan. 1992. "Aboriginal Communities, Aboriginal Rights, and the Human Rights System in Canada." In *Human Rights in Cross-Cultural Perspectives: A Quest for Consensus*, edited by Abdullahi A. An-Na'im, 221–252. Philadelphia: University of Pennsylvania Press.

Park, Han S. 1987. "Correlates of Human Rights: Global Tendencies." *Human Rights Quarterly* 9:405–413.

Rosemont, Henry. 1988. "Why Take Rights Seriously? A Confucian Critique." In *Human Rights and the World's Religions*, edited by Leroy Rouner, 167–182. Notre Dame, Ind.: University of Notre Dame Press.

Tu, Wei-ming. 1985. *Confucian Thought: Selfhood As Creative Transformation.* Albany: State University of New York Press.

Twiss, Sumner B. 1996. "Comparative Ethics and Intercultural Human-Rights Dialogues: A Programmatic Inquiry." In *Christian Ethics: Problems and Prospects,* edited by Lisa S. Cahill and James F. Childress, 357–378. Cleveland: Pilgrim Press.

_____. 1998. "A Constructive Framework for Discussing Confucianism and Human Rights." In *Confucianism and Human Rights,* edited by Wm. Theodore de Bary. New York: Columbia University Press. In press.

Twiss, Sumner B., and Bruce Grelle. 1995. "Human Rights and Comparative Religious Ethics: A New Venue." *The Annual of the Society of Christian Ethics*:21–48.

Wallace, Paul. 1994. *The Iroquois Book of Life: White Roots of Peace.* Santa Fe, N.Mex.: Clear Light Publishers. Originally published, Philadelphia: University of Pennsylvania Press, 1946.

Weston, Burns H. 1992. "Human Rights." In *Human Rights in the World Community: Issues and Action.* 2nd edition, edited by Richard Pierre Claude and Burns H. Weston, 14–30. Philadelphia: University of Pennsylvania Press.

Zion, James W. 1992. "North American Indian Perspectives on Human Rights." In *Human Rights in Cross-Cultural Perspectives: A Quest for Consensus,* edited by Abdullahi A. An-Na'im, 191–220. Philadelphia: University of Pennsylvania Press.

Chapter Seven

The Problem of Distributive Justice in World Religions

JAMES F. SMURL
Indiana University at Indianapolis

This chapter has three aims. One is to show why there is a problem in talking about distributive justice in most contemporary societies, cultures, and religious traditions. The second is to demonstrate how the beliefs and practices encouraged by many religious traditions point out the need, the demand, and the opportunities for just allocations of the benefits and burdens of lives knit together by resources and services known as social goods. The third and final aim is to suggest how, through scholarship, interreligious conversations, and practical programs, peoples of the world might make their own context-dependent expressions of distributive justice more widely intelligible and effective.

Problems in Talking About Distributive Justice

People around the world rarely use the term "distributive justice" when expressing their hopes for and disappointments with life in common with others. More often they talk about alleviating human suffering and promoting human betterment or they express their hopes for and disappointments with society in terms of social justice or human rights. Nonetheless, what they are talking about and calling for is, arguably, what I call distributive justice.

By distributive justice I refer to a just apportioning of the benefits and burdens in several spheres of social goods that people have in common. The spheres may be more private as are families, or more public as are education, law, health care, the economy, and politics. The benefits and burdens in these spheres include, to cite just a few illustrations, those associated with the husbanding of natural resources like land, water, and plant and animal life; and those that ensure that people have access to basic securities and provisions like public safety, food, and shelter. Distributive justice is not just a matter of who gets which of these resources, securities, and provisions, or when, where, and how they get them. It also is a matter of who pays, suffers, sacrifices, and bears the burdens of those benefits.

Benefits and burdens will come in different forms in spheres as varied as the family and the legal system, for example. The social goods being apportioned are different, as are the parties involved. In a legal contract for the purchase of an automobile, for instance, the contracting parties may have no ongoing relationship, and the risks or burdens of defaulting usually will fall heaviest on the one who defaults. Family members are closer to each other and share different social goods like food and shelter. The burdens for providing such benefits will fall more heavily on the adult members or on those best able to bear them. In families as in legal arrangements, however, the people involved exhibit a kind of solidarity in making common life flourish by accepting its responsibilities and sacrifices.

No matter which sphere of common life and shared social goods we consider, what's needed are not only just activities but also just people and just situations or social structures. The benefits and burdens associated with the social goods and services through which people relate to each other will be distributed justly only if and when the people involved are characterized by integrity and a commitment to justice and when they are making an effort to be fair. Still, even honorable people who try to behave in principled ways in distributing the benefits and burdens of the social goods in their trust can fail unless the social structures or the institutions they develop help sustain distributive justice. For instance, a tax structure that undermines the commitments of just people to allocate tax burdens fairly will interfere with and derail their commitments to distributive justice. But even just people living under relatively just social arrangements cannot always avert harm to their fellow citizens in the way they allot the benefits and burdens of social goods. In such a case, the best they can do is to alleviate any suffering and ensure that the harms are justifiable and proportioned to persons' capacities to sustain and recover from them.

Discussing such matters in terms of distributive justice can create problems for several reasons. Some people rarely experience a sufficient measure of such justice at home or in social spheres like education, law, health care, economics, and politics. They often spot problems of distributive justice too late or in ways that lead them to blame such problems on someone else. Often they identify the problem and its causes in highly charged rhetorical terms invoking human rights, equality, or social justice. Aggravating this already substantial list of problems is the fact that distributive justice is not well-understood in conventional Western theory and practical reasoning and is not sufficiently prominent either in comparative religious ethics or in interreligious dialogues.

This oversight in Western societies may be due in part to the fact that, because they are influenced by capitalism, conventional theory and practical reasoning generally assume that the primary subject of distributive justice is the allocation of income and wealth. As a result, interreligious and intergovernmental plans for action become so narrow in scope that they delimit considerations to economic wealth and poverty, to questions of redistributing wealth and income, and to divisions of rich and poor nations. Those surely are problems of distributive justice, but they are not the only problems, not even the most pressing and close to home. Should the increasingly global sharing of scholarship and dialogue hew to this traditional Western bias, some serious consequences would result. One would be the likelihood that research and dialogue, and the ensuing plans and actions, would become increasingly out of touch with the people they aim to assist. Another would be the irresponsible failure to acknowledge the importance of the theme of distributive justice in the narratives and practices of the world's religions. And a third would be the failure to consider—and the subsequent failure to take action to prevent—the conflicts that often arise precisely because of failures to approximate the ideals of distributive justice. Hoping to avoid such undesirable consequences, I next offer some reasons why distributive justice should be a more preeminent consideration in comparative religious ethics and interreligious dialogues

Distributive Justice in the World's Religions

Distributive justice as defined above has long been at least an implicit concern of the world's major religions. This is sometimes difficult to detect, however, since particular religions express this concern in ways shaped by historical, social, and cultural circumstances not similarly experienced by others. Furthermore, they express this concern in sources as varied as their respective foundational sacred texts, with doctrinal explanations coming from different times and places and with rituals and social practices, even within a single tradition, varying from region to region. Changes as well as continuities characterize traditions over the course of their distinct histories, and there can be significant differences between what they teach and what their practitioners actually do. As a result, scholars generally advise that one ask the following questions: Which form of a particular religion is being discussed? Which of its textual or other sources are used as evidence? Who best speaks for that tradition? From which era and locale does a particular expression come?

Given these daunting challenges and the relatively short space in which to address them, I have chosen an appropriately modest agenda for this part of the chapter. Only three religious traditions will be used as illustrations—namely, Buddhism, Christianity, and Islam. In all instances I will be careful to note which form of these religions we are considering and who best speaks for that part of the tradition. Specific eras and locale will be noted, textual and other sources will be identified, and some attention will be paid to a few contemporary expressions of distributive justice in these traditions

Buddhism

The oldest, most traditional form of Buddhism, Theravada Buddhism, is principally monastic and builds upon sacred scriptures written around the second century B.C.E. and collected in the official Pali canon. Theravada Buddhism often has been considered individualistic and bent on self-perfection, without much concern for the social good in general or for distributive justice in particular. That such is not the case in the foundational texts of the Pali canon has been argued by one who inhabits the world of Buddhism and has a scholarly reputation for the careful interpretation of its official texts—namely, the contemporary high-ranking Theravada Buddhist monk and textual scholar Phra Rajavaramuni from Thailand (Rajavaramuni 1990).

First, in a series of inferences drawn from Pali texts, Rajavaramuni shows how the benefits and burdens of social relationships should be distributed justly. Not only should the monastic community live in harmony; it should do so by, among other things, dividing gains and acquisitions equally among members. Furthermore, monks are bound to the laity because they are dependent upon them for food and other material necessities; in turn, the monks must teach and pray for the laity and, when necessary, offer them the hospitality of the monastery.

Next, Rajavaramuni identifies two traditional Theravadan themes that connect the good of society with the good of the individual. Both of these themes are arguably expressions of a deep and abiding concern for distributive justice. The first theme states that a society composed of people freed from attachment and pursuing perfection can be stable, secure, and peaceful. Conversely, such a society is conducive to the growth, development, and perfection of individuals. This kind of society can be maintained only when all members take responsibility for their own well-being. This duty will vary according to the extent of an individual's capacity to influence society. But all individuals must become just people and good citizens by developing the virtues, habits, and behaviors of good Buddhists—and that includes being economically, intellectually, and morally dependable. For his part, the king, at least in the Thai tradition, should maintain the social order by distributing wealth to the poor and by leading a life of royal virtue. And, finally, the monks should teach both the common people and the king how to acquire these virtues, how to act responsibly for the benefit of social welfare, and how to reach toward individual perfection.

The second theme deals with attitudes toward poverty and wealth. Poverty is seen as the primary source of crime, disorder, and greed; it is absent when there is an accumulation of wealth or economic sufficiency, which are prerequisites for a stable and secure society conducive to individual development and perfection. Hence, wealth is necessary and desirable as long as it is acquired legitimately and used to promote social as well as individual well-being. Laypeople who seek and gain wealth in upright ways and use it for the good and happiness of others as well as for their own needs are praiseworthy. It is assumed that wealthy people can do more for the social good than can poor people. But if wealth develops at the expense of or to the detriment of the community, then society should seek other ways to regulate its acquisition and distribution to ensure that it promotes individual and social development. Individual monks who become personally rich exhibit a form of greed and attachment inimical to Buddhist principles. Echoing claims often made in Western monasticism, Buddhist monks can justify material gains if such gains belong to the community as a whole.

In so reading these two themes in the foundational texts of Theravada Buddhism, Rajavaramuni makes a strong case that they are deeply concerned with distributive justice. But what evidence from history or contemporary living shows that this concern has been put into practice? Foundational texts are just that—foundational. Their interpretation and implementation over the course of centuries are marked by changes as well as continuities.

Approximately three centuries after the inception of Buddhism in the sixth century B.C.E., the Indian King Aśoka created a Buddhist state in which social welfare and the common good were dominant themes. His policies, or edicts, were engraved on rocks. Rock Edict II ordered the provision of medical facilities for men and women. Rock Edict III enjoined, among other things, generosity toward priests and ascetics, and frugality in spending. In Rock Edict V, Aśoka ordered his officers to work for the welfare and happiness of the poor and aged (Strong 1983, 4–5; Ling 1973, 183–212) In these edicts, Aśoka exemplified the concern for distributive justice found in the Pali canon of Buddhism's sacred texts.

At different times and in different locales, Buddhist societies had to find new ways of regulating wealth to ensure that it would promote social and individual development. Sometimes, as Frank Reynolds has observed, this included efforts to regulate the wealth of property-holding communities of monks as well as that of individual Buddhists (Reynolds 1990). Although societies in India, Sri Lanka, and Southeast Asia addressed them differently, some common themes and patterns appeared. Periods of monastic accumulation were followed by periods of reform. Reforms often were prompted by the fact that the monastic leadership was allied to economic and political elites. The laity, for their part, were supposed to acquire wealth in accordance with the Buddhist principle of productive activity. They were to manage and expend wealth in ways that benefited the community at large as well as themselves, but never wastefully or irresponsibly. To counterbalance their failures, laypeople were encouraged to practice giving or *dana* to show the community that they had achieved a measure of nonattachment. In sum, past records show that Buddhist societies redistributed natural resources and wealth to realign the benefits and burdens of social goods (Kemper 1990; Keyes 1990).

Sarvodaya Shramadana.   That Theravada Buddhism's historical record is being replicated in more recent times is evident in the activities of a Sri Lankan movement known as Sarvodaya Shramadana (which literally means "universal awakening through sharing of time, thought, and energy"). This movement was launched in 1958, ten years after Sri Lanka gained its independence from Great Britain. A. T. Ariyaratne, a young teacher in a Buddhist college in Colombo, together with a group of colleagues and teachers spent time in a depressed village to learn from it and then to use that knowledge to improve rural life. Subsequently, Ariyaratne launched a movement designed to awaken first individual personalities in villages, then whole villages, leading eventually to development activities and programs in the worst-off rural villages (Goulet 1988, 69; see also Ratnapala 1980, 470)

So stating his goals, Ariyaratne drew upon the traditional Theravada Buddhist teachings known as the Four Noble Truths, the fourth of which emphasizes how to end life's sufferings by pursuing the eightfold noble path to awakening, or enlightenment. Seen in this light, progress toward the goal of material development in villages hinges on villagers' progress toward awakening (in part by becoming more just persons) and on progress in creating just social conditions—two of the three legs in what I call the tripod of distributive justice. In addition to spiritual awakening, the movement also emphasized a moral element (right action and right livelihood as prescribed in the eightfold path), a culture that nurtures community spirit, the social means to achieve physical and mental health and knowledge, the political means to positively shape one's environment, and the economic means to meet basic needs. Village families understood these needs to include a clean environment, an adequate and safe water supply, basic clothing, a balanced diet, simple housing, health (spiritual, social, and physical), channels of communication, fuel, education, and cultural development. These benefits were not to be achieved through violent or illusory methods—that is, capitalist or socialist methods from their point of view—but only in a way that included the political participation of the masses in decisionmaking. Society's burdens were to be met through donated labor *(shramadana)* to accomplish tasks necessary for meeting community requirements. Implied in those ideals is the third leg in the tripod of distributive justice—namely, principles by which to guide the distribution of the benefits and burdens of a life lived in common, to benefit and not to harm others, to ensure that others will not be interfered with and will be accorded self-determination in solving their own problems locally (Goulet 1988, 70–71; see also Ratnapala 1980, 518; Smurl 1994, 144).

The philosophical basis of this movement is clearly Buddhist, as already noted above. One also should note that the movement builds on Buddhist notions about the nature of society and the virtues that must be cultivated to ensure that society is good and just. Society should be dharmic, or righteous; it should require both laity and the order of monks to encourage rulers to practice justice. The movement claims that the enlightenment it advocates encompasses an understanding that genuine socioeconomic development can occur only when individuals, local communities, and nations acknowledge the central importance of four virtues. These are: loving kindness toward all living beings *(metta),* compassionate action attacking the causes of suffering *(karuna),* joy in altruistic service more than in selfish gratification *(mudita),* and a serenity free both from a sense of self-importance and from the hurt felt from hostility and criticism *(upekka)* (Goulet 1988, 72, 80).

As its principles for distributing common benefits and burdens demonstrate, the Sarvodaya Shramadana movement is an outstanding illustration of how some contemporary Buddhists draw upon their religious traditions to promote and practice distributive justice. There is some uncertainty both about the movement's future and about its success in achieving its admirable and difficult goals. Goulet notes that the Sarvodaya Shramadana's future depends heavily on whether or not the Sri Lankan government's policies will remain consistent (1988, 73–79). The Sri Lankan sociologist Nandasena Ratnapala, who closely studied seven of the villages practicing the Sarvodaya Shramadana program, found some severe tensions between the goal of village self-reliance and the practice of centralized authority from afar (Ratnapala 1980, 471–472, 485–489) He concluded that the movement depended too heavily on external aid rather than on its own resources (499). But all who have observed this movement agree that it is a stunning example of religiously animated pursuit of a greater measure of distributive justice for people little able to solve their problems without such a push.

These Buddhist illustrations suggest that a tradition commonly regarded as more individualistic than communitarian may nonetheless contain some relatively sophisticated, even if culturally particular (as opposed to universal), forms of distributive justice. They also suggest the hazard of looking mainly to the foundational texts of a tradition, omitting further scrutiny of continuities and changes over the course of a tradition's history. Finally, they suggest that one look closely at the different ways a tradition is experienced and expressed in various times and places, in the present as well as in the past. These same lessons should be kept in mind as we turn now to consider some illustrations from the Christian and the Islamic religious traditions.

Christianity

As in the preceding Buddhist illustrations, the concern for distributive justice in the Christian tradition will not be treated exhaustively. Nonetheless, the following illustrations from texts sacred to Christians and from historical and contemporary developments that draw upon such texts and upon prior history should make Christianity's commitment to distributive justice clear.

Although I cannot speak authoritatively for the Christian tradition, from an academic point of view it appears that in searching for clues about the proper and just distribution of the benefits and burdens of the social goods communities hold in common, Christians look both to the Hebrew Bible (the Old Testament) and to the New Testament. Most of the clues in the Old Testament are to be found in the books of Exodus and Deuteronomy in what are called the Book of the Covenant (Exod. 20–24) and the Deuteronomic Code (Deut. 12–26).

Both of these passages are set in a context most clearly articulated in Deuteronomy, chapter 26, where the Jews are reminded that once, as slaves in Egypt, they had nothing, they were in bondage and were oppressed. Now, thanks to their God, they have inherited a land that he has made fruitful. In return, they are required to share with others some of the first fruits of all that is harvested in their land annually, and more of the same every third and still more every seventh or sabbatical year (Deut. 12:22–29, 15:1–11; see also Exod. 23:10–13). As in Exodus (21:1–6), additional requirements of the sabbatical year as specified in Deuteronomy focus on releasing people who have been enslaved for six years, recalling that the Jews were once slaves themselves in Egypt (15:12–18).

The sabbatical year requirements also include releasing debtors from outstanding loans (Deut. 15:1–6) and consecrating firstling male animals of herds and flocks to the God of Israel (15:19–23). To these requirements, passages in both Exodus and Deuteronomy add some remarkably explicit directives about protecting those who are relatively disadvantaged in society. These include Deuteronomy's directives to be fair to strangers and sojourners, to widows and orphans, by leaving some grain, olives, and grapes in the fields that they can harvest (24:17–22; see also Exod. 22:20–24). Also described in these passages are requirements to establish full and just weights and measures in commerce (Deut. 25:13–16), to pay hired workers' wages on the same day that they work (24:14–15), and, remarkably (at least for the twentieth-century reader), to prohibit the collection of interest on loans made "to your brother" but not on loans made to "a foreigner" (23:20–21).

In the Christian New Testament, one finds comparable major themes that emphasize the quality of relationships between neighbors and strangers and the sharing of possessions. The parable of the Good Samaritan (Luke 10:29–37) is emblematic of the New Testament's advice on how to be neighborly to those in need. Paul's letter to the Galatians states that there "is neither Jew nor Greek, there is neither slave nor free, there is neither male nor female; for you are all one in Christ Jesus" (Gal. 10:12). Finally, there are the memorable passages from the Sermon on the Mount that promote neighborly love in ways not previously emphasized (Matt. 5–7).

Although too extensive to recount more fully here, these classical texts, as in Theravada Buddhism, express the ideals of distributive justice that have been followed in the many forms Christianity has taken over the centuries and in different cultures. The tradition's concern to develop distributively just communities has taken many different forms and, as with other traditions, these efforts have waxed and waned. At times, religious authorities (monks and monasteries, bishops, popes, and Christian kings and princes) have amassed disproportionately large collections of social goods needed by all those under their control, but have not distributed the goods fairly. Reforms aimed at redistributing the burdens as well as the benefits of common lives and resources had to be initiated. The process continues to this day. That it does is evidence of the Christian tradition's ongoing commitment to the ideal of distributive justice. To see how it continues to be expressed, I will consider one contemporary illustration in some detail.

Habitat for Humanity. To illustrate how the symbols of the sacred texts of Christianity can be used to fashion contemporary philosophies and programs committed to distributive justice, consider the American-based movement called Habitat for Humanity. The leaders of this movement claim that 25 percent of the world's population lacks adequate shelter; they have set a goal of eliminating substandard housing throughout the United States and indeed throughout the world. Both their goal and their means of pursuing it bespeak a deep concern for the value of distributive justice as embodied in their partners as well as in their activities to reshape social structures (Fuller 1986, 38–46)

The Habitat story begins with Millard Fuller, who in 1965, at the age of thirty, had become a millionaire, but increasingly estranged from his wife and in search of a deeper and more spiritual purpose in life. At a farm called Koinonia (Greek for "community"), founded by Clarence Jordan in 1942 outside Americus, Georgia, Fuller found what he took to be a Christian community committed to action in accordance with biblical symbols and scriptures and modeled on the example of Jesus of Nazareth. According to the residents of Koinonia, Jesus not only preached the good news of salvation but also delivered good news to the poor in the form of food for the hungry, health for the sick, sight for the blind, and so on (Fuller 1986, 113–138).

From the mid-1960s to the mid-1970s, Fuller and his Koinonia partners tried to follow this example by creating housing for poor people. Starting in 1968, they raised the capital needed to build housing for their displaced rural Georgia neighbors. This capital came in the form of gifts from donors, no-interest loans from friends, and some of the profits from Koinonia's farms, industries, and housing; it was gathered into a trust fund called the Fund for Humanity. Anticipating the need for additional resources in the future, Koinonia's members also planned to recycle the mortgage payments from prospective partner-family homeowners and the small monthly administration fees attached to their no-interest, twenty-year home mortgages into the same fund (Fuller 1986, 47–72, 100–112).

The fund was established on the premises that the poor needed capital more than charity, coworkers more than caseworkers, and a hand up more than a handout; and that the wealthy needed a wise, honorable, and just way to divest themselves of their overabundance. In this way, Koinonia could help the rich heed the biblical admonition against laying up treasures on earth (Matt. 6:19–21), and, through their no-interest, no-profit building loan program, they would employ what they called "biblical economics" as found in the Jewish Torah's prohibitions on collecting interest on loans (Exod. 22:25). In these ways, Koinonia sought to put love into action—or love "in the mortar joints." Their intent was to achieve in reality the society idealized in the Jewish greeting "Shalom"—namely, a community perfectly ordered by God and marked by total spiritual and physical well-being, by love and justice, and by the peace of knowing that the needs of every person have been met (Fuller and Scott 1980, 85–99).

By 1969, Koinonia was offering housing assistance to the poor in their rural Georgia locale. In 1972 they built twenty-seven homes on land they owned, reserving some lots for a recreational area, a children's nursery, and development centers. Habitat for Humanity was officially launched in 1976 and in the same year helped house eight families in what was then Zaire. Since then, Habitat has delivered on its international and global goals by creating housing in Africa, Asia, and Central and South America, as well as in the United States.

A few other noteworthy elements of Habitat's philosophy should be mentioned. The group is interdenominational in organization and membership, emphasizing that whatever an individual's particular beliefs, doctrines, or practices, people at least can share a hammer—thus their "theology of the hammer." Habitat believes that the resources and the technology for adequate housing are available around the globe and simply need to be harnessed properly. It also contends that the materials used to construct

that housing should be appropriate for the locale and the culture involved—not made elsewhere and brought to the site at considerable expense and at risk of offending local sensibilities. Habitat emphasizes partnership and solidarity in the building and financing of homes, aiming to
build communities as well as housing. In describing the labor they require
of their partner homeowners as "sweat equity," Habitat underscores, and
perhaps epitomizes, a commitment to a just distribution of the burdens as
well as the benefits of adequate housing.

Islam

The Muslim religion has a rich and varied tradition of attending to distributive justice both in more private realms like the family and in more public
arenas like civil society. The recently deceased American Muslim scholar Isma'il al-Faruqi has noted how the sacred scriptures of Islam (in the Qur'an)
aim to promote distributive justice in families. Promoting context-bound
and, at least to Western eyes, sexist regulations about family wealth, mar-
riages and divorces, widows and orphans, and concerns about family members' capacities to bear burdens, the Qur'an offers a version of distributive
justice in terms rooted in seventh-century Arabic culture. In civil society, Islam has promoted forms of voluntary giving *(sadaqa)* and an obligatory,
tax-like form of alms *(zakat),* both designed to promote social well-being
and to alleviate the suffering of those who are least well off (al-Faruqi
1969, 359–377).

The Qur'an, Islam's most sacred text, records 114 recitations by the
Prophet Muhammad, believed to be divinely revealed. Now called chapters
or suras (cited as "S" in the text references that follow), these recitations reveal how Islam expresses its concerns for distributive justice in communities. Such concerns are to be seen in the light of the Qur'an's major themes:
God's bounty; human dependence on God and human responsibilities of
stewardship acting as God's deputies or vice regents; and distributive justice
as a form of worship and submission to God.

In the Qur'anic worldview, God is portrayed as a sustainer who creates
humans, the natural resources they need, and their children (S 74:11–13).
Principal among the natural resources that Muhammad recounts as the
beautiful and life-sustaining gifts of God are the lights of the sun, moon,
and stars; winds, water, and rain; soils and seed; and the growing power of
grains, olives, and dates (Ss 51–93, passim). Humans are not self-created;
God creates them—and from basic elements like a germ (sperm) cell (S
96:1). It is God who enables humans to possess what they have and to be
free from want (S 53:48).

The role humans are to play is characterized as stewardship, deputyship,
or vice regency *(khalifat)* (S 2:30). God's bounty in natural resources, but
also in the wealth humans possess that is to be understood as God's gift, is

to be used and distributed with accountability to God and with concern for the well-being of the community *(umma)* (Ss 3:104, 27:60, 42:38). Members of the community are equal and should walk the same pilgrim path (Ss 2:99, 49:11). Males and females should guard one another (S 49:13), but men have priority over women (S 4:34). Still, men should bear the burdens of sustaining women (Ss 2:237, 65:6) and providing their dowries (S 4:3), and fathers should bear the burdens of nursing mothers in proportion to their ability to do so (S 2:233, 286).

Parents, relatives, orphans, the destitute, and wayfarers all have claims on a community's resources (S 2:215). Especially pressing are the claims of disadvantaged persons like orphans (S 6:152). In fact, in some senses one's wealth belongs to the poor and the deprived (S 51:16).

Finally, to these rather clear illustrations of the proper distribution of the benefits and burdens of common resources, the Qur'an adds the religious duty of obligatory almsgiving, or *zakat*. Known now as one of the five pillars supporting the house of Islam, *zakat* is, like the other four pillars, a ritual practice required of Muslims. The Qur'an refers to *zakat* as a form of purification for the sake of one's soul (Ss 2:110, 9:103) and as a form of worship, similar to another of the pillars, prayer (S 2:277).

Ever since the classical period of Islam's flourishing (roughly, from the ninth to the twelfth centuries), the Islamic tradition has encouraged additional forms of distributive justice. For example, it has helped establish pious endowments or trusts *(awaqf;* singular, *waqf)* to support mosques, to promote learning, to reform practices that have led to unequal distributions of resources, and, in modern times, to maintain a range of social welfare services (Hourani 1991, 115–116, 163; Anderson 1976, 38–42, 162–171). The long and varied history of these endowments and how they have been reformed is recounted ably by Albert Hourani (1991) and Norman Anderson (1976). Rather than delving into historical considerations, it may be more fruitful to consider the modern role of some Islamic trusts.

Social Welfare in Contemporary Arab Territories.   In the last few decades, the heads of Arab nations and Muslim religious leaders alike have called for a greater measure of social justice. Since the 1950s, the Egyptian Gamal Abdel Nasser's way of expressing social problems and prospective solutions has become paradigmatic for many—including, most recently, Iraq's Saddam Hussein (Kelsay 1993, 9–10). That paradigm assigns blame for a nation's economic problems either to indigenous privileged elites or to foreign capitalistic powers. At the same time, it promises to redress those problems by nationalizing resources and production and by distributing wealth and social services more equitably (Esposito 1992, 71–73).

Since the time of Nasser, and more extensively in recent years, some Muslim religious leaders blame the woes of Arab and other Islamic peoples on two additional causes—namely, the secularization and Westernization of their governments and nations. Such is the rhetoric of a reform-minded Islamic group that began as the Egyptian Muslim Brotherhood, which was founded in 1928 by Hasan al-Banna. In the 1930s and 1940s, the brotherhood spread into the Palestinian territories, particularly the Gaza area, where it was popular because of its participation in the 1948 Palestine war. Throughout the 1950s, the brotherhood prospered in Gaza, where the population's density, harsh economic circumstances, and adherence to traditional social relations created a propitious climate for the brotherhood's reform message and its programs, which were launched with material support from the parent organization in Egypt and from the Saudi royal family. The organization was weakened between 1958 and 1967 by the tide of Arab nationalism, and many of its leaders were arrested in 1965, including Ahmad Yasin, who later would become the leader of the Islamic resistance movement known as Hamas. But, after the 1967 Israeli occupation of the West Bank and Gaza, the brotherhood generally, and Hamas in particular, was able to mobilize the masses and gain the sympathies of landowners, merchants, and shopkeepers (Abu-Amr 1994, 1–22).

In Egypt today, Islamic reform movements provide social services ranging from subsidized housing and food distribution to health care and legal aid as well as banking and investment services (Esposito 1992, 100, 139; Sullivan 1994, 8–9, 136–139, 153–160). The Egyptian Muslim Brotherhood launched similar endeavors in the West Bank and Gaza in 1967, about the same time that Habitat for Humanity was conceived in America. With financial support from Jordan and Saudi Arabia, the brotherhood managed schools, libraries, and sports clubs through its Islamic *waqf* office. It used funds from obligatory alms to help the needy, provided loans to college students, and supported numerous social and religious celebrations. It extended its influence still further by building large numbers of mosques and by using the tradition of the *waqf* to control an extensive network of property—such that *waqf* holdings currently are estimated at 10 percent of all real estate in the Gaza Strip, including hundreds of shops, apartments, garages, and public buildings as well as some two thousand acres of agricultural land (Abu-Amr 1994, 14–15).

Hamas, which is a brotherhood splinter group, has behaved similarly in Gaza. Hamas has acquired a shameful worldwide reputation in recent years because some of its members have siphoned funds away from the organization to support gruesome acts of terrorism in Israel and elsewhere, including the bombing of buses carrying innocent civilians. Despite the well-deserved scorn heaped on this violent segment of Hamas, the vast majority of the group's members are engaged in socially constructive activities that demonstrate their commitments to the ideals of distributive justice set out in the chapters of the Qur'an. Hamas continues the traditions of *zakat* and *waqf*— even to the extent that Article Eleven of the Hamas Charter refers to Palestine as an Islamic *waqf* given by God to generations of Muslims (Maqdsi 1990,

17). Like its parent organization, Hamas relies on the Islamic civil tradition of social welfare not only to spread its influence but also to redress unequal distributions of the benefits and burdens of life in Palestinian communities.

A 1994 American visitor to Gaza City painted a sad picture of that Palestinian community—dubbing it a city with dark alleys, twisting trails of potholes, more sheds and shacks and lean-tos than apartments, concrete refugee shelters, sweatshops, and mosques. Everywhere in Gaza City, this visitor found adults and children, donkeys and roosters alike moving about through endless piles of trash. However, the visitor noted that the city's current condition is due in part to its history, which has been dominated by Turks, British, Egyptians, Israelis, and, most recently, the Palestine Liberation Organization (PLO). Gaza's people seem not to have liked any of these interlopers and, instead, have found their own ways of doing things.

Their solutions are scarcely citywide, since Gaza is composed of a multiplicity of folkways practiced in neighborhoods; there is little, if anything, resembling a larger urban community. Tribes and factions define every family, block, and neighborhood. A few rich and powerful families dominate business, politics, and social institutions. They manipulate everything from home construction to medical care. Others "make a go of it" in the political black market by means of bribes and bartered favors. Gaza is not a city in any conventional sense; it does not even have a common, predictable water supply or waste disposal system, and no authority is charged with the responsibility to ensure that all residents are provided with certain basic protections and services.

But in at least one Gaza neighborhood, life is cleaner and safer, and residents are assured of at least some basic securities and provisions. This is a Hamas neighborhood, which boasts a private network of clinics, schools, day-care centers, mosques, small factories, and a welfare system helping widows, orphans, and handicapped persons who have suffered as a result of the *intifada* (the "shaking off") waged against Israel in the early 1990s (Kelly 1994, 56–63). This neighborhood well illustrates points that I have emphasized in this chapter, especially in the way a religiously oriented group can solve problems at the grassroots level (despite the terrorist activities of certain of its members). These problems and their solutions, common not only among Arabs in Gaza but among Buddhists in Thailand, Hindus in India, and Christians in America, arguably should also be the concerns of scholars in religious studies.

Finding Common Ground in Research, Dialogue, and Service

But how might these concerns be addressed effectively by those engaged in interreligious dialogue and comparative religious ethics? The principal aims of these endeavors, as I see them, are understanding the nature and structure of decent, livable communities and, to the extent possible, helping build such communities locally and internationally through scholarship, dialogue, and community action. If this understanding is correct, then the ways in which burdens are distributed and benefits are shared by people in these communities should be a major focus of scholarship, dialogue, and community action.

Scholarship

Some suggestions for further study have already been made. For example, scholars must consider the particular forms of religions being studied, their historical and geographical circumstances, who best speaks for them, and how their foundations may have been reinterpreted, as evidenced in the historical and anthropological studies of Buddhism discussed above. These and the other illustrations suggest that comparative studies of distributive justice need to pay as much, if not more, attention to the burdens associated with social goods as they do to the benefits. It is decisively important to know who "pays" and who gets hurt, and to what extent. The above illustrations also underscore the importance of identifying who is responsible for allocating benefits and burdens. It may be a king or a householder in a Hindu community. It may be a monk, a king, or a wealthy layperson in a Buddhist community. Or it may be a voluntarily organized group of community leaders such as Habitat in the United States, or the Egyptian Muslim Brotherhood or Hamas in the Middle East.

I can offer two more related sets of suggestions. The first, as indicated above, would be to encourage scholarship that not only identifies the people responsible for a distributively just social order but also the virtues that should characterize these persons. Such scholarship should focus on the duties that these persons should be expected to assume as much as, if not more than, it trains attention on the rights that people claim from them. With regard to virtue and character, as the Hindu Code of Manu puts it, if the king is not just, neither is his kingdom—and, by analogy, neither are the children of parents or the students of educators.

All of this suggests that distributive justice plays a role in more than economic spheres and that it requires just persons to put it into practice. It also suggests that a call for greater attention to the duties of the distributors of social goods need not impugn the legitimate claims of human rights—even when the case for those rights is made primarily in expressive and evocative, rather than in logical, terms. It does suggest, however, that a focus on rights, to the exclusion of attention to the obligations of those against whom these claims are made, may not only be vaporous; it also may be mistaken. Human rights claims often are unenforceable when the conditions or the resources required to honor them are not available. Sometimes claimants themselves fail to recognize that conventional or customary rights are at odds with what would prevail in an ideal society or would be provided by conscientious individuals when those with distributive authority like parents, teachers, and elected officials fail to make this recognition. Studies that aim to identify and help influence those responsible for acknowledging human rights would be useful tools for avoiding some of these missteps, especially since, as Twiss and Grelle have argued, the importance of human rights is undeniably central in comparative religious ethics (1995, 21–48).

A second set of proposals addresses the issue of particularity versus universality in the moral standards of distributive justice. This issue may arise mainly from the fact that the West has developed, and sometimes tried to impose, what it claims to be universal standards. If so, then it may be a largely rhetorical issue freighted with fears of Western imperialism appearing now in the domain of morality as it did previously in the sociocultural and political domains. To trouble too much about claims of universally applicable moral standards may be unproductive and may not make a practical difference in the way people live. For this reason, it may not be fruitful to concentrate too heavily on the goals expressed by the Global Ethic promulgated by the 1993 Parliament of the World's Religions (Küng and Kuschel 1993). But, as I shall suggest shortly, there well may be some universal expressions of distributive justice, even if no one has yet expressed them in terms intelligible to others living in equally contingent circumstances. Increased scholarly attention to the details of contingent lives, to the experiences of the people involved, to their stories, and to practices they developed to maintain and further their lives may make the commonalities in these matters more evident. For example, the problem in uncovering commonalities that can be universalized is often the fact that customs have schooled people to accept, or at least adapt to, less than just practices in their communities–or, alternatively, to fail to acknowledge, as Michael Walzer notes, that their putative universal standards of justice arose in fact from their own thickly embedded cultural particulars (1994). This is not to say, however, that there are no desires and needs for justice that can be made universal, or that pragmatic tests aiming to discover what people might agree to as ways of expressing principles of justice cannot be devised either through dialogue or through the experience of shared endeavor to create more livable forms of community.

Dialogue

If conversation partners hope to understand what they and the people they intend to represent have in common with respect to distributive justice— but *not* by asserting standards with which to whipsaw one other—they should begin with very concrete and rich descriptions of human experiences, lives, stories, and practices. These should include attention to the metaphors on which stories and practices rely. They should include stories and practices about families, workplaces, neighborhoods and communities, nations and religions. Through careful attention to such matters and by talking with, rather than at, each other, conversation partners should find some commonalities in an a posteriori, as opposed to an a priori, fashion, since the latter tends to impose on others what in reality are thick and culturally contingent statements of justice masquerading as universal principles (see Walzer 1994, 12; Rorty 1989). What I propose is similar to what Richard Rorty calls "imaginative identification with the details of others' lives, rather than [a call for] a recognition of something antecedently shared" (1989, 189). Such a procedure might help us uncover a global *ethos* rather than the scarcely attainable global *ethic* some others envision.

Of all the metaphors people live by, some from religious sources seem at once more problematic and more fruitful in conversations about distributive justice. Topping a far from exhaustive list of problematic metaphors are those that prop up the sometimes tainted claims of people hoping to justify their powers and possessions. Metaphors supporting male dominance in families; those dichotomizing people as kin and alien, neighbor and stranger; and those laying claim to promised lands come readily to mind.[1] Metaphors more conducive to conversations about distributive justice are those emphasizing sacred trusts, stewardship (or deputyship in Islam), and updated versions of, for example, Muhammad's transtribal community (the *umma*), experienced as transnational and transethnic by Malcolm X in a pilgrimage to Mecca. Equally productive would be ecological metaphors that highlight our increasingly interdependent physical, social, and economic environments; our electronic communications over the Internet; and our common human experience of being manipulated by social, economic, and political controllers who often fail to lead but never fail to make us pay for the consequences.

Community Service and Action

Scholars of religious ethics and their partners in interreligious conversations can be responsible public intellectuals, can mediate between disparate publics, and can alert people about forms of community service and action that promise greater measures of distributive justice. Here I will highlight two suggestions that might help people find ways to justly apportion the benefits and burdens of social goods in their communities.

The first is an alert to development funds instituted by oil-rich Arab countries to help finance improvements in social welfare, education, health services, transportation, and communications facilities in less developed

Arab countries. Similar funds have been established worldwide, and some are explicitly religious in origin and sponsorship. An Arab illustration is pertinent here because of the points made above about Saudi and Jordanian financial support for the Egyptian Muslim Brotherhood in Gaza. That support was channeled through one or more of the economic, social, agricultural, and technical funds established in the 1970s and after under the auspices of Saudi Arabia, Kuwait, and Abu Dhabi (see Raffer and Salih 1992). But how was it managed at the local level, what were its priorities, and to what degree did the intended beneficiaries participate?

The relevance of the answers to these questions is made evident by my second alert, namely to encourage the continuing growth of nongovernmental organizations (NGOs), grassroots organizations, and grassroots support organizations in developing countries. In a study of these organizations and their efforts to promote sustainable development, Julie Fisher noted that they do not seek to overthrow governments; rather, they challenge inequitable and repressive governments by enlarging peoples' participation in the conduct of civil society. Fisher estimated that, since the 1970s, more than 100,000 NGOs have been established in Asia, Africa, and Latin America—often by peasant women, professors, squatters, students, and farmers. Worldwide during the same time period, more than 30,000 support organizations have focused on development, the environment, the role of women, and primary health care and have channeled international funds to grassroots organizations that are highly egalitarian and participatory; women's organizations have been among the most successful of these groups (Fisher 1993, ix, 5, 182).

Fisher's study probably needs more corroboration, but it at least suggests that these grassroots organizations merit the attention of persons interested in religion, morality, and politics in general and distributive justice in particular—including scholars in comparative religious ethics and their conversation partners in interreligious dialogues, for the following reasons. Christian missionaries instituted grassroots organizations in Mexico as early as the sixteenth century among the Puerepas Indians. They helped local communities build and operate their own schools in Kenya in the nineteenth century and, since the 1980s, a majority of African grassroots support organizations have been tied to churches. Since the nineteenth century, agricultural colonies and credit cooperatives have been established by Christian missionaries in India; by the 1980s, these had become allied with Gandhian organizations that emphasized small-scale industries like shoemaking, weaving, and soap making. In the twentieth century, Buddhist monks in Sri Lanka have been active in ecology movements and in Thailand have promoted grassroots organizations pushing for rural development. Hundreds of Muslim-supported grassroots organizations are active in the West Bank, most with no ties to Palestinian liberation organizations; some 650 of these emerged during Lebanon's civil war. In Egypt, similar organizations emerged under the auspices of both Coptic Christians and Muslims. Palestinian organizations have grown rapidly in the absence of a Palestinian government and presently outnumber and have wealthier foundations than other Arab organizations established in the past two decades (Fisher 1993, 92). Some Egyptian Muslims have used Islamic investment companies to support hospitals, day-care centers, and schools; similar strategies have been employed in Saudi Arabia, Kuwait, Qatar, and the United Arab Emirates. Egyptian organizations have channeled the profits from farms and businesses to social services by using traditional Islamic religious endowments. Muslim leaders in Jordan declared that traditional Islamic obligatory alms could be dedicated to development activities. Similar stories come from Argentina, Brazil, Bolivia, Chile, Costa Rica, Guatemala, Peru, and elsewhere in Central and South America (Fisher 1993, 25, 28, 108, 110, 175; on Egypt, see also Sullivan 1994, 8–9, 57–98, 136–139, 153–160).

Among other things, these developments suggest that distributive justice is a worldwide issue and a most aggravating one in less developed countries. They also suggest that major world religions have found spiritual and other resources within their own traditions enabling them to take practical steps to alleviate if not always resolve such problems. It would be unfortunate if religious scholarship and dialogue were to overlook these developments. Equally unfortunate would be a failure to find ways both to express these problems and to develop mutually agreeable standards by which to guide activities aimed at alleviating such problems. As I hope to have shown in this chapter, such failures can be avoided if the problem of distributive justice is properly addressed both in comparative religious ethics and in interreligious dialogues, with sufficient attention drawn to the social and political implications of both endeavors. And, as I also hope to have shown, when properly addressed, distributive justice represents a call for just people and just situations in addition to just principles. When heeded, that call can lead to collaborative endeavors by people from different traditions—as we have seen in the case of Habitat, to cite just one example. And, perhaps more to the point of this volume, heeding the call of distributive justice can open potentially fruitful avenues of scholarship and conversation across religious and cultural traditions.

Notes

1. So too does Isma'il al-Faruqi's rendition of a passage from the Qur'an (Ss 4:135, 5:8): "If you change your language so as to avoid justice, or evade the doing of justice, remember that God knows all that you do" (al-Faruqi 1969, 364).

References

Abu-Amr, Zia. 1994. *Islamic Fundamentalism in the West Bank and Gaza: Muslim Brotherhood and Islamic Jihad.* Bloomington: Indiana University Press.

Anderson, Norman. 1976. *Law Reform in the Muslim World.* London: University of London, the Athlone Press.

Asad, Muhammad, trans. 1980. *The Message of the Qur'an.* Gibraltar: Dar-Al-Andalus.

Esposito, John L. 1992. *The Islamic Threat: Myth or Reality?* New York: Oxford University Press.

Faruqi, Isma'il Ragi al-. 1969. "Islam." In *The Great Asian Religions,* edited by Isma'il Ragi al-Faruqi, Joseph M. Kitagawa, and P. T. Raju, 307–377. New York: Macmillan.

Fisher, Julie. 1993. *The Road from Rio: Sustainable Development and the Nongovernmental Movement in the Third World.* Westport, Conn.: Praeger.

Fuller, Millard. 1986. *No More Shacks.* Waco, Tex.: Word Books.

Fuller, Millard, and Diane Scott. 1980. *Love in the Mortar Joints.* Piscataway, N.J.: Association Press.

Goulet, Denis. 1988. "Development Strategy in Sri Lanka and a People's Alternative." In *Wealth and Poverty Development and Development Projects in the Third World,* edited by Donald A. Attwood, Thomas C. Bruneau, and John G. Galaty, 61–83. Boulder: Westview Press.

Hourani, Albert. 1991. *A History of the Arab Peoples.* Cambridge: Harvard University Press, Belknap Press.

Kelly, Michael. 1994. "In Gaza, Peace Meets Pathology." *New York Times Magazine,* November 27, 56–63.

Kelsay, John. 1993. *Islam and War.* Louisville, Ky.: Westminster John Knox Press.

Kemper, Steven. 1990. "Wealth and Reformation in Sinhalese Buddhist Monasticism." In *Ethics, Wealth, and Salvation: A Study in Buddhist Social Ethics,* edited by Russell F. Sizemore and Donald K. Swearer, 152–169. Columbia: University of South Carolina Press.

Keyes, Charles F. 1990. "Buddhist Practical Morality in a Changing Agrarian World." In *Ethics, Wealth, and Salvation: A Study in Buddhist Social Ethics,* edited by Russell F. Sizemore and Donald K. Swearer, 170–189. Columbia: University of South Carolina Press.

Küng, Hans, and Karl-Josef Kuschel, eds. 1993. *A Global Ethic: The Declaration of the Parliament of the World's Religions.* New York: Continuum.

Ling, Trevor. 1973. *The Buddha: Buddhist Civilization in India and Ceylon.* New York: Penguin Books.

Maqdsi, Muhammad. 1990. *Charter of the Islamic Resistance Movement (Hamas) of Palestine.* Dallas: Islamic Association for Palestine.

May, Herbert G., and Bruce M. Metzger, eds. 1977. *The New Oxford Annotated Bible with the Apocrypha.* New York: Oxford University Press.

Raffer, Kunibert, and Mohamed Salih, eds. 1992. *The Least-Developed and the Oil-Rich Arab Countries.* New York: St. Martin's Press.

Rajavaramuni, Phra. 1990. "Foundations of Buddhist Social Ethics." In *Ethics, Wealth, and Salvation: A Study in Buddhist Social Ethics,* edited by Russell F.

Sizemore and Donald K. Swearer, 29–58. Columbia: University of South Carolina Press.

Ratnapala, Nandasena. 1980. "The Sarvodaya Movement: Self-Help Rural Development in Sri Lanka." In *Meeting the Basic Needs of the Rural Poor,* edited by Philip H. Coombs, 469–523. New York: Pergamon Press.

Reynolds, Frank E. 1990. "Ethics and Wealth in Theravada Buddhism." In *Ethics, Wealth, and Salvation: A Study in Buddhist Social Ethics,* edited by Russell F. Sizemore and Donald K. Swearer, 59–76. Columbia: University of South Carolina Press.

Rorty, Richard. 1989. *Contingency, Irony, and Solidarity*. New York: Cambridge University Press.

Smurl James F. 1994. *The Burdens of Justice*. With a foreword by Douglas Sturm. Chicago: Loyola University Press.

Strong, John S. 1983. *The Legend of King Asoka*. Princeton: Princeton University Press.

Sullivan, Denis J. 1994. *Private Voluntary Organizations in Egypt (Islamic Development, Private Initiative, and State Control)*. Gainesville: University Press of Florida.

Twiss, Sumner B., and Bruce Grelle. 1995. "Human Rights and Comparative Religious Ethics: A New Venue." *The Annual of the Society of Christian Ethics*:21–48.

Walzer, Michael. 1994. *Thick and Thin: Moral Argument at Home and Abroad*. Notre Dame, Ind.: University of Notre Dame Press.

Chapter Eight

"Teachers of Reality": Voices of Resistance and Reconstruction

JUNE O'CONNOR

University of California, Riverside

My future is in my children. . . . I hope they will use what happened to our family as a way to educate other people. I hope that they will be "maestros de la realidad," teachers of reality. (Tula 1989, 177)

In *Hear My Testimony*, Maria Teresa Tula of El Salvador invites us, as scholars and dialogue participants alike, to pay attention to her story and, by implication, to the stories of other Third World peoples whose struggles for survival provide a glimpse into the reality of daily life among the majority of the world's population. It is incumbent on those in the First World to pay sustained attention to Third World authors who are voicing their views about power and privilege, rage and resistance, suffering and struggle, hopelessness and determination. They want their stories and their efforts to be known, as the titles of their testimonials make clear: *Hear My Testimony* (Tula 1989), *Let Me Speak!* (Barrios de Chungara 1978), and "We Want Our Desires to be Respected" (New America Press 1989, 225–227), among others.

Scholarly reflection on the good and the right, together with community dialogues about moral issues, demand that we pay attention to those in relationship with us. Given North and South America's indigenous and European roots, given the historical, cultural, and religious ties among all peoples of the Americas, given socio-politico-economic interdependencies, and given the migration north of many from the south, Latin American sources are particularly important materials for ethical analysis and moral dialogue in the United States.

Testimonials

As we read and listen, it is useful to note several features of testimonial literature as a literary genre. Similar, though not identical, to autobiography, memoir, and oral history, testimonial literature is a self-conscious effort to communicate a set of messages as well as a set of facts. As personal narrative, it is a creative, constructive, and interpretive enterprise as well as a process of remembering, recollecting, and recording. Authors of testimonials are at once both creator and creation insofar as they select, interpret, and order the memories, meanings, and messages of their life stories. Experiences are highlighted, commented on, or omitted from the telling (Tula 1989, 8; Menchu 1984, 247). All personal narratives, including testimonial literature, rest on a select sample and an interpretation of a complex of experiences.

Second, authors of this literature characteristically claim that the tale told is not the story of a single individual but is the story of a people, of a whole community, who share in the testimonial because they face the same threats and embrace the same struggle as the author. In testimony, the author affirms the lives of many in like circumstances. What Rigoberta Menchu of Guatemala states is echoed by others: "My name is Rigoberta Menchu. I am twenty-three years old. This is my testimony. . . . I'd like to stress that it's not only *my* life, it's also the testimony of my people. . . . My story is the story of all poor Guatemalans. My personal experience is the reality of a whole people" (Menchu 1984, 1; see also Tula 1989, 227–228).

Third, because testimonials give voice to people whose experiences traditionally have been neglected, ignored, or misrepresented, they convey unique authenticity, authority, and insight. Gustavo Gutiérrez refers to this population as the "other side" and Elise Boulding as the "underside" of history (Gutiérrez 1990, 1; Boulding 1976). The authors are broadly known as "the poor," "the oppressed," and "the marginalized." The social conditions they portray, the inequalities and indignities they resist, and the future they work to construct are broadly corroborated by multiple and multidisciplinary research findings.[1] Testimonial literature grounds, details, and personalizes that research in narrative form.

Fourth, in addition to providing information, testimonial literature issues an invitation. It asks the reader to learn about but also to join the struggle to create a new society by working to reconfigure the international relations through which writer and reader are structurally related. Fifth, the production of this literature is a transnational and cross-cultural effort involving interviews, recordings, translations and transcriptions, and editing as well as publishing and printing. Many of these procedures occur within limited time frames and in carefully chosen locations, while traveling or seeking safe haven. Determining the exact contribution of these intermediary voices can be problematic, although some translators and editors make their procedures explicit and their presence visible in the final product (for example, see Tula 1989).

These stories speak to those in North America as well as those in Central and South America, for they regularly allude to North-South military interventions and economic interactions in the ways that citizens experience them. As they talk about themselves, these authors speak also about their neighbors. North Americans are one of those neighbors frequently spoken about—and spoken to.

By giving us vivid images of destitute poverty, hunger, terror inflicted by the state, violation of bodily integrity, and transgression of fundamental human rights as workers and citizens, as women, as prisoners, as children, these materials pull the curtains on widespread human misery and struggle for social change and transformation. Third World testimonial literature carries the potential to extend and deepen our understanding of human capacities for moral cruelty and moral nobility, moral creativity and moral collapse, resistance to moral evil and surrender to or compromise with such evil.

This literature challenges those in the First World to rethink moral axioms that are taken for granted and to rethink the moral categories with which we think. The purpose of this chapter is to enunciate four sets of issues that illustrate this claim: (1) that for these authors, solidarity rather than charity is the preferred virtue for our time; (2) that in a world of human rights violations, dialogue is not simply a goal or a process to be taken for granted; the very possibility of dialogue is a problem that needs to be addressed; (3) that religions function both to serve and to subvert human rights struggles and must themselves be accountable to moral norms; and (4) that scholarly efforts to understand other persons, cultures, and religions require the recognition of already existing historical, political, and socioeconomic engagements and interdependencies.

The first two issues, briefly addressed, appear to have special relevance to those involved in interreligious moral dialogues, where participants gather because of interest in practical moral questions about how to understand one another better, how to live wisely and well according to the golden rule, and how to be present to those in need; by gathering together they assume that dialogue is possible as well as valuable. The third and fourth issues, probed at greater length, are likely to have special interest for scholars in comparative religious ethics, because fascination with the functions and roles of religions in society, and with questions about method and approach, remain abiding concerns among religious studies scholars.

Solidarity Preferable to Charity

Elvia Alvarado, a Honduran campesina and author of *Don't Be Afraid Gringo: A Honduran Woman Speaks from the Heart,* makes her basic point baldly: "Hondurans don't want to be beggars. We're tired of begging from the United States. We want to be equals. And to be equals we need more than charity; we need solidarity" (1987, 106).

Elvia's granddaughter participates in a U.S.-sponsored program that provides a hot meal to five hundred children a day. "Every child has gringo godparents in the United States," Elvia explains:

> The gringos send the child a picture of their family, write letters, and send gifts once in a while . . . I'm very grateful to all these organizations in the United States, especially the private and religious organizations. I appreciate the food and clothing they send. I thank them sincerely for their willingness to help, and I know they do it with great love.
>
> But I'd also like to say that this relationship—where we're dependent on the goodwill of outsiders—isn't the kind of relationship we'd like to have. It's not our ideal kind of exchange.
>
> Because this way we're always waiting for handouts. We're always waiting for foreign institutions to come and give us food, to give us clothing, to give us dollars. In the long run, we're no better off.
>
> We're not going to solve our problem through handouts. Because our problem is a social one. And until we change this system, all the charity in the world won't take us out of poverty. (103–104)

Although "solidarity" is not a new term, it is assuming a distinctive prominence in our time as the actions and words of the poor compel worldwide attention and moral reflection (O'Connor 1993a, 1993b).

To enter into solidarity with the poor requires, among other things, that one work to view reality from their perspective. It demands that one listen well to the stories of their struggles, that one use one's moral imagination to picture, for example, the inadequate housing described at a meeting of the Assembly of Marginalized Women in 1988: "Our houses are shacks built with discarded tin, cardboard, plastic or other junk. Some of us live in one small room made of mud and sticks. We have to wrap our children in plastic so that they won't get wet. Our shacks are next to rivers filled with sewage. We live with the fear that the rains will carry our homes and children away" (Wright 1990, 80).

To view reality from the perspective of the poor requires us to recognize that many have resigned themselves to waking up and going to bed hungry, picking through garbage, witnessing bloated bellies from malnutrition and becoming accustomed to early childhood death.[2] To view reality from the perspective of those in resistance who work for social reconstruction is to take seriously the terrors and tortures that many experience at the hands of the state. In many of these countries, those who work for change are, by that very fact, considered subversives (Golden 1991, 122, 172, 184). "We have suffered because we demanded our rights—simply for thinking it was unjust to leave our children and to work for a minimum wage from sunup to sundown. That's the origin of our rebellion—simply that. The poor majority simply asked that we share in what the minority has gained through our labor and sweat" (Golden 1991, 102).

Maria Teresa Tula details the sufferings and intimidations endured by those who act on behalf of human rights. Describing the discovery of the body of Silvia Olan, a friend and coworker who disappeared and was later found dead, Tula writes: "There was evidence that she had been raped before she died. They had cut off part of her genitals and stuffed them into her nose. They cut off her breasts and her fingers as well. They had burned her eyes with acid, pulled out her tongue, and strangled her" (Tula 1989, 80). Beatings and sexual torture directed at women is common in many locations, as Tula learned from her own imprisonment and from exchanges with others:

> We women would talk to each other about all the horrible things that had happened to us. We had been tortured and raped by as many as eight or ten men, and some got pregnant as a result. . . . Some of the women were refugees who had been captured by the army. I remember one who was over 60 years old. They raped her with a flashlight over and over again. "Shove the flashlight in her vagina. See what she is hiding in there." These people suffered horrible things. . . . People had received electric shocks on their breasts, in their ears, and in their private parts. . . . I will never forget it. (161)

The impact of these stories on the storytellers themselves is often powerful, providing a prelude to moral conversion. After visiting her husband, who was sent to a Salvadoran prison because of his participation in a workers' strike, Tula muses, "I left prison that day with a great sadness, but a new vision of reality" (52). Having listened carefully to the stories of other mothers whose children and husbands had disappeared never to be seen again, she writes: "All of these stories entered my head and began to change the way I thought" (56).

Moving from unawareness and acceptance to explanation and analysis, Maria Teresa's narrative demonstrates why she became an advocate and activist on behalf of human rights as the wife of a victim and later as a member of CO-MADRES, the Mothers of the Disappeared. With this experience and commitment, she served as a speaker in Europe and the United States, promoting the international solidarity movement through which peoples throughout the world are invited to support and participate in the struggle for human rights and democratic self-determination.

Elvia Alvarado tells us exactly what she thinks solidarity means: "I'd say the best way to show solidarity with us is not by sending food or clothing or dollars. No. Show your solidarity by telling your government to get out of our country and leave us alone. And stand by us in our struggle" (Alvarado 1987, 106).

Ana Guadalupe Martinez of El Salvador articulates the hopes that give direction to this movement: "North Americans . . . want peace, justice, well-being, schools, education, work, health and religious freedom. Well, these are the same things our people want. They are the universal aspirations of the human race" (New America Press 1989, 160).

Yet support for these desires and for the ways in which they are formulated and pursued cannot be taken for granted, these women find, for many First World audiences find their testimonies about torture to be beyond belief and the destitute poverty in which many live to be outside of their experiences. Personalizing this dilemma, Tula reports an exchange with a woman she met in England, a pacifist who could not understand Tula's willingness to take up arms. Tula, by contrast, saw the use of arms as an understandable and legitimate act in defense of a people's life. "This time and every time we talked about Salvadoran politics we ended up shouting. Sometimes she would reproach me for what I said. I understood that she was a pacifist and wouldn't kill a fly. For her, hearing me talk about armed conflict was terrible. She couldn't accept it. I didn't understand her and she didn't understand me" (Tula 1989, 127).

Domitila Barrios de Chungara of Bolivia found this lack of understanding among First World peoples to be similarly problematic in that people simply "didn't see" and "couldn't see" what it is like to live in a society where basic human rights are not respected, where mine workers vomit their lungs bit by bit, where children are daily underfed, and where those working to change things are tortured (Barrios de Chungara 1978, 203).

These reports thus alert us to the difficulty of dialogue.

The Difficulty of Dialogue

Passionate about telling their stories, these women note that their sufferings and struggles are not always taken seriously. Maria Teresa Tula observes that people from the United States find it difficult to believe her accounts of torture and survival. They find such cruelty incredible. Journalists imply doubt as they report her words with qualification, claiming she "alleged" or "said" that she was tortured (Tula 1989, 176). Tula conjectures that this disbelief is largely due to the fact that people in the United States "have never lived in the middle of a war" (175). They often prepare for war in other countries and support wars elsewhere, she comments, but the majority lack direct experience of the cruelty that constitutes war. Tula and others provide the details that are necessary if we are to visualize more realistically and assess more knowledgeably the ways in which social conditions and class hostilities affect moral response and moral choice.[3]

Tula's observations spotlight the very notion of dialogue. Dialogue and other forms of verbal exchange are favored forums in the First World, where they are largely taken for granted. But the preconditions of dialogue include acceptance and trust, credibility and candor within an atmosphere of relative freedom. To the extent that a people's common experiences are beyond the moral imaginations of their listeners, let alone beyond their listeners' personal experiences, the possibility of dialogue is diminished. Second, dialogue can be dangerous for those who live in an atmosphere of intimidation, reprisal, and revenge. Dialogue is widely regarded as threatening or useless by those whose history is marked by being silenced, rejected, marginalized, ignored, or spoken for by those in power.

Enrique Dussel, an Argentine philosopher, historian, and ethicist, writes that efforts at intercultural communication must begin from the vantage point of alterity, from the standpoint of the other who has been excluded from dialogue or compelled into it (Dussel 1995). In some cases, the other may prefer silence and separation, given the asymmetrical positions of the parties present at the dialogue effort and given the historical experience of power inequities.

The testimonial literature that I cite does not take dialogue for granted as those in the First World tend to do. Those who live in developed countries tend to consider forthright exchange through dialogue to be possible, important, and achievable. But the literature that I refer to points to the fact that dialogue is a problem to be addressed, not simply a goal to be accomplished or a strategy to be assumed. Dussel asks the penetrating question we are tempted to rush beyond: What are the conditions for the possibility of dialogue? This is a question worth wrestling with—for scholars of comparative religious ethics and for participants in interreligious dialogues alike.

Nonetheless, a woman like Maria Teresa Tula, who has been disappointed by incredulous audiences and who knows well the difficulty of dialogue, presses for exchange, putting her hope in her children becoming "teachers of reality." She wants them to make known to First World "others" the human rights struggles her family has survived and the evils their experiences have exposed: "I want them to grow up in a different world. I don't want there to be war. I want there to be love, peace, and tranquillity. . . . I hope they will use what happened to our family as a way to educate other people. I hope that they will be 'maestros de la realidad,' teachers of reality" (Tula 1989, 177).

Tula alludes briefly to the way her religious faith strengthened her in the midst of her pain (151). She felt supported by the example of Archbishop Oscar Romero, who condemned human rights abuses in the name of God, who announced to soldiers that they were not obliged to obey orders contrary to God's law, and who begged, implored, and ordered the government and the military groups to stop the repression (Romero 1982, 1985; Erdozain 1981). Like many other Salvadoran critics, Romero was soon assassinated.

With respect to religion, Tula's testimony raises questions even as it conveys information. What roles do religions play in these human rights struggles? How do religious traditions, symbols, values, leaders, and institutions function in the testimonies told?

Religions and Human Rights

Elvia Alvarado places the origin of her human rights activities and involvements in church-sponsored programs. By means of these programs, she and others traveled to the countryside to instruct women on how to grow vegetables on their tiny plots of ground. Seeing the encouraging results of their work, they continued with commitment. But when she and other mothers started planting gardens, gathering construction materials, and building roads, support for the work abruptly ended. Their activities were seen as subversive by the government and as dangerous by the church. "They wanted us to give food out to malnourished mothers and children, but they didn't want us to question why we were malnourished to begin with. They wanted us to grow vegetables on the tiny plots around our houses, but they didn't want us to question why we didn't have enough land to feed ourselves" (Alvarado 1987, 16).

Given the current debate on religions and human rights,[4] a series of questions emerges: How are religions presented and portrayed in these stories? How do religions function in these human rights struggles from the peoples' points of view? Are religions in these settings the opiate of the poor, siding with the powerful, fostering the status quo, encouraging the masses to remain content with their lot and hope for a better life only after death? Or is religion a stimulus to change, an impetus to revolution, a grounding for dignity and justice that supports and fosters human rights efforts?

According to many of these testimonies, religion is both of these, oppressive in its passivity in one village, a liberating presence in another. Often enough, religions function as both passive-oppressive forces and liberating presences in the very same locale. Wrestling with competing visions of what it is to be religious and how best to understand religious responses to social evils is a struggle that takes place in multiple settings: between communities, within a single community, and within the mind of an individual person.

A base Christian community north of the Torola River in Morazan, El Salvador, reports its religious self-understanding in terms of a decisive shift in outlook and orientation. Initially, given the hardships of life due to floods and droughts, disease and unemployment, the people in this community took solace in prayer and ritual devotion because "praying made life more bearable." People prayed that life would improve, that the child would be cured and the crops would grow well. Religious beliefs and rituals were "a great relief" (Golden 1991, 40) for a people burdened by life and left to rely on their own resources.

> Since we didn't make a good impression or express ourselves well, no one listened to us *campesinos*. Nobody. Not even the priest with all his grandiosity, or the mayor with all his authority, or even less someone that was high up. In the chapel, alone, without a sound, God listened to the words that we said and those that remained embedded in our hearts. Nothing changed, everything continued to be just as ugly, but it made things more bearable to tell God our troubles and things seemed to get at least a little better. . . .
>
> If a visitor came by, a stranger to our parts, perhaps he would say, "And what good does so much praying do?" The stranger didn't understand the deepest parts of the well of faith. . . . It wasn't a matter of understanding, it was a matter of believing: we always kept our faith in God, in the God of the poor, in the God who would put a hand into our life and would perform the miracle of opening up a way out. (Golden 1991, 40–42)

The "way out" they looked for came in two forms: in "the word of God" believed to be present in the Bible, and in the community support that developed when "poor people began to have faith in other poor people" (Golden 1991, 42). This community credits the Second Vatican Council (1963–1965) with launching the liberating changes they experienced, which led them to discover and become a new sort of church.[5] Their discovery of the Bible became a decisive moment for this and many other communities among the poor. Rigoberta Menchu describes the liberating force of the Bible as a "weapon" (Menchu 1984, 130, 134), which she put to use in her nonviolent resistance in Guatemala. The Tarola community in neighboring El Salvador uses a different set of metaphors. These villagers describe the impact of the Bible on their lives to the flipping of a tortilla, to an earthquake, and to a breath that nourishes life-giving fire:

> This book of God is subversive because it turns the tortilla over, because it throws down the order of kings and empires and it puts the poor on top. This book with its stories of liberation, with its message of the prophets, with the life of Jesus that conquered death, with the stories of the first Christian communities, changed our life. This book taught us that we, the poor, are the preferred ones of God, that God wants the poor to stop being poor and that God calls us to work to change things. Our finding the Bible was like an earthquake. It changed the way things are, it changed the way of our thinking, of our doing things. It was the first breath that made the coals turn red. And in what seemed to be only ashes there was born a fire. (Golden 1991, 42)

Priests and religious people, pastoral agents and catechists came to the poor and prepared them to share and celebrate this word in their own communities. Then Archbishop Oscar Romero preached to them of justice and liberation in the midst of repression. "Through him . . . we were able to understand that the word of God spoke about our own life," they write. They began to see their faith as a "task" that carried an "obligation" (Golden 1991, 43) to create a future rather than as merely a "great relief" from the misery of the present (40). They explain: "And that is how we, poor men and women, began to stop believing in the false promises of outsiders, the great and the powerful, and we turned to our neighbors to reflect with them, and to organize with them, and to believe in them" (43).

Out of this belief in one another, groups of literacy teachers emerged, brigades of health care workers gathered, and community cooperatives organized to improve the food supply. Together they mobilized for education, health care, and nutrition; they asked hard questions about the status and fate of those who had disappeared; and they pressured those in power to honor their rights as workers, mothers, prisoners, and citizens.

For a time, these communities flourished; the people felt creative, and hope was fostered through visible, tangible gains. They looked out for the welfare not only of their own individual needs and family concerns but of one another as a community. "Never before had such marvelous things been seen, never before," they tell us (Golden 1991, 44). What they did not know at the time they began to organize, however, was that to do this work they would have to confront the Salvadoran army and other military groups supported by the landowning oligarchy who would regularly block their efforts.

Disappearances, imprisonment, bombings, and torture became common responses to the work of community organizers and activists. As the community continued to demand accountability from the government, they gained attention and garnered solidarity from regional and global human rights organizations that assisted their efforts in the face of repression. Many took up arms to defend themselves and their communities.

> In daily life we have seen that this action of God, of raising up the poor and giving them life, clashes with the powerful in this world. At first it didn't seem so clear to us, but now we know it well. . . . Our projects seem to us to be so good and so just, but they prohibit them, they want to destroy them. They continuously attack us and accuse us of being subversives. They threaten us. . . .
>
> To defend life . . . our people have had to take up arms to fight to hasten the day of justice for all and the day of true peace. They pushed us into this violence, they forced us into it. In this process toward peace our church of the poor lives now. (Golden 1991, 45)

Whether or not armed force hastens or slows justice and peace and whether the use of violence is morally legitimate are hotly contested issues across cultures. The point I wish to make here, rather, pertains to the way religion functions in the lives and work of the poor. The story told here makes it clear that however controversial their means and methods, the members of this community became mobilized by a vision of justice and peace that was fortified by religious texts and symbols, religious authorities and values.

Their newly discovered religious vision affirmed their dignity, condemned the unjust conditions of their lives, and offered a vision of justice and peace toward which to work. Contrasting the past with the present, this community cites a powerful shift in its religious attitude from passivity to activity, from waiting for God to act on their behalf to acting on their own behalf, even to the point of death: "They used to take our lives away and we didn't know how God would act to change things. Now we give up our life and we already know that God is on our side, that God is with us and that we are going to win" (Golden 1991, 45).

This communal account of a shift in the way religion operated in the lives of the poor makes visible the differences between religion-as-consolation in the midst of unalterable suffering on the one hand and religion-as-source-of-social-criticism and religion-as-stimulus-to-social-change on the other. When they took seriously the stories of the Bible, the villagers tell us, they saw themselves in the stories they read. From these stories, they gained a perspective about what life could be and should be. They acquired a new framework by which to examine and assess the social order in which they were immersed and in terms of which they had once felt helpless. The energy and creativity unleashed by this new religious awareness is marked—and marred—by a God-is-on-our-side enthusiasm that carries the potential for its own oppressiveness. The point to be noted simply pertains to a shift in the locus of power: These people feel empowered rather than disempowered by religious voices, stories, and perspectives.

Their archbishop, Oscar Romero, among others made clear to them that civil law, social practice, and cultural norms are not ends in themselves but are accountable to higher values such as justice, dignity, respect, responsibility, and love. Romero had preached to the government as well as the poor: "No soldier is obliged to obey an order contrary to the law of God. . . . I beseech you, I beg you, I order you, in the name of God, stop the repression!" (Romero 1982, 1985; Erdozain 1981). Like many Salvadorans in resistance, Romero was killed. His sociocritical perspective functioned to empower this community to disclose evil in the social circumstances of their lives, to transform attitudes of passivity, to engage in activities of resistance, and to take action on behalf of radical social change.

Not all the churches were in agreement on this approach. Elvia Alvarado, for example, criticizes Christians who are concerned with evangelization to the exclusion of community organization and social change. To those who quoted their pastor that it was sinful to be involved with community organizations and that religious people should focus on spiritual matters alone, Elvia responds: "Your pastor want to talk about sin? . . .

Does he tell you it's a sin to die of hunger? Does he tell you it's a sin that your children are malnourished? Does he say it's a sin that you can't give them a decent meal, decent clothes, a decent education? Does he say it's a sin for pastors to live as well as he does while his people go hungry?" (Alvarado 1987, 32).

Similarly, Rigoberta Menchu observes that "the Church in Guatemala is divided in two" (Menchu 1984, 245). On the one hand, there is the church of the poor, composed of Christians who condemn and denounce the injustices committed against the people; on the other, there is the institutional church represented by the officers and hierarchy who too often remain deaf to the suffering of the people and thus support the status quo out of loyalty or fear. Rigoberta explains her own choice:

> The world I live in is so evil, so bloodthirsty, that it can take my life away from one moment to the next. So the only road open to me is our struggle, the just war. The Bible taught me that. I tried to explain this to a Marxist *campanera,* who asked me how could I pretend to fight for revolution being a Christian. I told her that the whole truth is not found in the Bible, but neither is the whole truth in Marxism, and that she had to accept that. We have to defend ourselves against our enemy but, as Christians, we must also defend our faith within the revolutionary process. . . . This is what I have to teach my people: that together we can build the people's Church, a true Church. Not just a hierarchy, or a building, but a real change inside people. I chose this as my contribution to the people's war. I am convinced that the people, the masses, are the only ones capable of transforming society. (Menchu 1984, 246)

The authors of these testimonies press us to listen, learn, and develop a realistic sense of the struggles for survival and the terrible moral choices they face. Part of the process of collecting information on Third World sources involves recognition of an already existing engagement with them. This fact raises questions for scholars in comparative religious ethics about the ways in which we envision and approach our work.

Scholarly Standpoints

Although scholars regularly speak of the necessity of approaching their work in terms of "dispassionate research" from a position of "scientific objectivity" as (in terms of ethics) "ideal (distant) observers," Third World voices render these claims curious and questionable. Part of the latters' testimony is that the lives of outside observers are implicated in theirs. What does this ask of us, as heirs of an enlightenment tradition that honors "objectivity" as a scholarly ideal and operative norm for inquiry and investigation?

Although criticisms of enlightenment rationality are current in our time, emerging from feminist, environmentalist, pacifist, and postmodernist perspectives, among others, inherited notions of objectivity, impartiality, and neutrality persist in having a powerful hold on our thinking. Critics of these norms rightly note that "objectivity," "impartiality," and "neutrality" regularly mask the realities of geopolitical (and also gender, economic, cultural, and social) location and philosophical standpoint. I agree with this assessment.

A more apt description of the work of studying living persons and peoples, as well as relating to them in personal dialogues, I propose, is that scholars and dialogue partners alike are engaged in a study of subjects studying subjects, we studying us, both of whom are shaped by a history of intercontinental interactions and transnational exchanges.

To be a North American studying South Americans, for example, is not to be neutrally located but to be implicated in the lives of neighbors to the south by virtue of multiple international interdependencies. Intercontinental business practices, governmental interactions, and religio-cultural exchanges between North and South America create the matrix in which our relationships with one another are forged and in which investigation and representation of one another occur. Concretely, this is evident in the billions of U.S. dollars of military support that have been poured into countries like El Salvador. Daniel Santiago notes that $4 billion in U.S. military aid has not only supported military supplies, training, and maneuvers, but "has contributed to the militarization of all sectors of Salvadoran society. . . . For example, an association of retired and active military officers is now the largest real estate developer in El Salvador. Military officers control the most important agencies of the government. The military exerts control over the judicial system. Military values—conformity, acquiescence, unquestioning obedience to 'legitimate authority'—exert a great influence on popular culture" (Santiago 1993, 3).

By contrast, creativity, nonconformity, and community initiatives are regarded as subversive, and the price of subversion has often been death. Daniel Santiago, a Catholic priest at a San Salvador parish for six years who offers his own testimonial and an appraisal of the peace process begun in 1992, is not alone in concluding that "North Americans need to confront their culpability in this travesty of justice" (Santiago 1993, 4). Santiago notes that a month before his death, Archbishop Romero wrote a letter to U.S. President Jimmy Carter urging him not to send any more funding to the military. The funding continued.

Encoded in the language of objectivity, neutrality, and impartiality are critically important and nonnegotiable values such as accuracy in the apprehension of information and the display of insight, and honesty in reports and findings. But what the scientific paradigm lacks is the very ingredient that we are here being pressed to consider, namely, self-critical reflection. Studying others as the object and as the subject (matter) of our quest for understanding requires critical attention to our own standpoints as inquirers. When we North Americans study South Americans, or Asians, or Africans (or Third World communities within the First World) today, we are regularly being asked—by our subject matter—to investigate the changing forms of colonialism and neocolonialism that are inside of us the inquirers by virtue of our social location. We are being asked to interrogate attitudes of arrogance, control, and superiority that are intrinsic to these "isms." We are asked to face foreign policy complicity in the terrors these people undergo and to address our own naïveté about the force of self-interest and expressions of cruelty.

A Chinese proverb delivers a sobering observation: "Two-thirds of what we see is behind our eyes." Understanding the "other" requires us to look beyond our eyes, surely, but it requires us also to look behind our eyes to the inherited assumptions and chosen frameworks—about culture, class, gender, ethnicity, religion, and morality—that enable us to see anything at all. The limitedness of the scientific paradigm for scholarly work in the humanities in general, and the study of religions in particular, becomes increasingly more visible as we focus on *one another as other*, one another as the data for understanding.

When the data that we study, as testimonial literature makes clear, are *people's ways of seeing and suffering, surviving and coping, rebelling and repressing, valuing and acting, assessing and critiquing, dominating and resisting, destroying, creating, and transforming,* we are the wiser to note from the start that we are not studying objects objectively; rather, we are subjects working to understand the subjectivity of other subjects. To do this is to expand our cognitive, affective, and moral horizons. What people see and feel; why persons judge, choose, and act as they do; how humans exert power and process privilege; the strategies by which people deal with destitution and despair; the ways they exhibit creativity and hope—is knowledge that is difficult to access. But the testimonials cited here yield glimpses into those processes of initiative and response through which people express who they are and who they hope to become. Their reflections and yearnings are a mirror to us their readers.

This literature provides a rich database of information about the ways in which people approach one another morally and immorally in the midst of dramatic social, political, and gender inequalities. These inequalities are vividly displayed with respect to purchasing power, nutrition, education, and health care opportunities; with respect to a personal sense of bodily integrity and dignity in the family, the workplace, and the prison; and with respect to workers' rights, prisoners' rights, women's rights, and citizens' rights to initiate and to dissent. Since religions have commonly been influential sources of moral visions and values, and since religious institutions have commonly fallen short of, ignored, or abandoned their ideals in practice, the varying roles that religions play in the struggles taking place today in El Salvador, Guatemala, and other Third World countries provide important case studies.

The heritages of colonialism and neocolonialism, sexism and racism in which we ourselves are implicated by virtue of our geopolitical and social location, are now broadly recognized as critical factors that affect the ways in which we approach and therefore understand other persons, peoples, and cultures. The entire debate about the ways in which we perceive and present *the other* engages us in moral attentiveness, inquiry, and analysis.[6] How we approach *the other* morally is a question worth wrestling with in a wide range of contexts: international relations, domestic policy in a multicultural and multireligious society, daily life in workplace, neighborhood, and family life.

The *other* is, of course, a grand abstraction for the many persons from whom and with whom we differ. Although this chapter highlights materials from Latin America, similar struggles are reported by people in Asia, Africa, and from communities within First World countries as well. They write to expose gross inequities and to seek support for their human rights efforts and aspirations. The many differences we face in our attempts to understand and live with one another are briefly but vividly glimpsed in a broad-brush portrait of the world as global village.

Differences in Global Perspective

Downscaling the global village metaphor to a population of 1000 people, it is illuminating to note, for example, that 584 of these 1000 inhabitants are Asians; 124 are Africans; 95 East and West Europeans; 84 Latin Americans; 55 Russians, Lithuanians, Latvians, and Estonians; 52 North Americans; and 6 Australians and New Zealanders. The religious and a-religious loyalties are these: 329 of these 1000 are Christians, 178 Muslims, 132 Hindus, 60 Buddhists, 3 Jews, 86 members of all other religions (such as indigenous traditional religions as well as Sikhs, Jains, Zoroastrians, and Baha'is), and 212 are without any religion. The diverse religions named here thus characterize 788 of 1000 persons in the global village, while 212 persons out of 1000 have no religion.[7]

Additional estimates prompt further comparisons. An economic reading tells us that in this 1000-person community, 200 people receive 75 percent of the income whereas another 200 receive only 2 percent of the income. More graphically, only 70 of the 1000 own an automobile (and some of these 70 own more than one). About one third have access to clean, safe drinking water. Of the 670 adults in the village, half are illiterate (Meadows 1993, 168). The 1994 United Nations Development Report displays a dramatic difference in the ratio of poor to wealthy countries in the world: 60:1. In 1960, the ratio had been 30:1.[8] These figures dramatically demonstrate that the distribution of the world's wealth is narrowing, not expanding.

These facts, figures, and images put us in our place vis-à-vis one another with respect to religion, socioeconomic status, nutritional and educational opportunities, and the like. Through symbols such as the global village, through statistics that detail global inequities, and through stories that bring to life the misery of the majority, scholars and citizens with notable access to power and privilege have much to learn. Statistical figures are important for us to know. But it is in narrative description that we gain a sense of the moral impact that such conditions have on people. It is in the detail that our moral imaginations are stretched and our constructive moral thinking challenged.

For participants in interreligious moral dialogues, these materials can expand awareness and foster understanding not only about *the other* who is afar but also about *the other* next door. As more and more legal and illegal immigrants fleeing unrest and instability, actual and threatened persecution, move to North America, democratic citizens there are wise to do some homework in an effort to understand the whys and wherefores of those who are becoming new neighbors, fellow voters, and sometimes family members.

After traveling internationally as a "teacher of reality" to build solidarity for the human rights struggle in El Salvador, Maria Teresa Tula observed how easy it was even for her to "get disconnected from what the daily life of most people is like." She explains: "I learned many new things on these trips about other people and about El Salvador as well. I realized that there is so much about the life of people in my country that I don't even know. The work that I do takes me to certain places but I don't know everything that goes on. Even now that I have been doing solidarity work, I can get disconnected from what the daily life of most people is like" (Tula 1989, 129).

If an El Salvadoran civil rights activist can "get disconnected from what the daily life of most people is like," how much more are those who enjoy privilege in the First World likely to "get disconnected" from the world's majority, unless they allow themselves to learn from these "teachers of reality"?

I have proposed that scholars of comparative religious ethics and participants in interreligious moral dialogues take seriously testimonial literature of Third World, particularly Central American, peoples. By allowing them to be our teachers, we gain important information about the terrible realities of their lives and the possibilities they work to construct. In the course of doing so, we are challenged to think in new ways about our lives in relation to theirs, reconstruing the virtue of charity in terms of solidarity, for example, and facing the fact that dialogue is a task to be worked at, not a process to be assumed.

By reading these materials, we are positioned to notice with nuance the complex, changing, and sometimes conflicting ways in which religions function in people's lives. For those of us in the academy, these materials refute simplistic assumptions inherited from enlightenment critiques of religion that religion serves the masses only as an opiate. And we are led to notice anew the ways in which international interactions contextualize our work as scholars, pressing us to reconsider issues about starting point, standpoint, and viewpoint.

Other learnings, insights, and ways of thinking, stimulated by these materials, undoubtedly await attention and articulation. In a spirit of research and of dialogue, I invite fellow scholars and dialogue participants alike to report similarly on what you have learned from these teachers of reality.

Notes

1. See United Nations development reports, Amnesty International reports, and the work of social scientists, historians, and theologians on conditions in Latin America.

2. Reports from El Salvador inform us that almost 60 percent of Salvadoran children die before they reach the age of five and 73 percent of those under five are malnourished. Salvadorans have the lowest caloric intake per capita in all of Latin America. It is claimed that 2 million out of a population of 5.5 million live in extreme poverty. The death rate for women at childbirth is five times higher than for U.S. women. In 1977, before the war, there was one doctor for every 3,700 persons and one nurse for every 4,000 persons (Golden 1991, 106–107).

3. Mark Danner's *The Massacre at El Mozote: A Parable of the Cold War* (1994) offers an excellent investigation into one particular Salvadoran village massacre perpetrated by government forces. Utilizing eye-witness accounts, archaeological digs, and government documents exchanged between El Salvador and Washington, D.C., Danner provides vivid details. This book originated as the article "A Reporter at Large: The Truth of El Mozote," *The New Yorker,* December 6, 1993. A North American eye-witness report and testimony on the war in El Salvador is available in Charles Clements' *Witness to War: An American Doctor in El Salvador* (1985).

4. For a report on the struggle for human rights in Latin America in particular, see Penny Lernoux's richly informative and beautifully written *Cry of the People: The Struggle for Human Rights in Latin America* (1982). For broader discussions, see Kelsay and Twiss 1994; Twiss and Grelle 1995, 21–48; An-Na'im 1995; Küng and Moltmann 1990.

5. The Second Vatican Council convened Roman Catholic bishops from around the world at the Vatican to deliberate on ways in which these pastors might effectively address widespread poverty, war, atheism, and internal church conflicts, among other global and ecclesial issues. Attention to the sufferings of the poor was given special attention in "The Church in the Modern World," one of sixteen documents produced by the council.

6. Edward W. Said's *Orientalism* (1978) has been a causative force in this discussion. For a discussion that highlights the ethical dimension of the debate, see Armin W. Geertz, "On Reciprocity and Mutual Reflection in the Study of Native American Religions," *Religion* 24 (1994):1–22, with responses by June O'Connor, Kenneth Morrison, John W. Fulbright, and Lee Irwin and a response to respondents from Geertz.

7. Meadows 1993; also available in poster form from Value Earth Poster, c/o David Copeland, 707 White Horse Pike C–2, Absecon, NJ 08201; 609/641–2400. Donella Meadows is a systems analyst, journalist, and professor at Dartmouth College. Her book *The Global Citizen* (Washington, D.C.: Island Press, 1991) is a collection of short essays in which she elaborates on global statistics.

8. See United Nations 1994; see also Ruth Leger Sivard's annual *World Military and Social Expenditures* as well as *Hunger 1995: Causes of Hunger* (Silver Spring, Md.: Bread for the World Institute, 1994) for a wealth of statistics about poverty. For an excellent and accessible global view of current affairs regarding population, migration, life expectancy, poverty, nutrition, infant death, discrimination, unemployment, drugs, military power, censorship, and related issues, see Kidron and Segal 1995. Maps and graphics render these issues in comparative perspective.

References

Alegria, Claribel. 1987. *They Won't Take Me Alive: Salvadoran Women in Struggle for National Liberation*. Translated by Amanda Hopkinson. London: The Women's Press.

Alvarado, Elvia. 1987. *Don't Be Afraid Gringo: A Honduran Woman Speaks from the Heart*. Translated and edited by Medea Benjamin. New York: Harper and Row.

Angel, Adriana, and Fiona Macintosh. 1987. *The Tiger's Milk: Women of Nicaragua*. New York: Henry Holt.

An-Na'im, Abdullahi A., Jerald Gort, et al., eds. 1995. *Human Rights and Religious Values: An Uneasy Relationship?* Amsterdam and Atlanta: Editions Rodopi B. V.

Barrios de Chungara, Domitila, with Moema Viezzer. 1978. *Let Me Speak! Testimony of Domitila, a Woman of the Bolivian Mines*. Translated by Victoria Ortiz. New York: Monthly Review Press.

Boulding, Elise. 1976. *The Underside of History: A View of Women Through Time*. Boulder: Westview Press.

Cabastrero, Teofilo. 1985. *Blood of the Innocent: Victims of the Contras' War in Nicaragua*. Translated by Robert R. Barr. Maryknoll, N.Y.: Orbis Books.

Camara, Helder. 1969. *The Church and Colonialism: The Betrayal of the Third World*. Translated by William McSweeney. Kansas City, Mo.: Sheed and Ward.

Clements, Charles. 1985. *Witness to War: An American Doctor in El Salvador*. New York: Bantam.

Danner, Mark. 1994. *The Massacre at El Mozote: A Parable of the Cold War*. New York: Vintage.

Dussel, Enrique. 1995. *The Invention of the Americas: Eclipse of "The Other" and the Myth of Modernity*. Translated by Michael D. Barber. New York: Continuum.

Eck, Diana L., and Devaki Jain, eds. 1987. *Speaking of Faith: Global Perspectives on Women, Religion, and Social Change*. Philadelphia: New Society Publishers.

Erdozain, Placido. 1981. *Archbishop Romero: Martyr of El Salvador*. Translated by John McFadden and Ruth Warner. Maryknoll, N.Y.: Orbis Books.

Etzioni, Amitai. 1988. *The Moral Dimension: Toward a New Economics*. New York: The Free Press.

Evans, Robert A. and Alice Frazer Evans. 1983. *Human Rights: A Dialogue Between the First and Third Worlds*. Maryknoll, N.Y.: Orbis Books.

Galdamez, Pablo. 1986. *Faith of a People: The Life of a Basic Christian Community in El Salvador*. Maryknoll, N.Y.: Orbis Books.

Golden, Renny, ed. 1991. *The Hour of Women, the Hour of the Poor: Salvadoran Women Speak*. New York: Crossroad.

Gugelberger, Georg and Michael Kearney. 1991. "Voices for the Voiceless: Testimonial Literature in Latin America," *Latin American Perspectives* 18, 3 (Summer):3–14.

Gutiérrez, Gustavo. 1990. "Towards the Fifth Centenary." In *1492–1992: The Voice of the Victims [Concilium 1990/6]*, edited by Leonardo Boff and Virgil Elizondo. London: SCM Press.

Kelsay, John, and Sumner Twiss, eds. 1994. *Religion and Human Rights*. New York: The Project on Religion and Human Rights.

Kidron, Michael, and Ronald Segal. 1995. *The State of the World Atlas*. 5th ed., revised. New York: Penguin Books.

Küng, Hans, and Jürgen Moltmann, eds. 1990. *The Ethics of World Religions and Human Rights*. Concilium. London: SCM Press.

Lernoux, Penny. 1982. *Cry of the People: The Struggle for Human Rights in Latin America*. New York: Penguin Books.

Little, David, John Kelsay, and Abdulaziz Sachedina. 1988. *Human Rights and the Conflict of Cultures*. Columbia: University of South Carolina Press.

Meadows, Donella. 1993. "Who Lives in the Global Village?" In *A Sourcebook for the Community of Religions,* edited by Joel Beversluis, 168. Chicago: The Council for a Parliament of the World's Religions.

Menchu, Rigoberta. 1984. *I, Rigoberta Menchu: An Indian Woman in Guatemala*. Edited by Elisabeth Burgos-Debray. Translated by Ann Wright. London: Verso.

New America Press, ed. 1989. *A Dream Compels Us: Voices of Salvadoran Women*. Boston: South End Press.

O'Connor, June. 1993a. "Comforting the Sorrowful: From Charity to Solidarity." In *Rethinking the Spiritual Works of Mercy,* edited by Francis Eigo, 67–96. Villanova, Pa.: Villanova University Press.

_____. 1993b. "Stories from the South: The Voices of Latin American Women." *The Annual of the Society of Christian Ethics*:283–290.

Partnoy, Alicia, with Lois Athey and Sandra Braunstein. 1986. *Tales of Disappearance and Survival in Argentina*. Translated by Alicia Partnoy. Pittsburgh: Cleis.

Partnoy, Alicia, ed. 1988. *You Can't Drown the Fire: Latin American Women Writing in Exile*. Pittsburgh: Cleis.

Romero, Oscar A. 1982. *Martyr for Liberation: The Last Two Homilies of Archbishop Romero of San Salvador*. London: CIIR.

_____. 1985. *Voice of the Voiceless: The Four Pastoral Letters and Other Statements*. Translated by Michael J. Walsh. Maryknoll, N.Y.: Orbis Books.

Said, Edward W. 1978. *Orientalism*. New York: Vintage.

Santiago, Daniel. 1993. *The Harvest of Justice: The Church of El Salvador Ten Years after Romero*. New York: Paulist.

Sivard, Ruth Leger. Annual. *World Military and Social Expenditures*. Washington, D.C.: World Priorities.

Sturm, Douglas. 1994. "The Idea of Human Rights." *Process Studies* 23, 3-4 (Fall-Winter 1994):238–255.

Tula, Maria Teresa. 1989. *Hear My Testimony: Maria Teresa Tula, Human Rights Activist of El Salvador*. Edited and translated by Lynn Stephen. Boston: South End Press.

Twiss, Sumner, and Bruce Grelle. 1995. "Human Rights and Comparative Religious Ethics: A New Venue." *The Annual of the Society of Christian Ethics*:21–48.

United Nations. 1994. *Human Development Report*. New York: Oxford University Press.

Vigil, Maria Lopez. 1989. *Death and Life in Morazan: A Priest's Testimony from a War-Zone in El Salvador*. London: CIIR.

_____. 1990. *Don Lito of El Salvador*. Translated by Orbis Books. Maryknoll, N.Y.: Orbis Books.

"Voices of the Voiceless in Testimonial Literature, Part I." 1991. *Latin American Perspectives* 18 (Summer).

"Voices of the Voiceless in Testimonial Literature, Part II." 1991. *Latin American Perspectives* 18 (Fall).

Wright, Scott, et al., eds. 1990. *El Salvador: A Spring Whose Waters Never Run Dry*. Washington, D.C.: EPICA.

Chapter Nine

Piety, Politics, and the Limits Set by God: Implications of Islamic Political Thought for Christian Theology

JOHN KELSAY
Florida State University

At the outset, an explanatory note seems in order. While carrying out a bibliographic search for this project, I was struck by one of the subject headings under "dialogue." "Imagined conversations" read the heading, and a rather large number of titles were catalogued there.

The heading seemed provocative at first; upon reflection, however, its relevance seemed obvious. When we engage in dialogue, we imagine ourselves and the other: in collaboration, competition; over, against, and through one another. And all this suggested that the following, with its autobiographical cast, might present an interesting contribution to the theme of this volume, viz., the relationship between comparative religious ethics and interreligious dialogue.

Experience, Piety, and Obedience to Law

A Personal Note

I am sometimes asked how I came to my interest in Islam. When I am honest, I respond: pragmatically. While working on a ministry degree at a Presbyterian seminary, I determined to study ethics. My interest piqued by James Gustafson's work on the ways in which ethics might be "Christian,"

I had hopes of learning more about the ways Christian faith might be related to moral and political concerns. In a way, the goal was a type of self-understanding.

I also hoped, of course, to make a living. And so, in beginning graduate work at the University of Virginia, I spoke with teachers and colleagues about avenues of study that would allow me to pursue my original interests, while also enhancing my prospects for gainful employment. It was one of my colleagues who suggested that I take up a minor in Islamic tradition. Islam, he said, was "hot right now"—it was 1980, after all, and American hostages, whose fate helped bring about the election of Ronald Reagan, were being held in Tehran. After consulting with others, I began to read and to sit in on Abdulaziz Sachedina's courses. My motives, again, were pragmatic. Islam was, from my point of view, a way to speak about the motives of people behaving in ways that ran counter to American interests. Given time, I might be able to teach a survey of Islamic tradition; and if I worked hard enough, an understanding of Islam might play a role in any kind of analysis I developed of ethics and international relations.

By the end of a year's study, my perspective had changed. Having read as much as I was able in Islamic history and theology, and especially having developed a close association with Sachedina, I began to think in terms of Islam's power as a religious tradition. That is, I thought as much in terms of its conceptions of God, of humanity, and the relations between these; of Muslim perspectives on the moral and political life of humanity; and of the ways Muslim intellectuals had written about the relations between the religious and moral points of view, as I did in terms of the Islamic motives of contemporary activists. The two interests—in Islam as a religious tradition and in Islam as a clue in political analysis—belong together, of course. As my interest developed, however, I did experience a change in emphasis. If you like, you may say I found myself recognizing common ground in an Islamic "other." As I tried to understand, and continue to do so, I came to think of this common ground in terms of piety: a sense that, whatever human beings may be, they are creatures whose existence is characterized by the experience of limits. In Islam, as in Christianity—at least, in the Reformed variety from which my understandings spring—"God" stands as "that which sets the limits" within which we must order our lives. Such is our responsibility, and also our fate.

Recognition and Difference

As a tradition, Islam (as Christianity) is characterized by the acceptance of certain practices conceived as legitimate ways of ordering human existence in the light of this central insight—this piety, if you will. Even more, Islam is characterized by debates about practice, as those who take part in its development aim at responsibility, within the lines of a particular conception of the limits set by God.

Recognition, then, is the first lesson I drew from my study of Islam. As one shaped in particular ways by the practices of a Reformed, and more particularly, southern Presbyterian community, I recognized in Islam something akin to my own experience. Without such recognition, I must assume that my own analysis of Islam would have remained purely pragmatic. In some sense, I would then be developing this essay differently. I would present Islam as more alien, more purely "other" than now seems appropriate.

Now, the minute we speak of "recognition" (or, if you prefer, the possibility of empathy) between Christians and Muslims, we must also acknowledge the reality of difference (or the necessity of critical distance). Once one affirms a certain resonance between important strands of Islam and (to stay with the aforementioned examples) Reformed Christianity in terms of piety, one must also admit that there are important discontinuities. To take one example: Both Muslims and Reformed Christians emphasize the place of obedience to God's law as one of the most, if not the most important among those practices conceived as legitimate ways of ordering human existence within the limits set by God. But the form, the priority, and, most interestingly, the mood of this obedience is quite distinct. Muslims speak of comprehending the guidance God gives through signs *(ayat)*, most especially the Qur'an and the exemplary practice of the Prophet.[1] The discussion of *Shari'a,* or that guidance that leads to Paradise, is characterized by an agreement about these sources and about certain techniques of interpreting them (e.g., *qiyas* and *ijma',* "analogical reasoning" and "consensus"). In the background of this discussion are assumptions about the nature of human beings as those creatures God placed in the world in order to test their use of divinely given capacities to order life with justice. The theory of *usul al-fiqh,* or the "sources of comprehension" of divine guidance, points to the specially Islamic, and therefore most secure, way of pointing forgetful, self-centered humanity toward the "straight path" laid out by God from the day of creation. As such, the discussion of *Shari'a* is a means by which human beings are reminded and taught concerning the "natural religion" that is written on their hearts as an aspect of their character as creatures. The importance of obedience, in connection with the nature and destiny of human beings, makes the discussion of *Shari'a* or divine law a matter of utmost importance. We may characterize the mood that follows in terms of humility, tied to the acceptance of one's status as a creature. Such humility is also accompanied by a sense of dignity that comes from disciplining oneself, setting oneself apart from the common, run-of-the-mill existence of forgetful humanity. The law becomes a set of exercises of obedience that train one's heart and mind to focus on the inevitable, inexorable coming of the Day of Judgment. In this sense, perhaps the best single term to characterize the mood of obedience in Islam is *taqwa*—that sense of "godly fear" or "mindfulness" that indicates an awareness of the coming judgment.

With respect to Reformed Christianity, the predominant mood is one of gratitude, developed in terms of an apprehension of the gift God has given to the elect in Christ the Redeemer. Here we do not have such an extended treatment of the sources of divine law. The mood of obedience is set, rather, by the sense that human beings, set apart as those creatures capable of voluntary or free obedience to God's law, have come through their solidarity in sin to a state of inability to obey. This inability is not total. In John Calvin's treatise on Christian liberty, as in other places, one finds that human beings are capable of apprehending and observing those aspects of the law most basic to their social existence (Calvin 1960, III.xix). Further, humanity is driven by an inescapable sense, a kind of lingering memory of its obligation to worship the Lawgiver. Sinful humans cannot, however, apprehend with any surety the proper mode of such worship. Even more troubling, the obedience they are able to offer is corrupted by fear, resentment, and confusion. Created for voluntary obedience to the law of their nature, human beings suffer from a divided mind. Knowing that they are under obligation, they find themselves unable and unwilling to perform their duty. They are reluctant servants, at best. It is this divided mind that God addresses and, according to Reformed doctrine, heals through Christ the Redeemer. Or, to put it, as Calvin does, in terms of the "way we receive the grace of Christ the Redeemer": Through the experience of regeneration, God creates the possibility of a "new mood" of obedience. Instead of reluctance, unwillingness, and fear, we find joy and thanksgiving. I am hardly the first to note the significance of certain primary metaphors employed by the two traditions in connection with obedience—for Islam, the servant or slave of God; for Reformed Christianity, the children of God. For our purposes, these set obedience within a certain symbolic context, which, as James Gustafson might put it, correlates with particular dispositions or moods characteristic of Muslim or Christian piety (Gustafson 1975).

The great question for us is, of course, what to do with these findings. We can play out these aspects of recognition and difference, of empathy and critical distance, in a number of ways. We can, for example, continue our inquiry about the two traditions. We will find ways that Muslims speak about obedience to divine law that more closely resemble those of Reformed Christians than I have indicated thus far. Alternatively, we will broaden the scope of our discussion of Christian conceptions of obedience so that we find ways of speaking that make for closer analogies with Islam. We can, in other words, push toward identifying practices within each tradition that suggest the necessity of greater recognition, more empathy. For Christians, continued inquiry concerning Islamic practice might lead, for example, to the recovery of certain models developed by our forebears, but which have been discarded for one reason or another.[2] Alternatively, Christians might come to consider whether particular practices of the Muslim community might present a real alternative for them—a model that should, in other words, be affirmed as viable for Christians, as Christian.

In that last phrase we encounter a limit, however; or so it seems to me. However far we go in acknowledging recognition, however much we develop our capacities for empathy, certain boundaries remain important. To put it another way, even when we succeed in locating points of recognition and identification between Christianity and Islam, we cannot say we have done so in terms of a kind of "neutral territory." Even in the case where one might recommend that the Christian community adopt a practice historically identified with Islam, one does so because he or she is able to say: "This can be considered legitimate, in Christian terms." There is, it seems, a sense in which the "limitedness" characteristic of human existence extends to those boundaries of practice that define the communities we call "Christian" and "Islamic." So far as I am able to understand, the following holds true even when we have pushed the limits of recognition and empathy to the point where recovery, recognition, and transformation become possible: As a Christian, I am able to appreciate Muslim conceptions of law. I can learn to deliberate about matters of practice with Muslims. I can learn to make judgments, as a Muslim would. I can adopt certain judgments typical of Muslim jurists as a legitimate part of Christian practice. What I cannot do is make judgments and/or obey the law *as* a Muslim, without in some sense ceasing to be a Christian.

Reflections on Social-Political Thought

With respect to social-political thought, we can take this point further. Not only am I bound by identification with the Christian community, at some point. I am also bound or limited with respect to social and historical contexts. In a moment, I shall turn to some particulars connected with Islamic teaching on war and statecraft. It is worth saying at the outset, however, that I believe we shall find that, no matter how many resonances we discover between Christian and Islamic perspectives on these matters; no matter how much we find ourselves able to appreciate certain motifs of Islamic social-political thought; no matter how much the inquiry into Islamic perspectives makes us able to reconsider the historic development of Christian ethics, there are certain modes of social-political practice that are simply not viable, particularly in the United States. So I will argue, at any rate. Let me proceed, first with some general comments about Islamic political thought; second, with some comparisons of Christian and Islamic political thought; and third, with a few reflections on the implications of Islamic practice on these matters for contemporary Christian thought and for comparative ethics.

Islamic Political Thought

Muslims developed their most formidable positions on war and statecraft during the period of the High Caliphate (ca. 750–1258). It is this "classical" teaching that I have in mind when, for the purposes of this essay, I speak of Islamic social-political thought. In *Islam and War* I tried to describe the contours of this teaching as developed by the majoritarian, or Sunni scholars of the law.[3]

For our purposes, this earlier study provides an interesting example of the phenomena described above as recognition (or empathy) and difference (or distance). It is important, for example, to see Islamic teaching on war as a part of a theory of statecraft, or more generally of the political life of humanity. As classical jurists saw it, all human beings were called to submit to God, or to observe the limits set by their Creator. Further, all human beings were created with a capacity for understanding their obligations—if human beings will "reflect," argues the Qur'an again and again, they will understand their position and submit themselves to God.

In submitting, human beings accept the responsibility to construct a just social order. Rightly understanding themselves, they become "strivers" or "strugglers" *(mujahidun)* with respect to this goal. Most, however, do not so understand themselves. "Rivalry in worldly increase" distracts them; they do not "pause to reflect" on the meaning of life and their place in the universe.[4] Even when, given the "second chance" of guidance that comes through the preaching of God's "messengers" and the witness presented by the communities founded by the greatest of these "prophets," human beings receive a direct "reminder" of their destiny, most refuse to submit. This fact gives the "struggle" or jihad of those who do submit a new seriousness. For the good of all God's creatures, those led by a rightly guided prophet are called to "command good and forbid evil" through the construction and maintenance of a just social order. In particular, given the historic failings of its predecessors (primarily the Jewish and Christian communities), the *umma,* or Muslim community, is called to bear witness through the establishment of a social-political order that will testify to the natural religion of humanity—pure monotheism, reinforced by practices that instantiate the limits set by God.

In connection with this mission, the Muslim community controls territory, establishes institutions of administration, sends missionaries, and, under certain circumstances, employs military force. So the classical jurists held; we shall return to some issues raised by disagreements among Muslims on these matters a little later. The point here is to understand the connections between religion, statecraft, and war in the classical Sunni theory. In connection with the urgent task of constructing and maintaining a just political order, this theory held, it was incumbent upon the Muslim community to struggle to enlarge the territory within which Islamic values held sway. The Caliph, or head of state, was required to consider the best ways to achieve that goal. It was always appropriate for him to send emissaries to the courts of his counterparts, say, in southern and central Europe. Understood at least as "cultural missionaries," such emissaries served to increase knowledge of Islam, and under certain conditions to invite non-Muslim heads of state and their people to enter into formal relationships with the territory of Islam.

Should such an invitation be refused, however, the sending of emissaries could be construed as prelude to a formal declaration of war. Again, given the Caliph's judgment that conditions were right—i.e., that there was a reasonable hope of success in extending the territory of Islam and a reasonable relationship between this hope and the costs to be born—war could occur. When it did, the jurists indicated, it should be governed by the example of the Prophet.

> Whenever the Apostle of God sent forth an army or a detachment, he charged its commander personally to fear God, the Most High, and he enjoined the Muslims who were with him to do good [i.e., to conduct themselves properly].
> And the Apostle said:
> Fight in the name of God and in the "path of God" [i.e., truth]. Combat [only] those who disbelieve in God. Do not cheat or commit treachery, nor should you mutilate anyone or kill children. Whenever you meet your polytheist enemies, invite them [first] to adopt Islam. If they do so, accept it, and let them alone. You should then invite them to move from their territory to the territory of the *emigres* [Madina]. If they do so, accept it and let them alone. Otherwise, they should be informed that they would be [treated] like the Muslim nomads (Bedouins) [who take no part in the war] in that they are subject to God's orders as [other] Muslims, but that they will receive no share in either the *ghanima* (spoils of war) or in the *fay'*. If they refuse [to accept Islam], then call upon them to pay the *jizya* (poll tax); if they do, accept it and leave them alone. If you besiege the inhabitants of a fortress or a town and they try to get you to let them surrender on the basis of God's judgment, do not do so, since you do not know what God's judgment is, but make them surrender to your judgment and then decide their case according to your own views. But if the besieged inhabitants of a fortress or a town asked you to give them a pledge [of security] in God's name or the name of His Apostle, you should not do so, but give the pledge in your names or in the names of your fathers; for, if you should ever break it, it would be an easier matter if it were in the names of you or your fathers.[5]

Elsewhere, we find sayings of the Prophet that further indicate the limits of Muslim warfare:

He [of the enemy] who has reached puberty should be killed, but he who has not should be spared.

The Apostle of God prohibited the killing of women.

The Apostle of God said: "You may kill the adults of the unbelievers, but spare their minors—the youth."

Whenever the Apostle of God sent forth a detachment he said to it: "Do not cheat or commit treachery, nor should you mutilate or kill children, women, or old men."[6]

Now, one need not look very hard at this teaching, even in this short summary, to sense the possibilities of recognition between Christianity and Islam. If we think of the just war tradition, or more appropriately (in my view) the tradition of "just war thinking," in Western Christianity, there are some striking similarities between Christian and Islamic social-political thought. Thus, the notion that war serves the ends of constructing and maintaining a legitimate political community stands out, as does the conception of war as a rule-governed activity. The formal nature of the rules, or criteria, governing the use of war in statecraft is also strikingly similar in the two traditions: for example, conceptions that limit the right to wage war to particular, designated authorities; and conceptions that tie the authorities' decision to estimations of the probabilities of success in pursuing legitimate aims and to considerations of proportionality. If one notes, further, the restrictions on targeting indicated in the Prophetic sayings cited above, as well as considerations of *jus in bello* proportionality that appear in the reasoning of jurists, the formal parallel between the just war criteria and the requirements for just war in Islam is nearly complete. One has only to add the observation, assumed by the jurists, that in following the Prophet's exhortation to "fight in the name of God and in the "path of God," soldiers in the service of the territory of Islam would be fighting a special type of war (jihad) set off from the more general phenomenon *(harb)* in which human beings fought for wealth, power, fame, honor, and the like, to understand that the Muslim jurists, as the just war thinkers, were setting limits all around the human activity we call war, thus making the phenomenon of recognition stronger still.[7]

Comparisons with Christian Thought

As with piety, so with politics, however: Recognition and empathy must be accompanied by an acknowledgment of difference and distance. The first reaction a student of modern just war discourse is likely to have is that, whatever analogy is present between his/her tradition and the classical notion of jihad, a signal difference lies in the fact that the jurists were envisioning and legitimating a war of conquest rather than a war of defense. That concern can be dealt with in a number of ways; at this point it will suffice to indicate that, in my opinion at least, that is far from the most important difference between the two traditions. Much more significant, especially in terms of the connections between jihad and just war traditions' larger visions of political life, is the role religion plays in the Islamic case. Note, for example, the rationale for war: the expansion of a territory within which Islamic values are paramount. For modern just war thinking, religion is never a just cause of war. For Islamic thought, religion is the only just cause of war. That in itself is a striking fact, the import of which only gets stronger as we follow the ways the rules of jihad are colored by religious concern, through and through. Thus, when we come to consideration of the *jus in bello* criteria of discrimination, we find the Islamic analogue of noncombatant immunity tied to considerations of religious guilt, rather than to status vis-à-vis the war effort. Soldiers are legitimate targets, not because they are functionally central to the enemy's making of war but because their participation in the war effort indicates their resistance to the extension of an Islamic political entity. Similarly, women, children, the aged and infirm are not ordinarily legitimate targets; but the rationale for this is that they are presumed "less responsible" for the enemy's resistance to Islam. It would be more accurate to speak of them as "less guilty" than as "innocent," in the just war sense of that term. The religious tenor of discrimination is further shown in the distinction between rules governing wars between Muslims and non-Muslims, and between different Muslim parties. In the latter case, the jurists presumed that one of the parties must be in the wrong. Nevertheless, unless that party casts off its religion (and so becomes a party of apostasy), its fighters remain Muslims, and must be treated in such a way that reconciliation remains possible. The *jus in bello* restrictions are more tightly defined; even rebels are treated leniently, compared to non-Muslims.

The religious cast of the jihad tradition is part and parcel of the classical Islamic vision of political order. "Religion and politics are twins," the saying goes; although this saying does not, in and of itself, support the contemporary judgment that "there is no distinction between religion and politics in Islam," it can (and usually does) imply conceptions of a closer working relationship between the institutions of religion and of the state than those supposed in contemporary just war thinking. The role of religion in classical Islamic thought is closely tied to judgments about the relations between religion and morality, especially in terms of moral performance. Human beings, left to their own devices, are less likely to seek justice or look out for the common good. While they have a God-given capacity to understand and fulfill the obligations of their nature (and thus, the judgment "less likely" is in some sense experiential rather than a priori), the jurists understood the story of humanity to be one of forgetfulness and heedlessness. The Muslim community is in the position of the parent or elder sibling who, having received instructions from the physician concerning a prescription for the illness of the child or younger sibling, is obligated to perform the onerous task of making sure the medicine is swallowed, or more appropriately, the environment is altered so that health becomes more likely.

The presupposition of the classical vision of political order, then, is that the establishment of a state in which Islamic values—the values "natural" to humanity—are acknowledged as a matter of policy enhances the prospects for human beings to live together in peace and justice. Consider the symbolism in the jurists' division of the world. Where Islam prevails, we have *dar al-islam,* "the territory of Islam." It is not without import that the trilateral root on which *al-islam,* "the submission," is based is *s-l-m,* i.e., "peace."

Outside the territory of Islam, we have *dar al-harb,* the "territory of war." And it is war in the generic, undignified, and unrestricted sense. *Al-harb,* as mentioned, means war fought for human glory, or for merely human causes. The presumption is that outside the territory in which Islamic values are acknowledged, human beings will tend to lose sight of their position as creatures of God. They will justify considering their own wants over those of others, and their political life will be characterized by more or less constant strife. The resolution of this problem lies in the success of the Muslim community and its mission. The territory of Islam comes to be envisioned as a universal state in which all humanity is governed by Islamic values. Not that everyone becomes a Muslim. That would be wonderful, from the jurists' point of view; but it is unlikely. Indeed, one must be careful to stipulate that war is never to be used in a direct campaign to encourage conversion. The justification of jihad, in the sense of a military campaign, is always limited to the spread of Islamic territory. Government, not conversion, is the aim of war in the path of God.

The great difference between just war thinking and the rules of jihad, I have argued, is in the role of religion. And this difference signifies an ongoing difference between important strands of the more general tradition of Islamic social-political thought and its Christian counterpart. With Islam, we have a tradition committed to the notion that the moral and political life of humanity cannot be all it ought to be without the assignment of an official role to true religion. In contemporary just war thinking, by contrast, we have the assumption that the aspirations of humanity are best served by a regime of sovereign nation-states, hopefully with a tilt toward the institutions and values of democracy, including special provisions for the rights of religious minorities. Although such matters are controversial, I am inclined to say even more: The logic of contemporary just war thinking, for example in the hands of writers like James Childress or Michael Walzer, lends itself to assumptions about the priority of freedom of conscience and religious liberty. That is so even though it seems true, as Childress puts it, that the just war criteria are made to order for use in a number of different social-political contexts.[8]

Some Implications of Islam for
Christian Thought and Comparative Ethics

Once we have spoken of both recognition and difference, we move to the question of what to do. As with the general issue of obedience to God's law, so with social-political thought: We can push our descriptions of Islamic and Christian perspectives further than we have thus far and find or create tighter analogies. In the case of Islam, for example, we might begin to explore trajectories other than that set by the classical Sunni jurists and their schools. We might find interesting the work of dissenters and reformists, Sunni and Shi'i alike, who argue that the only appropriate motive for war is defensive. Shi'i jurists of the classical period, for example, argued that the notion of military jihad in connection with the Islamic mission was offensive—at least, in the absence of the divinely appointed imam, or leader. Subsequently, Shi'i jurists made a specialty of discussing the subtleties that necessarily accompany any realistic limitation of war to defensive purposes: Can defense include preemptive strikes, for example, or must it always be confined to reaction against an enemy who "fires the first shot"? Contemporary Shi'i jurists continue this line of thought, whether considering the war initiated in 1980 by Iraq when it crossed Iran's borders or the "irregular" war fought by Shi'i militias since Israel's invasion of Lebanon in 1982. Contemporary Sunni jurists also suggest that jihad as military action must be defensive, either in the sense of defending the borders of one's country or in the sense of intervention to defend the liberties and rights of Muslim peoples.

This last stipulation, of course, points us back in the direction of the classical teaching's insistence on the close relations between religious institutions and the state. Quite frankly, no matter how far we go in examining Islamic social-political thought, this feature is going to be a prominent one. I have argued elsewhere for the possibility of a more "separationist" view of religion and politics in Islam, based on the Qur'an and on Muslim testimony (Kelsay 1988, 1996a). There is no getting around the fact, however, that such a view is that of a minority. For most Muslims engaged in serious discussion concerning the relationship of their tradition and political matters, the importance of a collaboration between religion and state is assumed.

The fact of this assumption leads us, if we continue the inquiry, to an entirely different set of possible implications for Christian thought. We do not need to look far to consider that Christian tradition did not always assume the separationist tendency now taken for granted by most Americans. Indeed, we know that in the history of Christian social-political thought, the

U.S. model is quite the exception; although one can argue that certain strands in the tradition, carried out and developed for example in the more separatist congregationalist churches, contributed greatly to the U.S. model, other groups came very slowly and carefully (to say the least) to such a model. As in the Islamic case, such caution (not to say resistance) to organizing social and political life around the notion that "God alone is Lord of the conscience" was based in part on assumptions about the connections between religion and moral practice. Whether one thinks of Lutheran orthodoxy, of much of Roman Catholicism prior to Vatican II, or of the "imperial" Calvinism of the Massachusetts Bay Colony and elsewhere, the suspicion that sinful human beings need the clear directives and motivation supplied by established religion in order to limit their tendencies toward selfishness and libertine behavior was very strong in Christian social-political thought. In this sense, the Islamic insistence on the official role of religion in political life resonates with important strains in historic Christianity.

More interestingly, the twist that contemporary Muslims give to the importance of religion in political life bears comparison with certain Christian writers who offer strong criticisms of secularism and liberalism. Consider for a moment the following statement:

> There is a great difference between all the manmade forms of government in the world, on the one hand—whatever their precise nature—and a divine government, on the other hand, which follows divine law. Governments that do not base themselves on divine law conceive of justice only in the natural realm; you will find them concerned only with the prevention of disorder and not with the moral refinement of the people. Whatever a person does in his own home is of no importance, so long as he causes no disorder in the street. In other words, people are free to do as they please at home. Divine governments, however, set themselves the task of making man into what he should be. In his unredeemed state, man is like an animal, even worse than the other animals. Left to his own devices, he will always be inferior to the animals, for he surpasses them in passion, evil, and rapacity. As originally created, man is superior to all other beings, but at the same time, his capacities for passion, anger, and other forms of evil are virtually boundless. For example, if a person acquires a house, he will begin to desire another house. If a person conquers a country, he will begin plotting to conquer another country. And if a person were to conquer the entire globe, he would begin planning the conquest of the moon or Mars. Men's passions and covetousness, then, are unlimited, and it was in order to limit men, to tame them, that the prophets were sent. (Khomeini 1981, 330–331)

Here, the late Ayatollah Khomeini speaks, and he means to advance an Islamic critique of various characteristics of the secular state: its assumption that laws are a matter of popular consent; its distinction between public and private realms; its lowering of the demands of public morality to a bare minimum of requirements, held to be necessary for the maintenance of a naked public square. For Khomeini, as for many contemporary Muslims, the premise of a type of public order that eschews a public, established role for religion is terribly wrongheaded. It claims to liberate humanity from the shackles of oppressive religious authorities; in reality, the liberal or secular state opens humanity to oppressors far worse. In failing to hold up, in public ways, the exemplary guidance proffered by God through God's messengers, the secular state leaves humanity free only to sink deeper and deeper into the mire of heedlessness, in which everyone acts according to their immediate desire and everyone receives according to their capacity for ruthless disregard for others.

Now, there certainly are Muslims who disagree with Khomeini: It is not hard to find Muslims who say that Khomeini went too far, too fast, or that his version of Islamic government gave too much power to religious specialists. Nevertheless, the judgment on which Khomeini's statement is based is one that many Muslims share. Liberal politics, or secular politics, provides an insecure basis on which to sustain political life. Humanity needs the guidance of true religion if its members are to live together commodiously and to flourish. A state without an established religion is a half-state. It is insecure by definition. To support this judgment, contemporary Muslims cite a list of occurrences that, by their criteria, illustrate the evils lurking beneath the veneer of liberalism and secularity: the exploitation of "lesser civilizations" by European colonialists; the massacre of Armenians by Turks committed to the development of a "secular" state; two world wars, begun in "civilized" Europe; the Holocaust; the development and spread of Marxism; the hubris of the United States in its relations with postcolonial nations; and, most recently, the failure of the United States and the European Union to do anything to protect the Muslims of Bosnia or of Chechnya. Racism, greed, and violence are the outcome of the human experiment with secularity, according to this line of thought (cf. Kelsay 1996b). The expectation is that one day, the political order organized around this notion will implode. When that happens, the Islamic community will be present to pick up the pieces, and thus to put human civilization once more on the secure moral basis that flows from an acknowledgment of the unity between religion (i.e., Islam) and politics.

Such rhetoric is, in one sense, the stuff from which European and North American fear of Islam is constructed. Tone it down a bit, however, and one wonders: Is this so unfamiliar? Consider the following argument, which constitutes a kind of composite from several contemporary Christian writers: No society can survive for long without a religious consensus. Such a consensus is necessary for public morality. The United States, and more generally Western civilization, depends for its survival on the acknowledgment of Christian hegemony. Without such an acknowledgment, Western society becomes simply an economic arrangement in which each seeks the enhancement of personal fortune, defined in terms of the possession and consumption of material goods. A society without a soul leads to individuals with narrow, private visions. Christians, above all, ought not be afraid to affirm that statecraft is soulcraft and thus ought to build a social-political order around an acknowledgment of Christian values.

There are various versions of the argument, of course. In the hands of some writers, it is important to note the way that "Christian values" or "Christian hegemony" is crafted or modified to include at least a version of Judaism. Indeed, it is not strange, given the growing numbers of Muslims in the United States, to notice some arguing that the religious consensus necessary to sustain public morality should focus on the "common values of monotheism," or something to that effect. At this point, however, I simply want to press the question: Is the Muslim notion that the construction and maintenance of a just political order requires a collaboration between religious and political institutions so foreign to contemporary Christians?

Consider, for example, certain themes in the writing of Richard John Neuhaus. The well-known argument of *The Naked Public Square* asserts that a completely secular culture is an impossibility. Religious or quasi-religious assumptions are always present "at the heart" of human culture; the important questions have to do with the substance of these assumptions. As Neuhaus has it, much of the history and politics of the United States is inexplicable apart from the kinds of assumptions associated with the term "Christian America." Although this term has become problematic, the notion that "secular America" presents a viable substitute is wrongheaded. U.S. political life now seeks an alternative—a "heart" that will reflect Christian, or more generally, biblical assumptions about the nature of human beings, though with the important proviso that any contemporary "public religious consensus" must reflect respect between Christians and Jews (Neuhaus 1984).

I am aware that many will find it odd to compare Neuhaus with Khomeini; and it is certainly ironic that Neuhaus's comments in the journal *First Things* consistently express suspicion about the capacities of Islam to foster and sustain liberal democratic institutions. The reason for the strangeness (and perhaps also for the irony) lies, it seems to me, in a subtle but important difference in the precise contribution envisioned for religion in the writings of Neuhaus, on the one hand, and of someone like Khomeini, on the other. When Neuhaus speaks of a recovery of Christianity's historic role in U.S. cultural and political life, he is thinking of Christianity as a cultural entity rather than of the institutional Church as a direct political actor. In this recovery, religious institutions play their role more or less indirectly, as they help to shape character through the development and employment of a common moral discourse. The call is not for an establishment of particular religious institutions. Khomeini, rather differently, envisioned an establishment of Islam that required that the Majlis, or Parliament, in the Islamic Republic of Iran have a membership containing a specified number of persons with credentials as religious specialists. The Majlis would set policies that established the practices of Twelver Shi'ism as the official religion of the state; the rights of religious minorities were to be recognized and delimited according to Twelver juridical tradition. In matters ranging from tax policy to international relations, jurists were to "advise" policymakers, in the strong sense of that term.

One should probably say that Khomeini's position on these matters was extreme, even within the tradition of Islam. In particular, his notion of *wilayat al-faqih,* "deputyship of the jurist," by which the role of the religious specialists in the Islamic Republic was legitimated, is held by many Muslims to be an innovation. Such a judgment probably plays some role in the phenomenon, mentioned above, of current criticism of Khomeini and the religious specialists of Iran: They simply went too far in developing the public role of religion.

More significantly, for our purposes, it is important to note once again the dynamic of recognition and difference between Christian and Islamic social-political teaching. If Khomeini and others speak of the necessary role of religion in political life in ways that resonate with historic and contemporary Christian writing, Khomeini in particular also points to some differences in the two traditions.

From my point of view, what is most interesting about these differences is the way they instruct us about the relationship between traditions of social-political thought and historical context. One of the ways Khomeini justified his view of religion and state had to do with an appeal regarding the situation of Iran, and of Islam in general, in the modern world. Ideally, he argued, an Islamic state operates around a collaboration between the institutions of religion and of government. The collaboration works best when there is a recognition of the distinct functions of each set of institutions and of the unique specialties required by those who work in each. In the religious institution, the jurists function as the guardians of public morality, and of the Islamic identity of the nation. In the political institution, the head of state and various officeholders function to ensure public tranquillity and to provide for the common defense. That is the ideal. But, Khomeini would have continued, what should the jurists do when the political institution fails to carry out its duties? What happens to the notion of collaboration when the head of state not only refuses to consult with religious authorities but publicly demeans their discipline and imprisons and/or tortures those among the religious who speak publicly about political matters? What should the religious specialists do when the policies of the government do not make for tranquillity, but rather for injustice? Or when the government enters into arrangements with foreign powers that clearly instantiate and deepen the client role of an Islamic state in the international community?

In such a case, Khomeini held, the jurists must take a more active political role. They must assume the reigns of administration, against their specialization and, in a sense, their calling, until such time as the public culture has changed, so that political leaders once again develop a sensibility that makes collaboration possible. There is a necessary role for religion in public life, the late Ayatollah would have said. But the precise form of that role changes somewhat, depending on situational factors.[9]

Similarly, one might argue with respect to current (U.S.) Christian discourse. Here, one's options are limited, in a sense, by the First Amendment. Further, one is limited by the set of historical developments, and the cultural tradition that that amendment reflects and encourages. Finally, the way the aforementioned factors have played into immigration policies limits the options for thinking about the relationship between religion and politics by helping to create a situation of ever-increasing religious plurality. To put it bluntly: Certain options that were open to, and even preferred by, earlier generations of Christians and Muslims are not currently open to Americans. To my mind, at least, even the cultural version of Christian consensus envisioned by Neuhaus and some others is not really an option. It rests on the illusory judgment that Jews, Muslims, Buddhists, and even dissident Christians are ready to allow a coalition of religious conservatives to define the public morality of the United States.

Concluding Thoughts

Thus, what do Christians make of Islamic social-political thought, in the final analysis? I originally wrote this essay in response to the question: What would it be like to think that an Islamic perspective on politics were true, or the right one?[10] My answer is that this is a very difficult thought. It is difficult, not because of Christian triumphalism. We know enough about the history of Christian social-political thought and about the variegated relations between Christianity and democracy to avoid that. Nor is the difficulty caused by a lack of resonance between Christian and Islamic traditions on the political life of humanity. I hope I have said enough along the lines of recognition to defuse this particular argument, which is sometimes developed along the lines of notions of incommensurability. To my mind, the difficulty has to do with context. At a certain point, Western Christianity and Islam began to develop their social-political teachings in very different ways. In doing so, each was responding not only to Scripture and tradition—to the "basic insights," if you will—but to highly specific cultural factors. Those responses are with us still and lead to further interactions between traditions and culture that may ultimately drive Christian and Islamic ethics further apart, or closer together (the case is as yet unclear, and again depends to a great extent on particular contexts).

The import of this, it seems to me, is to reinforce those trends in religious thought that have, over the last two centuries or so, raised to consciousness the historical nature of human existence as one aspect of the limits God places upon us. I am not sure I have much to offer about this at present. It does, however, put one in mind of Ernst Troeltsch, who in his massive *Social Teaching of the Christian Churches,* as in most of the rest of his work, always had in mind the difference it makes to think of human beings as creatures bounded by history. For Troeltsch, the achievements of eighteenth- and nineteenth-century intellectuals in historical inquiry was a fact of inestimable importance to constructive religious thought. As he sometimes put it, the historical mode of thought is *the* characteristic way by which modern people frame their inquiries and develop their positions. That mode of thought suggests to us, first, that an inquiry into the practices of our ancestors is essential to understanding our own social and cultural position. Further, the historical mode of thinking teaches us that we must be careful to discriminate between those practices of our ancestors that are live options for us and those that are not. Finally, in so discriminating, we must not disparage the ways of our forebears. Properly employed, historical inquiry teaches us why our ancestors organized society in the ways they did. It shows us, even in cases where we cannot be or do not want to be like them, something of the variety of ways in which human beings can organize life. Historical understanding teaches us to appreciate our ancestors' justifications as well as to identify their rationalizations; it helps us to see how we are similar to yet different from them. Ironically, with respect to the issues I have been discussing, Troeltsch also thought that his study of Christian social teachings demonstrated the crucial role that religion has played in the development of Western culture. If, as he put it, it is not at present possible for Christianity to play quite the same role in public life as it once did, that is not to say that it will be permanently reduced to a private or semiprivate mode of spiritual cultivation—the type of practice Troeltsch called "mysticism." It may be, he wrote, that we are passing through a time of breaking down one type of Christian civilization, which will prove to be the prelude to another. The present notion of "radical individualism," Troeltsch wrote,

> will probably soon be an interlude between an old and new civilization of constraint. This individualism may be compared with the process of taking the materials out of a house which has been pulled down, sorting them out into the actual individual stones, out of which a new house will be built. What the

new house will look like, and what possibilities it will provide for the development of Christian ethics and of Christian social philosophy, no one can at present tell. (Troeltsch 1992, 2:992)

For all that Troeltsch says about history, substitute the words "comparative inquiry" and you have the gist of this essay. When it comes to thinking about Islamic social and political thought in relation to Christian ethics, we can affirm five things:

1. There is an important aspect of similarity between Christianity and Islam, so that one can affirm the phenomenon of recognition.
2. Such recognition is accompanied, at the same time, by a sense of distinction or difference.
3. When we speak about recognition and difference, we do so as creatures limited by historical, social, and other contexts. There is no neutral ground from which to articulate, appreciate, or assess these phenomena.
4. That said, once we move to the question: What shall we do?, we find, as we might expect:
   A. that we have some areas of overlap;
   B. that where we do or do not overlap, we have reason to marvel at the many sides of human wisdom in ordering existence; and
   C. that some judgments of Islamic social-political thought, as some of Christian tradition, are simply not options for us at present.
5. This, it seems to me, correlates well with the notion that human beings are creatures who define themselves and attempt to act responsibly within limits; as the Qur'an puts it, within "the limits set by God" (sura 2:187, 2:229).

Notes

1. The system of transliteration followed in this essay is a variation on one recommended by the *International Journal of Middle East Studies*. All diacritics are eliminated with the exception of *ayn* (') and *hamza* (').

2. These models have not been discarded by all Christians, of course. I am still speaking of the Reformed, and have in mind the loss of connection with the type of tradition outlined by Kenneth Kirk (1966).

3. Cf. Kelsay 1993. In that work, I also tried to describe the positions of dissenters (the various Shi'i groups) and of contemporary reformists, so as to present a more comprehensive picture of the Muslim discussion of the social and political responsibilities of the Islamic community and of humanity in general.

4. These phrases appear in a number of places throughout the Qur'an. Cf., for example, sura 102.

5. This version of a standard hadith (a report of Muhammad's *sunna* or exemplary practice) is taken from the translation of the Hanafi jurist al-Shaybani's *Kitab al-Siyar* by Majid Khadduri (Khadduri 1966, sec. 1). N.b.: *fay'* (untranslated in the citation), like *ghanima,* indicates booty. The distinctions between these categories are disputed. See Khadduri 1966, 48–49.

6. Khadduri 1966, secs. 28, 29, 30, 47.

7. I note here that the term *jihad* literally connotes "effort" or "striving" rather than "war" per se. In the context of Islamic discussions of war and statecraft, it is probably best to think of the term as indicating a struggle for justice, up to and including the use of lethal force in war under prescribed conditions.

8. It should be said, by way of qualification, that the political assumptions of contemporary just war writing often remain hidden or underdeveloped. My comments are an attempt to draw out the import of Paul Ramsey's suggestions that just war thinking constitutes the special "politico-military doctrine" of the "peoples of the West." (Ramsey 1983, 4) From my point of view, G. Scott Davis (1992) goes some distance in this regard. For Childress's discussion, see Childress 1982; for Walzer's, see Walzer 1977.

9. For an elaboration of these points, especially with respect to Khomeini, see Kelsay 1994.

10. This is the place to acknowledge the contributions to my thinking made by participants in a forum on comparative theology at the June 1995 meeting of the Catholic Theological Society of America in New York, where I first delivered a version of this essay.

References

Calvin, John. 1960. *Institutes of the Christian Religion.* Edited by John T. McNeill. Translated and indexed by Ford Lewis Battles. Philadelphia: Westminster Press.

Childress, James F. 1982. *Moral Responsibility in Conflicts.* Baton Rouge and London: Louisiana State University Press.

Davis, G. Scott. 1992. *Warcraft and the Fragility of Virtue.* Moscow: University of Idaho Press.

Gustafson, James. 1975. *Can Ethics Be Christian?* Chicago and London: University of Chicago Press.

Kelsay, John. 1988. "Saudi Arabia, Pakistan, and the Universal Declaration of Human Rights." In David Little, John Kelsay, and Abdulaziz Sachedina. *Human Rights and the Conflict of Cultures,* 33–52. Columbia: University of South Carolina Press.

_____. 1993. *Islam and War.* Louisville, Ky.: Westminster John Knox Press.

_____. 1994. "Spirituality and Social Struggle: Islam and the West." *International Quarterly* 1, 3 (Summer):135–151.

_____. 1996a. "Christianity, Islam, and Religious Liberty" (with David Little and Abdulaziz Sachedina). In *Religious Diversity and Human Rights,* edited by Irene Bloom, J. Paul Martin, and Wayne L. Proudfoot, 213–242. New York: Columbia University Press.

_____. 1996b. "Bosnia and the Muslim Critique of Modernity." In *Religion and Justice in the War over Bosnia,* edited by G. Scott Davis, 117–142. New York and London: Routledge.

Khadduri, Majid. 1966. *The Islamic Law of Nations: Shaybani's Siyar*. Baltimore: The Johns Hopkins University Press.

Khomeini, Ruhollah. 1981. *Islam and Revolution: Speeches and Writings of Imam Khomeini*. Berkeley: Mizan Press.

Kirk, Kenneth. 1966. *The Vision of God*. New York: Harper and Row.

Neuhaus, Richard John. 1984. *The Naked Public Square*. Grand Rapids, Mich.: William B. Eerdmans Publishing Co.

Ramsey, Paul. 1983. *The Just War*. Savage, Md.: Littlefield Adams.

Troeltsch, Ernst. 1992. *The Social Teaching of the Christian Churches*. Translated by Olive Wyon. Louisville, Ky.: Westminster John Knox Press.

Walzer, Michael. 1977. *Just and Unjust Wars*. New York: Basic Books.

Chapter Ten

Religions and the Ethics of International Business

RONALD M. GREEN
Dartmouth College

Ever since the publication of Max Weber's *The Protestant Ethic and the Spirit of Capitalism*, those studying the relationship between religion and business have focused on ways that religion affects the development of modern industrial and commercial life. This is the theme of the "work ethic," with its values of frugality, self-discipline, and devotion to one's worldly vocation. Although Weber emphasized the role that ascetic Protestantism, especially Calvinism, played in the West's development of this ethic, scholars subsequently recognized that other cultures possess analogs to the Protestant ethic that have contributed to modernization. Japan's medieval Samurai ethic of feudal fealty contributed greatly to the early development of that nation's economy, and Confucian values have been credited as facilitating the recent development of East Asian nations (Bellah 1957; Berger 1995).

I have no wish to contest this view of the importance of religious values in shaping a society's or culture's attitude toward economic life and business conduct. Indeed, in what follows, I will assume the Weberian perspective that, at a very basic "ethical" level at which a culture's attitude toward economic life is established, religious values play a powerful role. Nevertheless, I think it is also true that in the world today the relationship sometimes proceeds in the opposite direction. Specifically, I want to suggest that the attitudes, values, and norms driven by international business are shaping and transforming religiously based local traditions.

During the 1980s and 1990s, a global ethic of business has emerged that is making itself felt with increasing force throughout the world. Not only is this ethic conveyed internationally by the commercialized instruments of mass culture—press, television, and films—but its norms are reinforced and supported by the discipline of an interconnected global business community. The power of business to transform local traditions is obvious. Economic life reaches across national boundaries, and its demands press in on individuals and organizations with a force rivaled only by military power. Yet it should not be thought that the global business ethic to which I am referring is merely a new form of cultural imperialism. In many cases the values within this ethic are already present in local cultures and are merely brought to the fore by the demands of the international system. In other cases, these values reside within the indigenous system but are in tension with other traditional teachings. Here the global business ethic has the effect of precipitating or accelerating change in the local religious cultural system.

In what follows, I aim to do three things. First, I want to sketch an outline of the global business ethic and indicate some of the forces that have led to its emergence. Second, I want to verify the power of this global ethic with reference to at least one complex national example, the case of Japan. Finally, I want to review the ways in which developments in the Japanese context illustrate complex processes of continuity and change in religious ethical systems as they come to terms, through business life, with a larger community of moral relationships.

The Emerging Global Ethic

The past two decades have witnessed a remarkable transformation in the nature of international commerce. Although companies have traded across national borders for centuries, the recent past has witnessed the emergence of the truly "multinational" corporation. Wherever its home offices are located, the multinational is an entity that has substantial business operations in two or more nations and that, in a sense, is a "citizen" of several different national environments (Coates 1978).

The emergence of the multinational firm, combined with the sheer increase in the magnitude of global trade and communication, has led to a corresponding change in ethical practices. During the immediate post–World War II period, when multinational business was developing and firms, primarily based in Europe, the United States, and Canada, were first venturing beyond their borders, questions of conflict in ethical values were acute. During those years, the ethically and legally underdeveloped business environments of many poorer nations fostered unethical practices by transnational companies doing business there. One observer reports a contemporary assessment of multinationals during this period by quoting a critic who described them as embodying "almost anything disconcerting about modern industrial society" (Novak 1995, 785). On a theoretical level, it was also not clear that one could speak of ethical values transcending local cultures. Many voices, both inside and outside the business community, urged accommodation to local practices even when these ran counter to important norms in the multinational company's home culture. The problem was compounded by the fact that local values will always play a significant role in shaping the more discretionary features of business practices across cultures (Dunfee and Donaldson 1995, 176).

However, from the mid–1970s on a series of events precipitated change. Foremost among these were corruption scandals, beginning with the Lockheed episode in Japan and culminating with major crises that rocked the Italian political scene. These scandals unseated national governments and called into question the idea that values are merely culture-dependent. Not only was it apparent that host countries' citizens were not blandly accepting of serious business misconduct but it also became clear that there was a pressing need for multinational corporations to adopt standards of conduct that would apply to all their employees regardless of the operating environment. Changes in corporate practice, legislative initiatives in home countries, and the pressure of moral opinion both nationally and internationally accelerated these developments.

On the scholarly side, these transformations strengthened the confidence of business ethicists and others who have sketched the outlines of a code of international business conduct. Recognizing the need to respect indigenous values without utterly surrendering moral judgment to dictation by local conditions, writers like Thomas Donaldson (1989) and Richard De George (1993) have tried to establish a "moral minimum" in the form of a set of ethical norms or values reaching across national lines and grounding individuals' ethical expectations regardless of the cultural context. Thus Donaldson speaks of "fundamental international rights" that include such matters as the right to physical security, property ownership, and nondiscriminatory treatment. The attention given to proper business conduct in the Global Ethic enunciated in connection with the Parliament of the World's Religions of 1993 is a further sign of the maturation of thinking on this issue (Küng and Kuschel 1993).

The result of these social and conceptual developments is what I call the emerging ethic of global business. This ethic has three major components: a prohibition of corporate involvement in bribery and corruption; an opposition to discrimination in the conduct of business on the grounds of race, religion, ethnicity, or gender; and a commitment to the avoidance of activities that pose a significant threat to human life and health.

Before I describe these commitments in greater detail, I must observe that this business ethic does not live up to all the aspirations of ethical theorists. For one thing, this ethic is incomplete, omitting whole areas of moral life and relevant aspects of moral concern. As might be expected of norms that emerge from a concern with economic efficiency and open markets, it tends to ignore important questions of distributive justice and moral virtue. No standards of supererogation or conduct "above and beyond the call of duty" are enunciated. Even its limited ethical requirements are not fully implemented on the international scene. Although some of these requirements are more firmly established than others, the ethic as a whole has not been entirely accepted by the leading industrial nations. Finally, even where there is full formal commitment to these values, they are sometimes defied in practice by individual firms, especially smaller companies that find themselves unable to afford the "luxury" of ethical compliance. In listing the components of this global business ethic, therefore, I am at best signaling only an "aspirational" value system and a "work in progress." Nevertheless, it is significant that this ethic has achieved widespread support among leading multinational firms and that it is beginning to extend itself to companies in many different national environments.

Opposition to Bribery and Corruption

The first component of the global business ethic requires firms doing business on an international level to avoid complicity in bribery and corruption. This primarily refers to the bribery of political officials but it also encompasses a more generalized opposition to corrupt business practices. The United States led the way in the formation of this commitment with the passage in 1977 of the Foreign Corrupt Practices Act (FCPA), which criminalized the bribery of foreign governmental officials by representatives or agents of U.S. firms. This was in response to the disclosure of U.S. firms' involvement in major political scandals in Japan, Europe, and the Middle East. Although the FCPA was initially dismissed as an expression of American naïveté and as an invitation to foreign competitors to exploit business opportunities missed by U.S. firms, it has proven successful in many ways and has been only modestly revised since its passage (Pitman and Sanford 1994; Sheffet 1995). Because U.S. companies often competed principally against one another for the favor of foreign officials, their collective withdrawal from these activities was not necessarily injurious to their business interests. Energies devoted to corruption were replaced by a willingness to compete vigorously on grounds of price and quality, and this new focus has sometimes actually strengthened U.S. competitiveness overall (Pitman and Sanford 1994, 20). Recently, the FCPA has come to be regarded as a model for international imitation, with the introduction of similar United Nations and Organization for Economic Cooperation and Development initiatives (Bassiry 1990; Darlin 1993; Kimelman 1994; Sanger 1997).

Driving this globalization and legalization of standards of integrity is the awareness, derived from the basic rationale of market economies, that corruption introduces an irrational element into commercial decisionmaking and damages the business system as a whole. Although in the short run bribery can benefit a single firm, in the longer run it stimulates extortion and raises everyone's cost of doing business. Far from being "grease," illegal payments soon prove to be "grit" in the business system (Green 1994, 304). As a result, global standards of integrity have elicited support from business leaders as a form of "mutual restraint mutually agreed upon" (Hardin 1968). Multinational firms have a further important reason for committing themselves to these standards: their desire to prevent corruption at the periphery of their business from infecting core operations through the promotion and exchange of unscrupulous regional managers.

Nondiscrimination

The second value of this global business ethic is a commitment to nondiscrimination on the basis of race, religion, ethnicity, and gender in the conduct of business. Of these several forms of nondiscrimination, the formal opposition to racial discrimination is perhaps most firmly established in the international business community, reflecting the outcome of the decades-long struggle against the South African apartheid regime. In this case, geopolitical factors and widespread ethical revulsion in the United States and Europe combined to create change in South Africa and to establish strict terms of engagement, through codes like the Sullivan Principles (Washington 1986), for companies doing business there. In roughly similar fashion, but with considerably less success, political and legal pressure has been brought to bear on companies to avoid complicity in discrimination against citizens of Jewish background working for firms doing business in Arab countries. Provisions of the U.S. Export Administration Act of 1977 prohibiting religious discrimination have been applied against multinationals doing business in the United States (Rheingold and Lansing 1994). Some member nations of the European Union have adopted antidiscrimination statutes of their own.

Opposition to gender discrimination is even less advanced because this form of discrimination is firmly established in the cultures of some leading trading nations, notably many Arab states and Japan. Nevertheless, internal legal and ethical commitments to gender equality in many nations with advanced economies together with pressures on companies to avoid discriminating against female employees and managers who are assigned to foreign branches (sometimes called "transplant women" [Knapp 1996]) has created an increasing international presence of women managers. These pressures work, in complex ways, to reinforce a growing ethical opposition to gender discrimination in employment. The embarrassment experienced by the Japanese company Mitsubishi following charges of sexual discrimination in its U.S. operations illustrates the difficulty that multinational corporations face in trying to act on different standards from nation to nation (Elstrom and Brull 1996; Laabs 1996).

Protection of Human Life and Health

The third and final major component of this emerging global business ethic is a commitment to the avoidance of industrial and commercial activities that pose a significant threat to human life and health. A major event in the evolution of this commitment was the Bhopal disaster, in which a toxic gas leak killed thousands; one effect of this catastrophe was to put multinational companies on notice that they could no longer hope to insulate their core businesses and assets from liabilities incurred by foreign subsidiaries (Sharplin 1985; Gladwin 1986; Boatright 1993, 432). The major international boycott conducted against the Swiss-based Nestlé for its practices of marketing infant formula in the Third World also served to warn multinational corporations that they could not afford to be perceived as placing profits above life or health (McCoy 1995). Recently, worker health and safety have also emerged in controversies surrounding the use of child labor in overseas manufacturing operations (Nichols 1993; Tagliabue 1996; Greenhouse 1997). Relatively progressive companies like clothing giant Levi-Strauss reflect the importance of this issue in their efforts to establish human rights and labor standards for their international suppliers (Goll and Zuckerman 1993).

Like other aspects of the emerging global business ethic, of course, this area remains more aspiration than reality. Millions of children the world over are involved in production in ways that interrupt their education or threaten their health (*New York Times* 1996). U.S.- and European-based tobacco companies continue to try to expand their markets in less developed countries. Nevertheless, even these activities have come under international scrutiny or have met local resistance (Darlin 1993). The days when multinational businesses and local firms could act recklessly without opposition are fading. In the developed nations, most companies have become acutely sensitive to accusations of misconduct by their overseas subsidiaries or affiliates.

Local Accommodation to International Values:
The Case of Japan

This emerging global business ethic exerts great power to shape deeply entrenched cultural values, including those based on religious foundations. Recent developments in Japan help illustrate this. The outlines of Japanese business culture have become familiar in the West, partly because of the role Japanese practices have played in international trade disputes. Particularly noteworthy is the intense set of loyalties within and among business firms that make it difficult for foreign competitors to penetrate the Japanese market. These loyalties begin at the firm level and involve mutual commitments between the firm and its employees. The practice of lifetime employment that has characterized many of Japan's larger industrial and financial corporations, at least until the recent period of economic stress, finds its place here, as does the intense and sometimes health-threatening dedication that Japanese workers and managers show to their company (Palumbo and Herbig 1994).

Beyond the firm, loyalty plays a role in interfirm and intra-industry relationships. Many larger firms organize their business vertically, with suppliers and independent distributors in a tight circle of so-called *"keiretsu"* relationships. These involve a commitment to mutual support that can have the effect of reducing open competition. For example, if a supplier within the *keiretsu* circle experiences production limitations and therefore is temporarily unable to meet specifications for a new component, a Japanese manufacturer will seldom open bidding to unknown (or foreign) competitors. Instead, the manufacturer will cooperate with the supplier to help overcome the problems. In turn, if the manufacturer later encounters a crisis situation, the supplier may stretch its own production capacities to meet the customer's needs. On a larger and more attenuated basis, this kind of mutual support is also found in so-called "horizontal *keiretsu*" relationships involving a firm's primary bank, its fellow traders, distant affiliated firms, steady customers, and the like. Interlocking stock ownership is an important way of cementing these relationships.

Behind this business structure lies a system of social attitudes and moral values deeply influenced by Japan's religious culture. The Japanese perceive their social world in terms of four outwardly expanding concentric circles: an inner circle composed of family; a second, wider circle of colleagues (which includes friends and business associates); a third circle comprising the Japanese nation; and a fourth circle embracing the outside world (Taka 1994). Although there are values common to all these circles, each has its own distinct features, and the intensity of loyalty and commitment tends to diminish, albeit in irregular ways, as one moves outward from the center. The family circle *(ie)* normally commands intense devotion. It is characterized by moral ideals associated with filial piety, especially the care and responsive gratitude of the father-son relationship *(oyabun-kobun)*. Also characteristic is a willingness to avoid conflict and to defer to elders (even when their views are regarded as irrational) in order to preserve "harmonious unity" within the group.

The next circle includes friends, distant relatives, and superiors and colleagues in one's workplace. In premodern Japan, this circle was occupied by the local community *(mura)*, but today this has largely been replaced by

one's business organization *(kaisha)*, which also encompasses values and attitudes found at the family level *(ie)*. Although the workplace is characterized by far more reserve and caution than is found in the family circle, it,
too, can be a zone of intense loyalty. Family ideals of filial piety and a commitment to "harmonious unity" persist. Scholars observe that, even among
East Asian nations, the importance vested in this sphere is peculiar to
Japanese business culture (Berger 1995, 747). This results from the historical expansion of family-based commercial houses into large industrial corporations, the generalization of feudal ideals of loyalty, and the connection
between business and older community-based ideals. Because of the importance of loyalties in this sphere, Japan was able early on to establish commercial life on a broader base than the family-run enterprises that still remain prevalent in China, Taiwan, and Korea (Lodge 1995).

The third or "Japan" circle *(kuni)* is marked by a sense of loyalty but significantly less than that found in the two inner circles. Personal relationships move away from reserve and caution in the direction of greater aggressiveness. The fourth and final circle, the world community, elicits the
least loyalty and moral commitment. For ordinary Japanese, the world beyond Japan is a zone of moral uncertainty and ambivalence, "a chaotic
sphere, which threatens the cosmos of the inner circles" (Taka 1994, 60).
Here, attitudes of reserve, hostility, and respect intermingle, along with curiosity and an eagerness to understand and, in some cases, adapt foreign
practices or values to Japanese needs.

This moral and social structure, so important in the shaping of Japanese
business practices, traces its roots to deep religious motifs. Japanese culture
combines Buddhist, Shinto, and Confucian elements with aspects of modernization. Possibly foremost among the religious elements is the Confucian inspiration that Japan shares with other Asian societies. Marc Dollinger identifies four major Confucian motifs that have influenced Japanese culture:

> First, in its most essential form, Confucianism is a humanistic philosophy and
> the human being is regarded with dignity and respect. Second, Confucianism
> inculcates the values of harmony with its concurrent emphasis on loyalty,
> group and family identification, and the submergence of the individual. Right-
> eousness and the acts of righteous individuals within the framework of loyalty
> provide a third dimension. Lastly, there is the integrating theme of the morally
> superior person, the Chun-Tzu, who leads by example and is devoted to the
> other Confucian values. (1988, 576)

In the course of Japanese history, these religious themes have melded
with others derived from Buddhism and Shinto. To the essential humanism
of Confucianism, for example, Ch'an and other forms of Chinese Buddhism brought the notion of the "Buddhahood" of all living creatures and
the equal spiritual dignity of all human beings. To the Confucian theme of

loyalty to family, both Buddhism and Shinto added the idea that not just individuals but groups have their own unique spirit or numen. Indeed, since groups are regarded as connecting more directly with the spirit of the universe as a whole than individuals, participation in family, community, and work groups became a means of spiritual expression in Japanese culture.

Each of these motifs plays a role in Japanese business practice as it has evolved today. The Confucian sense of loyalty to family and filial piety, combined with the idea of the group numen, helps explain the quasi-familial (some would say paternalistic) atmosphere of many Japanese business firms. The ideal of lifetime employment with its commitment to employee retention and, where necessary, retraining, flows from this same moral source and the strong emphasis on the dignity of the individual human being. Confucian ideals inspire the leadership models of Japanese society. Leaders are constant and steady; they provide guidance for subordinates. Finally, the Confucian ideal of personal self-cultivation, renovation, and renewal fosters a commitment to the long-term goals of the organization and to a search for perfection without the pressure for immediate results (Dollinger 1988, 579). The Japanese ideal of *Kaizen* (continuous improvement of products, work procedures, and decisionmaking processes) and the famed Japanese work ethic (Misumi 1993) find much of their inspiration here. All these value commitments have played a role in the success of Japanese business.

This religiously influenced business culture also evidences limitations that can contribute to moral insensitivity and misconduct, as has been demonstrated to some extent in recent Japanese history. The intensity of loyalty within the inner circles of the moral universe generates, as its negative counterpart, a diminution of concern or responsibility for "outsiders." Within Japan, this has contributed to blatant discrimination against Koreans and other powerless non-Japanese who serve in the Japanese workforce. On the international scene, it has led, at best, to a reliance on free competition as the principal guide to conduct, constrained only by a poorly developed international judicial system; or, at worst, to a crass no-holds-barred competitiveness that has sometimes driven Japanese companies into patterns of behavior that have seriously undermined Japan's international reputation and its relationships with allies.

Inside Japanese corporations, the filial and hierarchical nature of relationships has also contributed to discrimination and misconduct. Business leadership has been viewed as a male affair. Women in business organizations are routinely assigned to the least important positions and are expected eventually to leave the firm in order to actualize their own sacred potential or numen within the sphere of home and family. Reliance on moral guidance from above and the emphasis on loyalty to the group have also tended to weaken the sense of individual responsibility for group misconduct. Commentators note that Japanese corporations have tended to be characterized by a sense of "diffuse responsibility" (Forbes 1996). Once corrupt practices are accepted or promoted by the leadership, there is little to check their spread. Within Japan, this has led to a series of financial scandals involving bribery, extortion, and insider trading that has unsettled governments and financial markets, and that has slowed Japan's recovery from recession. The dramatic fall of the Nomura Securities Company and the gross misconduct of senior managers of Daiwa Bank brought world-wide attention in the early 1990s to the questionableness of the business practices of Japanese financial firms (Fukunaga 1996).

Recently, there have been signs in Japan of a response to this string of ethical lapses. At the legal and regulatory level, new restraints have been imposed on business firms in their operations at home and abroad. Sentiment has coalesced within the financial community against business and political leaders found guilty of corruption (Shale 1994). Financial markets have been liberalized to make them more open to international participation. Insider trading laws and disclosure requirements have been toughened. These reforms seek to end the exclusionary control over financial markets exercised by a tight circle of Japanese firms and to render these markets "free, fair and global" (Mitsuzuka 1996). Under pressure from the United States, Japanese government and industry representatives have committed themselves to opening *keiretsu* circles to greater participation by foreign competitors (Forbes 1996).

Obviously, many of these changes have been driven by economic forces. For example, the Japanese financial services industry aspires to a global role, but the price of that role is accommodation to the norms and practices of global business. Favoritism and preference for those with whom one has established prior dealings may make ethical sense within a closed circle where expectations and responsibilities are mutually understood, but they can also impede the goal of encouraging powerful outsiders to participate in local financial markets.

What is interesting is that these changes at the business level are not regarded simply as a foreign imposition. They are being articulated and explained in terms of values as a legitimate extension of indigenous Japanese moral commitments. In a study of formal statements made by leaders of Japan's major business associations, Iwao Taka reports the emergence of a new emphasis on "fairness" in business dealings. The concept of "fairness" is not unfamiliar in Japanese business ethics. Traditionally, it has been applied to the set of attitudes and behaviors associated with the world of reciprocal moral obligations for those within each concentric circle of loyalty. For example, it is regarded as "unfair" for a manufacturer who has benefited from a supplier's past exceptional efforts on its behalf to offer future contracts to the lowest bidder. What is significant about the emergent use of "fairness" in recent authoritative official statements, however, is the recognition that the exclusion of outsiders by practices that systematically deprive them of the opportunity to enter circles of reciprocal relationships is also "unfair." Thus, the leader of one of Japan's largest business associations criticizes "economic activities based not on fair rules but on Japanese customs and practices that emphasize interpersonal relationship, such as unspoken communication and tacit mutual understanding." These activities, he asserts, "no longer hold water even in Japan." This executive urges his compatriots to make active efforts to familiarize outsiders with Japanese practices and expectations and to establish "fair rules and systems of the kind that can be understood by everyone" (Taka 1994, 78 n. 58, 77 n. 50).

On the international level, other business leaders have urged a greater role for Japanese corporations in assuming responsibility for the moral tenor of global business. Speaking in the wake of scandals that drew attention to Japanese business practices, the head of another of Japan's large business associations called on his associates to "moderate the aggressiveness that has been thought of as usual in business activities." He then went on to address Japanese business's international responsibilities: "We must consider more seriously our ways of business from the international point of view, as long as we do business in the international arena. For example, Japanese transnational corporations should understand the real needs of host countries, and take carefully thought-out measures for social contribution to them. We are strongly expected to show the credos which the international society can understand and support" (Taka 1994, 54). In a similar vein, Japanese companies have begun to talk about the need to be "good corporate citizens." Keidanren, an association of top Japanese business firms, has coined the term *kyosei* or "mutual survival" to underscore the need for attitudes of greater cooperativeness among Japanese firms and their host countries overseas (do Rosario 1992). Ryuzaburo Kaku, chairman of Canon, has made this concept the hallmark of his business philosophy, urging his fellow nationals to replace their creed of "one-nation prosperity" with a concept of global cooperation and social responsibility (Kaku 1994).

In his study of these public statements that indicate a shift in Japanese business ethics, Taka goes out of his way to underscore the religious sources of these transformations. Despite the concentrically prioritized set of traditional moral obligations, he observes, the Confucian morality on which Japanese civilization draws also possesses a sense of universal loyalty. Confucianism requires one to love those with whom one is most intimate most intensely because of the belief that such intimate loyalty is the precondition of all moral virtue: Those who cannot love in this way cannot love strangers either. It follows that an ethic which ignores the pressing claims of "outsiders" violates an important aspect of Confucian ethics.

Compassion and concern for strangers receive additional support from Buddhist ideals of the equal sanctity of all persons and from Neo-Confucian beliefs that each person is a microcosm of the universe.

The transformation of Japanese business ethics in the direction of the emerging global business ethic is still in its early stages. Although light is being cast on internal practices of favoritism and corruption, and new attention is being given to the demands of responsible conduct on the international scene, older attitudes continue to prevail. Within Japan, and in some foreign branches of Japanese firms, issues of sex discrimination remain persistent. Although more than half of Japan's married women now hold full-time or part-time jobs and women make up more than 40 percent of Japan's 64.5 million workers, only 5 percent of the presidents of companies are women. A recent Labor Ministry survey showed that 60 percent of women on a career track felt they were "treated unfairly in hiring, promotions, and job responsibility" (Russell 1996). Nevertheless, the global business ethic tends to work with inexorable force. The need to remain competitive, the impact of the global media, the proliferation of educational exchanges, and the increasing movement of people across national boundaries work together to erode support for traditional values that conflict with global norms. Although Japanese women are far behind their North American or European counterparts, like other women throughout Asia they will almost certainly play a much larger role in business in the future. Whether slow or fast, the pressure of the global business ethic imposes a directionality of change toward greater inclusiveness and universality.

Discussion

I have chosen the Japanese case as one illustration of a process whereby emerging business norms work in concert with indigenous values to effect moral transformation in a religiously based local culture. From the point of view of comparative religious ethics, what is important to note in this case is the *interaction* between indigenous and global values. Local, religiously based values are not overwhelmed by global culture. They are receptive to global values and provide a foundation on which these values can build. Global values are attractive not just because of the power that backs them up (although that certainly is a factor) but because they are perceived as legitimately complementing and supplementing indigenous traditions.

To understand this better, it is important to see that there is enormous ethical value in Japan's concentrically organized, religiously influenced business system. It is a source of the intense mutual loyalty between corporate stakeholders that is widely admired by Western business ethicists, whose ethical traditions tend to emphasize profit maximization above human values. From the Japanese perspective, the Western, especially American, subordination of trust relationships to profit, displayed in the conduct of corporate raiders and greenmailers like T. Boon Pickens, epitomizes unethical conduct because it emphasizes one fiduciary relationship, that between managers and shareholders, over all others. To the Japanese way of thinking, the American model eclipses important ties between managers and employees and between the firm and its suppliers, customers, and other financiers. As Alejandro Hazera observes, from a Japanese point of view, actions by managers that place the interests of outsiders, including independent shareholders, over those of the corporate organization are "considered a violation of their fiduciary responsibility to the 'company family'" (1995, 485). The great value to this ethical perspective is evidenced by its exportability to other cultural environments. The Japanese ideals of commitment to workers, to long-term planning, and to continuous improvement in products and processes *(Kaizen)* have already exerted enormous impact on global business practices. It can even be said that these ideals form a Japanese contribution to the emerging global business ethic.

When we understand its historical origins in family and community values, the traditional Japanese ethic made good sense. This ethic served the purpose of coordinating productive endeavor within the immediate community, the commercial enterprises, and the nation, which, for all intents and purposes, together defined the boundaries of the moral universe for most people. Even some of the discriminatory features of Japanese practice made sense in the traditional context. As was true in most premodern cultures, the emphasis on women's role in the home, and their corresponding subordination in the workplace, was not unreasonable in a context where lifelong childbearing and childrearing were women's destiny.

What the global business ethic has brought home to Japan is the recognition that parts of this indigenous ethic no longer fit contemporary reality. A company- and nation-based ethic will not ensure cooperative and productive relationships, the goal of ethics, when one's moral community includes important stakeholders beyond corporate or national boundaries. The subordination of women, which made some sense in an earlier familial and reproductive context, ceases to do so when women respond to global currents and demand a greater role in business matters, when discrimination runs up against international norms, and when one's competitors employ the talents of female managers to competitive advantage.

Recognizing all these facts, business leaders and others who form opinion in Japan are moving values and practice in the direction of the global business ethic. They are able to do so because many of the values of this ethic are already resident within Japanese culture and only require application to an enlarged vision of community. The redefinitions of "fairness" and "responsibility" found in the recent statements of influential business leaders illustrate this process of cultural development. More than a century ago, when Japan first opened its society to the West after a long period of imposed self-isolation, the hope was that all elements of traditional Japanese civilization could be retained and only the scientific and technological advances of Western culture imported. "Eastern ethics, Western science" *(toyo no do toku, seiyo no gei)* was the banner under which this transformation proceeded (Dollinger 1988, 576). However, recent events indicate that this compartmentalization of culture, science, and the economy is no longer possible. The economic, technical, and ethical imperatives of modern business work together inseparably. Recent changes in Japanese business ethics illustrate this.

In a deeper sense, this impingement of a global business ethic on indigenous religious cultures illustrates some fundamental dynamics of interest to students of comparative religious ethics. Although religious ethical systems frequently present themselves as unchanging and grounded in timeless, transcendent truths, they typically undergo significant transformation in their encounters with other cultures. Because ethics is the effort to facilitate a principled and noncoercive resolution of disputes, this religious ethical evolution usually moves in the direction of greater inclusiveness of competing interests and toward more universal values (Green 1987). By its nature, business is eminently suited to catalyzing ethical change of this kind. Not only does it draw on some of the deepest sources of human motivation but it makes a formal appeal to free consent as a condition of its activity. International commerce thus models the form of an expanded human community and extends a powerful invitation to indigenous cultures to transform themselves as required if they wish to participate in that community.

Obviously, not all features of modern business civilization are positive. Unfettered materialism and greed threaten local values, resources, and the environment in many less developed countries. Even in the Japanese context, it is by no means entirely clear that the values of the international business ethic will not do harm if they erode the multistakeholder perspective that has supported Japan's business system in the past. Nevertheless, the values borne by global business have their own contribution to make. To a significant extent, they represent a commitment to the equal dignity and worth of all persons that was originally inspired by the religious ideals of Europe and America. In this sense, global commerce is acting today as one of the leading arenas where religiously derived ethical positions are interacting and educating one another.

References

Bassiry, G. R. 1990. "Business Ethics and the United Nations: A Code of Conduct." *Advanced Management Journal* 55, 4:38–41.

Bellah, Robert. 1957. *Tokugawa Religion*. Glencoe, Ill.: The Free Press.

Berger, Peter L. 1995. "The Gross National Product and the Gods: The Idea of Economic Culture." In *On Moral Business,* edited by Max L. Stackhouse, Dennis P. McCann, and Shirley J. Roels, 743–753. Grand Rapids, Mich.: William B. Eerdmans Publishing Co.

Boatright, John R. 1993. *Ethics and the Conduct of Business.* Englewood Cliffs, N.J.: Prentice-Hall, 1993.

Coates, Jack. 1978. "Toward a Code of Conduct for Multinationals." *Personnel Management* 10 (April):41–43.

Darlin, Damon. 1993. "Pipe Dreams." *Forbes,* April 26, 45.

De George, Richard. 1993. *Competing with Integrity in International Business.* New York: Oxford University Press.

Dollinger, Marc. 1988. "Confucian Ethics and Japanese Management Practices." *Journal of Business Ethics* 7:575–584.

Donaldson, Thomas. 1989. *The Ethics of International Business.* New York: Oxford University Press.

do Rosario, Louise. 1992. "The Not Always Welcome Guests." *Far Eastern Economic Review,* June 18, 57–58.

Dunfee, Thomas W., and Thomas Donaldson. 1995. "Contractarian Business Ethics; Current Status and Next Steps." *Business Ethics Quarterly* 5, 2:173–186.

Elstrom, Peter, and Steven Brull. 1996. "Mitsubishi's Morass." *Business Week,* June 3, 35.

Forbes, Alasdair. 1996. "Business Ethics: Cleaning up Their Acts." *Asian Business,* June, 64–67.

Fukunaga, Hiroshi. 1996. "The Culture of Corruption: How Daiwa Bank Teamed Up with the Ministry of Finance to Deceive the US Government, World Stock Markets, and the Japanese Public." *Tokyo Business Today* 64, 1:4–7.

Gladwin, Thomas N. 1986. "A Case Study of the Bhopal Tragedy." In *Multinational Corporations, Environment, and the Third World,* edited by Charles Peason, chap. 10. Durham, N.C.: Duke University Press.

Goll, Sally D., and Laurence Zuckerman. 1993. "Levi Strauss, Leaving China, Passes Crowd of Firms Going Other Way." *Wall Street Journal,* May 5, A18.

Green, Ronald M. 1987. "Morality and Religion." In *The Encyclopedia of Religion,* edited by Mircea Eliade et al. Vol. 10, 92–106. New York: Macmillan.

_____. 1994. *The Ethical Manager.* New York: Macmillan.

Greenhouse, Steven. 1997. "Sporting Goods Concerns Agree to Combat Sale of Soccer Balls Made by Children." *New York Times,* February 14, A12.

Hardin, Garrett. 1968. "The Tragedy of the Commons." *Science* 162:1243–1248.

Hazera, Alejandro. 1995. "A Comparison of Japanese and U.S. Corporate Financial Accountability and Its Impact on the Responsibility of Corporate Managers." *Business Ethics Quarterly* 5, 3:479–485.

Hiraiwa, Gaishi. 1991. *Keidanren Review on Japanese Economy* 131 (October).

Kaku, Ryuzaburo. 1994. *Kyosei: A Concept That Will Lead the 21st Century.* Canon Inc., Document 1095P5.

Kimelman, John. 1994. "The Lonely Boy Scout." *Financial World,* Special Issue, August 16, 50–51.

Knapp, Gwendolyn. 1996. "Transplant Women On the Move." *Ward's Auto World* 32, 4:41–42.

Küng, Hans, and Karl-Josef Kuschel, eds. 1993. *A Global Ethic: The Declaration of the Parliament of the World's Religions.* New York: Continuum.

Laabs, Jennifer J. 1996. "Mitsubishi Faces Sexual Harassment Lawsuit by EEOC." *Personnel Journal* 75 (June):11.

Lodge, George. 1995. "The Asian Systems." In *On Moral Business,* edited by Max L. Stackhouse, Dennis P. McCann, and Shirley J. Roels, 754–757. Grand Rapids, Mich.: William B. Eerdmans Publishing Co.

McCoy, Charles. 1995. *Case 6: Nestlé and the Controversy over Marketing of Breast Milk Substitutes.* Columbus, Ohio: Council on Ethics and Economics.

Misumi, Jyuji. 1993. "Attitudes Toward Work in Japan and the West." *Long Range Planning* 26, 4:66–71.

Mitsuzuka, Hiroshi. 1996. "U.S.-Tokyo Trade Fight: Statement by Japan's Finance Minister." *Reuter News Service,* November 11, 1996.

New York Times. 1996. "U.N. Sharply Increases Estimate of Youngsters at Work Full Time." November 12, A6.

Nichols, Martha. 1993. "Third-World Families at Work: Child Labor or Child Care?" *Harvard Business Review* 45, 1:12–23.

Novak, Michael. 1995. "Toward a Theology of the Corporation." In *On Moral Business,* edited by Max L. Stackhouse, Dennis P. McCann, and Shirley J. Roels, 775–785. Grand Rapids, Mich.: William B. Eerdmans Publishing Co.

Palumbo, Frederick, and Paul Herbig. 1994. "Salaryman Sudden Death Syndrome." *Employee Relations* 16, 1:54–61.

Pitman, Glenn A., and James P. Sanford. 1994. "The Foreign Corrupt Practices Act Revisited: Attempting to Regulate 'Ethical Bribes' in Global Business." *International Journal of Purchasing and Materials Management* 30, 3:15–20.

Rheingold, Ruth N., and Paul Lansing. 1994. "An Ethical Analysis of Japan's Response to the Arab Boycott of Israel." *Business Ethics Quarterly* 4, 3:335–353.

Russell, Jack. 1996. "Working Women Give Japan Culture Shock." *Advertising Age International,* January 16, 1–24.

Sanger, David E. 1997. "Bribery Pact Is Ready for OECD Vote; Payoffs for Contracts Would Be Forbidden." *International Herald Tribune,* May 26, 15.

Shale, Tony. 1994. "Hammering Down the Nails that Stick Up." *AsiaMoney* 5, 1:12–14.

Sharplin, Arthur. 1985. "Union Carbide of India, Ltd.: The Bhopal Tragedy." *Case Research Journal* 198:229–248.

Sheffet, Mary Jane. 1995. "The Foreign Corrupt Practices Act and the Omnibus Trade Competitiveness Act of 1988: Did They Change Corporate Behavior?" *Journal of Public Policy and Marketing* 14, 2:290–300.

Tagliabue, John. 1996. "Europe Fights Child Labor in Rug Making." *New York Times,* November 18, D9.

Taka, Iwao. 1994. "Business Ethics: A Japanese View." *Business Ethics Quarterly* 4, 1:53–78.

Washington, Linn. 1986. "The Sullivan Principles." *Black Enterprise,* January, 23.

Chapter Eleven

Environmental Ethics in Interreligious Perspective

KUSUMITA P. PEDERSEN
St. Francis College

This chapter will offer a survey of resources for environmental ethics in a number of the world's religions. "Environmental ethics" is understood as moral teachings that can be used to guide policies and prescribe practices that benefit the environment. The approach is pragmatic and ethically descriptive. After attempting to establish what would in fact be beneficial for the environment, I will look in the traditions for religious and moral norms that may foster attitudes and require actions that have the needed results. Which religious beliefs, values, or practices could have a positive effect? Because of its practical emphasis, this account will give preference where possible to ethical statements that have communal significance: in foundational scripture, other sources that have recognized authority in a given tradition, official documents, and writings that have been the outcome of a consultative study process in a religious community or institution. These include both historically important teachings and recent efforts to recover, reread, and redefine religious values in ways that seem relevant to environmental concerns. New work in environmental ethics now constitutes a developed response to the environmental crisis by different religious communities. What this chapter will *not* do is compare the teachings of any group or institution with its actual practices, or assess the degree to which any given culture or religion has been environmentally successful. It also will not report on the many different environmental initiatives that religious communities throughout the world have organized,[1] a topic that would require a chapter in itself.[2]

An investigation of religious resources for environmental ethics shows that a diversity of fundamental beliefs, values, and practices in different traditions may be useful in arriving at a solution to the environmental crisis.

These do not necessarily center primarily on "nature" and respect for nature. Other norms such as justice, nonviolence, and an ideal of simplicity or asceticism may prove to be equally important. Also, religiously based anthropocentrism is not necessarily to blame for destruction of the environment. In fact, a contrast between anthropocentric (human-centered) and biocentric (life-centered) religious ethics may have been overdrawn in some past discussions of religion and the environment. This could be a red herring, a distraction from other important ethical questions. Each religious tradition, whether supposedly anthropocentric or biocentric in general orientation, possesses resources for the construction of what is now often called an "eco-justice" ethic,[3] an ethic that holds together concerns for the natural world and for human life, that recognizes that devastation of the environment and social and economic injustice go hand in hand, and that affirms that environmental rights and human rights are indivisible. I believe that this ethical approach is most effective in confronting the environmental crisis because it is comprehensive, and thus has the greatest capacity to integrate basic values and harness together their motivating power.

The Environmental Crisis

The present environmental crisis is unprecedented in at least two ways: in its rate of change and in its global reach. Human beings have always had some impact on their natural surroundings. This impact has sometimes been extensive and destructive (Dubos 1972; Weiskel 1980). But because of the huge increase in the sheer number of humans (which has an extensive impact on the environment even without industrialization)[4] and also because of new activities that are part of modern development, for the first time human life is impacting the nonhuman world not only on a regional but also on a planetary scale. Some of these effects are or may be irreversible. Species loss is one example. The possibility of global climate change is another. Vast social, economic, and political changes on all levels have also been a consequence of modern development. The speed of change, and also the acceleration of the rate of change, are new in human experience.[5]

The crisis is constituted by a now familiar list of issues. These include massive species extinction with decrease of biodiversity, the "greenhouse effect" mainly caused by the burning of fossil fuels, destruction of the ozone layer, pollution by toxic chemicals with far-reaching effects on human and nonhuman life, loss of topsoil, deforestation, desertification, declining health of ocean ecosystems, and depletion of nonrenewable resources. The goods and services used by modern industrialized economies (the lifestyle of "the North") are extremely energy- and resource-hungry, and their manufacture and use are poisonous and wasteful. Military industrialization has been a large part of this consumption and pollution. At the same time, the less material- and energy-intensive but pressing basic needs of the poverty-burdened South, with four times the population of the North, also deplete resources and degrade the environment. Environmental impact is no longer localized, as the increasingly rapid globalization of the world's economy has further developed "shadow ecologies" already created in the colonial period. Analysts often point out that the planetary ecosystem is closed and finite, and that as long as human population, consumption, and pollution continue to increase, we seem to be on a collision course with the limits of our habitat. We will exceed, or have already exceeded, the "carrying capacity" of the Earth (Cohen 1995).

The amount of data on these issues is immense at the same time that the rate of change is unfamiliar. Even with adequate data, it is impossible to say in a number of specific areas what the future is likely be, and in some cases essential information is not in hand; for example, "even rudimentary data on soil loss is almost completely unavailable for most countries of the South" (V. W. Ruttan, cited in Barney 1993, 19). The unpredictability of human behavior and the need for radical change during the next several decades make the future even more uncertain. Debates about the environment focus not only on "how bad" a situation is now—a judgment based on the facts—but on "how bad" it is likely to become later on—a judgment based on projections.[6] There have been repeated foretellings of catastrophe, even of the end of the human species and the destruction of life on the Earth. It is not my purpose here to repeat these apocalyptic warnings but rather to expose the elements of the crisis as a part of ethical inquiry and a search for solutions.

The external changes that would end the environmental crisis are not obscure. "We know what an environmentally sustainable economy would look like," Lester Brown affirms. He continues:

> In a sustainable economy, human births and deaths are in balance, soil erosion does not exceed the natural rate of new soil formation, tree cutting does not exceed tree planting, the fish caught do not exceed the sustainable yield of fisheries, the cattle on a range do not exceed its carrying capacity, and water pumping does not exceed aquifer recharge. It is an economy where carbon emissions and carbon fixation are also again in balance. The number of plant and animal species lost does not exceed the rate at which new species evolve. (Brown 1996, 11–12)

If one adds to this the elimination or greatly reduced use of harmful chemicals, and programs to restore damaged ecosystems (now called "eco-development"), a solution to the environmental crisis can be envisioned. Such a sustainable economy may not represent for some ecologists the best possible form of "human-earth relations,"[7] but the path from our present situation to the realization of any more radical ideals lies through this phase. All the same, many despair of achieving even this goal of moderate sustainability before the present crisis deepens into disaster. Why is it so difficult to get there from here? Jim MacNeill, a leading international authority on sustainable development, has written:

> Threats to economic well-being and national security from environmental breakdown, the desire to gain or protect access to scarce energy and other resources, and the potential collapse of life-support systems are greater today than any foreseeable threats from conventional arms. When these threats stem from military buildup by an unfriendly power, as in the Persian Gulf in August 1990, nations and regional defense blocs respond with a massive mobilization of diplomatic, military, and other resources. But to longer-term threats of environmental destruction and resource depletion, the world community seems incapable of mounting an effective response. Why?
>
> The reasons lie partly in the fact that awareness of the scale and consequences of environmental threats are only now beginning to penetrate world councils, and partly in the complexity of the issues of global changes. When these threats are considered against a background dominated by economic and ecological interdependence, and by rapid change and conflict, they emerge as complex geopolitical syndromes that challenge existing forms of governance. Measures to address them at their source confront values and aspirations, visions of the future, and codes of political behavior that are deeply rooted in our societies. (MacNeill, Winsemius, and Yakushiji 1991, 74)

It is significant that Jim MacNeill and others in the field of environment and development have not singled out lack of respect for "nature" as the cause of the crisis. "The environment" is what environs or surrounds us, and in common speech is often equivalent to nonhuman nature. But for as long as the environmental crisis has been construed as having primarily to do with nature, the issues have not gained a wide enough hearing. In her foreword to the landmark 1987 report of the World Commission on Environment and Development, Gro Harlem Brundtland observes: "The environment does not exist as a sphere separate from human actions, ambitions, and needs, and attempts to defend it in isolation from human concerns have given the very word 'environment' a connotation of naivety in some political circles" (World Commission 1987, xi). More recently MacNeill, the principal author of the same report, has noted that issues of "the environment," when first discussed internationally, were considered as an "add-on" to political, economic, and social issues, and "tended to be trivialized as 'externalities' outside the mainstream agenda of government" (MacNeill, Winsemius, and Yakushiji 1991, 53). From the context of Christian ecumenism, John Cobb has similarly commented: "The main problem now is not so much lack of good ideas [on the theology of nature] as the way this whole discussion is viewed by the larger church. There it appears, at best, as a side issue of legitimate interest to specialists, at worst, as a distraction from truly urgent priorities" (Cobb 1991, 261). In an official statement, Roman Catholic bishops of the United States have likewise said:

> For too long, we may have viewed environmentalists as single-issue advocates and dismissed their concerns as those of specialists. If we have done this, it has been to our detriment, for living in harmony with the natural world is fundamental to living in harmony with each other. We already fight wars over land and/or control of natural resources. If we concentrate on social harmony with little or no regard for eco-harmony, we may soon exhaust the planet's ability to support us. (U.S. Catholic Conference 1994, 11)

As these comments indicate, the view that environmental issues are mainly about nature, understood as the nonhuman physical world and as apart from human concerns, has been challenged. Within an eco-justice and human development perspective, many have drawn attention to the fact that the environment is not separate from human welfare but that the very opposite is true: It is inseparable from it. Policies and practices that are destructive to the environment, with the resulting breakdown of ecosystems, scarcity or maldistribution of resources, and pollution, are deeply interconnected with poverty, human rights abuses, armed conflict, and dangers to human health (Sachs 1995). Competition for resources and lebensraum has been a constant feature of human history; as resources become depleted, conflict becomes more acute (Homer-Dixon, Boutwell, and Rathjens 1993; MacNeill, Winsemius, and Yakushiji 1991; Westing 1986). Damage to or breakdown of ecosystems also may be a factor in violent conflict and further leads to movements of environmental refugees. Although it is still possible to read that the environmental crisis "will lead" to problems of environmental refugees, this has already been occurring (Homer-Dixon, Boutwell, and Rathjens 1993; MacNeill, Winsemius, and Yakushiji 1991, chap. 3). There is as well the ongoing phenomenon of "development refugees," populations amounting to ten million people each year that are displaced by development processes such as urbanization and the construction of roads and dams (Sachs 1995, 7, 30).

Everywhere in the world, toxic pollution, lack of resources, and destruction of habitat hit the poor and marginalized the hardest, with major burdens borne by indigenous peoples (Berger 1987). The majority of the world's people live in poverty. Two billion are in a condition termed "absolute poverty," unable to meet basic needs, including food, at even a minimally adequate level. Economic growth (which in many ways is destructive to the environment) has not lessened poverty but has actually increased the polarization between the world's rich and poor, according to the 1996 *Human Development Report* (UNDP 1996). The documentation of the human dimensions of the crisis of "the environment" is now extensive.

How much human suffering is acceptable? How much triage can we allow—or deliberately plan for? The situation poses these questions as much as it does questions of the preservation of nature, or the value of nature in itself. A human-centered ethic, as much as a nature-centered one, should be sufficient to designate the current situation a crisis, if not the "environmental" crisis then the "eco-social" crisis or the crisis of "environment and development."[8]

Although discussions of environmental ethics still contrast anthropocentric ethics with those that are ecocentric, or biocentric, it seems clear that even from an anthropocentric perspective, economic, political, and social issues must be seen in environmental terms. At the same time, if the state of affairs is seen from a biocentric or ecocentric perspective, environmental issues must be seen in economic, political, and social terms because human actions are the cause of the crisis: The crisis of nonhuman nature cannot be understood apart from human behavior and the reasons for this behavior.

The challenge that faces the human community cannot be characterized merely as lack of respect for nature, or "anthropocentrism" as such. As MacNeill points out, it may equally be the difficulty of seeing correctly a situation that is unfamiliar, moving quickly, and exceedingly complex—and then, based on new ways of seeing, transforming our desires and aspirations, and actually reinventing many of our most entrenched ways of living. The complexity and the unprecedented speed of events are met by resistance to change in behavior and what Timothy Weiskel has called "the difficulty of believing what we know." Not only new technologies but new national and international political and economic structures will be necessary to create a world order that can deal with the environmental crisis. To give only two examples, Paul Hawken has called for the replacement of our "extractive economy" with a "restorative economy," saying: "We need to imagine a prosperous commercial culture that is so intelligently designed and constructed that it mimics nature at every step" (Hawken 1993, 15). Larry Rasmussen has noted that "democracy," much as it is cherished, does not represent future generations, nonhuman life, or the Earth as a whole since it only governs the single nation-state (Rasmussen 1993, 202–203). Cultural and spiritual values must be redefined, and a new solidarity among human groups must be cultivated, but this will not be enough. As William Pedersen has pointed out: "Without a deep understanding of the political and institutional changes required to accomplish results, the public will not know what to demand and its representatives will not know what to supply." Therefore "relevant utopias" must be imagined, Pedersen says, as pictures of a workable future and as overarching frameworks for creative discussion. Within a "relevant utopia," opposing values can be contextualized and policy options tested (Pedersen 1994, 975–977). The Earth Summit held in 1992 in Rio de Janeiro and subsequent major UN conferences on different aspects of the global situation, as well as the current drafting of the Earth Charter, are activities taking steps toward these goals (Rockefeller 1996b). The emergence of a larger and stronger nongovernmental sector, with tens of thousands of nongovernmental organizations (NGOs) addressing different issues, is increasingly important in this process of reinventing ourselves as a sustainable global culture. Those NGOs affiliated with the United Nations that regularly attend UN conferences are a significant force, but they represent only a portion of the great number of people's groups and projects worldwide.

What can the world's religions bring to this collaborative undertaking? J. Baird Callicott believes that diverse religions and cultures contribute to an emerging "postmodern" evolutionary-ecological environmental ethic in which science is the unifying factor. Callicott believes (or hopes) that once this new environmental ethic is constructed, it will function globally as a transforming paradigm, coexisting with particular worldviews (Callicott 1994, chap. 9). More pragmatically, Brian Hehir has noted[9] that religions as transnational actors bring three things to the international arena: ideas about the meaning of life, international institutions, and living grassroots communities. Religion is an essential provider of identity, a definer of values, and a motivating force for hundreds of millions of people globally. As keepers of deeply held and age-old worldviews and moral teachings, religions are able to influence the larger part of the world's peoples. Religious communities must mobilize the entirety of their ethical and practical strengths and bring them to bear on efforts to find solutions to the environmental crisis. Happily, this engagement is now well under way. Let us now turn to a brief descriptive inventory of the particular ethical resources that several different religious traditions have and can draw upon in their movement to achieve sustainability and justice.

The Abrahamic Religions

The three Abrahamic religions are in agreement that no part of nature is in itself divine, though God is present in nature and can be known through nature. Although some exceptions or qualifications could be made, Jewish, Christian, and Muslim writers on the environment are generally clear in their refusal to compromise the foundational norm of the distinction between Creator and creation, and the prohibition against worshiping any part of nature. This distinction is not in itself, they say, the source of attitudes or practices harmful to the environment, and it is not negotiable, nor is a belief in the unique place of humans in God's creation. The idea of "dominion" by humans, however, is open to interpretation and has been undergoing a critical reexamination. Although the charge of anthropocentrism has indeed been brought against the Abrahamic religions, the response, once the question was worked through, has been that neither Judaism, Christianity, nor Islam is or could be anthropocentric, or human-centered; rather, all three traditions are theocentric, or God-centered, in their worldviews. Given this starting point, a viable environmental ethic is available in each of the traditions.

The Hebrew Bible

We begin with the earliest text, the Hebrew Bible. In spite of its paramount importance for both Jews and Christians, the vision of nature in the Hebrew Bible until recently has often been undervalued or misunderstood. Theodore Hiebert (speaking of both Jewish and Christian interpreters) has argued that this is so "because most past scholarship on the place of the natural world in biblical thought has been driven by several controlling ideas, ideas which are not as reliable, upon careful scrutiny, as they have generally been considered. The first of these ideas is the conception that biblical religion is concerned about history, not about nature," and that nature, serving merely as the stage for the drama of revelation and redemption in history, is marginalized. Hiebert quotes James Barr as saying that this idea "is one of our great modern orthodoxies," and that "historians in the future will look back on the mid-twentieth century and call it the 'revelation-in-history' period" (Hiebert 1996a). The second controlling idea about nature in the Bible has been that the original environment of the ancient Israelites was "the desert," which left an indelible imprint on their religion. Hiebert explains that both of these overshadowing ideas stem from nineteenth-century thought. Especially as a still-continuing attack on supposedly biblical ideas of human "dominion" over the nonhuman owes much to these received notions, Hiebert has called for a reevaluation of these preconceptions and their results. In *The Yahwist's Landscape,* he makes an important contribution to this reinterpretation. Hiebert has pointed out that "the biblical Hebrew language possesses no terms for 'nature' or 'history' . . . in fact, wherever one looks in the Hebrew Scriptures, divine activity and human experience are so interrelated with the world of nature (as we call it) that traditional [i.e., nineteenth- and twentieth-century] dualistic and highly anthropocentric readings of the biblical texts become problematic" (Hiebert 1989). Moreover, the ecological context of the ancient Israelites was not "the desert" at all but Canaanite hill country agriculture of the first millennium B.C.E., and for one biblical author, the Yahwist, the small farmer is the paradigmatic image of the human being in the world (Hiebert 1996b).

Because of the central role of agriculture, the Hebrew Bible gives expression to a deep, urgent, and immediate sense of dependence on rain and on soil, from which humankind is made (Gen. 2:7). This dependence is a part of the order of the world intended by God who made it. For biblical writers, contemplation of this order and of nature's beauty, majesty, and strangeness brings to mind the Creator and inspires praise, gratitude, and the wonder that Abraham Joshua Heschel calls "radical amazement" (Heschel 1955, 45). This contemplation of creation is sustained and profound, and continues throughout the Jewish tradition, as indeed it does in Christianity and Islam. Daniel Swartz notes the "extravagant use of natural metaphor" in the Bible, and its intimate knowledge of the natural world, and the fact that images from nature are used to refer to the divine itself.[10] Nature is not marginalized in the Hebrew Bible, and its essential worth is not in question, since the Genesis creation narrative states that "God saw all that He had made, and found it very good" (Gen. 1:31).[11]

There is disagreement, however, on just how far one may go in saying that nature has intrinsic value. In discussions of biblical religion and the environment, a tension persists between, on the one hand, an acknowledgment of mystical teachings of the divine immanence, and on the other, an emphasis on a "monotheism" wary of tendencies toward "pantheism" and "pagan" "nature-worship" that might seem to rear their heads in the quest of some environmentalists for a resacralization of nature.

There are biblical texts, however, that while they do not necessarily imply that nonhuman creatures have an equal status to humans, do seem to say that God has a relationship with them that is distinct from and independent of God's relations with humankind. In Genesis, God speaks directly to the sea creatures and birds created on the fifth day (before humans are created), saying "be fertile and increase" (1:22). The covenant made after the Flood is not only with Noah and his descendants but "with every living creature," or "all flesh." These phrases are repeated several times in ten verses (Gen. 9:8–17). Concerning the divine-nonhuman relationship, Robert Gordis and Eric Katz have argued that in the Book of Job, when God speaks to Job out of the whirlwind, God describes realms of creation explicitly *not* created for human benefit that are unknown to humans.

> Who cut a channel for the torrents
> And a path for the thunderstorms,
> To rain down on uninhabited land,
> On the wilderness where no man is,
> To saturate the desolate wasteland,
> And make the crop of grass sprout forth? (Job 38:25–27)

"And more than the useless rain where humans do not live," Katz says, "there are the animals, the great beasts 'behemoth' and 'leviathan,' which do not exist for human purposes; they lie outside the sphere of human life" (Job 40:15ff.; Katz 1993, 65–66). Psalm 104 (verse 26), indeed, says that God created the leviathan "to play," not to do anything with or for humans; the Talmud says that in fact it is God personally who spends the fourth part of each day playing with the giant sea creature (Avodah Zarah 3b, cited in Hertzberg 1991, 73). Both Katz and Gordis[12] see Job as a very strong affirmation of a theocentric religious ethic. There are in the cosmos vast realms that do not serve human purposes and are altogether beyond human experience. Although nature may encompass the stage of the drama of human redemption, this stage does not fill all of nature. There are other dramas, and God has other plans, even other covenants, within the totality of God's creation.

The Psalms, quoted in so many Jewish and Christian discussions of the environment,[13] also refer to the relationship of nonhuman creatures and their Creator as they describe such creatures offering praise to God. Monford Harris cites the rabbinic scholar Max Kedushin as well as the Hebrew Bible scholar J. Pedersen to support his view that "the attribution of personality to natural phenomena is a genuine element in the Hebraic world-outlook" (Harris 1976, 60). I suggest that such passages should not be seen as instances of anthropomorphic "pathetic fallacy" (the rhetorical device in which natural phenomena are said to reflect the emotions of humans) but as expressions of a religious vision that sees the world "not as a collection of objects but as a communion of subjects," in Thomas Berry's phrase, or what deep ecologists call "the biotic community." As we shall see, this view is also found in the religions of South Asia and those of indigenous peoples.

Judaism

The Hebrew Bible is the basis of environmental ethics in Judaism, and the fundamental biblical themes just outlined are powerfully reinforced in daily Jewish worship. The root "prayer," or witness of faith, in Judaism is the first line of the Sh'ma, the words: "Hear, O Israel, the Lord our God, the Lord is one" (Deut. 6:4). In daily morning and evening prayer services, this first line is followed by three passages, the second of which is Deuteronomy 11:31–21, including these lines: "If you will earnestly heed the commandments I give you this day, to love the Lord Your God and to serve Him with all your heart and all your soul, then I will favor your land with rain at the proper season—rain in autumn and rain in spring—and you will have ample harvest"; but if the people "turn to false gods in worship," God will "close the heavens and hold back the rain and the earth will not yield its produce."[14] The passage has powerful ecological resonance, associating the worship of "false gods" and the neglect of God's commandments (many of which concern the treatment of the land and its creatures) with a disruption of the balances of nature. It need not be interpreted only in narrowly voluntaristic terms of personal disobedience and punishment. Arthur Waskow has suggested that the passage refers specifically to the commandments re-

garding the sabbatical year, instructing that the land is to be left unculti-
vated every seventh year, and that thus the statement is intended literally:
Failure to keep these commandments actually would result in infertility of
the land.[15] It should also be noted that the passage may express what Gene
McAfee refers to as the "symbiotic relationship" often found in traditional
religious life among the ethical, the cosmic, and the ritual orders (McAfee
1996, 36). Whichever interpretation one prefers, the inclusion of this passage in twice-daily Jewish prayers makes it worthy of special attention in a
consideration of environmental ethics.[16]

Other key parts of traditional Jewish liturgy also have environmental dimensions. A blessing preceding the Sh'ma on the Sabbath says: "All creatures praise You, all declare, 'There is none as holy as the Lord.' . . . Creation reflects the rule of God, who is praised by the breath of all life." The
Amidah, recited at every Jewish prayer service, in different versions includes the words "May every living creature thank you and praise you
faithfully," while the Amidah for the High Holy Days contains the words
"Then all creatures will know that You created them, all living things will
comprehend that You gave them life, everything that breathes will proclaim, the God of Israel is King." The prayer Nishmat, recited in Sabbath
and holiday morning services, includes these words: "The breath of all that
lives praises You, Lord God. The force that drives all flesh exalts You, our
King, always" (Harlow 1989, 334). These prayers have not been reempha-
sized, revised, or written recently to enhance environmental "sensitivity"
but have been in regular use in these forms for many centuries, expressing
and fostering an ecological consciousness.

Numerous commandments in the Torah require specific practices that
provide for the environment. These include preservation of trees and arable
land, protection of animal welfare, conservation of water, and propagation
of dietary laws limiting the killing of animals (which some view as intended
ultimately to require vegetarianism). Rabbinic tradition elaborates extensively on all of these. A central principle that has developed throughout the
tradition is *bal tashchit,* "do not destroy," deriving originally from
Deuteronomy 20:19–20, which prohibits the destruction of trees, even by
an army laying siege to a city that owns them. Utilizing the fundamental
Jewish legal method of reasoning from the particular to the general, the
norm of avoiding destruction and waste is broadened and strengthened
throughout the rabbinic period and the Middle Ages. Contemporary Jewish
writers regard this principle as basic to environmental ethics in Judaism.

Another essential point elaborated in the rabbinic tradition is that humans do not own the Earth, which belongs to God; although Jewish law
acknowledges complex arrangements of possession, it does not acknowledge absolute ownership. The Hebrew language does not have "a single
word through which the concept of absolute ownership can be conveyed"

(Berman 1993, 16). Thus the fact of God's sole ownership of the land is reinforced. "Stewardship" (the responsible care of something one does not own but has been entrusted with) is a well-developed concept in Jewish law. It stipulates that the inherent worth of what is "possessed," or borrowed, must be maintained or, if damaged, restored (Swartz 1993; Berman 1993). In Genesis 2:15, God commands humans to "till and to tend" the earth, with Hebrew words that also mean "to serve," and "to guard" or "to watch over." This much-discussed text on stewardship is complementary to the equally debated and much-maligned verse on "dominion" (Gen. 1:28).[17] The controversy over whether Genesis 1 is to blame for the present environmental crisis is resolved, at least in Jewish terms, by looking at what the entire Jewish tradition teaches about normative practice. Thus, as Saul Berman concludes, "the various commentators—ancient, medieval and modern—who have discovered the essential complementarity of these two verses drew their awareness . . . from their recognition that much in the rest of biblical legislation requires this particular understanding of these verses" (Berman 1993, 15).

Finally, Jewish writers on the environment often point to two traditional practices that have significance for environmental ethics. The first is the recitation of a specific blessing, or *bracha,* on many designated occasions. These include acts repeated every day such as eating bread and other products of the earth, and drinking wine; as well as experiences that are less common, including seeing natural wonders such as the sea or a rainbow. Blessings foster gratitude and reverence for what humans receive from creation and acknowledge God as the source. The second practice is, as Ismar Schorsch has put it, "the absolute cessation of work that distinguishes the celebration of Jewish holy days," including the Sabbath. "The regimen of rest," he says, "is meant to restrict our strength as much as restore it, to deflate our arrogance as much as ennoble our spirit. The final intent of the opening chapter of Genesis is to pave the way for limits. It anchors the later and unnatural command to rest weekly in a cosmic act and induces us to acknowledge in deed, not word, that our dominion is only partial" (Schorsch 1992, 32–33). Schorsch and others find much ecological significance in teachings on self-limitation and discipline in every aspect of human activity, which constitute an overall ethic of restraint in the Jewish tradition.

Christianity

Much Christian discussion of the environment has been marked by a tone of repentance, a sense of finding the way back to something that has been lost or of remembering something that has been forgotten, because Christian resources for engaging this crisis, it is said, have been neglected. A generation of intense theological activity has been catalyzed by a recognition of the environmental crisis and the challenge it presents. Western civilization has often been held responsible for the environmental crisis, and Christianity is the dominant religious tradition in this civilization. This historical reality has occasioned a thoroughgoing reexamination of the role played in the crisis by values that are integral to Christianity. Christian ecologists have in due course concluded that Christians as sinful humans may be to blame, but they have not accepted the accusation that Christian teachings as such are the cause of the crisis. Both individual theologians and the churches have undertaken a rereading and redefinition of Christian norms to construct a Christian environmental ethic, and the outlines of a consensus now seem to be visible.

Wesley Granberg-Michaelson, in agreement with many, has characterized the "secularization" of nature over the past three centuries as a crucial theological mistake. As an example, he refers to a World Council of Churches document that as recently as 1966 stated:

> The biblical story secularizes nature. It places creation—the physical world—in the context of covenant relation and does not try to understand it apart from that relation. The history of God with his people has a setting, and this setting is called nature. But the movement of history, not the structure of the setting, is central to reality. . . . *The physical world does not have its meaning in itself.* (Granberg-Michaelson 1994)

"Creation was reduced to nature," as Granberg-Michaelson puts it, and was seen as the setting for the human drama and as raw material for human use. Many Christian environmentalists have come to regard this as a false step resulting from misinterpretation and wrong application of biblical verses to serve non-Christian aims of greed and power.

To correct this mistake, reclaiming the witness of the Hebrew Bible has been of first importance for Christian as well as Jewish environmental ethics. Thus Christian environmental ethics bears a strong family resemblance to that of Judaism. Christian writers cite the same texts from the Hebrew Bible, including the Genesis creation narrative, the covenant with Noah and "every living creature," the Psalms, and the Book of Job. Since God looked upon creation and saw that it was "very good," nature is of value because as creation it is God's gift. It is worthy of respect and care, and "dominion" must be interpreted as careful, reverent stewardship. Further, God's covenant is with creation as a whole, not exclusively with humanity. This wider view of covenant, developed by Granberg-Michaelson and others, now has broad currency (Granberg-Michaelson 1991). A powerful amplification of the Christian understanding of God's covenantal relation with all creation is found in chapter 8 of Paul's Epistle to the Romans, especially in the line: "Up to the present, we know, the whole created universe groans in all its parts as if in the pangs of childbirth" (8:22).[18] Paul here refers not only to God's relationship with all creation but also to the responsibility of humans to alleviate the suffering of the nonhuman world and to fulfill the promise of salvation in which the proper relations among God, humankind, and the natural world will be restored. Romans chapter 8 has proved to be a touchstone for Christians of diverse traditions and is cited repeatedly in contemporary Christian writings on the environment. In the New Testament, other texts with clear environmental significance include the sayings of Jesus on the sparrow and on the lilies of the field.

Especially in the 1990s, the ethical perspective known as "eco-justice" or "environmental justice" has emerged as central to Christian environmental ethics. Both a movement within the Christian churches and a theological approach, eco-justice has developed as a conscious refusal to see the environmental crisis merely as a question of nature or as "one more issue"; rather, it seeks to unite what is now recognized as the biblical valuation of nature with the biblical calls to justice and love of neighbor. As James Martin-Schram has put it: "The hallmark of an eco-justice approach is the attempt to hold together the twin imperatives of social justice and ecological integrity. Breaking down the traditional barriers between social and environmental ethics, an eco-justice approach attempts to discern and adjudicate various responsibilities owed to the poor, to future generations, to sentient life, to organic life, to endangered species, and to ecosystems as a whole" (Martin-Schram 1996, 140). Eco-justice is characterized by its integration of concerns for a number of "different" critical concrete issues— economic justice, militarization, human rights, race and gender issues, and the environment—within a single ethical analysis asserting that different forms of injustice spring from the same causes. For Christians, an eco-justice approach provides a firm footing for reflection and action on environmental issues, freed from reservations caused by a mistaken fear that essential Christian norms are compromised by an excessive or disproportionate emphasis placed on nature and possible de-emphasis of other core values.

Here the commitment to justice and love of neighbor are not decreased but rather can be expanded to nonhuman nature; as Paul Waddell has suggested: "Our neighbor is all of life, and just as we are called to care for and be responsible to other beings, we are called to care for the earth. . . . We have to draw the lines of community more broadly. We think community includes only other human beings, creatures like ourself; consequently, we conclude that justice extends no further than those like to us. But our sense of accountability grows when the boundaries of community are extended" (Waddell 1994, 60). Michael Himes and Kenneth Himes have similarly noted: "The theme of companionship, the relationship which exists not only between human persons but between humans and nonhumans, has been largely submerged in the stewardship theme. We need to recover it.

Companionship implies mutuality. It excludes the reduction of either side of the relationship to a tool of other's purposes." They find in the spirituality of St. Francis of Assisi a full expression of this sense of companionship. The fraternal creation spirituality of St. Francis is rooted not only in the immediate and concrete experience of communion but in a poverty of spirit "which recognizes that all creatures are united in the depths of their being by the fact of being creatures" and in the conviction that the unique dignity of humans is a free gift of God (Himes and Himes 1995, 275).

The mention of St. Francis should serve as a reminder that Christian asceticism does not necessary mean a devaluation of the natural world. The ascetic tradition in Christianity, closely identified with monasticism, has sometimes been held responsible for Western contempt of nature and failure to nourish environmental values because (the criticism goes) asceticism negates physical existence in order to attain a transcendent spiritual realm. It is possible, however, to argue the opposite. Excessive consumption, caused by greed, is one of the main causes of the environmental crisis. An ethic of restraint, whether lay or monastic (its more extreme form), directly addresses this issue. Here monastic asceticism should be placed on a continuum on which the Jewish ethic of restraint, Protestant lifeways of voluntary simplicity, and other similar norms may also be located. Religious law and custom as followed by traditionally observant or more "orthodox" practitioners in different religions, or the "Rule" under which monastics live in Christianity, Buddhism, or Hinduism, alike contain specific regulations on eating, food production and preparation, other industries, waste disposal, housing, clothing, and procreation. This is, in effect, a body of instructions for sustainable practice. The vocation of celibacy, though regarded as sacrificial and exceptional, may provide an ethical antidote to the pronatalist views of traditional agricultural societies that have been a factor in population growth. The complex rationales for the celibate vocation may challenge the assumption that procreation is a good in itself and should not be restricted (although in practice this antidote has not been much used; rather, monastic institutions and pronatalism have coexisted). Overall, a reduced level of consumption in monastic communities, a prescribed attitude of humility, the potential mitigation of pronatalism, and a high degree of intentionality in economic practices make monasticism an immense practical resource for environmental ethics. It should also be remembered that monastic vows of poverty in the Christian tradition have sometimes aspired not only to the restraint of sensual indulgence and worldliness but also to solidarity with the poor and the oppressed, thus uniting environmental and social concerns in a monastic embodiment of eco-justice.

Eucharistic theology is one more important element in Christian environmental ethics. Most often it has been taken to offer a cosmic vision of "sacramentality" in which Catholic writers affirm that the creation itself is a sacrament, "a world that discloses the Creator's presence through visible and tangible signs" (U.S. Catholic Conference 1994, 5). More specific to the Eucharist or Divine Liturgy itself, however, is the following striking statement by the Ecumenical Patriarch Dimitrios in an official teaching, "Orthodoxy and the Ecological Crisis."

> *Thine Own of Thine own we offer unto Thee.* .... In the form of bread and wine, material from creation moulded into new form by human hands is offered to God with the acknowledgement (spelt out in these words) that all of creation is God's and that we are returning to God that which is His. In the sense that this captures the primordial relationship of Adam to both God and Creation, it is a sight of the restoration of that relationship and even more than that, a foretaste of the eschatological state of creation. When we partake of the body and blood of Christ, God meets us in the very substance of our relationship with creation and truly enters into the very being of our biological existence. (The Ecumenical Patriarchate 1990, 7–8)

Here Patriarch Dimitrios states that participation in the sacrament that is at the heart of Orthodox and Catholic Christianity is itself a concretely ecological act. In the same message, the Patriarch also stresses the environmental importance of asceticism, which he emphasizes is central to the Orthodox tradition.

Islam

In Islam, the Qur'anic vision embraces an environmental ethic on which Muslim writers on the environment appear to be in strong agreement (Ammar 1995; Ba Kader et al. 1983; Khalid 1992; Nasseef 1986; Nasr 1992). The elements of this ethic could be described as follows. God is the sole Creator of all that exists, and God's creation is purposive and has a deliberate design: "We created not the heaven and the earth, and whatsoever between them is, as playing" (21:16–17).[19] In the order of nature, from the minutest physical detail to the greatest laws and patterns of the universe, each and every thing is the direct result of the consciously willed creative action of God, who "has only to say 'Be' and it is" (6:73, 2:117). God is the sole owner, or possessor, of all that God has created, and God directs all that takes place and will determine its end. The entire creation is itself a revelation of the divine, which has sometimes been called a second Qur'an (Nasr 1992, 88–89). Therefore, the entire creation is replete with "signs," which the Qur'an repeatedly exhorts the believer to ponder in order to learn of the divine nature; this perception is especially strong in the mystical tradition, which places special emphasis on the verse "Wherever you look, there is the face of God" (2:109). All creatures are under the absolute lordship of God. God is the Master *(Rabb),* each creature is God's servant (*'abd*), and all are united in a natural and cosmic *islam* or surrender to their Creator (Cragg 1969, 11). This is, it could be said, the Qur'anic statement of ecological oneness and "interdependence."

As in the Hebrew Bible, nonhuman creatures have their own relationships with God. The Qur'an explicitly states (in language surprisingly reminiscent of Native American understanding): "No creature is there crawling on the earth, no bird flying with its wings / But they are nations like unto yourselves" (6:38). The Qur'anic revelation is addressed not only to humans but to nonhuman creatures as well, since, as in the Bible, God at times addresses nature directly (for example, to give instruction to the bees, 16:68). And again as in the Bible, nonhuman creatures praise God, each in its own way:

> Hast thou not seen how to God bow all who are in the heavens and all who are in the earth,
> the sun and the moon, the stars and the mountains, the trees and the beasts, and many of mankind? (22:38)

> The seven heavens and the earth, and whosoever in them is, extol Him; nothing is, that does not proclaim His praise, but you do not understand their extolling. (17:44)

All creation has a common origin (21:30, 24:45), and there is no gap or ontological difference between humans and other creatures—the all-important ontological difference is between creatures and Creator. According to Seyyed Hossein Nasr, "traditional Islamic society has always been noted for its harmonious relation with the natural environment and love for nature to the extent that many a Christian critic of Islam has accused Muslims of being naturalistic" (Nasr 1992, 91). Humanity does, however, have a special role in the created order, as God's appointed "vice regent" (*khalifa*) on earth, although the human, as the angels foresaw, would "do corruption there, and shed blood" (2:30). Humans as beings who can choose between good and evil have a special responsibility to obey the divine will and to discharge the special responsibilities that come with the position of *khalifa*. They will be accountable to God at the final judgment. Nature is subservient to humankind (22:65, 67:15), but only to a limited degree.

Humans must act in relation to nonhuman nature in such a way as to maintain the harmonious unity and integrity of nature (Nasseef 1986), without waste or overindulgence (7:31), without harm, without pollution, and in accordance with Qur'anic commandments concerning water; in short, in all ways that are just and equitable for human society not only for the present but also for the welfare of future generations (Ba Kader et al. 1983; Khalid 1992). Thus an eco-justice ethic is inherent in the root scripture of Islam. This ethic is augmented in the hadith, or "traditions," which record the custom and practice of the Prophet Muhammad—including his compassion for animals, his close relationship with nature, and his humble and materially simple way of life—that set the example for Muslims. The later tradition of Islam further implements Muslim eco-justice with legislation on the treatment of animals, the prevention of overgrazing, the conservation of water and forest resources, and population limits for cities (Masri 1992).

This summary indicates that in spite of recent polemics, there is or can be an ecologically positive interpretation of the value of nature, of the human-nature relationship, of "stewardship," and of the elements of an eco-justice ethic in the three Abrahamic traditions. Humans are permitted to "use" nature for their own needs, as indeed they are in every culture, but nature has not been created only to serve these needs. The biblical and Qur'anic testimony is clearly that nature's purposes are not limited to human uses and human meaning. There is a significant distinction between acceptable and unacceptable treatment of nature, indicated by certain prescribed general attitudes and also spelled out in specific cases. The utilization of nature by humans is limited to legitimate use; selfish or destructive use is not justifiable. The criteria for distinguishing legitimate from illegitimate use, the fulfillment of real need from excess and exploitation, are set forth in the commandments and religious law of each tradition. No separate or "new" set of norms is needed to provide guidance for interacting with nonhuman nature. Instead, the moral norms for human life can be applied directly to environmental questions within an eco-justice perspective that embraces the well-being of both humans and the natural world.

South Asian Religious Traditions

The three ancient religions of South Asian origin—Hinduism, Buddhism, and Jainism—have in common a set of core values that determine their environmental ethics. These values are: first, the continuity of all forms of life; second, nonviolence; and third, the ascetic ideal. The values are in turn determined by certain basic beliefs. In this "regional ontology," one of the most important components of a shared worldview is the belief in repeated birth and death, rebirth or "reincarnation" as it is often called. The living being travels endlessly through the cycle of birth and death, or *saṃsāra*, until liberation from rebirth is achieved through the practice of the disciplines of yoga. In this view of the destiny of living beings, there is no difference in the essence of a human being, a god, a ghost, a demon, an animal, or a tree. Each of these species can and does transform into the other in a single moment. Religious teaching and folklore is full of stories concerning such metamorphoses.

Consider as an example a delightful story found in Buddhaghosa's *Visuddhimagga*, a major work of Buddhist commentary of the fifth century C.E. The Buddha was teaching on the shore of a lake and a frog listening to his discourse "apprehended a sign"[20] in the Buddha's voice. Then a cowherd, while leaning on a stick, pinned the frog's head under the stick and killed him. Instantly the frog was reborn in the Heaven of the Thirty-Three in a golden palace, surrounded by celestial nymphs. When he tried to remember what he had done to merit such a favorable rebirth, he recalled that he had attained a meditative state while listening to the Buddha's preaching. In his new form as a god, he appeared to the Buddha, explained what had happened, listened again to his preaching, and attained the state of spiritual progress known as "entering the stream" (Buddhaghosa 1976, 7:51).

The Jātakas, a corpus of more than five hundred stories about the Buddha's previous lives, contain many narratives of the future Buddha, or Bodhisattva, as an animal (Cowell 1990). These are attributed to the Buddha as narrator and traditionally carry his authority. The stories are far better known in Buddhist communities in Asia than are the finer points of Buddhist doctrine, and from early childhood and throughout life are told in communal settings as moral lessons and edifying entertainment.[21] More dramatic for the environmental question even than the Buddha's lives as an animal are his lives as a tree. The Jātakas include numerous stories in which the Bodhisattva is a "tree-spirit," which sometimes plays an active role in the story.[22]

This continuity of being among all forms of life and the absence of a gulf between humans and other living beings has led some to the conclusion that these three South Asian traditions have a strongly biocentric rather than anthropocentric worldview. (It is not possible to speak of Buddhism or Jainism as theocentric.) The biocentric conclusion is subject to some qualification. Humans are unique in that, according to traditional belief, only from a human birth can one attain liberation. Nonetheless, the teachings of the religions apply to living creatures of all kinds, not only to human beings. All beings are subject to the law of karma and share the basic desire to avoid suffering and attain happiness. At the same time, the popular belief that any being may have been a close relative or friend in a previous life fosters a sense of connection, the family of all beings or "web" of interdependent life so treasured by ecologists. The sense of mutual dependence is acknowledged in the various rituals of offering to deities, "spirits," and ancestors in the three traditions.

Intimately connected with this sense of solidarity with all living beings or "sentient beings" is the South Asian emphasis on nonviolence or *ahiṃsā*. Nonviolence emerges as a foundational norm for environmental ethics, and indeed all morality, in the three traditions.[23] As Christopher Chapple notes:

Regardless of religious distinctions, nonviolent action requires that the performer of any activity be aware of its implications. The concept of nonviolent action also presumes that another person is, in a fundamental sense, not different from oneself. Philosophically, the non-difference of oneself and others provides a theoretical basis for performing nonviolence. Within the context of the Indian quest for liberation, nonviolence provides an important step toward the direct perception of the sacredness of all life. (Chapple, 19)

Nonviolence as a norm does not apply in the same way to all beings or to all humans; its requirements differ according to one's nature and situation in life. For example, it differs for monks and householders, or from one social group to another. Nonetheless, the central importance of nonviolence as a value has broad positive implications for the environment. It traditionally has had the immediate practical results of protection of animals, protection of trees, and an inclination toward vegetarianism, which is environmentally helpful. Nonviolence also establishes as a general guiding principle avoidance of harm and destruction, and thus functions as an overarching norm in terms of which contemporary ethical arguments and practices can be, and are, defined from a Buddhist, Hindu, or Jain perspective. It is well recognized that of these three traditions, or indeed of all religious traditions, Jainism places more importance on *ahiṃsā* as a regnant principle than any other, and that this is the unique Jain contribution to environmental ethics.

South Asia is the home of one of the world's great ascetic and monastic traditions, which finds different manifestations in these three religions. As in Western monasticism just discussed, the ecological function of the ascetic vocation here is to uphold simplicity and nonconsumption as ideals that counteract innate greed and indulgence, and to devise particular practices that may be environmentally beneficial. Also, the prestige of asceticism and the presence of a strong monastic institution might even help (at least in theory) to reduce a given social group's net consumption if, as in Hinduism, some degree of renunciation is prescribed for three out of four of the classical stages of life, namely, for celibate student life, forest retirement, and full renunciation.

Hinduism

In Hinduism, a theistic tradition, there is a more pronounced ontological continuity between the divine and particular living beings than there is in the Abrahamic traditions.[24] Vedic and later accounts of creation are sometimes emanationist, implying a continuity of divine and natural existence, whereas the Upaniṣads set forth a foundational teaching of divine immanence, or the oneness of the divine reality and the world (variously interpreted in later philosophical systems). Hindu worship makes extensive use of concrete images of the divine in many forms. A nuanced discussion of this comparative theological question is not possible here, especially as a full account cannot be given by reference to written sources alone. There is, however, a clear contrast between the insistence of Abrahamic traditions on an uncompromised distinction between the Creator and the created, and the Hindu sensibility that might be called radically incarnational or sacramental, to use Western terms. Diana Eck has vividly described the ecological dimensions of this Hindu sensibility.

> One of the most striking aspects of the multitude of Hindu cosmogonic myths is the organic, biological vision that they express. The completed universe is imaged as a living organism, a vast ecosystem, in which each part is inextricably related to the life of the whole. And the whole is indeed alive: it is in constant process and movement, growing and decaying. There is no such thing as objectified "nature" or lifeless "elements," for everything belongs to the living pattern of the whole. . . . These are the images of a biological world-view, grounded in the Vedas, strengthened by the indigenous *yakṣa* and *nāga* traditions, and persisting still in the Hindu mythic imagination. It is a view in which the universe, and by extension the land of India, is alive with interconnections and meanings, and is likened to a living organism. There is no "nature-worship" here, but a sacramental natural ontology. (Eck 1995, 141)

It is usually commented in reflections on a Hindu environmental ethic that Hindus regard mountains, rocks, trees, and rivers, and the Earth itself, as sacred. If the Hebrew Bible and the Qur'an allow for an independent relation between God and creatures, who are conscious of God, praise God of themselves, and may even have a covenant with God, still it is prohibited to address any created being in prayer or to "worship" it (though one may bless it or praise it). No such prohibition is found in Hinduism, where a tree or river (as well as heavenly bodies) can indeed be invoked in the second person. The Ṛg Veda and Atharva Veda contain hymns to and mention of the waters, trees, medicinal plants, the goddess of the forest, the Earth, and Heaven and Earth.

In the Atharva Veda (12:1; Bloomfield 1897) is found the lengthy "Hymn to the Earth," especially noted by Hindu writers on the environment (Chapple 1993; Prime 1994; Singh 1986). This hymn praises and invokes Earth as a goddess and as the mother of humans. The hymn throughout clearly refers to the physical Earth, not to an abstraction; it is the firm and "all-supporting" Earth upon whom rivers run, creatures move, forests stand, people walk, battles are fought, and sacrifices performed. The hymn speaks of her brown, black, or reddish color; her "rock, earth, stone, and dust"; and her north, south, east, and west directions. With elaborate eloquence, the hymn praises the Earth's beauty, and asks for her bounty in all its manifestations (sometimes using the metaphor of "milk" from her breasts): pure water, abundant food, wide spaces, gems from the earth, orderly seasons, stability, and protection. She is the protector of the trees and the plants' support. The poet exclaims: "What I dig out of thee, O Earth, shall quickly grow again: O pure one, pierce thy vital spot, [and] not thy heart!" (Atharva Veda 12:35).

The idea of Earth as a goddess who is the mother of all creatures continues in the Purāṇas and later Hindu tradition (Kinsley 1986; Pintchman 1994). The orthodox Hindu, awakening in the morning, offers a series of prayers to God, the planets, the guru, and his higher and lower selves. Then, as he gets out of bed, he first places his right foot on the ground and says, "Oh Earth, the giver of all that is good to us, I bow before Thee" (Vidyanarva 1991, 6).[25] Contemporary Hindu environmentalists are keenly aware of the traditional belief in the divinity of the Earth and, like Vandana Shiva, may link abuse of the Earth to oppression of women by colonial and patriarchal forces of "maldevelopment," which destroy traditional and indigenous women's practices that are environmentally sound (Shiva 1989) and which have led to systemic social injustice and poverty as well as the destruction of ecosystems and sustainable agriculture. Gandhian thought has also been an important stream in environmental ethics in Hinduism and is influential in other areas as well.

An important area for further inquiry is the significance of trees, associated with female divinity, in religiously based ecological practices. Protected groves, often "sacred groves" associated with temples or shrines, have been a common method of conservation of forests, plants, and wildlife throughout India for many centuries. This traditional practice has now become the object of renewed attention and scientific study and is an instructive example of a fusion of religious meaning and environmental practice (Gadgil and Guha 1992; PTI 1996; Shiva 1989, 57; Sochaczewski and Rai 1993).

Buddhism

The distinctive contribution of Buddhist environmental ethics perhaps lies most in Buddhism's emphasis on the need to see all things as arising in dependence on causes and conditions. The doctrine of *pratītya-samutpāda,* or "interdependent co-origination," is noted prominently in many, if not most, Buddhist writings on the environment (for example Badiner 1990; Batchelor and Brown 1992; Davies 1987; Gross 1990; Namgyal 1986; Tucker and Williams 1997). This has a series of moral implications. In an environmental context, this doctrine is normally mentioned not in its more articulated, technical, and difficult form as the twelve-member sequence of interdependent co-origination (which is related to explanations of the process of birth and death), or in association with the concept of "emptiness" or *śūnyatā,* but rather as a well-known general metaphysical principle. This principle is then construed as a Buddhist worldview of "inter-being," to use Thich Nhat Hanh's expression, or as the causal interdependence and even interpenetration of all life and all things. The primary ecological principle of interdependence, advanced by environmentalists of all backgrounds, thus has an important Buddhist equivalent. The significance of the Buddhist emphasis on "conditionality" does not end, however, with this correspondence.

Buddhist thinkers associated with the movement known as "Engaged Buddhism" (Queen and King 1996) have taken the position that the Buddhist analysis of experience in terms of the Four Truths, the Five Precepts, the Three Poisons of greed, anger, and delusion, and other basic Buddhist teachings can and must be applied to human societies as whole systems. "The Buddhist principle of interdependence," Sallie King says, "is probably the most powerful tool used by the social activists to understand, express, and justify their perspective" (Queen and King 1996, 406). To discern accurately the causes and conditions of any problem, any form of suffering, will require analysis of the problem as structural. As Buddhadasa Bikkhu first pointed out, in terms of the Buddha Dharma it is not authentic to separate the spiritual from the social (Queen and King 1996, 155). Following Buddhadasa, Sulak Sivaraksa and other Buddhists (like Vandana Shiva and others in the Hindu context) have defined a critique of modern forms of industrial development and consumerism that constitutes a Buddhist eco-justice ethic (Sivaraksa 1992).

The orientation in Buddhist practice toward the discernment of causes and conditions and "seeing things as they really are" may give Buddhism a special strength in the urgent task of "reinventing" our entrenched but environmentally negative ways of life. Though I am not able here to include narratives of Buddhist environmental activism, the work of "development monks" in Asia and of "eco-Buddhists" in the West (as well as the partnership between these two groups) displays the achievements of Buddhist insight in environmental problem solving and community development. From the arena of Buddhist grassroots activism, as from so many other places, comes the message that "the health of the land depends upon the health of the people and the health of the people depends on the health of the land" (Wongkun n.d.). The practice of meditation to cultivate mental clarity is an important aid to practical discernment in the Engaged Buddhist approach, while meditation can also foster compassion and a palpable experience of the interconnectedness of living beings, a frequent theme of environmentally concerned Buddhists, which has been richly expressed in the anthology *Dharma Gaia: A Harvest of Essays in Buddhism and Ecology* (Badiner 1990).

East Asian Religious Traditions

The religious traditions of China, Confucianism and Taoism, may most usefully be considered together in an inquiry into environmental ethics, as

Mary Evelyn Tucker has suggested (Tucker 1993). These two traditions are in fact so closely interrelated that they can be regarded as two aspects of a single religious culture, which, like the South Asian traditions, is founded on certain pervasive concepts and values. Formal inquiry into the environmental resources of Chinese religious traditions has begun only recently, and at this time the literature is slim, but in the near future a substantial study will become available with the publication of papers presented at a 1996 consultation, "Confucianism and Ecology."[26] Some of these findings may be anticipated in the following comment by Tucker, who convened the consultation:

> Confucianism, in particular, has significant intellectual and spiritual resources to offer in emerging discussions regarding attitudes toward nature, the role of the human, and environmental ethics. Its dynamic, organismic world view, its vitalist understanding of *ch'i* (material force), its respect for the vast continuity of life, its sense of compassion for suffering, its desire to establish the grounds for just and sustainable societies, its emphasis on holistic, moral education, and its appreciation for the embeddedness of life in interconnected concentric circles are only some examples of the rich resources of the Confucian tradition in relation to ecological issues. (Tucker 1996, 151)

The basis of the Chinese ecological vision is the view of the universe as a single, living unity composed of a primal stuff, "material force" or *ch'i*, and functioning according to consistent primordial patterns of change.[27] In this unified cosmos, humans have a distinctive but not an isolated place; Wei-ming Tu, as Tucker notes, calls this the "anthropocosmic" vision. Chinese civilization, in traditional belief, was founded by Sage Kings who had attained realization of the cosmic harmony, and the goal of the religious and moral life in China has immemorially been to attune both the character of the human person and the order of human society to the greater pattern of the universe by following the "Way" of the sages. For the Neo-Confucian, the purpose of self-cultivation is to "form one body with the universe"; for the Taoist, that purpose has been to live in the same manner that the great "Way," or Tao, of nature acts. If alienation from nonhuman nature is found, the goal of Chinese religious practice must therefore be to overcome that alienation and to achieve a cosmic and "ecological" oneness with the world; this process also has social and political dimensions.

Since ancient times, Heaven and Earth have been looked upon as the parents of all things; they are still venerated today in village shrines (Paper 1997). This sense of close filial connection achieved one of its consummate expressions in the eleventh century "Western Inscription" of the Neo-Confucian Chang Tsai, which begins: "Heaven is my father and Earth is my mother, and even such a small creature as I finds an intimate place in their midst. Therefore that which fills the universe I regard as my body and that which directs the universe I consider as my nature. All people are my brothers and sisters, and all things my companions" (Chan 1963, 497). A sense of obligation to nurture the well-being of all things, and even to care for Earth and Heaven themselves, arises from *jen,* benevolence or love, which extends universally. For the early Confucian Mencius, as for Chang Tsai more than one thousand years later, benevolence is not directed to humans only. Mencius, speaking to King Hsüan of Ch'i about his capacity to become a benevolent ruler, locates the germ of benevolence in the King's inability to watch the suffering of an ox cringing in fear as it is led to be sacrificed (*Mencius* 1.A.7); it is this seed of compassion (better known through the example of the child about to fall into a well) that must be expanded into *jen* to enable rulers to govern justly and ultimately to unite Heaven, Earth, human beings, and all creatures.

The Chinese religious and philosophical disposition has always insisted on a grasp of practice and a testing of theories in social policy. Two examples from the early classics could be given as illustration. The first is from the *Tao Te Ching,* the earliest classic of Taoism. In chapter 80, Lao Tzu, traditionally considered the author, describes the ideal kingdom ruled by the Sage. In such a society, people would not use labor-saving machines, even if these were available to them. They would reject weapons of war, and "should be contented with their food, pleased with their clothing, satisfied with their homes, should take pleasure in their rustic tasks" (Waley 1958, 241). The passage is polemical and reflects the radicalism of the mystical ascetic the author may have been. But its concreteness about the simplicity of life in an ideal society is arresting, all the more so in juxtaposition with the famously enigmatic and mysterious sayings of Lao Tzu on the transcendent Tao itself. The second example of a focus on practice is from the first chapter of the *Mencius.* Mencius begins his conversation with King Hui of Liang on benevolent rule with a series of recommendations for agriculture and economy, starting with growing grain, fishing, and planting mulberry trees for silk cultivation (1.A.3). From this time on, as Tucker so concisely says, "the recognition that humane government rests on sustainable agriculture and maintaining a balance with nature is key to all Confucian political thought" (Tucker 1993, 158). Wei-ming Tu and other exponents of "New Confucianism" have constructed a contemporary Confucian ethic that both mounts a critique on what he terms "the Enlightenment mentality" of the West and at the same time outlines Confucian approaches to critical issues of the present, placing the environmental crisis in a broad social and political context (See Tu 1993, 1995).

Shinto, as the native religious tradition of Japan, shows certain characteristics that are similar to other indigenous traditions. Shinto, "the Way of the *kami,*" apprehends numberless numinous presences, "gods" or *kami,* in particular beings in nature including trees, rivers, rocks, and mountains.

The beauty of nature is taken to be in itself an experience of the sacred. The *kami* and their dwelling places are to be treated with reverence and care. This might mean, for example, that in the precincts of a shrine no trees may be cut down. The localization and particularity of the sacred presences give Shinto (like other indigenous traditions) a strong sense of place. A core value of Shinto, besides the well-known Japanese "love of nature," is purification, both physical and spiritual, which could provide a clear rationale and motivation for resisting pollution. Shinto also encompasses a shamanic tradition, which, in interaction with Buddhism, has for centuries produced ascetics of extreme rigor who in their austerities have forged deep bonds to special places and entities in the natural world of Japan.

Religious Traditions of Indigenous Peoples

Although the meaning of the word "indigenous," which has the sense "native," is not in question, there is debate about how and to what groups the term should be applied, especially as this has legal implications. The term "indigenous" is nevertheless now generally used in international affairs, in the United Nations system, and among NGOs.[28] Although still not entirely clear, the word is presently accepted and used by indigenous peoples themselves as one expression of their identity. In the study of religion, the adjective for both native peoples and their religions has evolved from "savage" in the nineteenth century and before, through "primitive" (still used in the 1970s), and on through such well-meaning locutions as "primal" or "animist" (both still in use), "basic," "microhistorical," and others. It seems preferable either to use the general term "indigenous" or to refer to a particular people or region by its proper name.

There are at least three obstacles to a short synoptic account of indigenous religions. The first is the great diversity of the hundreds of indigenous cultures found in different parts of the world. While it is impossible to obtain accurate figures, it is likely that over three hundred million people are practicing their traditional indigenous religions, even though some of these may also be nominal or even committed followers of another religion. Is it possible to generalize? This is an empirical question, which can only be answered by inquiring in detail into the traditions themselves. This brings one to the second obstacle, which is the state of the evidence. The literature of anthropology is enormous but mostly produced by nonnative scholars. It varies immensely in its accuracy, focus, methodology, and ideological bias, depending on the date of research and the author. An indispensable additional source for knowledge of religious traditions of indigenous peoples is the testimony and self-interpretation of native people themselves: in statements about their experiences and their values in their home settings, in conferences and other gatherings, in academic and other books and articles, and in literature and art. The third obstacle to presenting a general account of indigenous religions is conventional wisdom and stereotypes, which may be either positive or negative. Here one must watch out for what might be called a dialectic of the stereotypes, in which (for example) a notion of indigenous peoples as perfect ecologists arises, and then, with cautions about "romanticization," a reactive image of ecological destructiveness is put forward. It is only by looking deeply into the traditions themselves that such shallow polarization can be avoided.

Looking deeply when the record is so extensive, multifaceted, and ambiguous is not a simple matter, but the evidence in at least some quarters shows that the image of indigenous religions as essentially ecological is in many instances accurate. Let me take as a single illustration an important article by Christopher Vecsey, "American Indian Environmental Religions," in which the author presents a wide-ranging overview of North American Indian religions. Vecsey convincingly demonstrates common features of diverse Native American religions, with examples from specific peoples for each generalization and documentation copious enough to place the burden of proof on those who would demur that North American Indian religions are not environmental in basic orientation. He summarizes as follows:

> Ethics are limitations of freedom based on consideration for the welfare and feelings of others. They form a structure of morally proper action. American Indian attitudes toward the environment fit such a description. In their ethical relations with persons of nature, Indians assumed: first, that natural entities were essentially equal in value or worth to humans; second, that non-human persons expressed their intentions, needs, dislikes, and rights; third, that non-humans entered covenants with humans for mutual benefit; there were social contracts between humans and non-humans; and fourth, there was reciprocity in these relations between humans and non-humans. (Vecsey 1980, 20)

Vecsey then points out that both hunting and farming bring an inescapable moral tension into the relation between humans and animals, and between humans and plants. Native Americans are highly conscious of this dilemma of survival (Vecsey 1980, 23). Osage theologian George Tinker has written as follows on this tension and ways to resolve it:

> The necessity for reciprocity becomes most apparent where violence is concerned, especially when such violence is an apparent necessity, as in hunting or harvesting. Violence cannot be perpetrated, a life taken, in a Native American society, without some spiritual act of reciprocation. We are so much a part of the whole of creation and its balance that anything we do to perpetrate an act of violence, even when it is necessary to our own survival, must be accompanied by an act of spiritual reciprocation intended to restore the balance of existence. It must be remembered that violence as a technical category must extend to *all* one's relatives. (Tinker 1996, 160)

He continues with a discussion of ceremonies of reciprocation that Native American peoples perform on the many occasions when such rituals are appropriate. The ethics of Native American religions has indeed been ecological and sophisticated in its reflection on the dependence by humans on nonhuman life. The oneness in Native American traditions with the natural world is psychically profound but also pragmatic in its focus on survival and sustainability through elaborate localized systems of religiously mandated environmental practices.

The integration of worldview, ethics, and systems of environmental practices is essential to indigenous approaches to the environmental crisis, as is the historical experience of the link between "ecocide" and genocide. The collision of drastically different cultures, the continuing experience of oppression, and perception of a global crisis of environment and development generate not only critiques of the colonizing civilization but also fresh thinking on the renewal of indigenous lifeways. This thinking is not merely preservationist, a "return to the past," but seeks a feasible path into a sustainable future. Seneca historian John Mohawk thus joins his reflection on indigenous liberation theologies with an explanation of what he calls "liberation technologies":

> Technologies have political cousins. . . . Liberation technologies are those which meet people's needs within the parameters defined by cultures which they themselves created (or create), and which have no dependence on the world marketplace. . . . Liberation theologies are belief systems which challenge the assumption, widely held in the West, that the earth is simply a commodity which can be exploited thoughtlessly by humans for the purpose of material acquisition within an ever-expanding economic framework. A liberation theology will develop in people a consciousness that all life on earth is sacred and that the sacredness of life is the key to human freedom and survival. . . . A strategy for survival must include a liberation theology—call it a philosophy or a cosmology if you will, but we believe it to be a theology—or humankind will simply continue to view the earth as a commodity and will continue to seek more efficient ways to exploit that which they have not come to respect. . . . Our strategy for survival is to create and implement liberation technologies which are consistent with and complementary to a liberation theology which arises out of our culture and is a product of the Natural World. (Akwesasne Notes 1981, 75–78)

Religion, morality, politics, economics, and technology are all a single subject of concern here; that is, this is an eco-justice analysis. Its purpose is not only critical but also constructive. Impelled by the dissonance and danger that necessitate a "strategy for survival," a first step is taken toward imagining a "relevant utopia." In indigenous ethics, necessity is the mother of reinvention.

Summary and Conclusion

What conclusions can we draw from this overview of environmental ethics in religious traditions? This survey has attempted to cover the waterfront, and like a waterfront, it exhibits some continuity but less symmetry. This is inevitable, as my purpose has not been to present a neatly schematized plan but to draw a picture of a territory. It may be a messy picture, but if one stands back from it some large patterns emerge. I believe that the religious traditions we have reviewed do agree, to a greater or lesser extent, on the following important points:

1. The natural world has value in itself and does not exist solely to serve human needs.
2. There is significant ontological continuity between human and non-human living beings, even though humans do have a distinctive role. This continuity can be felt and experienced.
3. Nonhuman living beings are morally significant, in the eyes of God and/or in the cosmic order. They have their own unique relations to God and their own places in the cosmic order.
4. The dependence of human life on the natural world can and should be acknowledged in ritual and other expressions of appreciation and gratitude.
5. Moral norms such as justice, compassion, and reciprocity apply (in appropriate ways) both to human beings and to nonhuman beings. The well-being of humans and the well-being of nonhuman beings are inseparably connected.
6. There are legitimate and illegitimate uses of nature.
7. Greed and destructiveness are condemned. Restraint and protection are commended.
8. Human beings are obliged to be aware and responsible in living in harmony with the natural world, and should follow the specific practices for this prescribed by their traditions.

If there is even some consensus on these points, then the outlook in religious environmental ethics is very favorable. By adopting an eco-justice approach, which does not too narrowly circumscribe the question, it has been possible to inductively draw out these shared moral norms and religious ideas that are relevant to environmental ethics.

Since some might object that this account is overly optimistic, even naively so, it should be remembered that I first set out to investigate positive resources for environmental ethics in religious traditions. A description of the environmentally negative aspects of the religions was not part of the undertaking. I also stated that I would examine neither the gap between theory and practice nor the question of whether any given religion or culture has been environmentally successful. In this regard, it must especially be noted that the account given here is not gendered and that almost none of the factors (religious or otherwise) affecting the issue of population and consumption have been addressed. This critically important topic calls for separate treatment, and some ground has been broken elsewhere (see, for example, Coward 1995). I also have not looked at how the environmental ethics of the religions compare with the principles that have been defined in international law and by other secular institutions in the past two or three decades (Rockefeller 1996b). These are all significant omissions. Nevertheless, if the norms for environmental ethics just outlined can be seen as common to different religions, then this interreligious inquiry has rendered some service.

I should not close without considering once again the question of what difference religious teachings really make, or could make (since the ethical approach of this chapter was to be pragmatic). If the resources for environmental ethics are so abundant, why is the crisis so acute? The metaphor of "resources" is admittedly unfortunate for this discussion—but if resources are not exploited, what effect will they have? If religious traditions cherish these values and give these precepts, have these been put into practice, and if not, why not? The answer is not far to seek in any religion. This is a primordial spiritual question, named by the different traditions as sin, evil, or ignorance. Their answer is in the mystery of repentance and conversion. If one has not yet begun to repent, how can one awaken to repentance? If one has begun the work of conversion, how can one stay the course? If there is an antidote to the three poisons of greed, anger, and delusion, how can even one person, let alone the whole body of humankind, be made to take the medicine?

It also needs to be asked if something might be missing from the list of norms and ideas just given, although it is substantial. I think something *is* missing. Lethal as the poisons of greed and anger are, the poison of delusion may be the hardest to neutralize. The inability to see clearly where and what we are, and then to find our way out by devising whole new political and economic systems: This may be the new challenge of speeding change and complexity that religions in their present forms cannot easily meet. In the crisis of environment and development, religions are repeatedly called upon to provide "vision" and motivation, and to mobilize their communities to action. But *how* to act? Religion can and does provide values and motivation but cannot always provide methods and means. It has been said that the environment is a "transreligious" issue. It has also been remarked that our religions do not have teachings on "the environment" because this is a new and unfamiliar problem. These comments are both true and not true. We have been taught to "repent!" but we have not been taught to "reinvent!" Religious teachings can begin the task and can bring us far, but given the strangeness of the crisis, they may not by themselves take us the whole way. Religion needs to join forces with endeavors supposed by some not to be "religion": science, politics, commerce and industry, and the arts. Interreligious dialogue also has a crucial role to play as we reinvent ourselves, because it brings together the whole store of ethical resources that the religions offer to help us grapple with the crisis. As Larry Rasmussen says, "Earth's distress, after all, is the most ecumenical of issues. As such it requires a religious response of corresponding scope. No one religious tradition will suffice. Religions altogether will not save the planet, for that matter. Yet neither will the earth be saved without them" (Rasmussen 1996, 271).

Notes

1. The Alliance of Religions and Conservation has compiled information on 120,000–130,000 projects on religion and the environment worldwide (*The Economist* 1996, 108).

2. This space regrettably will not permit discussion of two important current movements, deep ecology and ecofeminism, although both have considerable bearing on environmental ethics in the religions.

3. This term became current in Christian churches in the 1970s but is now entering general use.

4. For example, a recent report in the *New York Times* attributes a disruptive global increase in "red tide" algae to an increase in human sewage (Broad 1996).

5. "Those of us born before 1950 have seen more population growth during our lifetime than occurred during the preceding *4 million years* since our ancestors first stood upright," says Lester Brown in "The Acceleration of History," the opening chapter of the 1996 *State of the World* report (Brown 1996, 3–20; emphasis added). The world's population has tripled since 1900 and has doubled since 1950. The way of life and the amount of consumption of a large part of this hugely increased number of people has changed completely from previous centuries. Since 1950 the consumption of grain has increased threefold, of seafood fourfold, of water threefold, of firewood threefold, of lumber, twice, of paper six times. The consumption of fossil fuels has increased fourfold since 1950 but since 1900 has multiplied thirty times. Since 1950 the world's economy has quintupled; since 1900 it has grown twentyfold (Barney 1993; Brown 1996).

6. The reader may notice (and some may object) that this chapter cites standard, or mainstream, sources for its analysis of the global environmental crisis. When one consults a variety of sources, there is a marked difference in *tone* between different reports, from radical and "doomsday" environmentalism to more conservative or "establishment" analysis. To the nonscientist's eye, however, it appears that different accounts differ not so much on the facts (they may cite the same data) as on the outlook for the future, the note of urgency or lack of it, the assignment of blame, and views on what should be done.

7. The phrase is Thomas Berry's.

8. UNDP 1996, chap. 2 usefully traces the evolution of the concept of "development" since the 1950s and the relation of growth to "development."

9. Brian Hehir, address at the Center for the Study of Human Rights, Columbia University, November 14, 1996.

10. As just one illustration, Swartz observes: "Today when we encounter God as a *nesher*, a griffin vulture (as we do in Deuteronomy 32:11), we must pause to examine just what is intended by the term. But we may surmise that then, when people first encountered that way of depicting God, they knew that the reference was to God as a fiercely protective parent, one who carries its young on its back to help them learn how to fly" (Swartz 1993, 2). The familiar phrase often translated as "on eagle's wings" is not poetic imagination or a prophet's vision of events in an occult spiritual realm but is based on detailed observation of living wild creatures. It conveys far more to those who share this deep acquaintance than to the modern city dwellers who know nothing of the *nesher*.

11. Citations from the Hebrew Bible are from the translation of the Jewish Publication Society.

12. Gordis goes so far as to say: "The Book of Job offers a religious foundation for the inherent rights of animals as co-inhabitants of the earth" (Gordis 1986, 119; Swetlitz 1990, 51).

13. Most frequently, Psalms 24, 90, 98, 104, and 148.

14. Quotations from the siddur, or Jewish prayer book, are from Jules Harlow, ed., *Siddur Sim Shalom,* the prayer book published by the Conservative Movement in the United States. As prayers occur repeatedly in different liturgies, in most cases no page numbers are given.

15. Arthur Waskow, personal communication, June 1996.

16. It is interesting to note that Rabbi Mordecai Kaplan, founder of the Reconstructionist Movement in Judaism, had removed the passage from the Reconstructionist prayer book published in 1945, but the passage was reinserted in 1989 because of its "ecological significance" (Goldman 1989).

17. Hayim Perelmuter points out: "Rabbinic commentary depends on a pun to interpret the passage. To be sure there is a Hebrew root *rada* that means 'rule.' But there is also a root *yarad* which means 'to descend,' and whose imperative form is also *r'du*. Here the pun comes to the rescue of ecology. Both the Midrash to this passage and the Rashi commentary tell us: 'If man is deserving, he rules; if not he is diminished.' The ultimate test for humankind therefore comes in its attitude to ecology and stewardship" (Perelmuter 1994, 131–132).

18. This citation is from the New English Bible.

19. Citations from the Qur'an are from A. J. Arberry's *The Koran Interpreted* (1973).

20. To "apprehend a sign" means to produce a mental "image" or counterpart of an external object of meditation. See Buddhaghosa 1976, 4:25.

21. The Venerable Kurunegoda Piyatissa, abbot of the New York Buddhist Vihara, has described to me the numerous social occasions in his native Sri Lanka as well as the educational settings (lay and monastic) in which the Jātaka stories are customarily read or told (personal communication, April 11, 1996). The Jātaka narratives have been part of moral formation and an important parat of national culture in Sri Lanka for many centuries.

22. I am indebted for this information to Matt Weiner.

23. In 1990–1992 I worked with other members of the International Coordinating Committee on Religion and the Earth (ICCRE) to draft an "Earth Charter" based on an interfaith consultation process carried out through studies and a series of dialogues and drafting meetings in different parts of the world. We found that the Indian Earth Charter as well as individual colleagues in India held up nonviolence as a core value for the environment, and that this was a distinctive South Asian contribution. See Braybrooke 1992, 138–142.

24. The charge of "pantheism," however, is false if by "pantheism" one means that God simply is the world and nothing more and that there is no transcendent divine being. Well-known authoritative texts, to say nothing of later literature, can be cited to lay this charge to rest, for example Ṛg Veda 10:90, or Bhagavad Gītā 9:4–5, 10:42.

25. Also, Swami Paramānanda Bhārati, personal communication, January 1990; this refers as well to the Śrī Vaiṣṇava tradition (Sharma 1996, 6).

26. This consultation was held at Harvard Divinity School in May 1996 as one of a series of meetings on the world's religions and the environment ending in October 1998.

27. These patterns are the subject of the *I Ching*, or *Book of Changes*, a classic more ancient in its earliest strata than Confucianism or Taoism as formal schools.

28. The International Labor Organization (ILO) has adopted the phrase "indigenous and tribal peoples," while the United Nations has been resistant to the word "peoples" but not to the word "indigenous." In areas colonized by the British, the term "native" has acquired an unwelcome connotation, but "indigenous" is now current globally.

References

Akwesasne Notes, ed. 1981. *Basic Call to Consciousness*. Revised edition. Mohawk Nation, via Rooseveltown, N.Y.: Akwesasne Notes.

Ammar, Nawal H. 1995. "Islam, Population, and the Environment: A Textual and Juristic View." In *Population, Consumption, and the Environment,* edited by Harold Coward, 123–136. Albany: State University of New York Press.

Arberry, A. J., trans. 1973. *The Koran Interpreted*. New York: Macmillan.

Badiner, Allan Hunt. 1990. *Dharma Gaia: A Harvest of Essays in Buddhism and Ecology*. Berkeley: Parallax Press.

Ba Kader, Abou, et al. 1983. *Islamic Principles for the Conservation of the Natural Environment*. IUCN Environmental Policy and Law Paper. Gland, Switzerland: International Union for the Conservation of Nature and Natural Resources (IUCN) and the Kingdom of Saudi Arabia Meteorology and Environmental Protection Administration.

Barney, Gerald O., with Jane Blewett and Kristen R. Barney. 1993. *Global 2000 Revisited: What Shall We Do? The Critical Issues of the 21st Century*. Arlington, Va.: The Millennium Institute.

Batchelor, Martine, and Kerry Brown, eds. 1992. *Buddhism and Ecology*. Worldwide Fund for Nature World Religions and Ecology Series. London: Cassell.

Berger, Julian. 1987. *Report from the Frontier: The State of the World's Indigenous Peoples*. Cambridge, Mass.: Cultural Survival.

Berman, Saul. 1993. "Jewish Environmental Values." In *To Till and to Tend: A Guide to Jewish Environmental Study and Action,* III:B. New York: Coalition on the Environment and Jewish Life.

Bloomfield, Maurice, trans. 1897. *Hymns of the Atharva-Veda.* Oxford: Oxford University Press.

Braybrooke, Marcus, ed. 1992. *Stepping Stones to a Global Ethic.* London: SCM Press.

Broad, William J. 1996. "A Spate of Red Tides Menacing Coastal Seas Worldwide." *New York Times,* August 27, C1, C5.

Brown, Lester R., et al. 1996. *State of the World: A Worldwatch Institute Report on Progress Toward a Sustainable Society.* New York: W. W. Norton.

Buddhaghosa Bhadantacariya. 1976 [1956]. *The Path of Purification (Visuddhimagga).* Translated by Bhikku Ñyanamoli. 2 vols. Boulder: Shambhala.

Callicott, J. Baird. 1994. *Earth's Insights: A Survey of Ecological Ethics from the Mediterranean Basin to the Australian Outback.* Berkeley: University of California Press.

Chan, Wing-tsit. 1963. *A Source Book in Chinese Philosophy.* Princeton: Princeton University Press.

Chapple, Christopher Key. 1993. *Nonviolence to Animals, Earth, and Self in Asian Traditions.* Albany: State University of New York Press.

Coalition on the Environment and Jewish Life. 1993. *To Till and to Tend: A Guide to Jewish Environmental Study and Action.* New York: Coalition on the Environment and Jewish Life.

Cobb, John B. Jr. 1991. "The Role of Theology of Nature in the Church." In *Liberating Life: Contemporary Approaches to Ecological Theology,* edited by Charles Birch, William Eakin, and Jay B. McDaniel, 261–272. Maryknoll, N.Y.: Orbis Books.

Cohen, Joel. 1995. *How Many People Can the Earth Support?* New York: W. W. Norton.

Coward, Harold, ed. 1995. *Population, Consumption, and the Environment.* Albany: State University of New York Press.

Cowell, E. B., ed. 1990 [1895–1907]. *The Jātaka or Stories of the Buddha's Former Births. Translated by Robert Chalmers. 6 vols. Delhi: Low Price Publications.*

Cragg, Kenneth. 1969. *The House of Islam.* Belmont, Calif.: Dickenson Publishing Company.

Davies, Shann, ed. 1987. *Tree of Life: Buddhism and the Protection of Nature.* Hong Kong: The Buddhist Perception of Nature.

Dubos, René. 1972. *A God Within.* New York: Charles Scribner's Sons.

The Economist. 1996. "Godliness and Greenness." December 21, 108–110.

The Ecumenical Patriarchate, assisted by the Worldwide Fund for Nature. 1990. "Orthodoxy and the Ecological Crisis." Istanbul: The Ecumenical Patriarchate.

Eck, Diana L. 1995. "Gaṅgā: The Goddess in Hindu Sacred Geography." In *Devī: Goddesses of India,* edited by John Stratton Hawley and Donna Marie Wulff. Berkeley: University of California Press.

Fragomeni, Richard N., and John T. Pawlikowski, eds. 1994. *The Ecological Challenge: Ethical, Liturgical, and Spiritual Responses.* Collegeville, Minn.: Liturgical Press.

Gadgil, Madhav, and Ramachandra Guha. 1992. *This Fissured Land: An Ecological History of India.* Delhi: Oxford University Press.

Goldman, Ari. 1989. "Reconstructionist Jews Turn to the Supernatural." *New York Times,* February 19, A26.

Gordis, Robert. 1986. "Ecology and the Jewish Tradition." In *Judaic Ethics for a Lawless World,* 113–122. New York: Jewish Theological Seminary. Reprinted in Marc Swetlitz, *Judaism and Ecology 1970–1986: A Sourcebook of Readings,* 47–52 (Wyncote, Pa.: Shomrei Adamah).

Granberg-Michaelson, Wesley. 1991. "Covenant and Creation." In *Liberating Life: Contemporary Approaches to Ecological Theology,* edited by Charles Birch, William Eakin, and Jay B. McDaniel, 27–36. Maryknoll, N.Y.: Orbis Books.

_____. 1994. "Creation in Ecumenical Theology." In *Ecotheology: Voices from South and North,* edited by David G. Hallman, 96–106. Maryknoll, N.Y.: Orbis Books.

Gross, Rita. 1990. "Buddhist Resources for Issues of Population, Consumption, and the Environment." In *Population, Consumption, and the Environment,* edited by Harold Coward, 123–136. Albany: State University of New York Press.

Harlow, Jules, ed. and trans. 1989. *Siddur Sim Shalom: A Prayerbook for Shabbat, Festivals, and Weekdays.* New York: The Rabbinical Assembly and the United Synagogue of America.

Harris, Monford. 1976. "Ecology: A Covenantal Approach." *CCAR Journal* 23:101–108. Reprinted in Marc Swetlitz, *Judaism and Ecology 1970–1986: A Sourcebook of Readings,* 59–62 (Wyncote, Pa.: Shomrei Adamah).

Hawken, Paul. 1993. *The Ecology of Commerce: A Declaration of Sustainability.* New York: HarperCollins.

Hertzberg, Arthur, ed. 1991. *Judaism: The Key Spiritual Writings of the Jewish Tradition.* Revised edition. New York: Simon and Schuster.

Heschel, Abraham Joshua. 1955. *God in Search of Man: A Philosophy of Judaism.* New York: Farrar, Straus and Giroux.

Hessel, Dieter, ed. 1996. *Theology for the Earth Community: A Field Guide.* Maryknoll, N.Y.: Orbis Books.

Hiebert, Theodore. 1989. "Ecology and the Bible." *Harvard Divinity Bulletin* 19, 3 (Fall):7–9.

_____. 1996a. "Rethinking Traditional Approaches to Nature in the Bible." In *Theology for the Earth Community: A Field Guide,* edited by Dieter Hessel, 23–30. Maryknoll, N.Y.: Orbis Books.

_____. 1996b. *The Yahwist's Landscape: Nature and Religion in Early Israel.* New York: Oxford University Press.

Himes, Michael J., and Kenneth R. Himes. 1995. "The Sacrament of Creation: Towards an Environmental Theology." *Commonweal,* January 26. Reprinted in Mary Heather MacKinnon and Moni McIntyre, eds., *Readings in Ecology and Feminist Theology,* 270–283. Kansas City, Mo.: Sheed and Ward.

Homer-Dixon, Thomas, Jeffrey H. Boutwell, and George W. Rathjens. 1993. "Environmental Change and Violent Conflict." *Scientific American,* February, 38–45.

Jewish Publication Society. 1985. *Tanakh: A New Translation of the Holy Scriptures.* New York: Jewish Publication Society.

Katz, Eric. 1993. "Judaism and the Ecological Crisis." In *Worldviews and Ecology,* edited by Mary Evelyn Tucker and John Grim, 55–70. Lewisburg, Pa.: Bucknell University Press.

Khalid, Fazlun, with Joanne O'Brien, eds. 1992. *Islam and Ecology.* Worldwide Fund for Nature Religions and Ecology Series. London: Cassell.

Kinsley, David. 1986. *Hindu Goddesses: Visions of the Divine Feminine in the Hindu Religious Tradition.* Berkeley: University of California Press.

MacNeill, Jim, Pieter Winsemius, and Taizo Yakushiji. 1991. *Beyond Interdependence: The Meshing of the World's Economy and the Earth's Ecology.* New York: Oxford University Press.

Martin-Schram, James B. 1996. "Population-Consumption Issues: The State of the Debate in Christian Ethics." In *Theology for the Earth Community: A Field Guide,* edited by Dieter Hessel, 132–142. Maryknoll, N.Y.: Orbis Books.

Masri, Al-Hafiz B. A. 1992. "Islam and Ecology." In *Islam and Ecology,* edited by Fazlun Khalid with Joanne O'Brien, 1–23. Worldwide Fund for Nature Religions and Ecology Series. London: Cassell.

McAfee, Gene. 1996. "Ecology and Biblical Studies." In *Theology for the Earth Community: A Field Guide,* edited by Dieter Hessel, 31–44. Maryknoll, N.Y.: Orbis Books.

Namgyal, Lungrug. 1986. "The Buddhist Declaration on Nature." In *The Assisi Declarations: Messages on Man and Nature from Buddhism, Christianity, Hinduism, Islam, and Judaism,* edited by Worldwide Fund for Nature, 5–7. Gland, Switzerland: Worldwide Fund for Nature.

Nasr, Seyyed Hossein. 1992. "Islam and the Environmental Crisis." In *Spirit and Nature: Why the Environment Is a Religious Issue,* edited by Steven C. Rockefeller and John C. Elder, 86–108. Boston: Beacon Press.

Nasseef, Abdullah Omar. 1986. "The Muslim Declaration on Nature." In *The Assisi Declarations: Messages on Man and Nature from Buddhism, Christianity, Hinduism, Islam, and Judaism,* edited by Worldwide Fund for Nature, 23–25. Gland, Switzerland: Worldwide Fund for Nature.

Paper, Jordan. 1997. "Chinese Religion and the Environmental Crisis." Paper presented at conference, Religion and Ecology: Forging an Ethic Across Traditions, Conference 3: East Asian and Pacific Religious Traditions, April 5, 1997, Boston Research Center for the Twenty-First Century, Boston.

Pedersen, William F. 1994. "'Protecting the Environment': What Does That Mean?" *Loyola of Los Angeles Law Review* 27, 3:969–979.

Perelmuter, Hayim G. 1994. "Do Not Destroy: Ecology in the Fabric of Judaism." In *The Ecological Challenge: Ethical, Liturgical, and Spiritual Responses,* edited by Richard N. Fragomeni and John T. Pawlikowski, 129–138. Collegeville, Minn.: Liturgical Press.

Pintchman, Tracy. 1994. *The Rise of the Goddess in the Hindu Tradition.* Albany: State University of New York Press.

Prime, Ranchor. 1994. *Hinduism and Ecology: Seeds of Truth.* 2nd edition. Worldwide Fund for Nature Series. Delhi: Motilal Banarsidass.

PTI (Press Trust of India). 1996. "Green Grounds for Temples in Kerala." *India Abroad,* August 16, n.p.

Queen, Christopher S., and Sallie B. King, eds. 1996. *Engaged Buddhism: Buddhist Liberation Movements in Asia.* Albany: State University of New York Press.

Rao, K. L. Seshagiri. 1995. "Revelation and Environment: A Hindu Perspective." Paper presented at conference, Revelation and the Environment, convened by the Ecumenical Patriarchate, September 1994, Athens.

Rasmussen, Larry L. 1993. "The Planetary Environment: Challenge on Every Front." In *Moral Issues and Christian Response,* edited by Paul T. Jersild and Dale A. Johnson, 98–208. New York: Harcourt Brace College Publishers. Originally printed in *Theology and Public Policy,* Summer 1990.

_____. 1996. *EarthCommunity, EarthEthics.* Maryknoll, N.Y.: Orbis Books.

Rockefeller, Steven C. 1996a. *Principles of Environmental Conservation and Sustainable Development: Summary and Survey.* Middlebury, Vt.: Steven C. Rockefeller for the Earth Charter Project.

_____. 1996b. "Global Ethics, International Law, and the Earth Charter." *Earth Ethics* 7, 3-4 (Spring-Summer):11–17.

Rockefeller, Steven C., and John C. Elder, eds. 1992. *Spirit and Nature: Why the Environment Is a Religious Issue.* Boston: Beacon Press.

Ruttan, V. W. 1991. "Constraints on Sustainable Growth in Agricultural Production: Into the 21st Century." In *Eleventh Agricultural Symposium: Agricultural Issues in the Nineties,* edited by Agricultural and Rural Development Department and Training Division of the World Bank. Washington, D.C.: The World Bank.

Sachs, Aaron. 1995. *Eco-Justice: Linking Human Rights and the Environment.* Worldwatch Paper 127. Washington, D.C.: Worldwatch Institute.

Schorsch, Ismar. 1992. "Learning to Live with Less: A Jewish Perspective." In *Spirit and Nature: Why the Environment Is a Religious Issue*, edited by Steven C. Rockefeller and John C. Elder, 28–38. Boston: Beacon Press.

Sharma, Arvind. 1996. "Attitudes to Nature in the Early Upaniṣads." Paper presented at conference, South Asian Religions and the Environment, convened by Lance Nelson, July 1996, University of San Diego.

Shiva, Vandana. 1989. *Staying Alive: Women, Ecology, and Development.* Atlantic Highlands, N.J.: Zed Books.

Singh, Karan. 1986. "The Hindu Declaration on Nature." In *The Assisi Declarations: Messages on Man and Nature from Buddhism, Christianity, Hinduism, Islam, and Judaism,* edited by Worldwide Fund for Nature, 17–19. Gland, Switzerland: Worldwide Fund for Nature.

Sivaraksa, Sulak. 1992. *Seeds of Peace: A Buddhist Vision for Renewing Society.* Berkeley: Parallax Press.

Sochaczewski, Paul Spencer, and Raghu Rai. 1993. "Pieces of Paradise." *Discovery,* June, 44–52.

Swartz, Daniel. 1993. "Jews, Jewish Texts, and Nature: A Brief History." In *To Till and to Tend: A Guide to Jewish Environmental Study and Action,* II:B. New York: Coalition on the Environment and Jewish Life.

Swetlitz, Marc. 1990. *Judaism and Ecology 1970–1986: A Sourcebook of Readings.* Wyncote, Pa.: Shomrei Adamah.

Tinker, George E. 1996. "An American Indian Theological Response to Eco-Justice." In *Defending Mother Earth: Native American Perspectives on Environmental Justice,* edited by Jace Weaver, 153–176. Maryknoll, N.Y.: Orbis Books.

Tu, Wei-ming. 1993. "Beyond the Enlightenment Mentality." In *Worldviews and Ecology,* edited by Mary Evelyn Tucker and John A. Grim, 19–29. Lewisburg, Pa.: Bucknell University Press.

——. 1995. "Global Community and Lived Reality." *Social Policy and Social Progress* (United Nations), Special Issue on the Social Summit (March):39–51.

Tucker, Mary Evelyn. 1993. "Ecological Themes in Taoism and Confucianism." In *Worldviews and Ecology,* edited by Mary Evelyn Tucker and John A. Grim, 150–160. Lewisburg, Pa.: Bucknell University Press.

——. 1996. "World Religions and Global Ecological Ethics: Contributions from Confucianism and Buddhism." *Earth Ethics* 7, 3-4 (Spring-Summer):14–16.

Tucker, Mary Evelyn, and John A. Grim, eds. 1993. *Worldviews and Ecology.* Lewisburg, Pa.: Bucknell University Press.

Tucker, Mary Evelyn, and Duncan Williams, eds. 1997. *Buddhism and Ecology.* Cambridge: Harvard University Press.

UNDP (United Nations Development Programme). 1996. *Human Development Report.* New York: Oxford University Press.

U.S. Catholic Conference. 1994. *Renewing The Face of the Earth: A Resource for Parishes.* Washington, D.C.: U.S. Catholic Conference.

Vecsey, Christopher. 1980. "American Indian Environmental Religions." In *American Indian Environments: Ecological Issues in Native American History,* edited by Christopher Vecsey and Robert W. Venables, 1–45. Syracuse, N.Y.: Syracuse University Press.

Vidyanarva, Srisa Chandra. 1991. *The Daily Practice of the Hindus.* New Delhi: Munshiram Manoharlal Publishers.

Waddell, Paul J., C. P. 1994. "Taming an Unruly Family Member: Ethics and the Ecological Crisis." In *The Ecological Challenge: Ethical, Liturgical, and Spiritual Responses,* edited by Richard N. Fragomeni and John T. Pawlikowski, 52–64. Collegeville, Minn.: Liturgical Press.

Waley, Arthur. 1958. *The Way and Its Power: A Study of the Tao Te Ching and Its Place in Chinese Thought.* New York: Grove Press.

Weiskel, Timothy C., with Richard A. Gray. 1990. "The Anthropology of Environmental Decline, Part 1: Historical Aspects of Anthropogenic Degradation." *Reference Services Review* (Summer):7–26.

Westing, Arthur H., ed. 1986. *Global Resources and International Conflict: Environmental Factors in Strategic Policy and Action.* Stockholm International Peace Research Institute and United Nations Environment Programme on Military Activities and the Human Environment. New York: Oxford University Press.

Wongkun, Pithaya. n.d. "Luong Pho Nan: Building Peace." Translated by Joshua J. Prokopy. Occasional Paper 3. Bangkok: Spirit in Education Movement in collaboration with Thai Interreligious Commission on Development and Santi Pracha Dhamma Institute.

World Commission on Environment and Development. 1987. *Our Common Future.* New York: Oxford University Press.

Worldwide Fund for Nature, ed. 1986. *The Assisi Declarations: Messages on Man and Nature from Buddhism, Christianity, Hinduism, Islam, and Judaism.* Gland, Switzerland: Worldwide Fund for Nature.

Chapter Twelve

From Genocide to Global Ethics by Way of Storytelling

DARRELL J. FASCHING
University of South Florida

Confronting Genocide and Ethical Relativism: A Personal Story

I have come to believe that in our postmodern world, after Auschwitz and Hiroshima, all theoretical reflection must be explicitly rooted in an author's own life story. None of us should be able to hide behind "objective" scholarship as if facts and theories were just "out there," a part of the landscape like trees and mountains. Authors must bear personal responsibility for the consequences of their thoughts and actions. So I feel compelled to begin with a personal story of how I became professionally involved in comparative religious ethics.

In my first year of teaching as an assistant professor at the University of South Florida, I offered a new course entitled "Judaism and Christianity After the Holocaust." On the opening day of class, I lectured students on the reality of genocide as the systematic, governmentally sponsored attempt to exterminate an entire people—not for any crime, not for any military or political advantage, but just because they exist. I explained how the Nazis attempted this by rounding up Jews and shipping them to the gas chambers for mass extermination. I affirmed that one of the reasons for studying the Holocaust was to better understand the human capacity for evil so that we could do our best to see that this would never again happen to anyone. In mid-sentence a young man raised his hand and interrupted me. "But Professor Fasching, maybe it was just the custom of Germans to kill Jews." I was dumbfounded. For a moment I did not know what to say. I then began to make the argument (somewhat awkwardly I am sure) that that is precisely the kind of ethical issue we must resolve; that after Auschwitz we cannot permit our openness to cultural diversity to lead to ethical relativism, lest we encourage such demonic customs.

By "demonic" I refer to acts that violate, degrade, or destroy other human beings, done not out of passion but out of cold, calculated rationality. Such acts are devoid of all capacity to identify with the humanity of the other and hence are devoid of all humanity; they are acts of atrocity committed by human beings against other human beings, as if the others were less than human and their lives of no more consequence than the lives of insects. In our age of mass slaughter, the twentieth century, the demonic has become commonplace. The trick in rejecting an ethical relativism that would tolerate such acts, of course, is to move beyond such relativism without falling into an absolutism that would treat others in an equally demonic fashion if they refuse to accept the offered "final solution" to the problem of relativism.

What I discovered at the very beginning of my academic career is that confronting genocide leads us immediately to issues of ethical relativism and the need for a cross-cultural and interreligious ethic in defense of human dignity. I began my career as one who did Christian ethics and very soon came to the conclusion that even Christian theological ethics, after Auschwitz, had to be done in such a way as to embrace the task of comparative religious ethics. This was true for at least two reasons. First, as a Christian who had been deeply alienated from my tradition by my confrontation with the Holocaust and the history of Christian anti-Judaism that led up to it, I felt I could no longer do Christian ethics in isolation from other traditions. I came to the conclusion that the only ethical way to do Christian ethics was to see and experience my own tradition as if I were a stranger; that is, through the eyes of others who would be affected by my tradition—beginning with the Jewish people. This "alienated" approach was the premise behind my book *Narrative Theology After Auschwitz: From Alienation to Ethics* (Fasching 1992). Second, I came to the conclusion that in a world of global interdependence it was not only the destinies of Jews and Christians that were intertwined but that of all peoples and religions. Therefore, the "alienated theological ethics" that had begun as a dialogue with post-Holocaust Jews had to be extended to engage the religious communities of Asia as well. That led to the sequel, *The Ethical Challenge of Auschwitz and Hiroshima: Apocalypse or Utopia?* (Fasching 1993). The substance of this chapter draws on arguments from these two books.[1]

Moreover, my cynical student's question about the "customs" of the Nazis continued to haunt me. I was convinced that in order to respond to the ethical relativism and cynicism of our students—who are quite diverse, religiously and ethnically—I needed to provide an ethical framework that would allow students to understand how people of diverse religions and cultures can take a common stand against the demonic cruelty of our age. Therefore, I developed a course, which I offer every semester, on comparative religious ethics, entitled "Religion, Ethics and Society through Film," which is normative rather than purely descriptive. I am now in the process of writing a textbook, *Comparative Religious Ethics: A Narrative Approach* (Fasching forthcoming) based on my experiences in teaching this course.

The underlying theme of this course is that the twentieth century is marked by two distinctive trends: on the one hand, the emergence across cultures of politically and technologically orchestrated mass death, symbolized by Auschwitz and Hiroshima, and on the other hand, the emergence of a cross-cultural and interreligious ethic of human dignity, rights, and liberation—an ethic of nonviolence symbolically forged by the lives of Tolstoy, Gandhi, and Martin Luther King Jr.

I teach this course with the conviction that a civilization that has no wisdom to offer the next generation is a civilization that is digging its own grave, and that the greatest ethical wisdom of the twentieth century is embodied in the emergence of a cross-cultural and interreligious tradition of human dignity and human rights. I do this with the conviction that it is a betrayal of the teaching vocation when ethicists teach ethics in a purely "objective and disinterested" fashion as a series of theories from which students are free to choose, as if they were picking selections out of a cafeteria line. If this is the only kind of ethics course that students are offered, we will end up teaching ethical relativism by default. Ethics will have been reduced to a matter of taste or preference.

For me, ethics became an experiment in alienation and dialogue. It began in alienation from my own tradition, an alienation rooted in a spontaneous identification with those who had been wounded by my tradition—beginning with the Jews. This pattern was powerfully facilitated by the fact that I married a Jewish woman, a fact of my biography that forced me, for the first time, to confront the history of anti-Judaism in the Christian tradition and to think through the relation of the two traditions—a relation that now became extraordinarily personal to me.

My alienation led me into a serious scholarly dialogue with post-Holocaust Jewish theologians, which helped me to see my own tradition through their eyes. The result was a movement from shock to *metanoia* (change of heart) to a felt imperative to reconstruct Christian faith and ethics in the name of justice. As I went through this process, I began to realize that my own biography had lessons to teach about doing theological ethics. The pattern of (1) alienation produced by my growing awareness of the ethical violations perpetrated by my own tradition, (2) identification and dialogue with the other, followed by (3) reform, I suspected, is a pattern that others might be able to identify with in relation to their own life histories and religious traditions.

I deliberately engaged in this pattern, which I described as doing "alienated theology"—namely, theology done as if one were a stranger to one's own tradition, seeing it through the eyes of those affected by that tradition. In fact, I have come to define ethical consciousness as the capacity to see and evaluate one's own actions from the viewpoint of the one affected by those actions. In this sense, alienation is an important moment in ethical consciousness, for unless we are de-centered or distanced from our own perspective, we will never be able to see our actions as though through the eyes of another.

My sense of constructive alienation was facilitated by another biographical factor as well. I did my Ph.D. degree in Christian theology within religious studies (at Syracuse University)—an inherently comparative discipline as opposed to a traditional seminary model. You cannot seriously do religious studies without going through a kind of illuminating alienation that distances you from your own tradition and provokes you to see your own tradition as others see it. Finally, the way I approach ethics was deeply shaped by two theologians who were both at Notre Dame when I was doing my doctoral work—Stanley Hauerwas and John Dunne. Both argued for the decisiveness of storytelling in shaping the ethical character of communities and persons. Hauerwas focused on the narrative power of the Christian story, whereas Dunne focused on the narrative power of stories from other traditions and how they might alter the insight and character of Christians. I found myself affirming both strategies as complementary to each other.

The upshot of this was that I came to think of alienated theology as a process of narrative ethics in a dialogical mode. Narrative ethics is rooted in the conviction that all ethical judgments are narrative dependent. Put differently, our understanding of good and evil is shaped by the kind of story we think we are in and the role we see ourselves playing in that story. I agreed with Hauerwas that our very ability to identify good and evil is deeply shaped by narrative. But I also agreed with Dunne that the example of Gandhi, for instance, shows us that, in our postmodern world, people's lives can be deeply shaped by not only the stories of their own tradition but the stories of the traditions of others.

The complementarity of these two approaches, I became convinced, was possible because, as Hauerwas insists, a central theme of the biblical narrative tradition is hospitality to strangers. Part of what this means, says Hauerwas, is that the Christian story should shape people whose character disposes them to make others' stories part of their own (1985, 197). Thus it became clear to me (even though Hauerwas does not seem to follow through on his insight) that hospitality to the stranger requires what Dunne describes as "passing over" into the religions and cultures of others in order to finally "come back" with new insight into one's own (1972, ix). This is what Gandhi did, he argued, when he passed over into the story of the Sermon on the Mount and came back to his own tradition with new insight into the nonviolent implications of the Hindu story of the Bhagavad Gītā.

I became very enthusiastic about the narrative approach to ethics, especially because it enabled me to make constructive use of still another form of alienation I had experienced in my life—an alienation from ethics itself. Throughout my undergraduate and graduate career, I had a strong distaste for ethics, primarily because I had never taken an ethics course that provided any real illumination for the actual life I had to live every day. All my courses seemed to involve endless abstract arguments, most of which were about the nature of ethics rather than about how one ought to live. Moreover, the various arguments seemed to stem from incommensurate theoretical perspectives that called "rationality" itself into question.

Finally, religious ethics, for the most part, seemed to be a pale reflection of philosophical ethics, having little to add to what reason concluded. The narrative approach seemed to me to be a strategy that understood the ethical power of religions, a power that lies (in large part) in the stories that religious communities tell, that constitutes their traditions, and that in fact deeply shapes the way human beings act in their everyday lives. From a narrative perspective, religion is not an addendum to ethics. Indeed, apart from the stories that shape a tradition (through myth and ritual), ethical thinking would not exist at all. In keeping with the postmodern mood of this school of thought, the primary mode of ethical reflection occurs in and through stories rather than through rationalistic logic (although reason and logic still clearly have a place). In this model, comparative religious ethics involved comparative storytelling and analysis.

The possibilities of narrative ethics as a way of doing comparative religious ethics seemed to me very exciting. But there remained for me one huge problem with this approach, the one raised by my cynical student: ethical relativism. If, as Stanley Hauerwas argues, all truth is narrative dependent and we live in a world of narrative diversity, then there are no universal truths. This puts an end, he argues, to all modern Kantian-style attempts to ground a universal ethic in universal reason—*including recent attempts to formulate a universal ethics of human rights*. Our postmodern situation is that we live in a narratively pluralistic world where all truth is relative to its narrative context.

The situation I found myself in, then, was that I agreed with Hauerwas that the Kantian quest for a universal rational ethic has failed. I also agreed that all truth is narrative dependent and that we have no metanarrative or neutral vantage point from which to adjudicate narrative-ethical differences. But I could not agree that this makes a cross-cultural and interreligious ethic of human dignity and human rights impossible. For me, such a conclusion was unacceptable. Instead, I concluded that each of us must find ways to stretch the language of our own traditions to accommodate the presence of the other through what John Dunne called "passing over and coming back." For reasons I hope will become clear, I argue that this can lead to an ethical coalition of diverse cultures and traditions that have in common at least one thing—stories of hospitality to the stranger. In the pages that follow, I attempt to outline my attempt at a solution to this dilemma as it has emerged out of my work on ethics after Auschwitz and Hiroshima.

Auschwitz and Hiroshima as Demonic Inversions of the Holy

If comparative religious ethics should not be done in abstraction from one's own life story (as if no one in particular were thinking these thoughts), neither should it be done in abstraction from our sociohistorical context. Whether we like to admit it nor not, the agenda of virtually all scholarship in any field is driven by contemporary sociohistorical concerns. And that is as it should be. For me this means that we cannot ignore the fact that we live in a technological civilization whose defining symbols are Auschwitz and Hiroshima.

How does this tie in with religion and ethics? A peoples' religiosity expresses their response to whatever they hold sacred—that is, whatever matters most to them. What typically matters most to human beings is their destiny: living rather than dying, and beyond that, living well. Thus, religion expresses their feelings of being "tied and bound" (the meaning of its Latin root, *religare*) in relations of obligation to whatever power(s) they believe govern their destiny. The specifics of what matters most can be quite diverse, but they are inevitably summed up in a "way of life" organized around whatever is held sacred and expressed in sacred stories and rituals.

At one time, human beings lived amid the unassailable powers of nature, on which they believed themselves to be dependent for their very existence. Their response to these powers was one of mixed fascination and dread—fascination at the powers' awesome supremacy in providing life in all its abundance (food, clothing, shelter, and so on) and dread at their awful potency in taking life away arbitrarily and capriciously through any number of "natural" disasters. Then science and technology emerged and demythologized and desacralized nature, only to create a new all-encompassing environment of awesome and awful powers—technological civilization. Human beings now think of themselves as dependent on these new powers for their existence and respond to them with a similar fascination and dread, knowing that the technological forces that drive our civilization can both provide the abundance of life and yet arbitrarily and capriciously end life with either a bang or a whimper—by either nuclear annihilation or ecological pollution. Technology has replaced nature as the new bearer of the sacred order, creating new sacred "ways of life." Technological civilization has filled us with utopian hopes and apocalyptic dreads. On balance, the age of modern and postmodern technological civilization has been dominated far more by the demonic than by the divine—a demonic symbolized by the names Auschwitz and Hiroshima.

After Auschwitz

In *The Cunning of History,* Richard Rubenstein makes the point that the Holocaust is not an aberration of history but rather the "expression of some of the most profound tendencies of Western civilization in the twentieth century" (1975, 21). Chief among these tendencies were the processes of bureaucratic rationalization. The turning point of the Nazi effort occurred after *Kristallnacht* (the Night of Broken Glass, November 10, 1938), when Jews were subjected to random and pervasive mob violence in the streets. Nazi Gestapo boss Heinrich Himmler rejected and suppressed the further use of mob violence that had been promoted by propaganda chief Joseph Goebbels. Himmler recognized that the only way to efficiently organize mass death was to remove the element of personal emotion and replace it with the cool and efficient operations of the impersonal techno-bureaucratic procedures that typified the death camps. Hatred is messy and inefficient. Unquestioning obedience to bureaucratic procedures would be necessary if killing on a mass scale were to be successful.

The nightmare of the death camps is vividly portrayed in a rich body of Holocaust literature, but undoubtedly the best known is Elie Wiesel's autobiographical work, *Night* (1958). In it, we get a glimpse of the horrific struggle to stay alive and retain one's humanity and religious identity in a techno-bureaucratic system organized for the express purpose of destroying first the dignity and then the life of its victims. In one of his most often cited passages, Wiesel describes the execution of a young Jewish boy and two other prisoners who had been discovered harboring arms.

> One day when we came back from work, we saw three gallows rearing up in the assembly place, three black crows. Roll call. SS all round us, machine guns trained: the traditional ceremony. Three victims in chains—and one of them, the little servant, the sadeyed angel. The SS seemed more preoccupied, more disturbed than usual. To hang a young boy in front of thousands of spectators was no light matter. The head of the camp read the verdict. All eyes were on the child. He was lividly pale, almost calm, biting his lips. The gallows threw its shadow over him. This time the Lagerkapo refused to act as executioner. Three SS replaced him. The three victims mounted together onto the chairs.

The three necks were placed at the same moment within the nooses. "Long live liberty!" cried the two adults. But the child was silent. "Where is God? Where is He?" someone behind me asked. At a sign from the head of the camp, the three chairs tipped over. Total silence throughout the camp. On the horizon, the sun was setting. "Bare you heads!" yelled the head of the camp. His voice was raucous. We were weeping. "Cover your heads!" Then the march past began. The two adults were no longer alive. Their tongues hung swollen, blue-tinged. But the third rope was still moving; being so light, the child was still alive. . . . For more than half an hour he stayed there, struggling between life and death, dying in slow agony under our eyes. And we had to look him full in the face. He was still alive when I passed in front of him. His tongue was still red, his eyes not yet glazed. Behind me, I heard the same man asking: "Where is God now?" And I heard a voice within me answer him: "Where is He? Here He is—He is hanging here on this gallows . . ." That night the soup tasted of corpses. (1958, 75–76)

The imagery of this story is powerful. And yet hanging was not the usual mode of extermination in the death camps. Although it was useful for enforcing camp discipline, it was too inefficient for perpetrating mass death. For that there were the gas chambers followed by the ovens. Or worse, sometimes the children were thrown directly into the ovens—alive. What Wiesel said of his first night in Auschwitz could be said of all nights by all the death camp prisoners.

Never shall I forget that night, the first night in camp, which has turned my life into one long night, seven times cursed and seven times sealed. Never shall I forget that smoke. Never shall I forget the little faces of the children, whose bodies I saw turned into wreaths of smoke beneath a silent blue sky. Never shall I forget those flames which consumed my faith forever. Never shall I forget that nocturnal silence which deprived me, for all eternity, of the desire to live. Never shall I forget those moments which murdered my God and my soul and turned my dreams to dust. Never shall I forget these things, even if I am condemned to live as long as God Himself. Never. (1958, 44)

Irving Greenberg has noted that it cost less than half a cent to gas each victim at Auschwitz and yet "in the summer of 1944, a Jewish child's life was not worth the two-fifths of a cent it would cost to put it to death rather than burn it alive" (Greenberg 1977, 11). He too suggests that Jewish faith has been consumed by those flames. The ovens of Auschwitz certainly evoke the most powerful and disturbing images. Before Auschwitz, he says, when Jews heard about a cloud of smoke and a pillar of fire, they thought of their liberation at the Exodus. But now, what Jew can hear of a cloud of smoke or a pillar of fire and think of anything other than the smokestacks and the ovens of Auschwitz? All that was holy and life-giving seems to have been replaced by that which is demonic and life-taking. The language of the holy has undergone a demonic inversion that seems to rob it of its spiritual and ethical power.

After Auschwitz and Hiroshima

If this is true for Auschwitz as a symbol of the Holocaust, it is also true of Hiroshima. With the surrender of Germany, the war came to an end in Europe, and some of the scientists who participated in the Manhattan Project to build the first atomic bomb raised serious questions about the need to use it against the Japanese. They had thought the Germans were close to developing their own bomb but they knew the Japanese were not. And yet a techno-bureaucratic logic, not unlike that which led to Auschwitz, prevailed. J. Robert Oppenheimer, who directed the Manhattan Project, argued: "Once you know how to make the bomb it's not your business to figure out how not to use it" (Wyden 1984, 150). We can call this "the technical imperative": If it can be done, it must be done. When one of the project scientists, Leo Szilard, tried to deliver a letter of protest from the scientists in Chicago to President Harry Truman, it was effectively subverted by bureaucratic processes "for security reasons." Technical experts were not supposed to raise ethical questions about mass death: They were supposed to follow orders with unquestioning obedience.

On July 16, 1945, at 5:30 in the morning, the first atomic bomb was exploded in the New Mexico desert at a site named Trinity. A fireball "infinitely brighter than the sun, its temperature 10,000 times greater, began an eight-mile ascent . . . turning night into day" (Wyden 1984, 212). The awesomeness of the sight inevitably elicited a religious response from the observers. One reporter, overwhelmed by this tremendous display of power, said that he thought of "the Lord's command, 'Let there be light.'" Whenever human beings encounter a power that they believe governs their destiny, the great comparative religions scholar, Rudolf Otto, suggests, they respond religiously with the ambivalent emotions of fascination and dread. The power of the bomb evoked emotions analogous to those of the holy. But the symbols of "light" and "life," drawn from the book of Genesis, were not really appropriate, for this event was no life-giving act of creation. It was rather a demonic inversion of the holy, revealing a power meant to produce total annihilation. It was Oppenheimer who captured its meaning most accurately. He recalled the line from the Bhagavad Gītā, spoken by the cosmic deity Vishnu, the lord of life and death: *"Behold, I am become death, the shatterer of worlds."*

August 6, the day the bomb was dropped, was the date for the feast of Transfiguration in the Christian calendar, a celebration of the revelation of Jesus as Son of God that provides a foretaste of his Resurrection, recalling how Jesus and his disciples climbed to the top of a high mountain where he was transformed before their very eyes. In that moment: "His face shone like the sun and his clothes became as white as the light," a light so bright that his disciples covered their eyes and fell down (Matt. 17:1–8). The telling of this event in the New Testament itself alludes to Moses coming down the mountain with the ten commandments—commandments that offer life. Here, too, "the skin on his face shone so much that they [the people] would not venture near him" (Exod. 34:29–35). These events recall formative moments in the history of Western religious experience. They recall the power of the Jewish God of history whose reality Christians sought to affirm with the doctrine of the Trinity. But after Auschwitz and Hiroshima, it seems as if the God of history has died. The symbols of "light" and "life" have been co-opted by the demonic and undergone an inversion of meaning.

This is no less true for Buddhists than it is for Jews and Christians. Once, enlightenment meant to experience the light of insight that liberates the self from suffering and death through the experience of *anatta,* or "no-self." But the total annihilation of all selves at Hiroshima brought about a demonic inversion of the experience of no-self. The *hibakusha* (literally, "explosion-affected person"), or survivors of Hiroshima and Nagasaki, speak of themselves as *mugamuchu,* meaning "without self, without center" (Lifton 1967, 26). However, they speak not of the humanizing experience of liberation or "no-self" that comes with Buddhist enlightenment but rather of the experience of total desolation that comes with total immersion in the kingdom of death, of which the survivors of Auschwitz were the first to speak. The dark night of Hiroshima brings no mystical fulfillment, only total immersion in a *shoah,* a time of desolation.

The observation of Irving Greenberg concerning the symbolic inversion of religious meaning after Auschwitz proves to be just as true with regard to Hiroshima. Thus, "light" and "enlightenment" no longer symbolize the giving of life. The cloud and the pillar of fire by which Israel was led through history no longer remind us of liberation and salvation but rather of both the gas chambers of Auschwitz and the mushroom clouds of Hiroshima and Nagasaki. Trinity no longer names the God of life but the place in New Mexico where planetary death was born. We live in a time of the demonic inversion of the holy. Now when a commanding voice speaks from a burning fire, it speaks not the language of being, *"I Am Who I Am,"* but of not-being, *"I Am Become Death."*

The Uniqueness of the Holocaust and the Ethical Imperative for Comparison

Some who have read my book *The Ethical Challenge of Auschwitz and Hiroshima* have been troubled by the book's title. I have been told that it is sacrilegious to place the word "Hiroshima" in the same sentence with the word "Auschwitz." This accusation itself is evidence of the religious power of these events. The Holocaust, many authors have insisted, is unique—even uniquely unique—and cannot be compared to other tragic events in history. To do so, they insist, is to trivialize its immensity and evade its uniquely demonic character by chalking it up to the general human capacity for evil. Indeed, at least one author is involved in writing a multivolume history whose purpose is to show that the genocide of the Holocaust is without comparison. It stands singular and alone. The message is clear: The Holocaust alone is the Holocaust—there shall be no others beside it.

The seriousness with which this argument is pursued and the singularity of the language all reinforce my observation—that although the Holocaust is a demonic event, it is also held sacred. It is held sacred in part because of its horrific awesomeness as a demonic *tremendum*. It is also held sacred, I believe, because the lives of those destroyed by it were infinitely precious. Their deaths should not be trivialized by a failure to understand the uniqueness and particularity of the evil events that led to those deaths. As Emil Fackenheim has argued in *To Mend the World,* their deaths should not be subsumed under the category of the general human capacity for inhumanity to others. To do that would be to allow those responsible to hide from responsibility for their actions. Such a tactic is, he says, "escapism-into-universalism" (1989, xiii). So we draw a sacred circle, establish an aura of taboo, around these events that forbids all comparison—the events are unique and singular.

Yet, although we are asked to treat the Holocaust as sacred and unique, we are also asked to remember the Holocaust so as to ensure that it will *never again* be repeated. Paradoxically, treating the Holocaust as sacred undermines this ethical imperative. The Holocaust is an ugly, profane, and demonic event. It does not deserve its protected status. If the Holocaust is an event that must *never again* occur, then it must be desacralized and made available for comparative study with other events of mass death. If we are serious about the pledge *"never again,"* then we must be able to understand the Holocaust's similarities and differences to other events involving religious and racial prejudice and mass death. If we are to understand the human capacity for the demonic, we need to see both what is unique and what is generalizable in each case. If the study of the Holocaust is to have an ethical impact, we must be able to make analogies where appropriate. Indeed, even Fackenheim recognizes that "not all are guilty of escapism who on hearing of the Holocaust, start thinking and speaking of children in Hiroshima or Cambodia. . . . To do such thinking and speaking is legitimate, however, only if it is accompanied by the recognition that the subject is being changed" (1989, xiii).

If the ethical command *"never again"* is to be taken seriously, then we must come to understand how and under what conditions the human capacity for the demonic erupts and how that capacity can be short-circuited and contained. This does not mean that there is nothing unique about the Holocaust. It appears to be singular in many respects. However, granting that, we must not conclude that it cannot or should not be compared to other events in which societies have exploited hatred and prejudice in order to engage in exercises of mass extermination.

Auschwitz and Hiroshima as the Formative Religious Events of Our Time

What is striking about the works of many of the post-Holocaust Jewish theologians, contrary to the insistence upon the absolute uniqueness of the Holocaust, is their linking of the particularity of the Jewish experience to the destiny of the whole human race. They persistently draw a connection between Auschwitz and Hiroshima. Again and again I have found authors such as Irving Greenberg, Elie Wiesel, Eliezer Berkovits, Richard Rubenstein, and Arthur Cohen linking Auschwitz to Hiroshima, not in order to draw exclusive attention to the plight of the Jews but, on the contrary, to interpret what happened to the Jews as a prophetic warning of the peril facing the whole human race.

As I read these post-Holocaust Jewish theologians, in the same breath with "Auschwitz" the name "Hiroshima" comes up again and again. The link between Auschwitz and Hiroshima turns out to be an inner link demanded by the analyses made by those who were, directly or indirectly, the victims of the *Shoah*. It is as if those who know something of the "desolation" of Auschwitz recognize that in some sense they have a kinship with those who know the "desolation" of Hiroshima. Also, more than once I have encountered an awareness of a logical as well as a psychological link between the two. This link is the progressive unfolding of a secularized technological civilization that no longer holds anything sacred, not even human life—nothing, that is, except what Jacques Ellul calls "the technical imperative": If it can be done, it must be done. The death camps were technically feasible and they came to pass. The atom bomb was technically feasible and it came to pass. A final total apocalyptic nuclear annihilation of the earth is technically feasible.

The movement from Auschwitz to Hiroshima is psychological, logical, and finally mythological, because Auschwitz and Hiroshima have assumed the mythological status of sacred events that orient human consciousness. They have become transhistorical and transcultural events that are shaping a global public consciousness of our common humanity. The horrifying irony of this is that they are not manifestations of the divine but of the demonic, and the common awareness they are creating is one structured by dread. The task of comparative religious ethics is to discover, through interreligious and cross-cultural dialogue, a common hope to unite us as a global human community, one that can carry us beyond our common dread.

We are the first generation to live in the shadow of the Holocaust. We are the first generation to live in the shadow of genocide. That a civilization of high culture, science, and learning could give birth to such a project—a rationally organized project to strip a subgroup of its own population of its property and legal rights, transport the members of this subgroup to death camps, and exterminate them with *the most efficient technological methods available*—leaves us overwhelmed. Like the mystic in the presence of an overwhelming God, the contemplation of this event fills us with both fascination and dread and leaves us speechless. We find ourselves doubting that we can find a language with which to adequately describe the event.

We are also the first generation to live in the shadow of Hiroshima. Although the dropping of the atomic bomb on Hiroshima was no act of genocide, it did give birth to the Cold War era, in which human beings were prepared to escalate the stakes from genocide to omnicide; an era in which the mass extermination of human life became thinkable as a "rational" and technologically feasible expression of foreign policy. And although the Cold War has thawed and melted in the 1990s, the use of nuclear weapons remains an option that nations East and West refuse to eliminate. The threat of apocalypse, which erupted at Auschwitz, is no longer limited to the West. Hiroshima symbolizes the globalization of the demonic in technological form, a globalization that forces a meeting of East and West.

In the mystical encounter with the immensity of the holy, language and imagination are defeated and individuals are left only with emptiness or "imagelessness." As Robert Jay Lifton's comparative analysis of the survivors of both Auschwitz and Hiroshima confirms, today it is another kind of immensity that defeats the imagination—the immensity of the demonic. Every attempt to capture, in either word or image, the experience of immersion in the kingdom of death created by the Holocaust, Elie Wiesel has suggested, seems entirely inadequate. Likewise, as one Japanese survivor of Hiroshima has put it: "There is no category for the atomic bomb experience. . . . One can find no words to describe it" (Lifton 1967, 404). Another survivor confessed that the immensity of the grotesque reality of death—the dead bodies, the smell—left him blocked, as Lifton reported it, "by a sense of the experience as sacred" (408). Once, silence was the language of the mystical encounter with the source of life. After Auschwitz and Hiroshima, it has become the language of the encounter with the kingdom of death.

Auschwitz and Hiroshima are the formative religious events of our modern and postmodern world. These events are paradoxically, at one and the same time, both sacred and profane. They have a profane, even demonic, aspect, and yet they elicit religious responses. Like the great classical events of religious history, they define a historical era—the one in which we live. Once we divided history into "before" and "after" Moses or Buddha or Christ. Now we divide history into "before" and "after" Auschwitz and Hiroshima. However, unlike the Buddha's Enlightenment, the Exodus led by Moses, or the Resurrection of Jesus, these new sacred events are demonic—a demonic inversion of the holy. They do not bring life and enlightenment but death and dehumanization.

The Demonic East and West:
Doubling and Killing in Order to Heal

When one stands back and tries to absorb the sum total of evil of the Holocaust, it is overwhelming. When one considers specific deeds of cold atrocity, this too is overwhelming. But when one examines the personal histories and day-to-day life of persons who committed such deeds, one is struck by how ordinary most of these persons were.

Robert Jay Lifton's study *The Nazi Doctors: Medical Killing and the Psychology of Genocide* (1986) offers some insight into how such an apparent contradiction is possible. Lifton's interviews with physicians who served in the death camps provides an intimate look into the lives and psyches of these professionals, who played a major role in operating the camps. Lifton tells of commenting to an Auschwitz survivor how he was struck by the "ordinariness of most Nazi doctors . . . neither brilliant nor stupid, neither inherently evil nor particularly ethically sensitive, they were by no means the demonic figures—sadistic, fanatic, lusting to kill—people have often thought them to be." To which the survivor commented: "But it is demonic that they were not demonic." The lesson of Auschwitz is that "ordinary people can commit demonic acts" (Lifton 1986, 4–5). It is demonic that people can kill devoid of all passion and emotion, and without a sense of personal involvement or responsibility.

Lifton set out to answer the question of how it was possible for the Nazi physicians who were assigned to do the selections for the death camps to assume such an attitude. Although they were typically unprepared for their assignment and had some initial difficulty in carrying it out, by the end of two weeks most had adjusted to their new task and were performing quite effectively. This is remarkable when one considers that these were all physicians who had taken an oath to heal and now had become practitioners of mass death. The transformation, Lifton argued, was made possible by two factors—a biomedical narrative, which enabled the physicians to think of killing as a form of healing; and a psychological process of "doubling," which enabled them to disown their own actions.

The narrative that enabled them to equate healing and killing stemmed from the biological myth of the pure Aryan race—a sacred narrative that saw the stranger (the Jews) as the agents of pollution. Viewing the Jews as less than human was not a form of prejudice because it was based in biological fact. As Lifton notes: "The nation would now be run according to what Johann S. [a Nazi physician] and his cohorts considered biological truth, 'the way human beings really are.' That is why he had a genuine 'eureka' experience—a sense of 'That's exactly it!'—when he heard Rudolf Hess declare National Socialism to be 'nothing but applied biology'" (129). It was this biological-racist narrative that legitimated the surgical excision of the Jews by means of the death camps. The Jews were viewed as "agents of 'racial pollution' and 'racial tuberculosis,' as well as parasites and bacteria causing sickness, deterioration, and death in the host peoples they infested. . . . The cure had to be radical: that is, (as one scholar put it), by 'cutting out the canker of decay'" (16). Just as the physician has to cut out a diseased appendage in order to restore a body to health, so the Nazi physicians had to cut out the Jews, who were a cancerous decay on the healthy body of the German people. The death camps were nothing but an exercise in public health built on the premise that to kill is to heal. And the authority of the physician, the embodiment of both modern scientific-technological and professional knowledge and skill, was essential to legitimate the sacral myth.

The psychological process of "doubling" accompanied this narrative as the means by which the physician was integrated into a new techno-bureaucratic social order. The physician had to adjust to the abrupt transfer from a social-institutional environment where he was a healer to a new social-institutional environment in which he was asked to kill. In order to do this, he needed not only a story to make sense out of his actions but also a way to relate his new role to his previous identity. This was done through the development of a second identity—a double. Alongside his previous self (as healer), the physician developed a second professional "killing self."

By doing this, the physician could say to himself: I am a good man, a healer, and in my personal life I continue to be that. But when I go to work, I act not for myself but according to my public duties as a citizen and professional. In performing my duty I surrender myself in total unquestioning obedience to a higher authority who is in a better position than I to know what I ought to do. Therefore, in this role, when I act, it is not I but some higher authority who is acting through me. Consequently, I am not responsible for what I do in my public and professional role. Moreover, what I do in my public role is not who I really am. Therefore, I can continue to think well of myself and I can go home and be loving and compassionate to my family and neighbors in the evening and go off the camps the next day and continue the mass exterminations.

Techno-bureaucratic order represents a kind of sacral order in which one participates by engaging in a total surrender of self in unquestioning obedience. The presence of the bureaucracy is experienced as awesome and overwhelming. The Nazi physicians typically said they felt that their refusal to perform their duties would not change anything. The bureaucracy was impervious to individual choice. If they did not do the selecting, someone else would. Moreover, they said they did not feel responsible because the Jews who arrived in the camps were dead already. Their fate had been sealed by bureaucratic decision long before they arrived. The physicians were merely cogs in the machine, instruments of a higher authority.

What doubling did was allow the individual physician to be integrated into the hierarchical order of a technical bureaucracy. Bureaucracy neutralizes our capacity to be ethical by separating ends and means. Unlike my personal life, where I choose both what I shall do (ends) and how I shall accomplish it (means), in a bureaucracy those in authority are believed to be in the best position to see the big picture and thus to choose the ends. Those technical experts lower down in the hierarchy are simply expected, with unquestioning obedience, to use their knowledge and skill to provide the means for carrying out those ends chosen by others higher up. Not having chosen the ends, one does not have to feel responsible for one's actions. As we heard again and again at the Nuremberg trials: "I am not guilty. I was just following orders." Thus, the demonic capacity to instigate mass death appears (at least in this instance) to be fostered by a total surrender to a sacred order, through a process of doubling accompanied by narratives that reconcile killing and healing.

Reading Lifton's study of the Nazi doctors in the light of my own knowledge of the history of Christian theology and ethics, I found myself deeply troubled by this pattern. For although the Nazi story had different content, I immediately recognized structural similarities between it and the ethics of Martin Luther. Given the profound influence that Luther's writings had in shaping German national culture and character, the relationship between the Nazi physicians' propensity to double and Luther's "two-kingdom" ethics seemed to me to be less than accidental.

Luther held that God rules the world with both his right and his left hand. With the right, he rules with compassion and forgiveness, filled with grace, over the individual human heart through the Gospel proclaimed by the Church. With the left hand, God rules with justice and wrath through the state in order to punish sinners. Paradoxically, God must always rule with both hands simultaneously because, at best, human beings are saints and sinners at the same time. The significance of this becomes clear in the context of this discussion when we look at what Luther had to say about the role of the public executioner. He argued that one could be a loving, forgiving, and compassionate Christian in one's personal life and still go to work every day as a hangman, conducting public executions. Unlike the medieval tradition, which argued that the public executioner must do penance after an execution, Luther argued that this was not necessary since in his public role the executioner was not acting for himself but for the state, and the state was acting for God. Thus it was not the individual but God who did the actual killing.

What is equally troubling is the narrative that accompanies Luther's two-kingdom ethic. Luther speaks of God as a hidden God with whom he wrestles (on the model of Jacob wrestling with the stranger in Genesis 32:23–32) in an inner struggle. This God reveals himself paradoxically through opposites. Luther tells us:

> *When God brings to life, he does it by killing;* when he justifies, he does it by making guilty; when he exalts to heaven, he does it by leading to hell. . . . And finally, God cannot be God unless he first becomes a devil and we cannot go to heaven unless we first go into hell, and cannot become the children of God, unless we first become the Devil's children. . . . We have spoken in extreme terms of this, and we must understand what is just as startling, that God's grace and truth, or his goodness and faithfulness, rule over us and *demand our obedience.* . . . For a little while I must accord divinity to the Devil, and consider our God to be the Devil. But this does not mean that the evening lasts for the whole day. Ultimately, his steadfast love and faithfulness are over us [Ps. 117:2]. (Ebeling 1970, 236–237; emphasis added)

This theme of bringing to life through killing did not originate with Luther but goes back to Augustine of Hippo, who in his *Confessions* interpreted his own inner struggles in wrestling with the God "who gives wounds in order to heal, who kills us lest we should die away from you" (Augustine 1963, bk. 2, 2).

The pattern of doubling and "killing in order to heal" has cross-cultural significance, which becomes apparent when we look at the story of the testing of the first atomic bomb. Oppenheimer's recalling the words of the Bhagavad Gītā at the Trinity test site is very revealing. It is as if in a moment of inverse enlightenment, or revelation, the religious symbols of East and West clashed and exploded within Oppenheimer's psyche, and he grasped the experience of the sacred as the demonic inversion of the holy. He apparently chose the name "Trinity" for the experimental bomb sight under the influence of the seventeenth-century poet John Donne, known for his poetic explorations of religion, death, and suicide. General Leslie Groves, Oppenheimer's superior, asked why he had chosen the code name "Trinity" for the site. Oppenheimer responded: "Why I chose the name is not clear, but I know what thoughts were in my mind. There is a poem of John Donne ["Hymn to God My God, in My Sicknesse"], written just before his death, which I know and love. From it a quotation: 'As West and East / in all flatt

Maps—and I am one—are one, / So death doth touch the Resurrection'"
(Rhodes 1986, 571–572).

The poem, says Richard Rhodes in his recounting of the event, suggested
to Oppenheimer the paradox that "dying leads to death but might also lead
to resurrection. . . . The bomb for [Niels] Bohr and Oppenheimer was a
weapon of death that might also end war and redeem mankind" (572). Oppenheimer, in his letter to Groves, admits that "'that still does not make a
trinity.' But in another, better known devotional poem Donne opens, 'Batter
my heart, three person'd God.' Beyond this, I have no clues whatever" (572).

Oppenheimer was not fully conscious of the connection between the two
poems that haunted him, but the link is clear when the two are compared.
For like the first passage, Donne's "Holy Sonnets" also explores the theme
of redemption through destruction.

> Batter my heart, three-personed God; for You
> As yet but knock, breathe, shine, and seek to mend;
> That I may rise and stand, o'rthrow me, and bend
> your force to break, blow, burn, and make me new. (Donne 1962, 785)

Donne's "Fourteenth Holy Sonnet" describes a narrative theme that we
should readily recognize—wrestling with the God who wounds in order to
heal and who slays in order to make alive. This is the metaphorical appropriation of the story of Jacob wrestling with the stranger. But this is the Christian version of that story, the version encountered in Augustine and Luther. It
is the version that inverts the meaning of the biblical narrative—the version
in which God not only "wounds in order to heal" but also "slays in order to
make alive." It is the version that allows the self (in this case, Oppenheimer)
to salve its uneasy conscience by doubling; that allows the second or professional self, through an ethic of unquestioning obedience, to do what it must
do no matter how distasteful this might be to the first self.

No doubt the unconscious, or barely conscious, apologetic that Oppenheimer had worked out in his own mind to justify the preordained conclusion of the Manhattan Project was expressed in his gravitation toward the
poems of John Donne and the code name "Trinity." Although the bomb
would do untold damage and unleash a terrible new power in the world,
still the very awesomeness of its power was seen as the necessary lethal
force that would bring an end to World War II and thus herald forth a new
life. But when, on the day of Trinity, the moment came and the experiment
became the reality of the bomb, it was not the Christian Trinity but the
words of Vishnu, one of the deities of the Hindu Trinity, that seemed more
appropriate—for in the Hindu Trinity, the divine and the demonic are one.

If we turn to the Bhagavad Gītā passage Oppenheimer quoted from
memory, we discover that the more common translation is "Time am I"
rather than "I am become Death" (Zaehner 1966, 297). Either, however, is

a legitimate translation of the original Sanskrit.[2] As the context makes clear, time is the power of death, the destroyer of worlds. But what follows is especially interesting. Vishnu says to Arjuna:

> Do what thou wilt, all these warriors shall cease to be,
> Drawn up [there] in their opposing ranks.
> And so arise, win glory,
> Conquer thine enemies and enjoy a prosperous kingdom!
> Long since have these men in truth been slain by Me,
> Thine is to be the mere occasion. (Zaehner 1966, 297–298)

We must remember that Arjuna is a Kshatriya, a warrior, who chooses not to go to war against his own relatives even though the war is just. He wishes neither to kill nor be killed. Krishna, his chariot driver, has been teaching him the paths to enlightenment so as to convince him that it is his caste duty as a warrior to fight. As long as he is not "attached to the fruits of his actions" (that is, as long as he does not act from personal motives such as ambition or greed) but rather does his duty selflessly, he will not accrue any negative karma. Indeed, "though he slay these thousands he is no slayer" (Prabhavananda 1972, 122).[3] And now, in chapter 11 of the Bhagavad Gītā, Krishna reveals his true identity as Vishnu. And what is his message? He is the real slayer of all men. All he asks of Arjuna is that he do his duty selflessly and in unquestioning obedience. He need not feel any guilt for killing his kinsmen, for he is not really their slayer. Here we have an archetypal example of the logic of doubling. This is the logic we found in Luther's hangman. We also found this same demonic logic among the Nazi doctors, only instead of God it was nature and bureaucracy that decreed life and death and absolved these physicians of responsibility for their actions, by in effect declaring: "Long since have these men in truth been slain by Me, Thine is to be the mere occasion" (Zaehner 1966, 298).

The point I wish to make is certainly not that the Bhagavad Gītā is somehow directly responsible for the behavior of the Manhattan Project scientists. This is hardly the case. What I am suggesting is that the unconscious link that Oppenheimer made between Trinity and Vishnu is more than accidental. It symbolizes the meeting of East and West at Hiroshima, religiously and culturally, in the eruption of the demonic. And it points to the presence of the phenomenon of doubling in more than one religious tradition. The point is that whether we are speaking of Eastern or Western religions, the predominant language of religion has been that of total surrender in unquestioning obedience to higher authority—a language that encourages doubling and the eruption of the demonic in some form of "killing in order to heal." After Auschwitz and Hiroshima, as Irving Greenberg says, there must be no unquestioning obedience, not even to God, for such obedience leads to Nazi-type loyalties.

The point to be grasped with regard to the convergence of religious experiences, East and West, at Trinity in the New Mexico desert is this: Whether we speak of the Hindu Trinity or the Christian Trinity, we are speaking of narrative traditions that sacralize death. Both the stories of Vishnu and of the Christian Trinitarian God we have referred to differ from the Jewish stories of wrestling with God in one important respect. The religious vision of the God of Arjuna, as well as the God of Augustine, Luther, and Donne, "wounds in order to heal and slays in order to make alive," whereas the God who comes as a stranger to wrestle with Jacob (Gen. 32:23–32) "wounds in order to heal" but does not slay in order to make alive.

Both Luther and Augustine (who stands behind Luther's piety) invert the meaning of this biblical story, in which Jacob is told that his new name will be Israel. In the story, Jacob is accosted by a stranger, who wrestles with him until daybreak. Jacob demands that the stranger identify himself but he will not. Instead, he requires Jacob to do so and then blesses Jacob, promptly renaming him "Israel," meaning *wrestler with God,* "for you have striven with God and with humans, and have prevailed" (Gen. 32:28). And as the sun rises and the stranger flees, Jacob walks away limping, resolving to call the place "Peniel," meaning "I have seen God face to face and yet my life is preserved" (32:31). The biblical version, as Jewish interpretation has faithfully recorded, emphasizes that although the stranger (God) is not defeated, Jacob prevails. He is the victor. This narrative strand within Judaism authorizes an audacious faith that dares to argue with God, to question God and demand that he keep his covenant promises.

In this story there is a profound transformation of identity—a conversion, or enlightenment (that is, Jacob becomes Israel). As with the typical Buddhist and Hindu forms of narrative imagination, so also in the Christian narrative imagination: Such a transformation can only occur if there is an utter death of the self and a total surrender of will in unquestioning obedience. And although one can find this theme in Jewish thought as well, here it is counterbalanced by a narrative strand that has become especially predominant after Auschwitz—the tradition of audacity, or "chutzpah." And although there are some parallels in other traditions, none from before the modern period that I am aware of have the continuity and prominence that one finds in Judaism. In this narrative strand, the Jewish imagination envisions a God who seeks not the total annihilation of the self but rather the discovery of its inalienable dignity. Jacob is wounded, but neither he nor the stranger are defeated. The stranger flees with the dawn and Jacob is blessed and can walk away suffering only a limp. The narrative strand of Judaism that advocates chutzpah seems to have grasped that no God worthy of the name would demand the total sacrifice of the self, because this would be the same as asking to forego the honor of being created in the image of God. In the Christian imagination of an Augustine, a Luther, or a Donne, by contrast, God must be the victor and humans must be defeated. The self must be defeated and slain so that a new and more obedient self can rise up to replace it.

These two ways of interpreting this story represent two ways of dealing with guilt and responsibility. The first leads to violence against the stranger and absolves the self of personal guilt through a total surrender to a higher will. "It is not I who slays but a higher one who acts through me." The second requires the self to take responsibility for its past through a repentance that wounds and heals, and in so doing leads to the path of nonviolent struggle, allowing both parties to walk away with their dignity intact. Jacob was wrestling with his guilt for the ways in which he had cheated his brother Esau in his youth. And now, after many years, they would soon be face to face. "The text says it clearly," Elie Wiesel tells us. He continues:

> Jacob is afraid. And Rashi, in his elegant manner, hastens to add that Jacob [like Arjuna] is afraid for two reasons: he is afraid of being killed and of having to kill. For he knows that one does not kill with impunity; whoever kills man, kills God in man. Fortunately, he is assaulted by an angel before he is assaulted by Esau. Who is the angel? Is it an angel at all? The text says "Ish," a man, but Jacob speaks of God. And though he emerges victorious from the struggle, his victory does not imply his adversary's defeat. Thus Israel's first victory teaches us that man's true victory is not contingent on an enemy's defeat. Man's true victory is always over himself. (Wiesel 1978, 155)

When approaching ethics through narrative, we must realize that everything depends on how the narrative is interpreted. The Christian interpretations of the Jacob story we have examined require an utter death of the self, a total surrender of will in unquestioning obedience to the God who slays. Out of this surrender then emerges an entirely new self. Through the despair of the dark night of the soul or the sickness unto death, the individual's own will is finally extinguished in a spiritual death experience. This is not fundamentally different from "the Great Death" of Buddhism or the total surrender expected of Arjuna by the God Vishnu in the Bhagavad Gītā. Such narratives—insofar as they embrace this mythic theme—are common embodiments of mythologies that sacralize death. If there is a universal and pervasive mythic theme in the history of religions from the primal myths of eternal return in tribal and early urban societies on through the great myths of Christianity, Islam (whose very name means "to surrender"), Hinduism, and Buddhism, it is that of life through death—death as total surrender of the self becomes the path to life. The one who is willing to embrace the God who is slayer will be led through death into new mode of being (such as eternity or nirvana).

Contesting the Demonic:
From Obedience to Audacity

There is a fundamentally demonic fascination in these traditions with the need for a total surrender to the God who slays. The Jewish narrative tradition of chutzpah stands as one of the few alternatives to this temptation. (The earliest stories of the Buddha's life also suggest a model of audacity, of questioning authority, but these seem not to have been utilized to the same extent by the later tradition.) This is a narrative tradition that has its roots in the story of Abraham's confrontation with God over Sodom and Gomorrah, in which Abraham expresses chutzpah in defense of the stranger. Fearing that God will slay the innocent along with the guilty, Abraham has the audacity to argue with God, insisting: "Shall not the judge of all, also be just?" (Gen. 18:25).[4] This tradition also draws upon the audacity of Job, who has the chutzpah to put God on trial, calling into question divine justice in the name of human dignity and integrity. Such chutzpah declares that no authority, whether sacred or secular, divine or human, may violate the dignity and integrity of a human being. For any authority to commit such a violation is for it to undermine its own authority—even if that be God. Emil Fackenheim sums up this powerful tradition:

> There is a kind of faith which will accept all things and renounce every protest. There is also a kind of protest which has despaired of faith. In Judaism there has always been protest which stays within the sphere of faith. Abraham remonstrates with God. So do Jeremiah and Job. So does, in modern times, the Hasidic Rabbi Levi Yitzhak of Berdiczev. He once interrupted the sacred Yom Kippur service in order to protest that, whereas kings of flesh and blood protected their peoples, Israel was unprotected by her King in heaven. Yet having made his protest he recited the Kaddish, which begins with these words: "Extolled and hallowed be the name of God throughout the world . . ." Can Jewish protest today remain within the sphere of faith? . . . In faithfulness to the victims we must refuse comfort; and in faithfulness to Judaism we must refuse to disconnect God from the *Shoah*. (1970, 76)

After Auschwitz and Hiroshima, only an ethic of audacity is appropriate. The world can no longer afford the luxury of unquestioning faith. Such faith is barbaric—it demands the sacrifice of life (whether animal or human) in order to promote life. Unquestioning faith is a nearly universal temptation of human religiousness around the world. Virtually all forms of religion have asked followers to sacrifice their will and surrender themselves to a higher reality. And all faith that asks for a total surrender of will is demonic. For all such faith is a training ground for fanaticism, which blurs the distinction between God and the techno-bureaucratic state (or other finite authorities) and leads to the dehumanization of the chosen victims of such authority. The only authentic faith is a questioning faith, a faith prepared to call even God into question. The difference between God and the idol is that idols will brook no dissent. The test of authentic faith is the possibility of dissent against all authority in the name of human dignity.

By surrendering to the myth of life through death, we have allowed our mythic consciousness, Western or Eastern, religious or secular, to shape our public policies along paths that lead not from the dark night of despair to new life and light but rather to the total darkness of planetary suicide. Our unconscious surrender to the sacral power of the ethnocentric techno-bureaucratic state has its training ground in the conscious surrender of our will and our whole being, advocated by the dominant forms of virtually all religions, Eastern and Western. After Auschwitz and Hiroshima, we can no longer afford the luxury of an unadulterated mythology of life through death, not even when it is sublimely transmuted, by Buddhist or Christian spirituality, into a language of self-transformation. We do not need an ethic that sacralizes death; rather, we need one that sanctifies life. We do not need a sacral ethic, but rather an ethic of secular holiness that champions human dignity, human rights, and human liberation against all mythologies that endorse *killing in order to heal* with audacious tenacity.

A Commanding Voice from Auschwitz and Hiroshima: The UN Universal Declaration of Human Rights

If the twentieth century has been the age of genocide and mass death, it has also been the age of the birth of human dignity and human rights. It was Emil Fackenheim who noted that Jews refused to give up their Jewishness even after the devastation of the *Shoah,* and who suggested that they had heard and responded to a silent yet commanding voice from Auschwitz forbidding them to grant Hitler a posthumous victory. "They are commanded to survive as Jews, lest the Jewish people perish. They are commanded to remember the victims of Auschwitz lest their memory perish. They are forbidden to despair of man and his world, and to escape into either cynicism or otherworldliness, lest they cooperate in delivering the world over to the forces of Auschwitz. Finally, they are forbidden to despair of the God of Israel, lest Judaism perish" (1970, 84). In claiming that Jews had heard such a command, Fackenheim was not so much advancing a theological hypothesis as making an empirical observation. He was simply acknowledging what, in fact, had already happened, because the visceral response to the *Shoah* by Jews, both religious and nonreligious, was a continuing affirmation of their Jewishness.

It is not implausible to suggest that the call for an ethic of human rights is related to the silent yet commanding voice speaking from both Auschwitz and Hiroshima—a voice directed, in this instance, to the whole human race.

The movement for human rights arose in response to the trauma of the Holocaust and the other forms of mass death perpetrated during World War II, including Hiroshima. This movement culminated in the formation of the United Nations in 1946 and the UN Universal Declaration of Human Rights (as well as the founding of the State of Israel) in 1948. The preamble to the declaration recalls the "barbarous acts which have outraged the conscience of mankind" and prepares the way for a strong affirmation of the unity of humanity in the main body of the declaration. Consequently, this document stands against all mythologies that would divide humanity, racially or otherwise, into sacred and profane in order to claim the world and its resources for any specific "sacred" race—as both the wartime German and Japanese mythologies sought to do. Human rights cannot be reduced to individual rights or community rights. The unity and sanctity of the human race, the declaration affirms, may not be denied or violated by any political order. Human dignity transcends all social, political, and cultural orders. This is the true measure of a just society—the limit that no authority may transgress.

The power of the ethical vision of human rights expressed in the UN declaration lies in the fact that it too is rooted in a visceral response, one that cuts across cultures and creeds. Unlike the language of most academic reflection on ethics, which remains technical and esoteric, human rights language is a language that has spontaneously taken root in cross-cultural public discourse. The language of human rights has become embedded in the language of politics and international relations. Even if in many cases the political usage of this language is hypocritical, this is the homage that vice pays to virtue, and it indicates that this standard has taken root in public life and can be used as a measuring rod for social and political criticism.

Indeed, the UN declaration codifies and gives international recognition to the ethics of hospitality to the stranger. Human dignity is that which cannot be defined but which all human beings share despite the differences that define them—differences of race, gender, religion, ethnicity, and so on. To participate in a story that reveres hospitality to the stranger is to participate in a story that recognizes the humanity of precisely the "other" who does not share one's own story. The declaration affirms this by implicitly insisting that human dignity is the limit which no story may transgress, regardless of whether that story takes on a nationalistic, ethnic, religious, or other form. It insists that the one who is profane—that is, outside of one's own sacred story—is human nevertheless. This is the lesson of every story of hospitality.

The indefinability of our humanity is a core religious insight, found in more than one religious tradition, that justifies offering hospitality to the stranger. For example, Judaism insists that human beings are created in the image of a God without image. In parallel fashion, Buddhism insists that the self cannot be defined, except negatively as "no self". Both of these traditions formed communities with an ethic of welcoming the stranger and the outcast. When such traditions act on this insight, they tend to undermine or desacralize the sacred orders of caste and class in society. For, as Max Weber recognized, religion can assume different patterns. In some forms it sacralizes the existing order of society (routine), and in other forms it desacralizes, disenchants, and secularizes the social order (charismatic).

I have adopted the strategy of scholars such as Jacques Ellul and Gabriel Vahanian in using the term "sacred" for the former and "holy" for the latter. From this perspective, the sacred divides the world into a dualism of the sacred and the profane, whereas the holy desacralizes (i.e., secularizes) every sacred order. Unlike the sacred and the profane, the holy and the secular are not opposites but complementarities that promote diversity rather than uniformity by encouraging hospitality to the stranger. They do so, I would argue, to preserve the dignity of every person whose humanity cannot be named or imaged and so cannot be confined to the categories of any particular sacred order. Phenomenologically, we find a parallel recognition of the indefinability of our humanity in the contemporary social sciences, which argue that no society has ever been able to completely socialize (to define and confine to social roles) even one of its members. In every society, the core of our humanity, our dignity, resists definition and remains indefinable.

The covenant embodied in the UN declaration is at once both holy and secular. It cuts across the religious and the secular, winning adherents both religious and nonreligious. It is unique in its ability to challenge the privatistic and relativistic attitudes of modern and postmodern consciousness, eliciting and creating a public transcultural holy community-of-communities of all those called out to champion human dignity. It has created its own secular organizations to champion this dignity, even as it works cooperatively with religious organizations. Such organizations include the United Nations itself, especially the UN Commission on Human Rights and its various subcommissions, as well as the International Court of Justice and regional conventions on human rights in western Europe, the Americas and Africa. Then there are the governmental offices of individual nations that monitor each other for rights violations and use this information to political advantage. (Motivations of self-interest aside, this political game does keep the pressure on to observe human rights.) Finally, there are nongovernmental voluntary organizations such as Amnesty International, the Anti-Slavery Society, and the International Committee of the Red Cross. Also in this category are religious communities (such as churches and synagogues), labor organizations, and professional associations.

Human Rights and Narrative Ethics: From Abraham and Siddhartha to Tolstoy, Gandhi, and Martin Luther King Jr.

One can scarcely speak of human dignity, human rights, and human liberation in our world without thinking of the extraordinary accomplishments in the tradition of nonviolence forged by three individuals from diverse religions and cultures: Tolstoy, Gandhi, and Martin Luther King Jr. What the lives of these three individuals suggest to us is that it is possible for narrative diversity to generate a shared ethic without sacrificing the diversity of particular traditions.

Arthur Cohen once argued that after Auschwitz we have come to realize that all human beings are bound to each other by their experiences of the demonic *tremendum*. "Auschwitz or Hiroshima or Vietnam or Cambodia or Uganda—what does it matter as long a each person knows the *tremendum* that bears his name; and it is one name only, for the rest what endures beyond the name and binds each human being in abjectness and torment to the other is that the configurations overlay, the *tremendum* of the Jews becomes the *tremendum* of the nations" (1981, 36). But if it is true that the configurations of the demonic overlay, perhaps this is also the case for the configurations of the holy, with their diverse narratives of hospitality to the stranger. Indeed, this is the insight we gain from the lives of Tolstoy, Gandhi, and King.

When one thinks of nonviolence one thinks first of all of Mahatma Gandhi. It is no secret that Gandhi's encounter with Jesus' Sermon on the Mount was a major factor motivating him to turn to the great Hindu narrative from the *Mahabharata,* the Bhagavad Gītā, in order to find the message of nonviolence within his own religion and culture. But people do not always recall that it was Gandhi's encounter with the writings of the great Russian novelist Leo Tolstoy that drew his attention to the power of the Sermon on the Mount.

Tolstoy came from the wealthy classes of landed gentry in Russia, and his novels brought him not only fame but fortune. And yet in the middle years of his life he underwent a conversion. As a result he freed his serfs, gave away all his wealth, and spent the rest of his life serving the poor and attempting to live by the teachings of the Sermon on the Mount. While Gandhi's Hinduism was clearly influenced by Tolstoy's Christianity, it is equally important to note that Tolstoy's Christianity in turn was deeply indebted to Buddhism. For Tolstoy's conversion was brought about in part by reading a story from the lives of the saints about a monk named Barlaam who brought about the conversion of a young Indian prince named Josaphat. The historian of religions Wilfred Cantwell Smith has traced the history of this story. He notes that Tolstoy was converted to the Christian life as spelled out in the Sermon on the Mount upon hearing a thinly disguised version of the life of the Buddha that had made its way into the lives of the saints (Smith 1981, 6–11).

The story is that of Josaphat, a wealthy young prince who gave up wealth, power, and family in order to seek an answer to the problems of old age, sickness, and death. In the midst of his urgent quest he met a Syrian monk, Barlaam, who told him a parable about a man who falls into a well and is hanging on for dear life to two vines. Along come two mice, one white and one black, who begin to chew on the vines so that before long they will be severed and the man will plunge to his death. This parable depicts the man's spiritual situation: The mice represent night and day, the forces of time eroding his life and bringing him surely to his death. The paradox, spiritually speaking, is that instead of waiting for death to come he must learn to let go now, for if he no longer clings to his life but gives it up to God, his spiritual death will lead to new life.

A century before Tolstoy, in Japan, the great Zen master Hakuin (1685–1768) told a similar story about a man clinging to the side of a cliff who had to learn to let go so as to experience the "Great Death" of enlightenment, or nonattachment; a "Great Death" that paradoxically gives way to the "Great Joy" of achieving "No-Self" (Dumoulin 1963, 258–259). The parallel between these two stories is no accident, for the same story and the same parable made its way not only from India to China and Japan but also from India through Persia to the Mediterranean world and eventually to northern Europe. Versions of the story can be found in Greek, Latin, Czech, Polish, Italian, Spanish, French, German, Swedish, Norwegian, and Icelandic, as well as in Arabic, Hebrew, and Yiddish. The story seems to have worked its way into virtually all the world's religions. The Greek and Hebrew versions came from the Arabic. The Muslims, in turn, got it from the Manichees in Persia, who got it from the Buddhists in India. The Latin *Josaphat* is a translation of the Greek *Loasaf*, which is a translation of the Arabic *Yudasaf*, which is a translation of the Persian *Bodisaf*, which is a translation of the Sanskrit *Bodhisattva*, which is, of course, a title for the Buddha. The parable of the man clinging to the vine appears to be even older than the story of the Buddha and may go back to Hindu, Jain, and even pre-Aryan sources (Smith 1981, 6–11).

The story of the prince who renounces the world and the accompanying parable allow us to see the profound ways in which the narrative traditions of the world's religions can be interdependent. If Gandhi came to appreciate the message of nonviolence through exposure to the life and teachings of Tolstoy, it turns out that Tolstoy's conversion itself represents a convergence of the life stories of two of the greatest teachers of nonviolence in the history of religions—Siddhartha Gautama and Jesus of Nazareth. But what Gandhi found lacking in Tolstoy's understanding of the Sermon on the Mount he found present in the Bhagavad Gītā, namely the notion of nonviolence as an active rather than a passive virtue—that is, as capable of producing an active resistance to evil. The spiritual genius of Gandhi was to transform the metaphor of warfare in the Bhagavad Gītā from one that authorized killing in order to heal into one that authorized and demanded an audacity on behalf of the stranger. In so doing, Gandhi transformed the

Bhagavad Gītā into a story of nonviolence on a par with the story of Jacob wrestling with the stranger and Jesus' Sermon on the Mount. Wrestling with a stranger does not have to lead to conquest any more than turning the other cheek has to lead to cooperation with evil. Both actions can be combined in an audacity on behalf of the stranger, which is expressed in active civil disobedience against unjust laws and on behalf of human dignity.

When Martin Luther King Jr. embraced Gandhi's teachings on nonviolence, he was in fact drawing on the mystical and ethical insight of at least four great religious traditions: Hinduism, Buddhism, Christianity, and Judaism (the Sermon on the Mount is rooted in the Jewish ethic of welcoming the stranger and showing audacity on behalf of the stranger). Both Gandhi and King also explicitly drew on the Socratic witness to civil disobedience as an expression of audacity. What Gandhi's and King's ethic of nonviolence illustrates is that narrative traditions are not mutually exclusive. Moreover, Gandhi's life illustrates that even narrative traditions of total surrender and unquestioning obedience can be rehabilitated and transformed into traditions of audacity, the way Gandhi transformed the Bhagavad Gītā from a story that authorized killing in order to heal into a story of radical nonviolent resistance (the audacity of civil disobedience) to evil. And yet some questioned whether he was audacious enough. The chief framer of India's secular constitution, Dr. B. R. Ambedkar, who was also the leader of the Mahars (untouchables, or outcasts), broke with Gandhi because he did not find him audacious enough on the issue of caste. Ambedkar then led his people (in 1956) to embrace the Buddhist *sangha* as the more appropriate (holy) community to champion their dignity and equality in the sacral world of caste.

The spiritual adventure of passing over into the life of the stranger and coming back with new insight into our own is not a parlor game for dilettantes; it is a world-transforming process whose results have been keenly felt in the emergence of a global ethic of nonviolent resistance to all incursions on the sanctity of human dignity. This process illustrates the way in which comparative religious ethics can advance a normative ethic through cross-cultural dialogue.

Where Do We Go from Here?

Our postmodern situation is such that we now recognize that there is no neutral vantage point from which to do comparative religious ethics. We shall each have to stretch the language of our own tradition to make room for the other. After Auschwitz and Hiroshima, speaking as one shaped by biblical narratives, it may seem that we live in a time of a new covenant with the whole of humanity, a covenant whose saving remnant is composed of holy communities such as those found within narrative traditions that advocate audacity and hospitality. These narrative traditions can be found in Judaism, Christianity, Buddhism, and many other traditions, both religious and secular. These various communities, in response to the silent yet commanding voice heard from Auschwitz and Hiroshima, are called to a new covenant, which renews the covenant of Noah so that "never again" will we seek to visit destruction on the human race or any portion of it. These are the communities that have separated themselves from the dominant sacred order of their societies to embrace a transcultural ethic that measures justice by the indefinable measure of human dignity. These are the communities that sustain human dignity and equality through an ethic of audacity on behalf of the stranger. In the global ecology of an emerging world civilization, it is the unity-in-diversity of such kindred traditions that promises to form the creative leaven for the promotion of a human rights ethic.

Alfred North Whitehead once estimated that approximately 10 percent of the European population participated in the Renaissance, and yet the Renaissance transformed Europe. The global ethic that I am imagining does not envision itself as a totalitarian ethic in which everyone must adhere to the same story. Ten percent of the world's population, engaged in passing over and coming back, working through the presence of diverse holy communities—Buddhist, Jewish, Christian, and other kindred religious and secular communities—can be a saving remnant. This remnant would be sufficient to create the public order necessary for the unity-in-diversity of a global civilization—a public order that answers to the measure of human dignity, protects human rights, and brings about human liberation.

The ethical commitment to human dignity and secular holiness that I am espousing is one that best thrives in the context of multiple communities and diverse stories, religious and nonreligious, theistic and nontheistic. It is precisely this diversity in story and community (mythos and ethos) that can make a universal ethic of human rights possible as an ethic of human liberation capable of shaping public policy on a global level. If a human rights ethic were to be rooted in any one communal narrative alone, the danger of a religious and cultural imperialism would quickly arise. But the diversity of communal narrative traditions, overlapping in their common commitment to welcoming the stranger, makes it possible for them to create a mutually correcting, mutually balancing moral ecology for an emerging global civilization.

As I look for opportunities for the emergence of global ethics through interreligious dialogue, I look in a direction that I see as promising and that I wish to explore in the future. For as we approach the coming of a new millennium, we ought to pay special attention to the African-American community, out of which Martin Luther King Jr. came, as an important point of dialogical convergence for the emergence of a global interreligious ethic. In King's nonviolent philosophy, not only do most of the world's major religions have a place but also—as the work of Peter Paris and Lewis Baldwin suggests—the African tribal religions and their kindred cousins around the world.

Moreover, King's turn to Gandhi was not an isolated event out of sync with the African-American churches. On the contrary, Sudarshan Kapur has shown that beginning in the 1920s the African-American community followed the efforts of Gandhi with keen interest in an ongoing dialogue (not the least of which was between Howard Thurman and Gandhi); they saw in Gandhi's struggles a mirror of their own. The only tradition that seems to be obviously missing from this dialogue is that of Islam. But that religious tradition made itself felt through the Black Muslim movement that gave rise to Malcolm X and, more importantly, through Sunni Islam, to which Malcolm X converted near the end of his life. When Martin Luther King Jr. and Malcolm X met and shook hands "for the first and only time" on March 26, 1964 (Cone 1991, 2) at the Capitol Building in Washington, D.C., the entire history of the world's religions symbolically converged in an ethical dialogue about the just use of violence in a post-Holocaust and post-Hiroshima world, a dialogue that is unfinished and whose outcome, I believe, will shape the face of the globe in the coming millennium.

Notes

1. Part of the argument of this chapter is also adapted from my paper "Historical Consciousness, Religion and the Social Order: Can We Make Normative Judgments?" (Fasching 1994).

2. I thank my colleague in Asian religions, Nathan Katz, for checking the Sanskrit and confirming this for me.

3. R. C. Zaehner's translation reads: "Were he to slaughter [all] these worlds, [he] slays nothing. He is not bound" (Zaehner 1966, 319).

4. Ronald Green has pointed out that, contrary to the typical "modern" Christian-Kierkegaardian interpretation, namely, that God can give commands that "suspend the ethical," "Jewish thinkers refused to relinquish a moral conception of God." Green's point is that a Kierkegaardian interpretation violated the rabbinic sense of who God is, and so Jewish thinkers appealed to a variety of midrashic stories to circumvent such an interpretation. See Green 1982, 17, 9; see also Green 1988, chaps. 4, 5, which respectively survey Jewish and Christian exegeses of the *Akeda.* Here Green points out that, prior to Kierkegaard, Christian exegesis also circumvented the Kierkegaardian conclusion of a religious suspension of the ethical.

References

Augustine. 1963. *Confessions.* Translated by Rex Werner. New York: Mentor Books, New American Library.

Baldwin, Lewis. 1991. *There Is a Balm in Gilead: The Cultural Roots of Martin Luther King, Jr.* Minneapolis: Fortress Press.

Cohen, Arthur. 1981. *The Tremendum*. New York: Crossroad.

Cone, James. 1991. *Martin & Malcolm & America: A Dream or a Nightmare*. Maryknoll, N.Y.: Orbis Books

Donne, John. 1962. "The Holy Sonnets." In *The Norton Anthology of English Literature*, edited by M. H. Abrams et al. Vol. 1. New York: W. W. Norton.

Dumoulin, Heinrich. [1959] 1963. *A History of Zen Buddhism*. Boston: Beacon Press

Dunne, John. 1972. *The Way of All the Earth*. New York: Macmillan.

Ebeling, Gerhard. 1970. *Luther: An Introduction to His Thought*. Philadelphia: Fortress Press.

Ellul, Jacques. 1975. *The New Demons*. New York: The Seabury Press.

Fackenheim, Emil. 1970. *God's Presence in History*. New York: Harper Torchbooks.

_____. 1989. *To Mend the World*. Bloomington: Indiana University Press.

Fasching, Darrell J. 1992. *Narrative Theology After Auschwitz: From Alienation to Ethics*. Minneapolis: Fortress Press.

_____. 1993. *The Ethical Challenge of Auschwitz and Hiroshima: Apocalypse or Utopia?* Albany: State University of New York Press.

_____. 1994. "Historical Consciousness, Religion and the Social Order: Can We Make Normative Judgments?" In *Religion and the Social Order*, edited by Jacob Neusner, 235–255. Atlanta: Scholars Press.

_____. Forthcoming. *Comparative Religious Ethics: A Narrative Approach*. Oxford: Blackwell.

Green, Ronald. 1982. "Abraham, Isaac, and the Jewish Tradition: An Ethical Reappraisal." *Journal of Religious Ethics* 10, 1 (Spring):1–21.

_____. 1988. *Religion and Moral Reason*. New York: Oxford University Press.

Greenberg, Irving. 1977. "Clouds of Smoke, Pillar of Fire: Judaism, Christianity, and Modernity After the Holocaust." In *Auschwitz: Beginning of a New Era?* edited by Eva Fleischner. New York: KTAV.

Hauerwas, Stanley. 1985. *Against the Nations*. Minneapolis: Winstron Press.

Kapur, Sudarshan. 1992. *Raising Up a Prophet: The African-American Encounter with Gandhi*. Boston: Beacon Press.

Lifton, Robert Jay. 1967. *Death in Life*. New York: Basic Books.

_____. 1986. *The Nazi Doctors: Medical Killing and the Psychology of Genocide*. New York: Basic Books.

Paris, Peter. 1995. *The Spirituality of African Peoples*. Minneapolis: Fortress Press.

Prabhavananda, Swami, and Christopher Isherwood, trans. [1944, 1951] 1972. *The Song of God: Bhagavad-Gītā*. New York: Mentor Books, New American Library.

Rhodes, Richard. 1986. *The Making of the Atomic Bomb*. New York: Simon and Schuster.

Rubenstein, Richard. 1975. *The Cunning of History*. New York: Harper and Row.

Smith, Wilfred Cantwell. 1981. *Toward a World Theology*. Philadelphia: Westminster Press.

Wiesel, Elie. 1958. *Night*. New York: Avon Books.

_____. 1978. *A Jew Today*. New York: Random House.

Wyden, Peter. 1984. *Day One: Before Hiroshima and After*. New York: Simon and Schuster.

Zaehner, R. C., trans. 1966. *The Hindu Scriptures*. New York: Dutton, Everyman's Library.

Chapter Thirteen

Commentary on Part Two

DENNIS P. McCANN
DePaul University

The papers presented in Part 2 of this volume show how comparative religious ethics can make a practical difference by helping to define a range of critical moral issues that ought, and often do, enjoy top priority in interreligious dialogue on a global scale. The most recent dramatic example of such dialogue, of course, is the 1993 Parliament of the World's Religions, which endorsed a statement, drafted by the noted Roman Catholic philosopher Hans Küng, *Toward a Global Ethic (An Initial Declaration)* (Council for a Parliament of the World's Religions 1993; Küng and Kuschel 1993; Küng 1997). This declaration clearly has stimulated interreligious dialogue, not just among the parliament's participants and well-wishers but also among all of us for whom a new consciousness of global moral obligations and responsibilities is dawning. As these essays demonstrate, comparative religious ethics can contribute to the development of a Global Ethic by showing how the Global Ethic emerges from, and is rooted in, the moral concerns expressed in diverse religious traditions and cultural perspectives.

Each of the essays focuses on a particular area of moral concern that is crucial to the development of a Global Ethic. Sumner B. Twiss wants to use comparative religious ethics to promote the universal recognition and implementation of human rights. James F. Smurl seeks to show convergences in the ways a variety of traditions approach the challenge of distributive justice. June O'Connor's study of "the teachers of reality" in El Salvador reminds us that the Global Ethic will lack both credibility and authenticity so long as it ignores the experience of the poor and the marginalized. John Kelsay seeks to promote world peace by understanding religion's relationship to politics and its role in legitimating, but also in providing ethical constraints upon, warfare among nations. Ronald M. Green shows how the prospects for a Global Ethic may be enhanced through the socially transformative activities of multinational business corporations. Kusumita P.

Pedersen notes how the world's religious traditions contain important resources for developing the global vision capable of sustaining environmental ethics. Darrell J. Fasching insists that the debilitating ethical relativism, which all too often is mistaken for global awareness, can be overcome only by rooting the Global Ethic in religiously subversive narratives that challenge us to imagine and morally affirm our common humanity.

Each chapter thus succeeds in illuminating crucial areas of moral concern for a Global Ethic. But each also makes certain assumptions about interreligious dialogue and the role that practitioners of comparative religious ethics may play in it. Although each perspective has its own distinct profile, I hope to show how they are complementary. Each illuminates part of the challenge that any scholar is likely to face in developing comparative religious ethics in the context of interreligious dialogue focused on a Global Ethic. There are likely to be any number of ways of presenting these complementarities. Here are the ones that seem most compelling to me: (1) moral advocacy versus ethical analysis as the basic posture for comparative religious ethics; (2) the role of narrative in comparative religious ethics; and (3) the ethics of interreligious dialogue. The first two of these may strike the reader as "old hat" in that they have been prominent in methodological discussions about religious ethics for at least a generation. They do, however, serve to remind us that whatever else comparative religious ethics may be, it is not in general methodologically distinct from religious ethics, which has always involved making comparisons of some sort, if only among various authors within the same religious tradition. The third point, however, may seem new, or at least may be viewed as offering a new twist to the perennial problem of scholarly accountability. The challenge here emerges from the new context in which comparative religious ethics is unfolding. Does comparative religious ethics seek simply to understand interreligious dialogue or to take an active role in shaping it? How our authors position themselves on the third issue, I hope to show, depends on where they are already positioned relative to the first two.

Moral Advocacy Versus Ethical Analysis in Comparative Religious Ethics

Although these terms, moral advocacy and ethical analysis, have often been posed as a dichotomy—a decisive either/or to be faced in developing one's methodology for, say, Christian social ethics—they are more usefully seen as a continuum capturing both normative and descriptive tasks in religious ethics. An advocacy approach to comparative religious ethics is one that starts from a practical commitment to some overarching ideal, like human rights or liberation, which is affirmed as an absolute ethical norm or imperative. Comparative religious ethics as moral advocacy seeks to compare and assess critically the relative validity of religious moral systems (and the communities that espouse them) in light of that commitment. The point of an advocacy approach is to mobilize religious resources in order to change the world more to the liking of those committed to the ideal. Analysis, on the other hand, is more concerned to understand the world rather than to change it. As an approach within comparative religious ethics, it seeks to promote understanding for its own sake or, perhaps, for certain unstated goals like world peace. The difference between these two is more one of emphasis rather than a tightly logical dichotomy.

The essays in Part 2 all line up on the advocacy side of this continuum. I was struck by the depth of the moral passion that animates them. Each of the authors is committed to one or another aspect of a global moral vision that is centered on human rights. The various other good causes—distributive justice, liberation, economic empowerment, and environmental responsibility—are sometimes explicitly, but always implicitly, related to a comprehensive understanding of human rights. The only possible exception is John Kelsay's essay on Islamic political thought. Kelsay's priority is to understand Islamic assumptions about politics, government, and the morality of warfare, but even Kelsay writes in the hope of challenging stereotypes and thus advancing the cause of peace. The authors, in short, share the view that comparative religious ethics must be more than an exercise in descriptive ethics, which promotes the understanding of different moral belief systems and cultures for its own sake. Comparative religious ethics, for them, is and ought to be animated by certain normative, socially transformative goals. The question is, of course: What warrants the norms that they have made central to their conception of comparative religious ethics?

The question is not whether human rights advocacy is a morally worthy cause. But what are the tacit assumptions governing its critically central role in comparative religious ethics? None of the authors demonstrate that human rights are universally valid; for the most part it is assumed, along with the universal validity of the other imperatives that they advocate. Sumner B. Twiss's essay makes reference to such arguments, but he assumes that the relativizing critique of human rights—as if such were merely an expression of Western moral ideology—is not persuasive. His argument, instead, tries to overcome the relativizers' suspicion, by showing that even the religious and cultural traditions usually considered most alien to Western moral ideology, in fact, contain openings for the development of human rights doctrine. Darrell Fasching, on the other hand, tacitly makes concessions to ethical relativism, based on his experience of teaching sophomores who accept ethical relativism as a moral absolute. He will not waste time trying to reconstruct their views in order to refute them philosophically; instead, he believes that a unique historical narrative—the subversive memory of Hiroshima and Auschwitz—is sufficient to warrant the universal claim for human rights.

Both strategies are quite promising, particularly if one assumes, say, with Alasdair MacIntyre (1981), that conventional philosophical arguments warranting universal moral absolutes are, and must ever be, inconclusive. But the suspicion of imposing the agenda of Western moral ideology is particularly acute in the context of global interreligious dialogue. Perhaps the world is already at a stage of development where the imperatives honored by these essays are universally recognized as the authentic expression of many different religious and cultural traditions. But I doubt it. Interreligious dialogue, if it is to be genuine, cannot be based upon a moral consensus that has already been achieved, as it were, over the heads of its diverse participants. It is useful to note in this context that *Toward a Global Ethic (An Initial Declaration),* endorsed at the 1993 Parliament of the World's Religions, is not framed explicitly in terms of human rights or any of the other imperatives advocated by our authors. To be sure, the declaration raises the ethical questions to which many feel that human rights doctrine is the answer, and it seeks to go behind the United Nations' Universal Declaration of Human Rights to highlight the human concerns that animated it as well. But those who want to develop comparative religious ethics as a contribution to interreligious dialogue may want to reflect on the parliament's circumspection here. Was it motivated by a prudent fear that interreligious dialogue might break down over a premature commitment to Western moral ideology?

The Role of Narrative in Comparative Religious Ethics

Of the essays featured in Part 2, three represent an approach in which narrative, personal or otherwise, is prominent: the essays by O'Connor, Kelsay, and Fasching. Of the remaining four, only Smurl's, Green's, and Pedersen's completely suppress the author's narrative perspective, thus conforming to the conventional expectations of scholarship. Twiss's essay stands between the two groups in that it explicitly emerges from the author's experience in the Project on Religion and Human Rights, seeking to respond to certain challenges that surfaced as the project unfolded. Even the essays by Smurl, Green, and Pedersen develop their arguments by interpreting the narrative expressions of a variety of religious communities. It seems fair to say, then, that our authors share the view—increasingly prominent in Christian ethics (see Hauerwas and Jones 1989)—that reasserts the centrality of narrative in ethical reflection.

Nevertheless, there is sufficient diversity in the use of narrative among our authors to allow us to map its possible roles in comparative religious ethics and their implications for interreligious dialogue. As already indicated, Fasching's essay contains a telling answer as to why narrative has become so important in religious ethics. It is not just that the religious traditions under examination are themselves usually constituted in narrative form. Narrative, or storytelling, is a nearly universal form of first-order religious discourse. It is impossible to do comparative religious ethics without some sensitivity to and skill in the interpretation of religious narratives. But the significance of the narrative approach lies elsewhere. What is the form that critical ethical reflection, or second-order moral discourse, should take? Should the insights of a narrative tradition be translated into abstract concepts capable of being tested in conventional moral argument, or should these insights be recast into yet another narrative that, among other things, reflects the author's personal appropriation of them? Fasching is convinced that conventional moral argument is too weak to overcome the complacency of ethical relativism. He explicitly resorts to a narrative approach in order to warrant a postmodern commitment to universal moral absolutes, which he hopes will be socially transformative. But given the obvious relativity characteristic of narrative perspectives, only the most extreme or unique narrative can supply such warrants. Hence his perspective focuses on the memory of Auschwitz and Hiroshima as the defining narrative for postmodern religious ethics. The other authors are also grappling with the significance of narrative in religious ethics, but they reflect approaches that differ from Fasching's in interesting ways.

Of the three essays in which narratives are central, O'Connor's suppresses her own narrative stance in order to create the space in which her readers can absorb the testimonials of her "teachers of reality." Kelsay and Fasching, and to some extent Twiss, take the opposite course. They introduce their personal narratives precisely in order to facilitate the reader's understanding of the narratives they propose to interpret. Both strategies reflect certain challenges that are bound to intensify as comparative religious ethics develops in the context of interreligious dialogue. The central issue, it seems, is one of moral authority. Here, it is best seen in the problem of selectivity. If religious narrative confers moral authority, why should this particular narrative be so honored? What warrants the selection?

Recognizing the moral authority of a particular narrative or narrative tradition, of course, is a central issue in interreligious dialogue. As a Roman Catholic, I may be pledged to uphold the dogma of papal infallibility (which is warranted ultimately by a particular interpretation of New Testament narrative) and defer to papal authority in matters of faith and morals, but must I insist that you also acknowledge the pope as a precondition for interreligious dialogue? And if I do so insist, what sort of "dialogue" is it likely to be? Would the possibilities of dialogue be enhanced if, beyond explaining the dogma of papal infallibility, I were to share with you a personal narrative recounting the vicissitudes of my experience as a decidedly liberal Roman Catholic thinker? This analogy, at any rate, kept popping into my mind as I read June O'Connor's essay. Must I acknowledge the moral authority of her "teachers of reality," that is, grant a hermeneutic privilege to their interpretation of the civil war in El Salvador, in order to enter into dialogue with her or with the poor of El Salvador? Just because O'Connor finds these particular narratives uniquely authoritative, why should I? There is an interreligious dimension to this, of course. Why should O'Connor accept at face value her teachers' negative views on Protestant evangelicals in El Salvador, who are more or less dismissed as agents of Yanqui imperialism? Better yet, why should I? To acknowledge any person, social group, or institution as "teachers of reality," in the emphatic sense that O'Connor intends, does confer a moral authority that seems beyond criticism. It asserts, as far as I can tell, a functional substitute for papal infallibility. But is either assertion warranted?

The moral conversion to which O'Connor summons her readers may not have seemed such a stark choice, had she, like Kelsay, situated the narratives of her teachers in relationship to her own personal narrative. Kelsay, more effectively than some of the other authors, tries to anticipate the difficulties that his readers may have in coming to a fresh, less prejudiced understanding of his subject, namely, the role of religion in Islamic politics. Kelsay's personal narrative is useful precisely because it puts his own tradition in play as an equal participant in interreligious dialogue. Islam no longer stands under judgment from the hermeneutically privileged perspective of Western moral ideology but is situated in an irenic conversation with Kelsay's own tradition of Reformed Christianity. This dialogue is genuinely open and thus risks sacrificing the claim of unquestioned moral authority for either tradition; but it also yields fresh insight by showing how Islam and Reformed Christianity share certain affinities in their ideas about God that translate into similar views on the relationship of religion and politics. Reformed Christianity, no less than Islam, historically promoted a militant understanding of the role of government in enforcing religiously based morality. I found that the modeling of interreligious dialogue that Kelsay offered prompted me to revisit the history of Catholic social teaching on these issues. I accepted his invitation to put my own tradition in play and started making notes in the margins suggesting parallels between Islamic political thought and the claims of the papacy typical of pre–Vatican II Catholicism. Kelsay's use of personal narrative did not insist that I accept the representatives of either Islam or Reformed Christianity as teachers of reality; but I found myself learning from them, precisely because his narrative tended to mute the claims to moral authority typically associated with both traditions.

The use of narrative to establish moral authority or to subvert it, either way, is risky business. O'Connor, I assume, wants to effect in her readers a socially transformative moral conversion. If we take as gospel the views of her teachers of reality, how could we not be moved to some kind of social action in solidarity with the oppressed, if not in El Salvador, then certainly in our own backyards? I suspect that she knows full well the risks involved in asserting a hermeneutic privilege for her informants but that she finds the call for revolutionary solidarity so compellingly urgent that these theoretical risks can responsibly be set aside. Kelsay's approach to understanding Islam seems to require taking the opposite risk. He pursues the satisfactions of theoretical reflection, offering a list of five conclusions that allow us to make peace with ourselves and with Islam, but leaving for another day the adjudication of certain conflicts, whose resolution, as he says, is simply not an option for us at present. An awareness of moral complexity is affirmed, but predictably at the risk of postponing the socially transformative praxis that may be necessary to a realistic politics of social justice and peace.

The problem of authority or selectivity in the use of religious narrative also surfaces in Darrell Fasching's essay. Fasching styles himself an "alienated" Christian ethicist. He believes that Christian complicity in the horrors of Auschwitz and Hiroshima makes it impossible to continue the project of Christian theology in any other context than comparative religious ethics. He sees in these narratives of Holocaust an "ethical imperative for comparison" and thus has schooled himself in contemporary Jewish religious thought in order to reconstruct Christian theology. Fasching infers that Christian theology stands in need of a massive overhaul, relying on a rather tortuous argument in which Christianity's classical understanding of God, and obedient submission as the primary expression of faith in Him, come to be regarded as ultimately responsible for the diabolical evils symbolized by Auschwitz and Hiroshima. He finds crucial evidence for this interpretation of classical Christianity in, of all places, John Donne's fourteenth Holy Sonnet, where Donne makes his submission:

> Batter my heart, three-personed God; for You
> As yet but knock, breathe, shine, and seek to mend;
> That I may rise and stand, o'rthrow me, and bend
> your force to break, blow, burn and make me new.

In Fasching's perspective, Donne's poetry discloses the classical Christian perversion of Biblical faith, common from Augustine through Luther and beyond, that "wrestles with the God who wounds in order to heal and slays in order to make alive." Apparently, Fasching feels that this familiar paradox of orthodox Christian mysticism incites some, if not all, Christians to murder and ultimately to deliberate acts of genocide. Fortunately, there is an alternative: an audacious faith, rather than a submissive (or passive-aggressive) one, which can be reconstructed by learning from a Jewish theology of "chutzpah." Such an audacious faith, Fasching hopes, will allow Christians to repent of their complicity in the radical evils of the twentieth century and join with other audacious religious dissenters like Tolstoy, Gandhi, and Martin Luther King Jr. in order to build a "moral ecology" for a new global civilization.

Fasching's hope for the future is as breathtaking as his interpretation of the Christian past is provocative, and perhaps not always helpfully so. At issue here, however, is the selectivity of his reading of biblical narrative. He invokes the Book of Job as a template for the audacious faith that Christians should appropriate from Jewish tradition, with little apparent concern that the Book of Job is also a major source of the submissive faith from which he is alienated. Job not only dares to question God; in the end, he also comes to repent of his questioning, submissively affirming: "Though he slay me, yet will I trust in Him." The Book of Job, along with other books of the Hebrew scriptures, thus would seem to be a major source for the classical theism that Fasching calls on Christians to abandon. Yet how can classical theism be eliminated without also suppressing the biblical template for Fasching's audacious faith? The point is neither to refute nor vindicate Fasching's interpretation, but to highlight the kinds of questions that are likely to emerge when either strong theoretical claims or demands for strong action are made on a narrative base that, to say the least, may be criticized as idiosyncratic. The difficulties inherent in Fasching's readings of either the Book of Job or the Holy Sonnets of John Donne cannot be resolved by recourse to Fasching's personal narrative. Fasching's narrative of religious alienation may explain his tendentious readings, but it cannot render them persuasive.

The uses of religious narrative in these essays lead me to conclude that, while personal narratives can be an effective invitation to interreligious dialogue, they are not likely to create consensus around any given set of universal moral absolutes. The epistemological difficulties of conventional moral argument are not overcome by the adoption of a narrative approach, but are merely deflected. If narratives are to provide the warrants that conventional moral argument cannot deliver, they must possess an authority that reasoned justification cannot confer. But how and why is that authority recognized? Neither O'Connor nor Fasching give reasons for their submission to the authority of either the testimonials of the El Salvadoran teachers of reality or the subversive memory of Auschwitz and Hiroshima. Yet reasons must be given, unless, of course, one already stands among the converted.

By contrast, John Kelsay's use of narrative seems more promising precisely because it invites us to engage in dialogue, rather than summoning us to conversion. Narrative provides perspective, which is always limited, and hence warrants only soft claims. Because it is dialogical, it is also open-ended. It cannot claim definitiveness for any one narrative or perspective. Kelsay tacitly admits this by opening his own faith tradition to critical

scrutiny, as we follow his exploration of Islamic social thought, and by concluding that, beyond the convergences illuminated by the critical comparisons, it remains unclear how some serious differences will ever be resolved.
Kelsay, in short, for the sake of interreligious dialogue, is willing to rela-
tivize his own perspective in order to create a climate of mutuality in which
new learning can emerge. The use of personal narrative, in short, can be
disarming, and intellectual disarmament may be just what is required for
interreligious dialogue to advance.

The Ethics of Interreligious Dialogue

The previous methodological reflections in no way should be construed as
minimizing the important contribution that comparative religious ethics
can, and in this case, already has made to interreligious dialogue. I would
like to conclude, then, by returning to the practical intention motivating
this collection of essays, the role of comparative religious ethics in interreligious dialogue. What and how do these essays contribute to the development of the kind of Global Ethic envisioned by the 1993 Parliament of the
World's Religions? As a member of the steering committee that made the
initial proposals for a parliament, and as a participant in its proceedings, I
continue to believe that comparative religious ethics is crucial to the kind of
interreligious dialogue that the parliament's founders originally intended. It
was clear from the beginning that the dialogue was meant to go beyond the
implicit goal of increasing mutual understanding among various communities of faith. The dialogue was to be about the world we all live in, and
whether interreligious dialogue could give rise to new forms of practical
collaboration among the world's religions for addressing the world's problems. The attempt to create a Global Ethic was not peripheral to the parliament's agenda; it was central, and it still stands at the global level as an invitation to the kind of practical collaboration that many of the Parliament's
local sponsors in Chicago were able to initiate, among other things,
through the creation of a new institution for a genuinely inclusive ecumenism, the Metropolitan Assembly.[1]

Given the practical intent of the interreligious dialogue that culminated
in *Toward a Global Ethic (An Initial Declaration)*, the question motivating
this volume is how can scholars practicing the discipline of comparative religious ethics make a contribution to the further development of this ethic?
To answer this question, it may be useful to remind ourselves what the declaration is and is not. It is not a systematic treatise in moral theology, and it
is not a primer in the discipline of comparative religious ethics. It makes a
good-faith attempt to avoid the impression that, when all is said and done,
it is simply another expression of late-twentieth-century Western moral ideology. As a result, its formulations tend to be vague and open-ended. It

takes the form, first of all, of conscientious protest. "The world is in agony . . ." is how the preamble begins, and most of its formulations are negative in form: ". . . we have learned . . . that rights without morality cannot long endure, and that *there will be no better global order without a global ethic*" (Council for a Parliament of the World's Religions 1993, 1, 4; italics in original).

In seeking to identify the "fundamental consensus on binding values, irrevocable standards, and personal attitudes" sufficient to warrant a Global Ethic, the declaration proceeds in negative terms. The "fundamental demand" animating the declaration is first couched in negative terms familiar from both rabbinic Judaism and Confucianism: "What you do not wish done to yourself, do not do unto others" (1993, 5). The same is true of the "irrevocable directives" proposed as "four broad, ancient guidelines for human behavior which are found in most of the religions of the world": "1. Commitment to a Culture of Non-violence and Respect for Life," which the declaration draws from the negative universal prohibition, *"You shall not kill!"*; "2. Commitment to a Culture of Solidarity and a Just Economic Order," from *"You shall not steal!"*; "3. Commitment to a Culture of Tolerance and a Life of Truthfulness," from *"You shall not lie!"*; and "4. Commitment to a Culture of Equal Rights and Partnership Between Men and Women," derived from *"You shall not commit sexual immorality!"* (1993, 6–9). To be sure, each of these negative formulations is immediately followed by a positive statement, but the overall impression is that the use of the negative is meant, as it is in rabbinic tradition, to define a minimal set of nonnegotiable moral limits that the world's religions must insist upon if they are to remain true to their mission in the world.

Given these limits, what *Toward a Global Ethics (An Initial Declaration)* does not say is as interesting as what it does say. Here, too, the need to maintain the maximum feasible consensus serves as a constraint upon how far the declaration is willing to go beyond protesting overt immorality. The declaration avoids the current conundrums of Western moral ideology. It neither endorses nor condemns socialism, liberation, or feminism. To be sure, it joins those committed to these perspectives in denouncing "class thinking, racism, nationalism, [and] sexism," but it describes these as forms of "egoism" or "selfishness" (1993, 5), and remains deliberately agnostic about their social systemic dimensions. Perhaps the most interesting example of this tendency is the declaration's observations under the heading "Commitment to a Culture of Equal Rights and Partnership Between Men and Women." The document explicitly condemns "sexual exploitation and sexual discrimination" (1993, 9); yet it is careful to use language that supports traditional religious understandings of gender role, marriage, and family life. The document's agnosticism is a deliberate attempt to focus on those perceptions that unite, say, Roman Catholics and Muslims as well as

Congregationalists and Reformed Jews, rather than what divides them. The moral consensus may be broad, but just how deep is it?

This reading of the parliament's initial declaration suggests that, indeed, there is much that comparative religious ethics can contribute to the development of a Global Ethic through interreligious dialogue. The Global Ethic, it turns out, is very tentative, and the challenge facing scholars in the field of comparative religious ethics is just how far the interreligious moral consensus can be pushed through critical, comparative study of the world's religious traditions. Each of the essays in Part 2 tries to push forward, but in a different way.

Twiss implicitly challenges would-be parliamentarians to consider whether an explicit and comprehensive understanding of human rights ought to be made the centerpiece of the Global Ethic. His reading of the openness of Chinese and indigenous religious traditions to an ethic of human rights may be persuasive to some and dubious to others, but it does challenge us to consider whether and how the Global Ethic can get beyond the limits of negative protest and define a positive agenda for social transformation.

Smurl's essay on distributive justice could be read as offering a somewhat different ethical paradigm than Twiss's. But its chief contribution to interreligious dialogue, I think, is in providing useful information on how local religious communities can organize themselves actually to do something to stimulate economic development. Making such information available—especially in the form of comparative studies—to participants in interreligious dialogue not only helps overcome lingering stereotypes, for example, about the activities of the Muslim Brotherhood in West Bank and Gaza but also may challenge them to develop similar programs in their own communities.

O'Connor's essay reminds us that the results of any dialogue inevitably depend upon who is invited to the conversation and who is excluded. One wonders what *Toward a Global Ethic (An Initial Declaration)* would have been like had O'Connor's informants participated in the parliament and in the dialogues preparatory to it. The issue here is not political, but epistemological, as O'Connor insists. Even if the other participants are hesitant to grant a hermeneutic privilege to O'Connor's informants, they still need to listen to and learn from them, and on that basis, begin to teach them as well.

Kelsay's essay provides a model of critical reflection that may or may not be second nature to scholars devoted to comparative religious ethics, but the ability to open one's own tradition to critical scrutiny in order to facilitate dialogue is still problematic—as several incidents at the parliament itself suggested[2]—among those who represent organized communities in interreligious dialogue. He challenges participants in the dialogue to discover what openness may entail, and why it can lead to a deeper understanding and commitment to one's own faith tradition, rather than simply undermining it.

Green's contribution challenges those who conceive the Global Ethic as developing exclusively on the basis of shared religious principles. He shows how ostensibly secular institutions, multinational corporations acting within an emerging global marketplace, not only have made important strides in developing a global business ethic but have shown that such an ethic can be more effective in addressing some of the Global Ethic's concerns, for example, economic empowerment and sexual discrimination, than are the ethical traditions of various religious communities. Those who would develop the Global Ethic need to consider Green's argument, for the parliament's declaration does create the impression that interreligious moral consensus is being achieved at the expense of denigrating the ethical achievements of modern, secular institutions. Like Smurl's, Green's major contribution to the dialogue may simply be the dissemination and interpretation of important information about nonreligious institutions and their ethical agendas, which rarely, if ever, surface in interreligious dialogues focused particularly on economic development and social justice.

Pedersen, like Green, points to unsuspected resources for developing the Global Ethic. Pedersen recognizes that the challenge of developing an environmental ethic has been particularly difficult for religious communities, particularly in the West, because they have been accused of promoting attitudes that, in celebrating the moral dignity of humanity, in effect leave their disciples "environmentally challenged." Pedersen invites participants in interreligious dialogue to take a fresh look at environmental ethics by suggesting that each of the major religious traditions already do possess intellectual and spiritual resources that promote environmental responsibility. Here, too, the main contribution may be modest, but crucially important: the dissemination and interpretation of invaluable information that can help shape the priorities for a Global Ethic.

Last, but by no means least, there is the work of Fasching. Fasching's contribution to interreligious dialogue is that of a prophet. As an alienated participant, he approaches his role, like the Hebrew prophet Jeremiah, with the aim of shaking things up. He reminds all of us that none are innocent, that none of us can approach the task of developing a Global Ethic without confronting our own complicity in the evils that the Global Ethic is meant to address. Religious traditions and the moral attitudes they promote may be part of the solution to our global problems, but, as Fasching reminds us, they are also part of the problem. A full and credible statement of the Global Ethic cannot pretend otherwise.

Notes

1. The Metropolitan Assembly was founded during the week of deliberations at the parliament with the express purpose of redefining ecumenism in Chicago on a

more inclusive basis that would elicit the collaboration and support of Chicago religious communities—particularly minorities and recent immigrant communities—not represented in the ecumenical relationships that already have been institutionalized among mainline Protestants, Roman Catholics, and representatives of conservative and reformed Judaism. The Metropolitan Assembly seeks particularly to broaden the civic coalitions working on a host of social problems, such as racism, poverty, and urban violence.

2. Despite intensive efforts by the parliament's organizers to ensure a favorable climate for growth in interreligious dialogue, the week's deliberations, among other things, witnessed a fiery confrontation over alleged religious persecution in Kashmir, the dramatic withdrawal of representatives from the Greek Orthodox Church incensed over the parliament's decision to recognize representatives from Wicca and other neopagan groups, and protests from some Jewish groups over the inclusion of a delegation, including the Reverend Louis Farrakhan, from the Nation of Islam. The passions aroused by these incidents, nevertheless, should be read as a sign of just how seriously all parties regarded the significance of their participation in the parliament.

References

Council for a Parliament of the World's Religions. 1993. *Toward a Global Ethic (An Initial Declaration)*. Chicago: Council for a Parliament of the World's Religions.

Küng, Hans. 1997. *A Global Ethic for Global Politics and Economics*. London: SCM Press.

Küng, Hans, and Karl-Josef Kuschel, eds. 1993. *A Global Ethic: The Declaration of the Parliament of the World's Religions*. New York: Continuum.

Hauerwas, Stanley, and L. Gregory Jones, eds. 1989. *Why Narrative? Readings in Narrative Theology*. Grand Rapids, Mich.: William B. Eerdmans Publishing Co.

MacIntyre, Alasdair. 1981. *After Virtue: A Study in Moral Theory*. Notre Dame, Ind.: University of Notre Dame Press.

About the Editors
and Contributors

Marcus Braybrooke, copresident, World Congress of Faiths, and team vicar, Dorchester Team Ministry, Diocese of Oxford; author of *Pilgrimage of Hope: One Hundred Years of Global Interfaith Dialogue; Together to the Truth; Time to Meet;* and *Faith in a Global Age.*

Darrell J. Fasching, professor and chair, Department of Religious Studies, University of South Florida; author of *Narrative Theology After Auschwitz: From Alienation to Ethics* and *The Ethical Challenge of Auschwitz and Hiroshima: Apocalypse or Utopia?*

Ronald M. Green, John Phillips Professor, Department of Religion, and director, Ethics Institute, Dartmouth College; author of *Population Growth and Justice; Religious Reason; Religion and Moral Reason; Kierkegaard and Kant: The Hidden Debt;* and *The Ethical Manager: A New Method for Business Ethics.*

Bruce Grelle, associate professor, Department of Religious Studies, California State University, Chico; coeditor of *Christianity and Capitalism: Perspectives on Religion, Liberalism, and the Economy;* director, Religion and Public Education Resource Center; past president, Chico Area Interfaith Council.

John Kelsay, professor and chair, Department of Religion, Florida State University; author, coauthor, or coeditor of *Human Rights and the Conflict of Cultures; Cross, Crescent, and Sword; Just War and Jihad; Islam and War;* and *Religion and Human Rights;* coeditor, *The Annual of the Society of Christian Ethics.*

Sallie King, professor and head, Department of Philosophy and Religion, James Madison University; coeditor of *Engaged Buddhism: Buddhist Liberation Movements in Asia.*

Dennis P. McCann, professor and chair, Department of Religious Studies, DePaul University; author of *Christian Realism and Liberation Theology; New Experiment in Democracy: The Challenge for American Catholicism;* coauthor of *Polity and Praxis: A Program for American Practical Theology;* coeditor of *On Moral Business: Classical and Contemporary Resources for Ethics and Economics;* executive director of the Society of Christian Ethics.

Kate McCarthy, assistant professor, Department of Religious Studies, California State University, Chico; author of papers on liberation theology and religious pluralism, global ethics, and women in Buddhism; consultant to Global Theological Consultation on Land, Sri Lanka, 1991.

June O'Connor, professor and chair, Department of Religious Studies, University of California, Riverside; author of *The Quest for Political and Spiritual Liberation:*

A Study in the Thought of Sri Aurobindo Ghose and *The Moral Vision of Dorothy Day: A Feminist Perspective.*

Kusumita P. Pedersen, assistant professor and chair, Department of Religion, St. Francis College, Brooklyn; author of articles on Asian traditions and interreligious dialogue as well as "An Earth Charter: An Interfaith Perspective" (Global Forum of NGOs, UN Conference on Environment and Development); formerly executive director, Temple of Understanding (New York); joint secretary, Global Forum of Spiritual and Parliamentary Leaders on Human Survival; and executive director, Project on Religion and Human Rights.

James F. Smurl, professor, Department of Religious Studies, Indiana University, Indianapolis; author of *Religious Ethics: A Systems Approach* and *The Burdens of Justice.*

Sumner B. Twiss, professor and chair, Department of Religious Studies, Brown University; coauthor of *Comparative Religious Ethics: A New Method;* coeditor of *Genetic Counseling: Facts, Values, and Norms; Experience of the Sacred: Readings in the Phenomenology of Religion; Religion and Human Rights;* and *Religious Diversity and American Religious History: Studies in Traditions and Cultures;* coeditor of *The Annual of the Society of Christian Ethics;* book discussion editor, *Journal of Religious Ethics.*

Index

Abington School District v. Schempp
  60, 62
Abraham (biblical), 312
Abrahamic religions, 259–270, 272,
  273. *See also individual religions*
Absolutism, 109, 123–125, 157, 292
Abu Dhabi, 193
Accountability, 92, 160, 206, 269, 323
Adams, Robert Merrihew, 123, 132
Africa, 157, 167, 185, 193, 210, 211,
  241, 320
African Americans, 48, 319, 320
Agriculture, 260, 274, 277
Akan tradition (Ghana), 169
Alienation, 276, 292, 293, 295, 329
  alienated theology, 294
Almsgiving (*zakat*), *186, 187, 188,
  194*
Alvarado, Elvia, 199–200, 201, 204,
  207–208
Ambedkar, B. R., 318
"American Indian Environmental
  Religions" (Vecsey), 279
Anderson, Norman, 187
Anger, 275, 282
Animals, 261, 270, 271, 272, 279,
  284(n12)
Anonymous Christians, 86, 87
Anthropocentrism, 254, 258, 259–260
Anthropology, 278
Anthropomorphism, 262
Anti-Defamation League, 101
Anti-Semitism, 91
Appleby, R. Scott, 83
Aquinas, Thomas, 86
Arab states, 241
Ariyaratne, A. T., 181

Asceticism, 254, 267, 268, 270, 272,
  277, 278
Asia, 157, 167, 180, 185, 193, 210,
  211, 237, 248, 292
  East Asian religions, 275–278
  South Asian religions, 270–275
  See also individual religions
Asoka (Indian king), 131, 180
Assembly of Marginalized Women, 200
Atomic bomb, 299, 307, 308. *See also*
  Hiroshima; Nuclear weapons
Audacity, 312–313, 317, 318, 319,
  328, 329
Augustine of Hippo, 307, 308, 310,
  311
Auschwitz, 293, 296–300, 302–304,
  312, 313, 319, 328
Automobiles, 211

Baldwin, Lewis, 320
Banna, Hasan al-, 188
Barlaam (monk), 316, 317
Barney, Gerald, 54
Barr, James, 260
Barrios de Chungara, Domitila, 202
Barrows, John Henry, 88
Barth, Karl, 76–77, 87
Beliefs/believers, 15, 35, 80, 104, 109,
  167, 176, 202, 223, 270
Bellah, Robert, 46–47, 67
Beneficence, 119
Berkovits, Eliezer, 302
Berman, Saul, 264
Berry, Thomas, 262
Bhagavad Gītā, 295, 299, 307,
  308–309, 311, 316, 317–318
Bhopal disaster, 242

Biases, 24
Bible, 75, 79, 95, 111, 207, 270, 273,
    294
  Book of Job, 261, 262, 265,
    284(n12), 312, 329
  Exodus/Deuteronomy, 183, 262,
    263, 284(n10), 298, 300
  Genesis, 260–262, 264, 265, 299,
    310, 312, 326
  New Testament, 83, 94, 183, 184,
    266, 300
  Psalms, 261, 262, 265
  as a weapon, 205
Blessings, 264
B'nai B'rith, 101
Bonney, Charles, 146
Boulding, Elise, 198
Braaten, Carl, 78
Braybrooke, Marcus, 134, 143, 146
Bribery, 240–241. See also
    Corruption
Brown, Lester, 255, 283(n5)
Brundtland, Gro Harlem, 256
Buddhadasa Bikkhu, 275
Buddhaghosa, 271
Buddhism, 83, 89–90, 163, 244, 245,
    248, 271, 278, 300, 310, 314,
    316, 318, 319
  Buddhists, 78, 82, 83, 100, 102, 106,
    112(n5), 189, 193
  and distributive justice, 179–183
  Engaged Buddhism, 275
  and environmental ethics, 267, 270,
    272, 274–275
  Great Death in, 311, 317
  life of Buddha, 312, 317
  and non-violence, 131
Bureaucratic rationalization, 297. See
    also Techno-bureaucracy
Burma, 136
Business, 237–250

CAIC. See California, Chico Area
    Interfaith Council
California, 50, 62–63, 69(n16)
  California State University, Fullerton
    Center for the Study of Religious

Chico Area Interfaith Council
    (CAIC), 51–53, 58–59, 69(n14)
  State Department of Education,
    60–61, 64
  Three Rs Project in, 62
Callicott, J. Baird, 259
Calvin, John, 220
Capitalism, 84, 178, 187
Carter, Jimmy, 70(n), 110, 209
Caste, 318
Catholicism, 48, 77, 78, 86–87, 100,
    101–103, 110, 326, 327
  Declaration on the Relationship of
    the Church to Non-Christian
    Religions (1965), 101, 113(n7)
  U.S. Catholic Conference (1994),
    257
  World Day of Prayer for Peace
    (1985), 102
  See also Second Vatican Council
Celibacy, 267
Center for Global Ethics, 118, 127,
    128, 139(n3)
Chang Tsai, 276–277
Chapman, Colin, 111(n3), 276
Chapple, Christopher, 271–272
Charity. See under Solidarity
Chico Enterprise-Record, 52
Children, 160, 171, 197, 199, 202,
    223, 224, 225, 301
  in El Salvador, 200, 203, 213(n2)
  in Holocaust, 297–298
Childress, James, 226–227
China, 164, 275–276, 317
Christian Coalition, 51, 52, 53, 58,
    100, 101
Christianity
  and Buddhism, 316
  and distributive justice, 183–186
  and environmental ethics, 264–268
  and Hinduism, 144
  and Islam, 218–221, 224–232, 234,
    327
  social-political thought, 227–228,
    229–230, 232
  See also Catholicism; Exclusivism,
    Christian; Inclusivism, Christian;

Pluralism, Christian; Protestants; Reformed Christianity
Christianity and the Encounter of the World Religions (Tillich), 112(n5)
Christology, 75, 85, 91, 94–95. *See also* Jesus Christ
Church of Jesus Christ of Latter-day Saints, 48
Chutzpah, 312, 328. *See also* Audacity
Citizenship, 35, 36, 40, 41, 45, 46, 47, 60, 64–66
Civil disobedience, 318
Clark, Tom, 60
Coalitions, 102, 147, 296
Cobb, John, 256–257
Cohen, Arthur, 302, 316
Cold War, 303
Colonialism, 85, 91, 101, 126, 157, 161, 162, 210, 211, 255
Commitment, 99–101, 108–109, 120–121, 143, 144, 177, 186, 239, 243, 245, 331
Common good, 36, 40, 56, 62, 150, 225
Common morality, 123, 125, 128, 132, 138
Communitarianism, 162, 164
Community action, 190, 192–194
Comparative methods and theory, 12, 19–20, 23–24, 25, 33
Comparative religious ethics, 212, 248, 250, 292, 295, 296, 322
    approaches to, 1. *See also* Curricular paradigms
    and distributive justice, 177, 178, 194
    and human rights, 191
    and interreligious dialogues, 2–3, 4, 41–49, 59–64, 133, 150, 159, 217, 303, 318, 323, 325, 326, 330, 332
    as intersection of academic/public agendas, 40, 64, 66
    literature of, 39
    moral advocacy vs. ethical analysis in, 323–325

narratives in, 323, 325–330. *See also* Narrative ethics; Storytelling
    and public intellectuals, 36–41
    secondary venues for, 49–64
    teaching, 4–5, 11–28, 30–33, 148
    themes in, 123–125
Compromise, 57, 59
Confessions (Augustine), 307
Confucianism, 163–167, 173(n6), 237, 244, 245, 247, 331
    and environmental ethics, 275–276
Cunning of History, The (Rubenstein), 297
Consensus, 110, 119, 121, 126,129, 130, 131, 162, 163, 166, 172, 229, 230, 265, 325, 332
Conservative white Christians, 105
Consumerism/consumption, 43, 267, 272, 275, 283(n5)
Continuity of life, 270, 271, 272, 273, 276, 281
Cooperatives, 206
Corporations. *See* Multinational corporations
Corruption, 239, 240–241, 246
Council for a Parliament of the World's Religions, 145. *See also* Parliament of World's Religions
Covenant on Civil and Political Rights, 159
Covenant on Economic, Social, and Cultural Rights, 159
Crises, 83, 98–99, 100, 160
    environmental, 254–259, 264–265, 266, 280, 282
Critics, 36, 65–66, 67(n6)
"Cross-Cultural Environmental Ethics" (course), 42–44
Cultural wars, 52, 53, 56, 105
Curricular paradigms, 12–28, 30–33, 148
    assessment of, 20–28
    presuppositions of courses, 13, 19, 29(n2), 44
    See also individual approaches
Cyprian (bishop of Carthage), 76

Daily News Record (Harrisonburg, Virginia), 137
Danner, Mark, 213(n3)
D'Costa, Gavin, 88, 113(n9)
Dean, William, 39–40, 49, 67(n6)
Death penalty, 102
Declaration Toward a Global Ethic, 126, 127. *See also* Parliament of World's Religions, Global Ethic Declaration of
De George, Richard, 239
Delusion, 275, 282
Demonic, the, 292, 299, 301, 302, 303, 304, 309, 312
Deserts, 260
Destruction, avoidance of, 263, 272, 281
Development, 282
   funds for, 192–193
   refugees of, 257
   sustainable eco-development, 255–256
Dialogues, 36, 54, 163, 170, 172, 178, 190, 191–192, 194, 199, 217, 292, 293, 294, 319, 320
   difficulty of , 202–204
   See also Hermeneutical dialogical approach; Interreligious dialogues
Differences, 2, 14, 23, 64, 84, 85, 98, 111, 219, 222, 224, 314
   models of religious difference, 74, 92–93, 97. *See also* Exclusivism; Inclusivism; Pluralism, as model of religious differences
   See also Diversity; Pluralism
Dignity, 168, 169, 172, 207, 219, 245, 250, 267, 292, 293, 296, 297, 310, 312, 313, 314, 315, 318, 319
Dimitrios (Ecumenical Patriarch), 268
Disappearances, 201, 206
Discourses, 56, 57, 66
   bridge, 49–50
Discrimination, 160, 239, 241, 245, 248, 249, 331
Distributive justice, 176–194, 332
   in Christianity, 183–186
   in world's religions, 178–189

Diversity, 22, 48, 50, 91, 97, 98, 111, 134, 158, 160, 292, 316, 319. *See also* Differences; Pluralism
Dollinger, Marc, 244
Dominion theme, 259, 260, 264, 265
Donaldson, Thomas, 239
Donne, John, 307–308, 310, 311, 328
Don't Be Afraid Gringo: A Honduran Woman Speaks from the Heart (Alvarado), 199–200
Doubling, 304, 305, 306, 307, 308, 309
Driver, Tom, 91
Dualism, 156, 315
Dunne, John, 294–295, 296
Duran, Khalid, 129–130, 135
Durkheim, Emile, 34, 64–65
Dussel, Enrique, 203
Dworkin, Ronald, 125

Earth Charter, 285(n23)
Eck, Diana, 273
Eco-justice. *See under* Environmental issues
Ecumenism, 121, 256, 283, 330, 333(n)
"Editorial: Toward a 'Universal Declaration of Global Ethos'" (Swidler and Küng), 121
Education, 37, 41–45, 101, 122, 148, 166, 206, 276, 293. *See also* Comparative religious ethics, teaching; Curricular paradigms; Public schools; Universities
Egypt, 188, 194
Egyptian Muslim Brotherhood, 188, 193
Elites, 84, 97, 98, 126, 187
Ellul, Jacques, 302, 315
El Salvador, 197, 201, 202, 203, 204–208, 209, 212, 213(n2), 327
Empathy, 219, 220, 221, 222, 224
   empathetic understanding, 15, 18, 21, 22, 25, 45
Enlightenment, 74, 76, 90, 181, 182, 208, 300, 309, 310, 317

Environmental issues, 42–44, 98, 111, 122, 163, 167, 168, 171, 192, 193, 208, 253–283, 333
  eco-justice, 254, 257, 266, 267, 269, 270, 275, 280, 281
  solution to crisis, 255–256
Equality, 107, 120, 132–133, 172, 177, 210, 241, 318, 319, 331
Ethical Challenge of Auschwitz and Hiroshima, The: Apocalypse or Utopia? (Fasching), 292, 300–301
Ethical naturalism, 14. *See also* Historical enquiry, historical comparative approach
Ethical theory vs. normative ethics, 125
Ethnocentrism, 13, 15, 21
Eucharistic theology, 267–268
Europe, 240, 317
European Union, 241
Evangelicals, 73, 75, 77, 78–79, 101, 111(nn 2, 3), 129, 207
Everett, William, 49
Exclusivism, 91, 99, 130, 143, 144
  Christian, 75–80, 100–101
  and commitment, 99–101
  and fundamentalism, 82–85
  non-Christian, 80–82
Executioners, 306–307
Exploitation, 98, 121, 133, 331

Fackenheim, Emil, 301, 312, 313
Facts/values, 13, 21
Fairness, 246–247, 249
Faith, 13, 112(n5), 312–313
Families, 243, 244, 245, 249
Family values, 79, 83
Farley, Margaret, 128
Farquhar, J. N., 144
Faruqi, Isma'il al-, 186
FCPA. *See* Foreign Corrupt Practices Act
Feminism, 97, 128, 169, 208
Financial markets, 246
Finding Common Ground (Haynes and Thomas), 61–62
First Amendment, 60, 61, 62, 70(n), 232

First Things journal, 230
Fisher, Julie, 193
Focus on the Family, 100, 138
Ford, Gerald, 69–70(n17)
Foreign Corrupt Practices Act (FCPA), 240
Formalist-conceptual approach, 1, 12–14, 17, 20–21, 24, 26–27, 28, 30–31
Four Noble Truths, 90, 181, 275
Francis of Assisi (Saint), 267
Frankfurt Declaration, 77–78
Fraser, Nancy, 49
Freedom(s), 121, 122, 123, 137, 159, 162, 172, 226
  Four Freedoms, 169
Fuller, Millard, 184
Fundamentalism, 82–85, 108, 129–130, 142, 143
  and human rights, 155, 156, 157, 171–172
Fund for Humanity, 185
Fusion of moral horizons, 1, 18, 23, 68(n10), 149

Gandhi, Mohandas (Mahatma), 96, 293, 294, 295, 316, 317–318, 320
Gaza Strip, 188, 189
General revelation, 85, 86
Genocide, 156, 160, 291, 292, 301, 303
Ghana, 169
Girl Scouts, 137–138
Global ethic, 2, 118–139, 318, 319, 322, 330, 333
  of business, 237–242, 248, 249, 250
  vs. global ethos, 192
  uses of, 133–138
  See also Parliament of World's Religions, Global Ethic Declaration of; "Universal Declaration of a Global Ethic"
Global Ethic Foundation, 148
Global village, 211
God, 92, 94, 96, 112(n6), 113(n9), 137, 186, 188, 205, 207, 220,

259, 268, 284(n10), 300,
310–311, 312, 313, 328
commandments of, 262–263,
320(n4)
God-centered worldviews, 260
and Holocaust, 298
and Jacob story, 310
limits set by, 218, 219, 233, 234
and nonhuman creatures, 261–262,
263, 265, 269
and two-kingdom ethics, 306–307
See also Ultimate reality
Goebbels, Joseph, 297
Golden Rule, 106, 119–120, 121, 146,
199
Gómez-Ibáñez, Daniel, 119, 132, 136
Good Samaritan parable, 184
Gordis, Robert, 261–262, 284(n12)
Goulet, Denis, 182
Government sector, 40, 49
Graff, Gerald, 47
Granberg-Michaelson, Wesley, 265
Grassroots organizations, 193–194
Great Britain, 134, 142–143, 147–148,
149
Greed, 229, 250, 265, 267, 275, 281,
282
Green, Ronald, 320(n4)
Greenberg, Irving, 298, 300, 302, 309
Greenburg, Blu, 81
Groves, Leslie, 307
Guatemala, 194, 198, 205, 208
Guilt, 311
Gustafson, James, 217, 220
Gutiérrez, Gustavo, 198

Habitat for Humanity, 110, 184–186,
194
Habits of the Heart (Bellah), 46–47
Hakuin, 317
Hamas, 188–189
Harris, Monford, 262
Hauerwas, Stanley, 294, 295
Hawken, Paul, 258
Haynes, Charles, 61–62
Hazera, Alejandro, 249
Health, 239, 242, 257, 275, 305

health care, 193, 206, 213(n2)
Hear My Testimony (Tula), 197
Hehir, Brian, 259
Hermeneutical-dialogical approach, 1,
5, 12, 16–19, 20, 22–23, 24–25,
25–26, 26–27, 28, 32, 42–45,
148, 149
problems with, 23, 68(n10)
Heschel, Abraham Joshua, 261
Hess, Rudolf, 305
Hick, John, 92–93, 94, 97, 127
Hiebert, Theodore, 260
Himmler, Heinrich, 297
Hinduism, 96–97, 295, 310, 311
and Christianity, 144
Code of Manu, 190
and environmental ethics, 267, 270,
272–274
Hindus, 78, 82, 83, 111, 189
See also Bhagavad Gītā
Hines, Michael and Kenneth, 266–267
Hiroshima, 293, 296–297, 299–300,
302–304, 309, 312, 313, 319, 328
History, 233, 260, 296, 300, 304
historical-comparative approach, 1,
12, 14–16, 17, 21–22, 24, 25,
26–27, 28, 31–32
Hogg, A. G., 144
Holism, 22, 276
Holocaust, 291, 296, 300–302, 303
death camp physicians, 304–306,
309
See also Auschwitz
Honduras, 199–200
Hospitality to strangers, 294, 296,
314–315, 318, 319
Hourani, Albert, 187
Housing, 184, 188, 200. *See also*
Habitat for Humanity
Hubbard, Benjamin, 48
Humanism, 244
Human rights, 119, 121, 128,
155–172, 177, 190–191, 199,
201, 202, 203, 242, 257, 293,
296, 313–315, 325, 332
covenants/treaties concerning,
159–160, 161, 169

generations of recognition of, 161–162
nongovernmental organizations for, 158, 206
and non-Western traditions, 163–171
and religion, 204–208
universality of, 135–137, 155, 157–159, 171, 295, 319, 324
See also under Fundamentalism
Humility, 219, 267
Hussein, Saddam, 187
"Hymn to the Earth," 273–274

Ichimura, Shohei, 90
Identity, 83, 84, 99, 100, 104, 109, 156, 157, 168, 259, 278, 310
Idolatry, 82
Illiteracy, 211
Imperialism, 106, 124, 127, 138, 157, 191
Inclusivism, 75, 91, 99, 101–103, 107, 143, 144
  Christian, 85–88, 94, 113(n9)
  convictions of, 88
  non-Christian, 88–91
Income, 178, 211
India, 82, 147, 180, 189, 193, 242, 274, 285(n23), 317
Indigenous peoples, 155, 160, 163, 257, 285(n28)
  and environmental ethics, 278–280
  and human rights, 167–171
Individualism, 233
Information, 48–49, 198, 208, 210, 212, 255
Intellectuals, 36, 38, 39–40, 67(n6), 233. *See also* Public intellectuals
Interdependent co-origination, 274–275
Interest payments, 184, 185
Interfaith Alliance, 51, 52–53, 58, 59, 69(nn 12, 14)
Interfaith Council. *See* California, Chico Area Interfaith Council
Interfaith movement/activity, 50–59, 66, 88, 103, 104, 105, 141, 142, 143, 145, 147, 149, 150
International Bill of Human Rights, 159

International Coordinating Committee on Religion and the Earth, 285(n23)
International Court of Justice, 315
International Interfaith Centre, Oxford University, 69(n11), 141, 148
International Jewish Committee on Inter-Religious Consultations, 81
International law, 160
Internet, 127, 128, 139(n3), 192
Interpretation of Religion, An (Hick), 93
Interreligious dialogues, 1–2, 35, 79, 80, 106–111, 129, 130, 141, 199, 212, 283, 319, 322, 327, 329–330, 333
  and Buddhism, 90
  and distributive justice, 177, 178, 194
  ethics of, 330–333
  and exclusivism, 78, 99, 100
  and fundamentalism, 84
  and inclusivism, 87–88, 101
  intrareligious dialogue, 110–111
  Jewish interest in, 81
  and pluralism, 92, 95, 97, 104–105
  and power arrangements, 107–108
  value of, 73–74
  weaknesses in, 2
  See also Dialogues; *under* Comparative religious ethics; Universities
Intifada, 189
Intuitionism, 124–125, 130
Iran, 129, 227. *See also* Khomeini (Ayatollah)
Iranaeus, 85
Iraq, 227
Iroquois Confederacy, 169
Islam, 76, 80–81, 81–82, 89, 135, 217–234, 311, 328
  Black Muslims, 105, 192, 320. *See also* Nation of Islam
  and distributive justice, 186–189
  and environmental ethics, 268–270
  High Caliphate, 222
  militant, 83, 156

Muslims, 78, 82, 100, 105, 111, 129, 144, 147, 193–194
and non-violence, 131, 132
political thought in, 221–232, 234
Sunni/Shi'i traditions, 222, 223, 227, 231, 320
See also Muhammad (Prophet); Qur'an; *under* Christianity
Islam and War (Kelsay), 222
Israel, 82, 188, 227, 314
as name, 310
Italy, 239

Jacob (biblical), 310, 311, 318
Jacoby, Russell, 36, 37, 46
Jainism, 270, 272
Japan, 237, 238, 239, 240, 241, 242–250, 277–278, 317
circles of social world in, 243–244, 246
Jātakas, 271, 284(n21)
Jesus Christ, 75–76, 77, 78, 79, 82, 83, 92, 100, 104, 109, 112(nn 5, 6), 113(n13), 184–185, 220, 299–300, 317. *See also* Christology
Jesus Seminar, 94
Jews. *See under* Judaism
Jihad, 222, 224–225, 226, 227, 235(n7)
John Paul II, 102
Jordan, 188, 193, 194
Jordan, Clarence, 184
Josaphat (Indian prince), 316–317
Journal of Ecumenical Studies, 121
Judaism, 80–81, 85, 89, 143–144, 230, 310, 313, 314, 319, 331
chosenness concept in, 97
and environmental ethics, 262–264, 267
Jews, 48, 100, 101, 183, 241, 291, 292, 305. *See also* Holocaust
Reconstructionist Movement in, 284(n16)
Justice, 109, 110, 122, 124–125, 132, 159, 172, 191, 206–207, 225, 226, 266, 274, 293. *See also*
Distributive justice; Environmental issues, eco-justice
Justin Martyr, 85

Kaku, Ryuzaburo, 247
Kaplan, Mordecai, 284(n16)
Kapur, Sudarshan, 320
Karma, 271, 309
Kashmir, 334(n2)
Katz, Eric, 261–262
Kedushin, Max, 262
Keidanren, 247
Keiretsu relationships, 243, 246
Kenya, 193
Khomeini (Ayatollah), 228–229, 230, 231–232
Killing as healing, 304–305, 307, 313
King, Martin Luther, Jr., 316, 318, 319–320
King, Sallie, 106, 275
Knitter, Paul, 91, 107–108, 110, 126
Koinonia (farm), 184–185
Kollek, Teddy, 142
Kraemer, Hendrik, 77
Kristallnacht, 297
Krupnick, Mark, 37
Küng, Hans, 105, 113(n8), 118–121, 127, 132, 150–151. *See also* Parliament of World's Religions, Global Ethic Declaration of
Kuschel, Karl-Josef, 129
Kuwait, 193, 194

Language, use of, 36, 44, 59, 66, 83, 99, 123, 126, 132, 158, 160, 161, 163, 194(n), 260, 278, 284(n17), 285(n28), 309, 314, 331
Lao Tzu, 277
Latin America, 193, 194, 197
Law(s), 55, 122, 134, 135, 160, 166, 221, 222
divine law, 219, 220, 228
religious, 270
See also Shari'a
Leadership, 245
Lebanon, 194, 227
Lemon v. Kurtzman, 62

Levi-Strauss company, 242
Liberalism, 100, 130, 228, 229
Liberation theology, 109, 280
Liddy, G. Gordon, 52
Lifton, Robert Jay, 303, 305
Little, David, 124–125, 130
Loans, 184, 185
Lockhead, David, 91
Logos tradition, 85
Love, 109, 110, 122, 123, 184, 185,
    207, 247, 266, 277
Loyalty, 243, 244, 245, 247
Luther, Martin, 306–307, 308, 310,
    311

McAfee, Gene, 263
MacIntyre, Alasdair, 325
MacNeill, Jim, 256, 258
Malcolm X, 192, 320
Malnutrition, 200, 204, 213(n2)
Market sector, 40, 49, 246
Martinez, Ana Guadalupe, 202
Martin-Schram, James, 266
Marty, Martin E., 83, 156
*Massacre at El Mozote, The: A Parable
    of the Cold War* (Danner), 213(n3)
Materialism, 250
Meadows, Donella 214(n7)
Media, 49, 50, 52, 120, 150, 248
Medieval period, 86, 263
Meditation, 275
Menchu, Rigoberta, 198, 205, 208
Mencius, 165, 277
Metaphors, 192, 205, 220, 273, 308
Methodology, 1, 3, 24, 27, 28, 323
Metropolitan Assembly, 330, 333(n)
Mexico, 193
Middle Ages. *See* Medieval period
Middle East, 157, 240
Minnery, Tom, 138
Minorities, 128, 142, 147, 155, 226,
    231
Missionary work, 123, 193
    cultural missionaries, 223
Mitsubishi corporation, 241
Modernity, 42, 43, 65, 105, 125, 157,
    172

Modernization, 237, 244
Mohawk, John, 280
Monasticism, 267, 272
Monotheism, 80, 89, 222, 230, 261
Moral theory/doctrine, 12, 13. *See also*
    Common morality
Morgan, Peggy, 35, 147, 149
Mothers of the Disappeared, 201
Muhammad (Prophet), 82, 131, 186,
    192, 219, 223–224, 270
Multinational corporations, 238–239,
    240, 241–242, 247
Muslim Brotherhood. *See* Egyptian
    Muslim Brotherhood
Muslims. *See under* Islam
Mutombo, Nkulu, 137
Mysticism, 268, 277, 328

Naked Public Square, The (Neuhaus),
    230
Narrative ethics, 294, 315–318
Narratives, 323, 325–330. *See also*
    Narrative ethics; Storytelling
*Narrative Theology After Auschwitz:
    From Alienation to Ethics*
    (Fasching), 292
Nasr, Seyyed Hossein, 269
Nasser, Gamal Abdel, 187
Nationalism, 98, 188, 331
Nation of Islam, 48, 79, 334(n2)
Native Americans, 105, 269, 278–279
Natural Law theory, 102
Natural resources, 176, 186
Nature, 256, 257, 258, 259, 260, 262,
    265, 266, 269, 270, 273, 281, 296
    alienation from, 276
    beauty of, 278
    nature-worship, 261
*Nazi Doctors, The: Medical Killing and
    the Psychology of Genocide*
    (Lifton), 304
Neff, David, 78–79
Nestlé corporation, 242
Neuhaus, Richard John, 230–231
NGOs. *See* Nongovernmental
    organizations
Night (Wiesel), 297–298

Non-Christian religions, 73, 80–82, 157, 163. *See also* Exclusivism; Inclusivism; Pluralism, as model of religious differences; *individual religions*

Nongovernmental organizations (NGOs), 158, 193, 259, 278

Non-violence, 120, 124–125, 131–132, 205, 254, 270, 271–272, 285(n23), 293, 295, 311, 316, 317–318, 331

Nuclear weapons, 303. *See also* Atomic bomb; Hiroshima

Nuremberg trials, 306

Obedience, 219–220, 307, 309, 310, 311, 312–313, 318, 328

Objectivity, 39, 144, 208–209, 291, 293

O'Connor, June, 126, 130–131, 134

Olan, Silvia, 201

On Being a Christian (Küng), 113(n8)

Openness, 103–106, 107, 292

Oppenheimer, J. Robert, 299, 307–308

Organization for Economic Cooperation and Development, 240

Origen, 85

Orthodox Rabbinical Council of America, 81

Orthodox tradition, 268, 334(n2)

Orthopraxis, 80, 82

Other(s), 15, 18, 24, 25, 45, 83–84, 92, 97, 104, 109, 110, 111, 138, 144, 156, 172, 192, 203, 210, 211, 212, 247, 292, 294, 296, 314

Otto, Rudolf, 299

Outka, Gene, 125

Ownership of Earth, 262–263

Palestinian territories, 188, 194

Panikkar, Raimon, 93–94, 145

Pantheism, 261, 285(n24)

Papal infallibility, 326, 327

Paris, Peter, 320

Parliament of World's Religions
Global Ethic Declaration of (1993), 105–106, 110, 118–121, 123–139, 145, 146–147, 148, 150–151, 191, 239, 322, 325, 330–332
of 1893, 78, 88, 96, 146
of 1993, 2, 4, 50, 54, 78, 105, 145, 148–149, 334(n2)

Patriarchy, 168, 170, 171

Paul (biblical), 184, 265–266

Paul VI, 102

Peace, 122, 131, 172, 206–207, 226

Peace Council, 145

Pedersen, William, 258, 262

Perelmuter, Hayim, 284(n17)

Phenomenology, 15, 149

Phillips, W. Gary, 111(n3)

Physicians. Holocaust, death camp physicians

Piediscalzi, Nicholas, 62

Piety, 218, 219, 220

Pilgrimage of Hope (Braybrooke), 149

Pinnock, Clark, 78, 111(n2)

Piyatissa, Kurunegoda, 284(n21)

Placher, William, 104–105

Plaskow, Judith, 97

Pluralism, 4, 15, 17, 22, 50, 57, 60, 78, 79, 87, 135, 142, 143, 144, 149
as academic, 95
Christian, 91–95, 104–106
criticisms of Christian, 104–105, 105–106
intrareligious, 74
as model of religious differences, 75, 91–98, 99, 103–106
non-Christian, 95–98
and openness, 103–106
See also Differences; Diversity

Policy issues, 43, 50, 156, 231, 257, 319

Population growth, 283(n5). *See also* World populations

Postmodernism, 95, 98, 99, 103, 108, 208, 259, 295, 315, 326

Poststructuralism, 37

Poverty, 55, 143, 180, 185, 187, 198, 199, 200, 202, 205, 206, 213(n2), 274
  absolute, 257
  ratio of poor to wealthy countries, 211–212
  vows of, 267
Power issues, 107–108, 126, 128, 150, 203, 207, 265
Prayer, 204–205, 262, 263, 273, 274
Problems, 55
  global/intercultural, 17, 99, 103. *See also* Crises
Professionalism. *See* Universities, professionalization and specialization in
Profits, 248–249
Project on Religion and Human Rights, 136, 155, 158, 159, 172(n)
Property, 188
  property rights, 122, 123
Prospects for a Common Morality (Outka and Reeder), 125
Protestant Ethic and the Spirit of Capitalism, The (Weber), 237
Protestants, 48, 77, 87, 100, 105, 110, 237, 267. *See also* Luther, Martin
Public intellectuals, 35, 36–41, 45, 46, 49–50, 56, 59, 65, 66, 149, 150
  vs. academic intellectuals, 39–40
Public life, 38, 42
Public schools, 59–64, 134–135

Qur'an, 111, 186–187, 194(n), 219, 222, 234, 268, 269, 270, 273

Racism, 144, 211, 229, 305, 331
Radhakrishnan, Sarvepalli, 96, 97, 143
Rahner, Karl, 86–87, 112(n6)
Rajavaramuni, Phra, 179
Ramsey, Paul, 235(n8)
Rapes, 201
Rasmussen, Larry, 258, 283
Rationality, 13, 15, 21, 22, 85, 86, 208, 292, 295
Ratnapala, Nandasena, 182
Reeder, John, 26–28, 125

Reformed Christianity, 219, 220, 327
Refugees, 160, 201, 257
Reincarnation, 270–271
Relativism, 1, 22, 23, 93, 109, 134, 135, 136, 138, 292, 293, 295, 315, 324
  vs. absolutism, 123–125
Religions, moral similarity among, 130–131
Religious studies approach, 38–39, 67(n4), 294
Research and writing, 45–48
Respect, 61–62, 122, 142, 170, 171, 172, 207, 331
Responsibility, 61–62, 120, 122, 165, 166, 177, 179, 207, 218, 219, 245–246, 247, 249, 266, 291, 306, 311
  and the Holocaust, 301, 305
Reynolds, Frank, 180
Rights, 55, 61–62, 120, 122, 123, 133, 135, 160, 161, 200, 239
  civil-political/socioeconomic, 161–162, 165–166, 167, 210
  collective, 166, 168–169, 170, 171
  See also Human rights; *under* Women
Roman Empire, 76
Romero, Oscar (Archbishop), 203, 205–206, 207, 209
Roosevelt, Franklin D., 169
Rorty, Richard, 192
Rubenstein, Richard, 297, 302
Ruether, Rosemary, 91

Sabbath, 264
Sachedina, Abdulaziz, 218
Sacramentality, 267–268, 273
Sacredness, 278, 296, 297, 302, 303, 304, 310, 315
Salvation, 74, 75, 76, 77, 78, 79, 80, 85, 86, 89, 97, 112(n6)
Samartha, Stanley, 144–145
Santiago, Daniel, 209
Sarvodaya Shramadana movement. 181–182
Saudi Arabia, 188, 193, 194

Scandals, 239, 246
Scholarship, 35, 36, 37, 39, 40, 41, 45,
    46, 47, 54, 64–66, 178, 190–191,
    194, 199, 208–211, 260, 296
Schorsch, Ismar, 264
Schweiker, William, 17, 22
Schwöbel, Christoph, 104
Science, 50, 250, 259, 296
Second Vatican Council, 86, 205,
    213(n5)
Secularism, 228, 229, 230
Self-cultivation, 164, 165, 245, 276
Self-determination, 169, 170, 182
Self-interest, 56, 57
Selves, 122, 123, 310–311, 314, 317.
    See also Doubling
Seminars, 18, 20
Separation of church and state, 105,
    227–228
Separatism, 81
Sermon on the Mount, 184, 295, 316,
    318
Sexism, 211, 248, 331
Sexuality, 121, 124–125
Shadow ecologies, 255
Shahadah, 80
Shari'a, 135, 219
Shema, 80
Shinto tradition, 244, 245, 277–278
Sikhs, 82, 147
Simplicity, 254, 267, 272, 277
Sivaraksa, Sulak, 275
Sizemore, Russell, 13
Smith, Wilfred Cantwell, 316
Sobrino, Jon, 109
Social goods/needs, 176–177, 181, 184,
    190, 192, 211, 257
Social science, 64, 65, 69(n16), 315
*Social Teaching of the Christian
    Churches* (Troeltsch), 233
Society for Values in Education, 147
Solidarity, 120, 162, 167, 168, 169,
    186, 206, 328, 331
    vs. charity, 199–202, 212
Soteriology, 74, 131. *See also* Salvation
South Africa, 241
South America, 194, 209, 210

Southern Baptist Convention, 77,
    101
Specialization. *See* Universities,
    professionalization and
    specialization in
Spretnak, Charlene, 108
Sri Lanka, 82, 83, 180, 181, 182, 193,
    284(n21)
Statecraft, 221, 222, 223, 224, 230
State of the World Report (1996)
    (Brown), 283(n5)
Stepping Stones to a Global Ethic
    (Braybrooke), 146
Stewardship, 264, 265, 266, 270
Stoics, 85
Storytelling, 291–320. *See also*
    Narratives; Narrative ethics
Stout, Jeffrey, 67(n5)
Strangers. *See* Hospitality to
    strangers
Subjectivism, 22, 23
Sullivan Principles, 241
Sunyata concept, 90
Sustainable economy, 255–256
Suu Kyi, Aung San, 136–137
Swartz, Daniel, 261, 284(n10)
Swearer, Donald, 83, 91
Swidler, Leonard, 91, 113(n16), 118,
    121–122, 123, 127, 128, 132,
    133, 146
Szilard, Leo, 299

Taka, Iwao, 246, 247
Talmud, 262
Taoism, 275–276, 277
Tao Te Ching, 277
Taqwa, 220
Taxation, 177
Teachers, 63, 64, 206
Team teaching, 16, 18, 63
Techno-bureaucracy, 297, 299, 305,
    306, 313
Technology, 98, 99, 280, 296–297, 302,
    303
Terrorism, 188, 199, 200
Testimonial literature, 198–199, 203,
    210, 212–213

"Testing/Trialling the Global Ethic" project, 148, 149
Thailand, 179, 189, 193
Theological approach, 38
Thick theory of the good, 167
Third World, 197, 199, 208, 210, 212, 242
Thomas, Oliver, 61–62
Three Poisons, 275, 282
Three Rs projects, 61–62
Thurman, Howard, 320
Tillich, Paul, 86, 87, 112(n5)
Time to Meet Braybrooke), 143–144
Tinker, George, 279–280
Tolstoy, Leo, 316
To Mend the World (Fackenheim), 301
Torah, 263
Torture, 200, 201, 202, 206
"Toward a Global Ethic (An Initial Declaration)," 127. *See also* Parliament of World's Religions, Global Ethic Declaration of
"Toward A Universal Declaration of a Global Ethic" (Swidler), 113(n16), 118, 127
Traditionalists, 142
Treaties, 160
Trees, 270, 271, 272, 274, 278
Tremendum, 316
Trinity doctrine, 82, 88
Trinity test site, 299, 307–308, 310
Triumphalism, 77, 81, 92, 112(n5)
Troeltsch, Ernst, 233
Trusts, 187, 188, 192
Truths, 108, 122, 123, 144, 145, 157
Four Noble Truths, 90, 181
as narrative dependent, 295
truthfulness, 120, 124–125, 331
two-truths doctrine, 89–90
Tu, Wei-ming, 276, 277
Tucker, Mary Evelyn, 276
Tula, Maria Teresa, 197, 201, 202, 203–204, 212
Twiss, Sumner B., 42
Two-kingdom ethics, 306–307
Typology, 28, 75

Ultimate reality, 74, 92–94, 144–145, 272–273. *See also* God
UN. *See* United Nations
Understanding. *See* Empathy, empathetic understanding
Unificationists, 147
Unitarians, 147
United Nations (UN), 142, 240, 259, 278
Commission on Human Rights, 315
Conference on Human Rights (Vienna), 136
Development Report (1994), 211
Draft Declaration of Indigenous Peoples Rights, 169–170
Universal Declaration of Human Rights, 122, 128, 135, 159, 160, 173(n6), 313–315, 325
United Religions Initiative, 142, 145–146
United States, 134, 189, 229, 232, 240, 241, 249
"Universal Declaration of a Global Ethic" (Swidler), 121–122, 123, 127, 128, 132, 133, 146
Universal interests, 57, 69(n15)
Universalism/universality, 1, 21, 27, 57, 128, 138, 143, 191, 192, 248, 250, 301. *See also* Human rights, universality of
Universities, 36–37, 39, 40, 41–45
and interreligious dialogues, 48–49, 69(n11), 150
professionalization and specialization in, 37–38, 45, 46–47, 67(n6)
Upaniṣads, 272
Upaya doctrine 90
Urbanization, 257
U.S. Export Administration Act of 1977, 241

Vahanian, Gabriel, 315
Values, 146, 150, 156, 157, 160, 161, 162, 163, 166, 168, 172, 207, 209, 223, 225, 226, 230, 237, 238, 239, 240, 242, 243, 245,

248, 249, 250, 253, 254, 258,
    265, 270
Vanderbilt University, Freedom Forum
    First Amendment Center, 62
Vecsey, Christopher, 279
Vedas, 272, 273, 285(n24)
Vegetarianism, 263, 272
Victims, 107
Violence, 50, 52, 55, 82, 98, 111, 122,
    130, 143, 148, 149, 155–156,
    172, 188, 206, 229, 257, 297,
    311, 320
  and spiritual reciprocation, 279
  See also Non-violence
Virtues, 164, 167, 179, 182
Vishnu, 309, 310
Visuddhimagga (Buddhaghosa), 271
Vivekenanda (Swami), 96

Waddell, Paul, 266
Walzer, Michael, 191, 226
Waqf tradition, 187, 188
War(s), 221, 223, 257
  just wars, 224, 225, 226–227,
    235(n8), 309
  See also Jihad
Waskow, Arthur, 262–263
Water, 211, 270, 283(n5)
Wealth, 178, 180–181, 185, 187,
    211–212
Weber, Max, 237, 315
Weiskel, Timothy, 258
Western traditions, 13, 14, 27, 42, 95,
    161, 233
Whitehead, Alfred North, 319

Wicca, 79, 334(n2)
Wiesel, Elie, 297, 302, 303, 311
Williamsburg Charter, 61, 69(n17)
Women, 91, 92, 97, 122, 128, 129,
    132–133, 168, 187, 193, 199,
    224, 225, 274
  childbirth death rates, 213(n2)
  in Japan, 245, 248, 249
  rights of, 159, 160, 170, 171,
    331
  transplant women, 241
Work ethic, 237, 245
World Commission on Environment
    and Development report (1987),
    256
World Conference on Religion and
    Peace, 146
World Council of Churches, 77, 265
World Jewish Council, 101
World Missionary Conference (1910),
    77
World populations, 211, 283(n5)
World War II, 160

Yahwist's Landscape, The (Hiebert),
    260
Yasin, Ahmad, 188
Year of Interreligious Understanding
    and Cooperation, 142
Yes to a Global Ethic (Küng), 127
Yitzhak, Levi (Rabbi), 312

Zaire, 185
Zakat. See Almsgiving
Zionists, 156